How To Break An Egg

How To Break An Egg

1,453 Kitchen Tips, Food Fixes, *Emergency Substitutions*, and Handy Techniques

BY THE EDITORS, CONTRIBUTORS, AND READERS
OF *Fine Cooking* MAGAZINE

The Taunton Press

The Taunton Press
Inspiration for hands-on living®

The Taunton Press, Inc., 63 South Main Street, PO Box 5506, Newtown, CT 06470-5506
e-mail: tp@taunton.com

EDITOR: Pam Hoenig
JACKET/COVER DESIGN: Richard Oriolo
INTERIOR DESIGN & LAYOUT: Richard Oriolo
PHOTOGRAPHER: David Lazarus
FOOD STYLIST: Pamela Sorin

Fine Cooking® is a trademark of The Taunton Press, Inc.,
registered in the U.S. Patent and Trademark Office.

Library of Congress Cataloging-in-Publication Data
How To Break An Egg : 1,453 kitchen tips, food fixes, emergency substitutions, and handy
techniques / from the editors, contributors, and readers of Fine cooking magazine.
    p. cm.
 Includes index.
 ISBN 1-56158-798-2
1. Cookery. I. Taunton's fine cooking.
 TX651.C36 2005
 641.5--dc22
                         2005011616
Printed in the United States of America
10 9 8 7 6 5 4 3 2 1

The following manufacturers/names appearing in *How To Break An Egg* are trademarks: Braun®,
Bundt®, Calphalon℠, Cuisinart®, Demarle®, Frog Hollow Farm®, Gold-Plum®, Grip Liner®,
Krups®, Microplane®, Pyrex®, Scotch-Brite®, Silpat®, Sitram®, Toll House®, Tupperware®,
Vise-Grip®

Acknowledgments

Special thanks to the readers, authors, editors, copyeditors, and other staff members of *Fine Cooking* who contributed to the making of this book.

Contents

Introduction

What if you could download the collective wisdom of hundreds of great cooks? Better yet, what if those cooks were the readers, authors, and all-around cooking enthusiasts who populate the pages of *Fine Cooking* magazine? If this sounds like a pie-in-the-sky idea, I'm happy to tell you it's not. *How To Break An Egg* is an amazing collection of over 1,400 tips, tricks, advice, and solutions straight from the pages of *Fine Cooking*.

Need a gentle way to melt chocolate? Use a heating pad. Want a quick tool for making fresh breadcrumbs? Try a coffee grinder. Butter frozen? Grate it onto a plate to soften it quickly. A handy way to fill a pastry bag? Use a tall glass to hold it. The best way to store crusty bread? In a paper bag. How can you tell if an artichoke is fresh? It'll squeak when you squeeze it! *How To Break An Egg* is packed with time-saving and problem-solving gems like these.

It's not just the "Aha!" moments that make this book special, though. It's the source of those ideas—our unique collection of authors. From our readers—the clever contributors to our popular "Tips" department—come many of the best solutions. But we've also distilled the sage advice of our editors, our test kitchen staff, and the talented chefs and cooking experts who write our features, too. Great ideas from great cooks, all organized into an easy-to-reference format you'll find indispensable.

How To Break An Egg is incredibly useful, to be sure. You won't want to miss the chapter on troubleshooting; if you suffer from lumpy gravy syndrome or are fed up with pie dough that's too sticky or that cracks when you roll it, this is the place to turn to. And with an entire chapter of handy kitchen prep techniques illustrated with step-by-step color photos, you'll master everything from cutting a chicken into serving pieces to trimming artichokes in no time. But just like *Fine Cooking* magazine, *How To Break An Egg* will also just plain get you excited about messing around in the kitchen. I wouldn't keep this book too far from the stove; you'll likely use it every day. Though I must admit, it makes great bedtime reading, too.

SUSIE MIDDLETON
Editor, *Fine Cooking*

Cookware, Appliance, and Utensil Tips

Don't let your nonstick pan go up in smoke

One of the fastest ways to ruin a nonstick surface is to overheat oil to the point that it smokes and leaves a hard, dark, difficult-to-clean film on the pan. Nonstick pans are *especially vulnerable* since we tend to use less oil in them, and less oil heats up faster. Plus, the dark surface makes it hard to see what's happening with the oil. To avoid carbonized oil buildup, use refined vegetable oils, which tolerate higher degrees of heat. Generally, canola, safflower, sunflower, soy, and corn oils won't begin to smoke until they reach 420°F. Olive oil has a lower smoke point of around 360° to 380°F. (Frying temperatures are typically around 325° to 375°F.)

—Maryellen Driscoll, *Fine Cooking*

Protect nonstick pans during transport

As a personal chef, I need to carry my nonstick cookware to my clients' kitchens, and I worry about damaging the surface during transit. My simple solution is to place a layer or two of *paper towels between the pans* so they don't get scratched. I also do this in my own kitchen when these pans are stacked during storage.

—Terry Palsha, via email

Seasoning cast iron

Cast iron is slightly porous, so it needs to be seasoned if it's new. This process takes about 20 minutes. Use a paper towel to spread a generous amount of *canola oil over the entire interior surface* of the pan. Set it over low heat for about 5 minutes. Remove the pan and wipe it out with clean paper towels. Repeat this process at least twice.

—Abigail Johnson Dodge, *Fine Cooking*

And another way

I found an easy way to season my cast-iron cookware in my gas oven. After coating the pan with a thin layer of oil, I put it in the *lower broiler section* of my oven. Since the broiler heats up whenever I use the oven, my cast-iron cookware is seasoned as I do my regular baking. I reseason my pans a couple of times a year as they need it. For new pans, I repeat the oiling process three or four times until I have a well-seasoned pan.

—Cynthia A. Jaworski, Chicago, IL

Cooking on a Grill Pan

Because the ridges are the only direct source of heat in contact with food on a grill pan, food can be slow to cook through. Here are some ways to deal with that problem, along with tips on how to prevent sticking.

FOR BEEF AND PORK:

- Steaks should be relatively thin and preferably boneless.
- Chops should be thin, about ½ inch.
- Burgers should be shaped slightly flat (they'll plump as they cook and will shrink in diameter).

FOR CHICKEN:

- Avoid bone-in pieces.
- Boneless thighs or breasts should be pounded to make them more even and thin; butterflying boneless breasts is another option.
- Chicken tenderloins are your best option.

FOR VEGETABLES:

- Cut vegetables so they lie flat.
- A thick vegetable, like a portobello mushroom, will cook through faster if sliced.

TO PREVENT STICKING:

- Heat the pan over medium heat for at least 3 minutes before adding the food.
- Brush oil on the food rather than on the pan (this also helps prevent burnt-on oil and smoking).
- After adding food to the pan, don't move the food for at least the first minute.

—Maryellen Driscoll, *Fine Cooking*

Deep-frying to season a wok

I season my wok by using it to *deep-fry*. It's an ideal frying tool; a wok gives me the depth I need without the threat of oil bubbling over. And after just one batch of french fries, I discovered that I also had a very well-seasoned wok.

—Robert Ponsi, Eustis, FL

Caring for cast iron

I recently bought a cast-iron pan. Can you tell me more about how to best care for it?

—Tina Lujan, Colorado Springs, CO

Mara Reid Rogers, author of *Cooking in Cast Iron*, replies: You should use your cast-iron pans often because it's actually the cooking process that perfects the surface; over time, the pan will develop a beautiful, deep black, shiny patina and become practically nonstick. The first few times you use the pan, cook foods that are high in fat, such as sausage or bacon. Avoid foods with a high water content at first.

Don't cook acidic foods, like tomatoes or wine, in your pan. They react with the iron, causing degradation of the pan's surface and giving the food a metallic flavor or off color. For the same reason, never marinate food in cast iron.

When you remove the pan from the heat, don't leave the hot foods covered—the steam can diminish the seasoning on the pan's interior. Always clean, wash, dry, and rub your pan with oil immediately after each use. Many people never let their cast-iron piece come into contact with soap because it removes some of the seasoning; they simply rub it clean with salt, then rinse and dry it. I think it's fine to use a mild dishwashing liquid and water to clean the pan. Use a stiff, nonmetal scouring pad or brush to remove any stubborn food particles. Never soak cast-iron cookware in water or any other liquid and never wash it in the dishwasher.

Don't allow cast-iron cookware to air dry because it will rust. Dry it in a warm (300°F) oven for about 20 minutes, then turn off the oven and let the pan cool down inside the oven. Once cool, rub the pan with a very thin layer of vegetable oil or shortening. Lay a paper towel flat on the inside of the pan to absorb any moisture or excess oil and to help prevent rust. Store it in a dry place, uncovered so that moisture won't collect inside.

For a nonstick pan, use butter and oil

Here's a way to duplicate a nonstick surface on a regular "stick" baking pan. Rub the pan with butter, freeze the pan for a few minutes, then coat the pan with vegetable oil. This *double-layer coating of fat* works as well as any nonstick pan.

—Shirley O. Corriher, *Fine Cooking*

An easier way to lift a heavy pan

I find that it's much easier to lift a single-handled heavy pan—like a cast-iron skillet—if I hold the pan with my thumb pointing toward the end of the handle and my palm facing the pan. This way, my *wrist isn't stressed* by the weight of the pan, and I don't need to have a strong arm to cook with a cast-iron pan.

—Doris Hsu, via email

Use a painter's trick to prevent dripping pans

When I pour gravy or tomato sauce out of a small saucepan, a little sauce always ends up dripping down the side of the pan. But here's a tip for pouring that prevents the drip. First I tilt the pan to pour all the contents out, then I continue *turning it in the same direction*, essentially flipping it until it's right side up again. (Keep your grip a little loose, as it's the handle rather than your hand that's turning.) By making the pan do a 360-degree flip, the drip gets caught inside the pan's lip.

—Perry Weddle, Sacramento, CA

Pan substitution

If you're following a recipe that calls for a small flameproof roasting pan and you don't have one, a large *heavy-duty ovenproof skillet*, preferably with straight sides, makes a fine substitute. Remember, though, not to grab the hot handle without protection.

—Jennifer Armentrout, *Fine Cooking*

Another use for cast-iron skillets

If you're making a delicate sauce and you don't have a heavy pan or a heat tamer, use a cast-iron skillet to buffer the pan from the heat. Over gentle heat, any *saucepan set inside a cast-iron skillet* is transformed into a piece of heavy-duty equipment.

—G. R. Scialoia, Mt. Snow, VT

Use a roasting pan as a stovetop griddle

I use my nonstick, heavy-duty flameproof roasting pan on the stovetop as a griddle for breakfast foods such as pancakes, French toast, eggs, and breakfast meats. *Straddled over two burners*, the pan makes an efficient, extra large cooking surface that keeps the food contained while allowing it to brown. It also does a great job of browning chicken and pork chops.

—Tiny Shuster, St. Johnsville, NY

Picking a Baking Sheet

Overwhelmingly, the baking pros I've spoken with across the country advised cooks to buy heavy, durable rimmed aluminum baking sheets (also known as half sheet pans).

"When you're in a store, pick up a baking sheet and see how heavy it is," says Nancy Silverton, cookbook author, pastry chef, and owner of La Brea Bakery. "Try to find heavy-duty, restaurant-quality aluminum sheet pans with a lip around them. And whatever you do, don't go near the supermarket. It's a false savings to buy inexpensive baking sheets, because they start warping over 300° F."

Adds Nick Malgieri, author of *How to Bake* and chairman of the baking program at the Institute of Culinary Education in New York, "I use [half sheets] at home, I use them at work, and I develop all my recipes on them. They're durable and affordable." Kathleen Stewart, owner of The Downtown Bakery in Healdsburg, California, says she loves them because they conduct heat well, "so evenly, but not *too* quickly—perfect for cookies."

And according to cookbook author Abby Dodge, half sheet pans "give you the biggest bang for the buck"—they don't warp, you can freeze things on them, and they're handy for a multitude of other uses.

Because most pros use parchment paper to line their sheets, a nonstick surface isn't important to them. But if nonstick is a key feature for you, by all means, get it, but be aware that if you put oil on it, it will result in a sticky buildup you won't be able to remove and that the dark color of nonstick can result in overbrowning.

And finally, before you buy your baking sheet, heed veteran baker Flo Braker's advice and measure the racks in your oven. You'll get the best results if your baking sheet has 2 inches of room on each side of it for air to circulate. If you're going to be using your sheets only for cookies, you'll get superior air circulation with unrimmed cookie sheets.

—Susie Middleton, *Fine Cooking*

Improvising a tube pan for cakes

I don't own a tube pan, but that doesn't keep me from making cakes that call for one. To improvise my own tube pan, I set an *empty, clean metal food can* in the center of a deep cake pan. I fill the can with beans so it's heavy and doesn't move around. Then I grease the pan and can as the recipe instructs and pour in the cake batter around the can.

—Florence Sarnoff, New York, NY

Mark baking pans with their volumes

I mark the volumes of all of my baking pans, flan tins, cake tins, etc., on the back of the pan *with a permanent marker*. The best time to do this is when you've just bought the pan and you can copy the volume measurements from the packaging labels. To measure the volume of an old baking pan, fill the pan with water to within ¼ inch of the rim, then pour the water into a liquid measuring cup like a Pyrex® measure that's marked with cup measurements and fluid ounces.

—Jane Becktel, via email

Warning for hot pots

After removing a pot from the oven, I always wrap *a hand towel around the handle.* This ensures that if anyone tries to pick up the pot, he or she won't get burned.

—Howard Goldberg, Manalapan, NJ

Make your own pot handle covers

To move around hot pots and pans with heat-conductive metal handles, you can either fumble with a towel or potholder or else do what I've done: make your own pot handle covers. *Fold a regular potholder in half* and sew up the side and one end. Then you can slip the holder right onto the handle and use it to safely move hot pots and pans without getting burned.

—Kathy Rudman, Etna, NH

Protect wooden-handled skillet with foil

I inherited a cast-iron skillet with a wooden handle and couldn't wait to use it for baking cornbread and chicken. To protect the wooden handle in the oven, I wrapped it with heavy-duty aluminum foil and had no problems (the foil and the handle got very hot, but *the wood didn't crack*).

—Rosalind Foyer, Encino, CA

Glass vs. Metal Baking Pans: Your Choice Affects Cooking Times and Crustiness

Size isn't the only thing that counts when choosing a pan from the many in your cupboard. The material it's made of will affect both the baking time and the color of your breads, pies, cakes, and brownies.

Glass pans give food a darker, browner crust, so they're generally best for breads and pies, which benefit from a deeply baked exterior. Because of the way glass transfers heat in the oven, it will bake both faster and darker than most metal pans (the exceptions are very dark, heavy-gauge metal pans, like the black steel pans used in professional kitchens. These intense heat conductors cook quickly and will also turn out appealing, dark crusts).

Lighter-colored pans give you a paler crust, which is what you want with delicate cakes and brownies. Light-colored aluminum and shiny stainless-steel pans reflect more heat than glass and dark metal pans. This may mean your baked goods will need a bit more time to finish cooking, but it also means the sugar and chocolate in these pastries won't be as likely to burn.

Avoid flimsy metal pans, which often bake unevenly and tend to warp at high temperatures.

—Molly Stevens, *Fine Cooking*

Old pans bake unevenly

If your baking pans are scarred with blackened, baked-on spots, consider replacing them. Those dark areas can cause uneven baking.

—Gayle Roberson, Hightstown, NJ

Use a pot lid as a shield

When adding foods to hot liquids (such as potatoes or vegetables into simmering soup stock), use the lid of the pot to scrape the vegetables off the cutting board and into the hot soup. The *lid creates a shield* for any hot liquid that splashes up.

—Jeremy Garrison Ross, Brooklyn, NY

Securing a pasta machine

To clamp down a pasta machine securely without risking damage to your counter-top, *clamp the machine to a cutting board*. Put a piece of nonslip material—the kind you put between a rug and a slippery floor—between the cutting board and the countertop. Your pasta machine won't budge when you crank it. The nonslip material is available at carpet and hardware stores for about a dollar a square foot.

—J.J. Jackson, Victoria, British Columbia, Canada

Use a flexible mat to move appliances

I love my heavy-duty stand mixer but hated having to drag or lift the heavy thing from the back corner of my kitchen counter to the front so I could use it. The mixer also left scratches on my tile counter each time I moved it, so I took a thin, *flexible plastic chopping mat* (the ones that cost only a couple of dollars) and slid it under the appliance to cushion my counter. The mat I bought is a translucent white, so it barely shows against the tiles. My mixer now rests in its corner of the mat, and all I have to do is grab the mat to glide the mixer to the front. Then, when I'm done, I just push the mat to slide the mixer back into the corner again. A word of caution: Don't leave your mixer unattended while it's running, and if you have a long mixing job to do, remove the mat so the mixer can rest securely on the counter.

—James Kerr, via email

What not to use an immersion blender for

Don't try using your immersion blender to make mashed potatoes, whipped cream, cookie or cake batters, herb butter, ground meat, or ground nuts. We found it's not effective, despite some manufacturer's claims.

—Joanne Bouknight, *Fine Cooking*

Splatter-free immersion blender

An immersion blender is a great tool for quickly blending a sauce or puréeing a soup, but it can also splatter food if you're not careful. To avoid creating a mess, I slip a *plastic bag over the bowl* or pot. Then I make a slit in the bag that's large enough to wiggle in the blade end of the immersion blender. The power button stays above the bag. When I turn it on, the ingredients stay inside the pot and the bag acts as a kind of lid.

—Joan McRae, Chesapeake, VA

Guidelines for Using a Convection Oven

- When following a recipe designed for a conventional oven, heat the convection oven to a temperature 25°F lower than the recipe suggests.

- Expect food to be done in less time (as much as 25% less) than it would be in a conventional oven, even with the 25°F reduction. The longer you're cooking something, the greater the time savings; for instance, a turkey may cook an hour faster in a convection oven than in a regular oven, but you may shave off only a minute or two when baking cookies.

- Use baking pans with low sides to get the full benefits of convection.

- Go ahead and fill every rack in the oven, but still keep an eye on browning. Depending on your oven, you may have to rotate the pans for even cooking.

- Most ovens let you turn convection on and off. Play around with it. If you want a well-browned roast that's also slowly cooked, turn the convection on at the start or at the end but off during the rest of the cooking.

- The fan sometimes blows parchment or foil around; use a metal spoon or fork to hold it down.

—Susie Middleton, *Fine Cooking*

Easier, safer microwaving

Instead of using plastic wrap to cover your dish before microwaving, use a very damp (but not soaking) *paper towel* to cover the dish. It works great on reheated rice. The paper towel doesn't collapse or melt onto the food like plastic wrap, nor does it shrink-wrap itself onto the dish. It lets just enough steam escape and contributes just enough moisture for the best results. The paper towel also absorbs splatters, and there's no risk of steam burns that can occur while trying to vent plastic. Use a good-quality brand in plain white.

—Susan Asanovic, Wilton, CT

Keep it sharp

Check the blades on your food processor. As a food processor ages, so do its blades, which begin to *dull with use.* In the case of pesto, for example, blunt blades bruise herbs and other pesto ingredients, causing them to oxidize and darken quickly.

—Tony Rosenfeld, *Fine Cooking*

Food processor blade stays put while pouring

How many times have I struggled to pour out the contents of my food processor bowl without letting the blade fall out, too? I finally discovered that the solution in the video that came with my Cuisinart®. Just plug your finger into the hole under the bowl and the *blade will remain secure* while you pour or scoop out the contents.

—Sierra Decatur, Cheshire, CT

Plastic wrap keeps processor lid clean

To keep the top half of your food processor clean while you're processing, put a piece of *plastic wrap over the bowl* before putting on the lid. This works like a charm on many processing jobs, with the exception of those that require use of the feed tube.

—Christina Stuccio, Weehawken, NJ

How Not to Break Your Hand Mixer and Other Tips

- At all costs, resist the temptation to cream cold, hard butter with your hand mixer. It's one of the most common ways people burn out their machines. Instead, cut the cold butter into small pieces and let it sit out on the counter for 20 to 30 minutes or until it's softened to 65° to 68°F

- If your butter is adequately softened, add it to the bowl in pieces and not as one big stick for more even and less arduous creaming.

- When mixing mashed potatoes, a stiff dough, or a double batch of cookie dough, use a large bowl with a wide base. The mixer can move better through ingredients when they're spread out rather than piled up.

- Never stick a spoon, spatula, or your hands in the mixing bowl while the mixer is running. It seems like an obvious point, but it happens all the time.

- When beating cream or egg whites, start with a slow speed and gradually build to a high speed. This avoids spatter and helps stabilize the foam.

- When adding flour or confectioners' sugar to a batter, turn off the mixer and blend the ingredient in by hand just enough so that it won't scatter in a poof when you turn on the beaters.

—Maryellen Driscoll, *Fine Cooking*

Blending 101

In the process of researching and testing blenders, we learned that a lot of good blenders will splatter, leak, jam, and even break because of common user errors. The following are some basic do's and don'ts of blending.

- Load liquids and soft ingredients first, solid ingredients last. Solids should be no larger than 1-inch chunks.

- When you start, start slow and gradually build speed to lessen motor stress.

- Use the pulse button, if available, when blending frozen drinks.

- Immediately stop blending when ingredients jam.

- To blend hot ingredients without splattering, remove the cap on the lid's fill hole and wrap a thick dish towel over the lid; add a minimal amount of liquid; start at a low speed and increase gradually. (Ideally, let hot ingredients cool before blending.)

- Never wiggle the jar to jostle lodged ingredients when the blender is running.

- To prevent jams when adding ice cubes or frozen fruit, drop the cubes or fruit one at a time through the lid's fill hole while the blender is running.

—Maryellen Driscoll, *Fine Cooking*

Preventing waste in your food processor

After using the food processor for sticky things like purées, the blade is left with a lot of food on it. To prevent this mess and waste, remove the contents from the processor bowl, replace the blade, and *pulse the empty processor* for a few seconds with an empty bowl. You'll get clean blades and whatever was left on the blades will be on the bowl, which you can easily scrape out with your spatula.

—Rose Marie Olaechea, Lima, Peru

Skewer a food processor blade to make washing safe

Washing a metal food processor blade by hand can be tricky. Instead of trying to hold the blade with one hand while sponging it with the other, I wedge the *handle of a wooden spoon* into the cavity on the underside of the the the spindle and hold the spoon, keeping my fingers (at least on the hand that's not holding the sponge) a safe distance from the sharp blades.

—Maryellen Driscoll, *Fine Cooking*

Pressure cooker safety

Some manufacturers caution that grains may foam up and clog the steam vents. To prevent this, add *a tablespoon of oil or butter* per cup of dry grain and fill the cooker just to the halfway mark.

—Jan Newberry, *Fine Cooking*

A watched slow cooker doesn't cook

Avoid removing the lid of a slow cooker during cooking. Stirring isn't usually necessary, but if you do need to lift the lid, you may need to add 15 to 20 minutes to the cooking time, depending on how much heat was lost. Also, when you lift the lid, don't tilt it; rather gently lift it straight up to avoid spilling condensation into the crock and diluting the cooking liquid.

—Maryellen Driscoll, *Fine Cooking*

If you do need to lift the lid, you may need to add 15 to 20 minutes to the cooking time.

Tips for Using the Microwave

- Use glass, ceramic, or plastic containers that are approved for microwave use. Microwaves can't penetrate metal cookware—you'll get a show of fireworks rather than cooked food.

- Contrary to popular belief, cookware can become very hot in the microwave. Always use potholders when checking or removing food.

- Microwaveable glass measuring cups are very handy—they're available in a variety of sizes (from 1- to 8-cup capacities), have handles for easy use, and can serve as mixing bowls when stirring in additional ingredients.

- Microwaveable glass pie plates work well for foods that need to be spread out for even cooking, such as nuts or shredded coconut.

- Ingredients right out of the refrigerator or freezer will take longer to cook than those at room temperature.

- I usually set the microwave timer for the total cooking time when I'm able to stand by and tend foods. This is more convenient than resetting the timer after each short check, but the key is that you must stay nearby to check progress.

—Judy Rusignuolo, *Fine Cooking*

Adapting Recipes for the Slow Cooker

Here are some tips for adapting regular stovetop-simmered or oven-braised recipes for the slow cooker:

- Brown meats and poultry in a skillet on the stovetop before adding them to the cooker. This boosts flavor, adds color, and renders some fat.

- Use the low heat setting for tough cuts. Turning the heat to high will shorten the cooking time but won't deliver nearly as tender results.

- Root vegetables are slow to cook through, so cut them into pieces no larger than 1 inch and put them in the bottom of the cooker so they'll be surrounded by hot liquid.

- In a slow cooker, liquids have no way to evaporate and foods release yet more liquid as they cook. If you have excess liquid at the end of the cooking time or if the flavor is diluted, simmer the liquid in a saucepan until it has the consistency and flavor intensity you want.

- Add more fresh herbs and spices to taste at the end of cooking (and reducing) to boost flavor and freshness.

- Avoid adding milk, cheese, or sour cream until the last hour of cooking. With the exception of processed cheese, dairy products will separate with long cooking. Evaporated milk is a safe substitute.

—Maryellen Driscoll, *Fine Cooking*

Make breakfast in your slow cooker

I love having hot oatmeal for breakfast in the fall. Before bedtime, I put a cup of steel-cut oats (like the kind imported from Ireland) into my slow cooker with 4 cups of water and 1 teaspoon of cinnamon or apple pie spice, plus ½ cup of raisins or other dried fruit. Then I cover the cooker and put it on low to cook overnight. In the morning, I just give the oatmeal a quick stir and add milk and maple syrup for a hot, hearty breakfast.

—Donald Matesz, Toledo, OH

I cover the cooker and put it on low to cook overnight.

Knives and Kitchen Shears

A stiff knife is a safe knife

One of the most important attributes of a kitchen knife is *lateral stiffness.* A flexible knife blade is dangerous because it can twist while cutting, changing direction unpredictably and possibly cutting the user. While a flexible blade can be appropriate for some purposes, such as filleting a fish, a general-purpose knife should be a stiff as possible. To test a knife, hold the handle as normal with the cutting edge of the blade parallel to a hard surface, then press down firmly on the tip. A good knife will deflect no more than ½ to ¾ inch—any more than that and the knife should be avoided. Bread knives that pass this test are extremely rare.

—Davis Yetman, Newtown, MA

Use the sharp "heel" of the knife

In a perfect world, your knife would always be sharp. But when faced with a dull knife, use the part of the blade closest to the handle. Because it sees less use, it will be *sharper than the middle* of the blade, which gets more of a workout.

—Eric Reinfelder, Topsham, ME

Use a knife's spine to scrape food from a board

After slicing, dicing, or chopping your vegetables, turn your knife over and *use the dull side of the blade* to scrape the vegetables off the cutting board and into your pan or bowl. Your knife will stay sharper longer, and you won't be shaving tiny bits of plastic or wood from the cutting board onto your food.

—Jenna Roses Zimkus, Boston, MA

Grapefruit knife for easy bagel cutting

When cutting a bagel, I use a curved, serrated grapefruit knife. By using a sawing motion, the curved blade helps keep the bagel in place and easily cuts it in half.

—Linda Sclafani, New York, NY

Cutting a bagel safely

To slice a bagel in half without risking a cut to your hand, place the *bagel on its side* on a sturdy cutting board and hold the top steady. With your other hand, push the point of a sharp knife into the top of the bagel below your fingers and use a sawing motion to slice the bagel in half.

—Christine Landi, Santa Ynez Valley, CA

Keeping an edge

My honing steel doesn't work as well as it used to. Do I need to replace it?

—Matt Soban, via email

Norman Weinstein, the knife skills instructor at the Institute of Culinary Education in New York City, replies: A honing steel restores a knife's bite by straightening the microscopic "teeth" at its edge, which can fold with use. A steel can be used on a straight-edged knife with practically every use or whenever you feel the knife's bite is gone. Over time, however, repeated use will degrade the grooves of a honing steel, making it virtually useless. To test, run your thumbnail around the circumference of the tool. If you can feel the grooves, your steel still has some life in it.

Honing steels are magnetized and pick up the microscopic filings that come off the blade. Run a soft cloth up the steel after each use to keep the grooves from getting clogged. If you hone the knife with food particles on it, wash the steel with a soft, soapy cloth and rinse and dry it thoroughly. If a knife doesn't respond to honing, it's likely time to have the culprit sharpened.

Cleaver blade guard

If you've lost (or never had) a blade guard for a large knife such as a cleaver, try buying a clear plastic report cover like those used to hold school term papers. Its long plastic clip can be trimmed to the knife blade's length, and it slides easily and fits snugly over the exposed blade.

Try buying a clear plastic report cover.

—Mark F. Hillger, Buffalo, NY

Cork your knives

A knife block or cutlery rack is the best way to store sharp knives. But if you don't have one of these, you can safely store knives in a drawer by sticking their *sharp points into a cork*. The cork protects the knife tip and helps keep the blades from knocking into one another.

—Randy Bard, Washington, DC

Shear Genius

Here are some of our favorite uses for kitchen shears:

- Cutting a whole chicken into parts
- Trimming the fat from a chicken or duck
- Snipping slices of bacon into small pieces
- Chopping up canned whole tomatoes (just leave them in the opened can and snip away)
- "Mincing" a handful of fresh chives or "slicing" rounds of scallions
- Snipping off the ends of green beans or snow peas
- "Chopping" up tough, large pieces of dried fruit
- Trimming away the tough outer leaves on artichokes
- Slicing homemade pizza
- Trimming crusts and cutting bread into cubes
- Trimming pie dough before crimping
- Cutting slashes into shaped bread dough

When buying a pair of kitchen shears, look for these features:

Serrated and notched blade: Many shears have one blade that's serrated, which helps when gripping slippery items; we found it particularly handy for trimming fish and cutting out the back of a chicken. A notch near the fulcrum is useful for breaking through small bones.

Break-apart blades: Many shears let you separate the blades at the fulcrum, which is incredibly useful for cleaning.

Rounded handles: Too many shears have plastic handles with edges that aren't rounded and they can be downright painful to use. Look for rounded edges.

Snug handles: A smaller circular hole for the thumb is particularly helpful when you need to apply pressure.

—Maryellen Driscoll, *Fine Cooking*

Your cupboard is probably full of some of the best knife sharpeners around

I'm talking about the unglazed rims on the bottoms of many bowls, plates, saucers, and mugs. When ceramic ware is removed from the kiln and cooled, its bottom is typically ground flat. This removes the glaze along the rim and exposes *a very hard, abrasive surface* that's perfect for putting fresh edges on knives and cleavers. To sharpen a knife on the bottom of a plate, flip the plate over and hold it in one hand along your forearm. Holding the knife in your other hand (at an angle of about 25 degrees to the plate), slide the knife forward, heel to toe, along the rim, as though you were trying to take a thin slice off the plate. Turn the knife over every few strokes to hone the opposing edge. The rim of the plate will begin to darken as it cuts away steel from the blade. When it gets really dark, which means the ceramic is clogged with filings, move to an unused part of the rim. Running the plate through the dishwasher will remove most of the metal and keep stains off your good linens. But a brown stain—residual rust deposits—will remain on the rim.

—Albert Pound, New Haven, CT

Play the mandoline, safely

I bought a professional mandoline, but I found the safety guard to be very limiting. A few tries without the guard put my fingers in terrible jeopardy and reminded me why I bought the guard in the first place. A solution is to use a moistened Scotch-Brite® pad to hold the vegetable you're cutting. The pad's rough surface grips the vegetable, while its flexibility lets it conform to the vegetable's shape, creating a real comfort zone. Just place the pad in the palm of your hand, and don't let your fingers extend beyond the pad; if you slip, the pad gets sliced, not your hand. Now I can slice, julienne, and waffle with confidence (waffling with confidence doesn't come easy). With a sure hand and the proper stroke, anyone can play a mandoline.

—G. Robert Jackson, Alexandria, VA

Use a moistened Scotch-Brite pad to hold the vegetable you're cutting.

Kitchen Tools and Cutting Boards

Tongs and their myriad uses

I use my *spring-loaded tongs* to pull out the hot oven rack to check on a dish because they let me grab the rack more securely than a stiff potholder does, and they allow me to keep my distance from the oven's heat. Of course, I also use the tongs for things like turning a piece of meat without puncturing it, sautéing vegetables, and gripping a single piece of ziti to check for doneness. To my mind, tongs are the next best thing to having heatproof hands (now that would be a great invention).

—Susie Madison, Stuart, FL

Avoid tong fatigue

Spring-loaded kitchen tongs are among my favorite cooking tools. I use them for everything from turning pork chops to tossing vegetables in the sauté pan, plating and garnishing a main dish or dessert, and even serving salad. I learned early on to avoid a tired hand and forearm by "choking up" on the tongs so my *hand is nearer to the blades*. This gives me more control over the tong blades and results in less fatigue and stress on my hand.

—Lydia Nieves, Nogales, AZ

Store tongs in PVC collars

Large tongs are one of the more useful kitchen tools, and I have several pairs. Unfortunately, if the locking mechanism breaks, they're a pain to store. I finally came up with an inexpensive, simple solution. At the hardware store, I bought several ¾-inch *PVC collars* (connectors for plastic pipe) for less than 50 cents each. The collars slip over the handle of the tongs but won't go over the gripping end.

—John L. Wilson, Houston, TX

And another way

I have an alternative method to *storing tongs* that won't close. Just save the cardboard tube from a roll of paper towels. Cut off about 2 inches, insert the tongs, and store them in a drawer. The tongs won't catch on other utensils.

—Bernard Latasiewicz, Detroit, MI

Use a potato masher for fruit, too

The next time you need slightly mashed fruit for a recipe like strawberry short-cake, try using a potato masher. It *squashes the fruit* without turning it into juice or a purée, as a food processor will do.

—Peggy Makolondra, Sturgeon Bay, WI

Choose the right peeler for the job

I keep two types of peelers on hand: one with a swivel blade and another that doesn't swivel. I use the *swivel peeler for vegetables* with thin, delicate skins, such as carrots and asparagus. The *fixed blade peeler* is better for thicker-skinned eggplant, turnips, and apples. For vegetables like celeriac with coarse, craggy skins, I use a paring knife.

—Sophie Stepanskiy, Fairfield, CT

Use a ladle for faster straining

The process of putting food through a strainer goes much faster when you press a metal ladle against the solids and move the ladle in a circular motion.

—Terry Hahn, Boston, MA

"Brand" wooden spoons as sweet or savory

I like to keep my *wooden spoons segregated*—those for sweet things separate from those for savory foods. In order to tell them apart, I "brand" the handles of the savory spoons in the flame of my gas burner. It takes but a few seconds and makes them forever identifiable.

—Maggie Carter, Sowney, CA

Spoons that stay put

I know it's a bad habit, but I love to leave my wooden spoon resting on the edge of a sauté pan as my sauce simmers away. The real problem is that, as the sauce reduces, the spoon often slides down into the pan when I'm not looking. Then I have to fish it out and wash it off. To keep my spoons from sliding into the saucepan, I've *cut a small notch* in each just about where they naturally rest on the pan's edge.

—Gloria Gerstein, New York, NY

Fill a pastry bag neatly

To easily fill a pastry bag, put the tip in place and put the *bag into a tall glass*. Turn the top of the bag over the edge of the glass to make a cuff and hold the bag steady. Fill the pastry bag, turn up the cuff, and pipe away. You'll appreciate this method when you have to refill the pastry bag.

—Jeanie James, Mukilteo, WA

Fill pastry bags easily

To fill a pastry bag hands-free, put the pastry tip in the bag, tuck some of the material near the tip into the tip itself (to prevent the filling from falling through), and support the pastry bag in a *large measuring cup or straight-sided bowl*. This also prevents the bag from falling over.

—Lisa Jung, San Rafael, CA

Why use a wooden spoon?

Many recipes specify a wooden spoon for stirring or other uses. What is the advantage of a wooden spoon over metal or plastic?

—Robert Shorter, Winston-Salem, NC

Abigail Johnson Dodge replies: "Mix with a wooden spoon" is something of an old-fashioned phrase that remains ingrained in modern recipe parlance. In the past, wooden spoons were the mixing utensil of choice because they were large enough to mix a batter, heatproof enough so they wouldn't melt, nonreactive so they wouldn't have adverse effects on acidic foods, and soft enough so they wouldn't scratch the surfaces of pots and pans.

Nowadays, we continue to see this phrase in recipes even though we have many other utensils that can do the same job as wooden spoons. The newest addition to the modern kitchen arsenal, heatproof silicone spatulas, are great for stirring and scraping hot ingredients on or off the stove, and they won't scratch nonstick surfaces. Rubber spatulas and plastic spoons can be big enough to handle many mixing tasks as long as no heat is involved—they'll still melt. Large stainless-steel spoons are nonreactive and strong enough to mix almost anything.

That said, a wooden spoon is still an essential tool. It's sturdy and fits comfortably in the hand, plus its rounded business end is often the best for the stirring task at hand. The next time you see the phrase, "stir with a wooden spoon," by all means use one if it's available. But if your wooden spoon is otherwise engaged, consider your other tools. You probably have something else ready and waiting to play stand-in.

Shiny or dull side of aluminum foil?

When you're cooking with aluminum foil, will the food take longer if the shiny side faces away from the food, deflecting the heat?

—Todd Luft, Petoskey, MI

Carol Owen, former director of consumer services for the Reynolds Metals Company, replies: We're often asked this question. It makes no difference which side faces out or in during cooking. We've tested it in our laboratory, and though our lab equipment picked up a very slight reflectivity difference, the difference is so small that it doesn't affect cooking.

Get the most out of a piping bag

Whether I'm using a zip-top bag or a pastry bag to pipe out icing, ganache, or caramel sauce onto a dessert, I find that *a dough scraper* is the perfect tool for getting at the dregs that stick to the sides of the bag. The wide dull blade of the scraper forces every last bit down toward the hole—much more effective than using my fingers.

—Rose Levy Beranbaum, *Fine Cooking*

Rinse cheesecloth before using it

Before using a new piece of cheesecloth for any cooking task, it's a good idea to *shake out any lint and dust*. If I'm using the cloth to line a colander or sieve, I also rinse it with water, which makes the cloth stick to the strainer so it doesn't slide around as I begin pouring in hot stock.

— Robert Danhi, *Fine Cooking*

How to unwrap a roll of plastic wrap

When I can't find the edge on a roll of plastic wrap, I rub a little flour around the roll. The flour catches along the hidden edge and helps you grab it.

—Abby Muller, Newport News, VA

Nonstick aluminum foil

When I'm making something with a sticky, cheesy top, like lasagna, that needs to be covered in foil before baking, I like to *spray the foil with cooking spray* before placing it on top of the pan. This keeps the cheese from sticking to the foil and pulling off all that good topping.

—Julie Black, Dexter, MI

Uncurling parchment

To straighten rolled parchment, cut a piece to size, place one half of the sheet *over the edge of the counter*, and put your forearm lightly over the paper. Pull the bottom end of the parchment over the counter's edge toward the floor, then reverse the parchment and repeat to uncurl the other half.

—Carol Bradshaw, via email

Pinching down parchment

All of us who like to use parchment must have had the problem of sliding parchment, and I have coped with it in various ways. I like to clip the parchment to the rim of the baking sheet with a common *spring-loaded clothespin* in each corner. As soon as the item to be baked is safely on the baking sheet, whether it be a batch of cookies or a couple of loaves of hearth-baked bread, the item itself will hold the paper down, and the clothespins can be removed before putting the batch in the oven.

—James Hunter, Traverse City, MI

Choosing and Caring for Rolling Pins

- When picking out a pin, roll it on a counter and examine it at eye level, to make sure that it isn't warped or nicked, advises Abby Dodge.

- To clean a rolling pin, just brush it off with a dry cloth, or use a damp sponge to wipe it off and then dry it thoroughly with a cloth. Rolling pins need no oiling at all. Never soak them in water, which causes warping and cracking.

- To keep a rolling pin from getting dings or nicks, Flo Braker advises suspending the pin horizontally from a rack, either on a free wall, under a counter, on a closet door, or even under a kitchen cart.

—Maggie Glezer, *Fine Cooking*

Anchoring kitchen parchment

Call me a control freak, but I like to be in complete control of the baking parchment when I do my baking. There's nothing worse than trying to work with parchment that slides all over the baking sheet because it doesn't quite fit the pan. Whenever I make biscotti, cookies, or *pâte à choux* (cream puffs), I use a little of the *dough or batter to glue the corners* of the paper to my baking sheet. After baking, the paper comes off easily, and cleanup is a breeze. Isn't that the reason they made baking parchment?

—Eric Hoey, San Pedro, CA

Quick parchment rounds

When I make a parchment round for my cake pan, I avoid the tedious step of outlining the pan with a pencil and then cutting the parchment. Instead, I put a cake pan on a large sheet of parchment on a cutting board and run the point of a sharp pair of scissors around the outside edge of the pan to *score the parchment*. Then I separate the parchment round from the rest of the sheet. I have a perfect round for my cake pan, and I avoid getting pencil "lead" in my baked goods.

—Diana Almeida, via email

Making a nonskid cutting board

A cutting board that skids while you're slicing or chopping is aggravating at best, unsafe at worst. It's a good idea to lay a *slightly damp dishtowel underneath* your cutting board before you work. The single layer of dishtowel makes the cutting board nonskid, and if your board is a tiny bit warped, the towel helps level it. As an additional benefit, any juices that run off your food are likely to be absorbed by the towel, instead of dripping onto the counter.

—Morgan Gallagher, Cleveland, OH

Mark a clear chopping mat to cut vegetables precisely

I used a permanent marker to *write ruler measurements* like ½ inch, ¾ inch, and 1 inch *on the back* of my cheap, flexible, translucent chopping mat. Then, if a recipe calls for carrots diced ½ inch, for example, I can use the marks to guide me without having to pull out a ruler. This helps me prep my ingredients more precisely so they'll cook evenly. Be sure to write the numbers backward so they'll read properly on the good side of the mat. I also draw measured circles on another mat for rolling out pastry dough.

—Ken Fruehstorfer, Palatine Bridge, NY

Using Cutting Boards Safely

About ten years ago, a study suggesting that wooden cutting boards have antibacterial properties got national attention and sent people running out to buy wooden boards. More recent studies by the same scientists seemed to demonstrate that bacteria such as salmonella get absorbed into the wood within a few minutes, leaving the exposed area of the unwashed board free of the potentially harmful microbes. (Many more bacteria were recoverable from the unwashed plastic cutting boards in their experiments.) If the wooden board is well dried after washing and remains dry, the absorbed bacteria eventually die. But because different tests (including those performed by NSF International, a nonprofit certifier of products relating to public health, and by the U.S. Food & Drug Administration) have reported contradictory results, the FDA continues to recommend plastic boards mainly because of the ease of cleaning, since they are dishwasher safe.

While the research—and the debate—continues, the best approach to safety is to clean any cutting surface after it comes in contact with raw meat or poultry either in a dishwasher, for plastic cutting boards that fit, or by hand with a solution of 1 teaspoon bleach in 1 quart of water. By the same token, don't be lulled into haphazard, quick cleaning by plastic boards that boast having antibacterial properties: as must be stated on those boards' labels, the treatment protects the *plastic* from the bacteria and not necessarily the *user*. So wash well. Better yet, dedicate one board to meat and poultry and one to everything else.

Prevent cracks by oiling wooden boards with food-grade mineral oil when they start to look dry. If a wooden board shows signs of wear, have it resurfaced (if it's a thick butcherblock type) or get a new one. A well-worn plastic cutting board should also be replaced: its grooves and scratches can harbor bacteria.

—Joanne McAllister Smart, *Fine Cooking*

You Use That to Do What?

Cook corn on the cob in an asparagus steamer

I've found that my asparagus steamer is great for steaming or boiling other vegetables too, especially sweet summer corn. Three regular or four small ears fit perfectly.

—Sally Bushwaller, Chicago, IL

Pasta insert is handy for straining stock

I've discovered a handy use for my pasta insert while preparing stock. I put all the ingredients (bones, vegetables, etc.) into the insert and put the insert into the stockpot. When the stock is finished, I *simply lift the insert, drain*, and deposit the waste into the trash. Then I pass the liquid through a strainer lined with cheesecloth. No more awkward maneuvers to pour the scalding liquid and bones out of the stockpot.

—Laura Mack, Boise, ID

Oven rack doubles as cooling rack

When I'm baking loaves of bread, cake layers, or cookies, I transfer the lower *oven rack to a countertop before heating* the oven. The rack is a great size for cooling, and it goes right back in the oven when I'm finished baking.

—Martha Davis, Inman, SC

An oven rack doubles as a pasta drying rack

I love to make fresh pasta but since I don't own a pasta drying rack, I press an oven rack into service. I just put one rack in the top position in the oven and remove the other rack. Next, I *drape strands of pasta over each wire of the rack*, letting the two halves hang down between the wires. Once I'm done, I push the rack back into the oven and close the door. This gives my pasta an out-of-the-way place to dry, protected from dust and pets. I also tape a note to the oven door, reminding me not to turn it on!

—Rex Browning, Mercer Island, WA

Cooling rack doubles as drainer

I use an 18-inch-long cooling rack for more than just cooling baked goods. It *makes a great drainage rack* when set over the sink, particularly for rinsing food that gets cramped in a colander. And since it effectively turns the sink into another work surface (the cooling rack can support a cutting board or baking sheet), it's also an efficient use of space for people who have small kitchens.

—Sheri L. Castle, Raleigh, NC

Cool blanched vegetables quickly on a wire rack

When I was blanching sugar snap peas recently, instead of draining them in a colander, I *straddled a wire cooling rack over the sink* and poured the pot of hot sugar snap peas over it. The peas drained easily, and I was able to spread them out and have air circulate around them so they cooled more quickly. I do this instead of shocking them in cold water so they won't get waterlogged.

—Katy McCabe, Ipswich, MA

Pastry cooling rack doubles as a trivet

I love using my slow cooker to make braises and stews, but I noticed that the counter under the cooker gets quite hot during the long hours it's cooking. Since I don't have a trivet large enough to hold the cooker, I used my biggest, sturdiest *pastry cooling rack as a trivet*. I sometimes also use a heavy-duty, aluminum baking sheet with 1-inch-high sides set upside down as a trivet for the cooker.

—Elena Reddic, Washington Crossing, PA

A trivet in a pinch

For those times when I need one more trivet than I have available, I improvise one with aluminum foil. I *scrunch up the foil* into a long, 1-inch-thick rod and then I shape it into a ring or a Z-shape. It may not be very attractive, but it does the job.

— Robert Danhi, *Fine Cooking*

A roasting rack doubles as a cookbook holder

My large V-shaped roasting rack makes a great makeshift cookbook holder. I rest the *open book in the V-groove* against one of the angled sides. The rack holds the book up but back at enough of an angle that the pages stay open to where you want without flipping back.

—Ken Fruehstorfer, Palatine Bridge, NY

Flour your baking equipment with a puff

I keep a new cosmetic powder puff in my flour canister to dust my pastry boards and rolling pin lightly and evenly with flour before beginning my pastry work.

—Pat Swart, Bridgeton, NJ

Use an ice-cream scoop for muffin and cookie batter

For uniform and professional-looking cookies and muffins, use an ice-cream scoop. It saves time, *makes equal portions*, and is much neater than scraping batter off a spoon.

—Lisa Jung, San Rafael, CA

A coffee scoop for measuring

I received a very nice stainless-steel, long-handled coffee scoop. Since I already have a few coffee measures, I've stored this one with my measuring spoons. The scoop measures 2 tablespoons exactly, and it's handy for use in recipes that call for 2 tablespoons of olive oil or other ingredients. (Check your scoop, though—not all measure 2 tablespoons exactly.)

—Jack Farrell, Lansing, MI

Spray-bottle liqueurs make haste, not waste

When you want to moisten cake layers with liqueur, use a spray bottle to *mist the layers evenly*. Use a funnel to pour any extra liqueur back into the original bottle.

—Mary Sullivan, Coronado, CA

Butter makes a cheese plane useful

Remember that cheese plane in the back of the gadget drawer? Run it across a stick of cold butter for a thin, quick-melting *ribbon of butter*—perfect for buttering your toast or bagel.

—Philippa Farrar, Santa Barbara, CA

Cold soda bottle rolls out a sticky dough

When I need a rolling pin for a small job, I fill a one-liter *soda bottle with cold water*. The weight of the bottle and the cold of the liquid inside tames even the stickiest of doughs. If the dough does stick, I just add a little flour.

—Nancy Smith, New Buffalo, MI

Invert a salad spinner to cover a cake

I often make old-fashioned layer cakes. Finding myself without a proper cake cover, I've discovered that the outside bowl of my salad spinner, *turned upside down*, fits perfectly over a 9-inch cake.

—Brooke P. Cole, Stone Ridge, NY

Tortilla press rolls out mini tart shells

While I was making miniature tart shells for a party, I discovered a better way to roll out the dough. The recipe said to use my fingers to pat the walnut-size balls of dough into the tart pan, but the rough, uneven texture bothered me; I wanted a thin, crisp crust. After my rolling pin failed to give me what I wanted, I tried a tortilla press. I cut open the seams of a zip-top bag (plastic wrap was too thin), floured the bag lightly, positioned the dough balls between the floured pieces of the bag, and applied a slow, even pressure. The result was perfect. The dough was thin and manageable, slipping right into my mini tart pan or muffin tin. And all the tarts were uniform.

The dough was thin and manageable, slipping right into my mini tart pan.

—Mary Hooten, Richmond, VA

Blow-drying fruit

If you're making a dish in which fresh fruit must be washed and then completely dried, such as chocolate-dipped strawberries, rinse the fruit gently and lay it out on a clean terry-cloth dishtowel. Lay another towel on top and gently pat the berries to absorb as much moisture as possible. Then remove the top towel and finish drying the berries using a blow dryer *on its "cool" setting*.

—Phyllis Kirigin, Croton-on-Hudson, NY

Cut fruit with an egg slicer

I don't like boiled eggs very much, but I have found another use for my egg slicer—it works wonders *on soft fruit*. I use it all the time for slicing peeled kiwis since they're just the right size. It works for bananas, too.

—Zach Townsend, Irving, TX

It slices, it dices...

For *perfectly sliced* mushrooms in a flash, I use my egg slicer. Set the mushroom on its side (stem pointing toward you) and slice. Some of the slices will stick together, but they're easy to separate. The egg slicer also comes in handy for shredding packaged mozzarella (not fresh) for pizzas. Put an egg-size chunk into the slicer, slice, turn the cheese 90 degrees, slice again, and *voilà*—perfect shreds. You can even turn the cheese once more and slice to create a beautiful dice.

—Jennifer Winston, Fishkill, NY

Potato ricer squeezes out liquid

To remove almost all the liquid from cooked spinach or grated zucchini, I use a potato ricer. I put a handful in at a time, give it *a few gentle squeezes*, and the vegetables are virtually dry.

—Janet Fee, San Jose, CA

Squeeze more than garlic in a garlic press

When I want to *add an extra boost of flavor* to a soup, sauce, or salad dressing, I reach for my garlic press. I don't just use it for garlic, though. I also press chile peppers, citrus peel, and herbs like fresh rosemary at the same time that I press the garlic.

—Tom Spofford, Davis, CA

Use a melon baller for coring

A medium-size melon baller can do double-duty removing pear and apple cores. Cut pears in half lengthwise and apples in halves or quarters. *Scoop out the core* and the stem ends with the melon baller. It's faster and easier than using a paring knife, and very little fruit is wasted.

—Lillian Main, Victoria, British Columbia, Canada

Melon baller doubles as caper spoon

For a convenient caper spoon, I use my double-ended melon baller. The *smaller end fits into most caper jars*, and the hole in the bottom of the scoop lets the brine drain out.

—Bob Bollinger, Eugene, OR

Potato peeler reaches into caper jar

My potato peeler comes in handy to scoop capers and small olives out of their *narrow jars*. (This works only with old-fashioned straight peelers, of course, not the newer Y-shaped ones.) I also use my peeler to scrape the gills from the underside of portobello mushrooms.

—Joyce A. Foti, Wading River, NY

Getting rid of those sticky fruit labels

For years, I tried to find an easy way to remove those little produce stickers from tomatoes, stone fruit, apples, and pears without tearing the fruit's skin. When I recently bought *a serrated peeler*, I discovered that I could use it to lift the edge of the label away from the fruit and peel it off without taking a chunk of fruit with it.

—Charlotte Kornhauser, Clark, NJ

Pierce whole veggies with corn-cob holders

When microwaving whole potatoes or winter squash, it's usually a good idea to pierce the vegetable several times so that it cooks more evenly. But trying to pierce tough skin with a fork can be difficult. I've found that corn-cob holders are *the perfect piercing instrument*—much more effective than a fork. I also use corn-cob holders to prick the skin of duck or geese before roasting them so the excess fat can run out.

—Diana M. Tarasiewicz, Grand Junction, CO

Zester as cheese grater

When I want to grate just a little Parmesan cheese, I use my lemon zester instead of my cheese grater. With the zester, I can *shave off a small amount* quickly enough, and I'm not left with the chore of washing the grid panel of the grater.

—Steve Hunter, *Fine Cooking*

Charcoal starter decorates cakes

In a pastry class, my teacher used a hot electric charcoal starter to decorate a layer cake. First she dusted the top of the cake with confectioners' sugar. Then she made caramelized lines on the cake by touching one side of the red-hot burner to the sugar. Done in both directions, this *created a lovely lattice design*. I now use my charcoal starter for this purpose only. One word of caution: The starter gets very hot, so set it on a ceramic tile or hot plate while it's warming up and cooling down.

—Lilia Dvarionas, Kanata, Ontario, Canada

Easy-to-open, airtight jar lids

Lately, I've been making batches of vanilla extract that I store in glass jars; I need to check the progress of the flavor occasionally, but the lids can be difficult to open, especially if sugar or other ingredients create a sticky seal. I've found that if I place a *small plastic sandwich bag* between the lid and the jar rim, I can seal it tightly yet when I want to open the jar, the two layers of the plastic bag slide against each other and make the lid easy to remove.

—Mina Yamashita, Albuquerque, NM

Grip jar lids with sandpaper

Get a good grasp on tough-to-open jar lids and bottle tops by covering them with a piece of sandpaper.

—Howard Wiener, Spring Hill, FL

Rubber gloves help open stubborn jars

My dishwashing gloves do more than just protect my hands during cleanup. Their *rubbery, textured surface* helps me get a grip on tight jar lids. And I also don a clean pair when mixing up cold ground meat to make meatballs, burgers, or meatloaf.

—Alan Pelikan, Summit, NJ

Rubber jar openers steady bowls

If you're whisking ingredients in a small bowl (to make a vinaigrette, for example), and the bowl keeps spinning around, try setting a round *rubber jar opener under the bowl*. The rubber disk will steady the bowl and keep it from moving around as you whisk.

—Maureen Gamble, Overland Park, KS

Soda-bottle funnels

I make funnels for filling small-mouth jars from the tops of one-quart or half-gallon plastic bottles.

—Jeanne F. Schimmel, Hobe Sound, FL

Use a can for a cake stand

Since I don't own a cake pedestal, I usually improvise one to make frosting a cake easier. I take a *large can of tomatoes or beans* out of my pantry and put the metal round from the bottom of a cheesecake or tart pan on top of it. (You can also use a cardboard cake round.) I secure the metal round to the can with a bit of duct tape. Having the cake up high really makes frosting it easier.

—Cameron Butler, Lewes, DE

Mustard bottle makes a great garnishing tool

I like to reuse my clear plastic mustard squeeze bottles by washing them and filling them with sweet or savory sauces to *garnish everything* from desserts and appetizers to main courses.

—Buffet Campbell, Agawam, MA

Make bread crumbs in a coffee mill

When I need a cup of fresh bread crumbs for meatloaf or for coating fish or chicken, I use my coffee mill. I simply tear bread into small pieces, toss them in the coffee mill, and pulse. I get *perfectly even bread crumbs* in seconds.

—Bill Sweet, New Bern, NC

Use wooden skewers to lift waffles

To remove my waffles from the waffle iron without damaging them, I stick one *wooden skewer into each side of the waffle* and gently lift up. This prevents any tears or visible puncture marks on the waffles so I can serve them proudly to my guests.

—George Magladry, Eureka, CA

Use ice packs to chill a water bath

The next time you use an ice bath to shock vegetables, stick *an ice pack or two* in a bowl of tap water for a few minutes; they'll chill the bath just as efficiently as ice cubes. This way, you'll always have enough ice on hand for drinks, instead of emptying your freezer trays of precious cubes.

—Rog LaTouche, San Diego, CA

Frozen cold packs have many purposes

When I'm making a custard, an Italian meringue, or any food that needs to be cooled quickly, I use a first-aid cold pack that I always keep in my freezer. I prefer the pack to ice cubes since it doesn't melt or leak, and it's easy to hold in my hand (with a dishtowel). I can also set a bowl on top of the pack and stir a mixture to cool it. For Italian meringue, I rub the pack along the bottom of the bowl of my stand mixer.

I prefer the pack to ice cubes since it doesn't melt or leak.

—Hillary Thagard, via email

Frozen rocks keep crudités cool

To keep my crudités crisp and cold, instead of ice cubes, I use *small white rocks that have been scrubbed*, rinsed, and stored in the freezer in a plastic bag. Smooth river rocks are ideal. I layer the chilled rocks in a bowl or on a platter and pile the vegetables on top. It makes a beautiful presentation, and, best of all, the rocks don't melt.

—Robin Brisco, Tustin, CA

Shake up a vinaigrette in a "sippee" cup

Now that our kids have outgrown spillproof "sippee" cups, I've discovered that they're perfect for making *small batches of vinaigrette or other emulsions.* Just dump in the ingredients, screw on the top, and shake.

—Sheldon Pressman, via email

Blend a slurry in a cocktail shaker

When I need a quick thickener for sauce or gravy, I make a slurry by putting flour and water in a *regular cocktail shaker and giving it a few good shakes*. This produces a much smoother mixture than I've ever been able to make by stirring. And the shaker has a built-in strainer, which keeps any lingering lumps of starch from getting into the sauce.

—Jessica Buker-Vincent, Windham, ME

Paper plate spouts

Inexpensive, flexible paper plates have become valuable helpers to me for small chores in my kitchen. I sift flour and other dry ingredients onto them. Then, holding the plate with one hand and *folding up the sides*, the plate becomes a neat and stable pouring spout. I also use a paper plate as a trough to fill the pepper mill. It works great—the peppercorns don't roll all over the kitchen.

—Evelyn M. Brown, Norfolk, VA

Make a spice shaker from a canning jar

A pint-size, wide-mouth canning jar with *screening wire fitted into the screw-on band* makes a good shaker for dry barbecue spices, jerks, and rubs. It dispenses a wide, even shake and can also be used to store the spices if it's sealed in plastic to keep out moisture. Regular screening wire is sold in hardware stores (just be careful when cutting the sharp edges).

—Dixie Wilson, Olive Branch, MS

A tea infuser doubles as a sugar or spice shaker

While looking for a sifter to dust some paprika over my chicken, I picked up my spring-loaded tea infuser instead. I dipped the infuser into my jar of paprika and shook it over the chicken. It did a great job, *distributing just the right amount* of paprika with no mess. Then I tried it with confectioners' sugar and it worked just as well. To clean the infuser, just give it a quick rinse under the tap.

—Genevieve Jaskiewicz, Stoney Creek, Ontario, Canada

Rulers in the kitchen

I always keep one ruler in a kitchen drawer and another with my wooden spoons on the counter. This way, they're *always handy when I need to measure* a baking dish or casserole. (At our house, we need two rulers since one often disappears at homework time.)

—Ellen Sandberg, North Vancouver, British Columbia, Canada

Crack holiday nuts with Vise-Grip® pliers

Vise-Grip pliers are great for cracking nuts for holiday baking. The design *greatly reduces the force needed* to crack hard-shelled nuts. Turn the adjustment knob to handle different shapes and to apply precise pressure to leave the nut meat intact.

—David Fong, Long Beach, CA

Pliers in the kitchen

I use pliers to remove skin from chicken, to pull off the tough membrane from a rack of ribs, or for any other job that requires *a lot of grip*. I wash the pliers in the dishwasher and keep them with my kitchen shears and other utensils.

—Ann Elder, Fennville, MI

A gold mesh coffee filter works overtime

My kitchen is very small, so I try to get the most out of every kitchen tool I have. I recently discovered that my reusable gold mesh coffee filter can do *double-duty as a strainer*. After steaming clams, I wanted to reserve the broth but saw sand in the bottom of the pot. The coffee filter happened to be within reach, so I used it to strain the broth. Now I also use the filter for straining small quantities of sauce and gravy.

—Tonya Rubiano, Westfield, NJ

Mousepads are all-purpose kitchen tools

Too many freebie mousepads? I use extras to *prevent pastry boards from slipping* and bowls from "creeping" when I'm whisking or beating. Mousepads are also great on the table under hot pots, casseroles, and plates, and when used to prevent appliances from damaging the counter. The only thing mousepads are no good at is trapping mice.

—Susan Asanovic, Wilton, CT

Keep cookbook on a music stand

I found that a good way to keep a cookbook out of the way of splatters and spills is to rest it on a sturdy music stand. *The stand is adjustable* to a good reading height for standing or sitting, and if needed, it comes with a lamp. By positioning the stand on my left (since I'm left-handed) and about 3 feet from where I'm working, I can keep the book at a safe distance, yet it's still handy. To find one of these music stands, call or visit a music store that caters to professional musicians.

—Renee Tate, St. Louis, MO

Rubber bands secure a casserole lid

When I need to bring my favorite casserole to a potluck, I use stout, thick rubber bands (the heavy-duty ones from broccoli are good) to keep the lid on the dish and make it *easier to transport*. I just hook a rubber band over one of the casserole handles and crisscross it over the lid knob, and then I do the same on the other side.

—R. B. Himes, Vienna, OH

Clothes hanger as paper towel holder

My paper towel dispenser is the most low-tech system imaginable: a wire clothes hanger. It's easy to make and use. Use wire cutters to snip the hanger in the middle of the bottom side (the longest side of the triangle). Slip both sides of the wire through a roll of paper towels. The paper towels *roll easily*, and you can move the hanger wherever it's most convenient. I keep mine hanging on a hook off my pot rack.

—Barbara Hom, Night Owl Catering, Sebastopol, CA

Sheet protector + binder clip = recipe holder

Many of my recipes are on single pages printed off the Internet, which I keep in plastic sheet protectors. For handy reference while working at the stove, I attach a *binder clip to the inside of the cupboard door* closest to the range, where I can conveniently hang my recipe at eye level while cooking. This also saves a bit of precious counter space.

—Laura Minne, Boise, ID

Cheap, handy kitchen clips

Binder clips, which are available in office-supply stores, are a big help around the kitchen. They make *great closures for bagged foods and pastry bags,* can hold recipe cards on the stove vent hook, and will clip papers onto refrigerator magnets.

—Russell Shumaker, Richmond, VA

Wood scraper gives icing a smooth finish

For finishing icing on the sides of a cake, I depend on a *6-inch scraper*, which you can buy in hardware stores or at a lumberyard. It's smaller than a spatula and much easier to hold straight. I position the scraper perpendicular to the side of the cake and hold it gently as I rotate the cake's turntable. The scraper also works beautifully on square and triangular cakes, as it can make sharp, perfect corners.

—Krista Stanley, Mt. Kisco, NY

Paint scrapers in the kitchen

I use a paint scraper to cut and scrape dough, to scoop up diced and chopped ingredients, and to clean dough from the work counter when I'm finished baking.

—Bill Moran, San Diego, TX

Shoveling chopped veggies

For years of cooking just for me, I used the flat of my chef's knife or cleaver to transfer chopped vegetables from the cutting board to the pan on the stove. Since I got married and started cooking for two (or more if we have company), the flat blades aren't large enough and I started dropping lots of chopped veggies on the floor with annoying regularity. For a while I tried using a pastry scraper as I had seen on Graham Kerr's show, but it was also too small. While having part of the house rehabbed, I discovered the right tool for the job. I watched a drywaller pick up spilled nails by using a *6-inch drywall knife*, known as a "taping knife," as a shovel. I went to the hardware store and found my own for $7. It has a comfortable handle, flexible steel blade, and is washable. It's large enough for 5 chopped carrots. I get odd looks from guests in my kitchen, but they know me and understand. My main problem is keeping my wife from using it for patching the walls as we rehab the rest of the house.

—Mark Beard-Witherup, Chicago, IL

Use an artist's palette for your ingredient prep

I use a paint palette to hold seasonings and garnishes when I prep ingredients for a dish. The *palette has little wells* that can keep my chopped shallots separate from my minced garlic until I'm ready to use them. The palette keeps all my ingredients at hand so I don't forget to add anything while cooking, and it eliminates the need for numerous small bowls.

—Christine Zieleniewski, Ramsey, NJ

Pillowcase becomes salad spinner

If you don't have a salad spinner, you can make your own with an old cotton *pillowcase and a little centrifugal force*. Put the rinsed greens in the pillowcase and take them outside. Grasp the end of the case in one hand and spin the case in a windmill-like motion next to your body. In about 30 seconds the greens will be dry and the pillowcase will be damp. It looks a little silly, but it's incredibly efficient, especially when you're making large amounts of salad.

—Mark Petroni, Weston, CT

Improvise a salad spinner

You can improvise a salad spinner with a *plastic grocery bag*. Pick out a strong bag with no holes and stuff several paper towels inside. Then place the lettuce in the midst of the paper towels, grab the handles, check for stray guests and children, and twirl the bag around, as if you were going to rope a calf, about ten times. The paper towels will soak up the water, and the lettuce will come out nice and dry.

—Karl Kaufmann, Balboa, Republic of Panama

Improvise a jar lifter for pickles

While sterilizing pickle jars, I realized I didn't have a good jar lifter to get the jars out of the boiling water. I took *thick rubber bands* (the kind used for lobster claws and produce) and wrapped them *around the tips of the tongs*. The wrapped tongs gripped the jars securely so I could pull them out of the boiling water safely and easily.

—Jeanne Schimmel, Hobe Sound, FL

A medicine dropper measures out extracts

I like using flavored extracts in my baking but find it wasteful and irritating when the extract runs down the sides of the bottle when I'm trying to measure it out. Now I use a *child's medicine dropper* to measure extracts. The droppers are marked on the sides with incremental measures of a teaspoon so it's easy to get precisely the amount called for in the recipe. Many pharmacies will give you a medicine dropper if you request one.

—Whitman Kramer, via email

A new use for an old pillowcase

While making a jellyroll, I found I didn't have a dishtowel large enough *to turn the cake onto*, so I used a clean cotton pillowcase. I dusted the pillowcase with cocoa powder to keep it from sticking, flipped the cake onto it, and rolled it up. It worked beautifully. The pillowcase provided plenty of over-hang to keep the cake covered. Afterward, I shook the extra cocoa out of the pillowcase, threw it in the wash, and it came out perfectly clean.

—Robin Hart, via email

Versatile zip-top bags

The most valuable tool in my kitchen is a freezer bag with a zip top. Lightly *coat the inside of a gallon-size freezer bag with vegetable spray* and let yeast dough rise in it. Seal the bag and put the dough in a warm place.

There's no cleanup of messy greased bowls. Put chopped chocolate in a bag, seal it, and put it in hot water for about 5 minutes. Remove from the water, dry the bag, and knead it with your hands for about a minute. When the chocolate is smooth and creamy, snip a small hole in the corner of the bag and squeeze the chocolate onto cakes, pastries, or bar cookies to decorate. When filling mini muffin cups or madeleine tins, put the batter in a gallon-size bag, seal, and snip a $3/4$-inch opening from one corner of the bag. Then simply pipe the batter into the prepared tins. Also, you can use the gallon-size freezer bags to steam green beans and asparagus in the microwave. Prep the vegetables; rinse them with cold running water; and seal, with water still clinging to them, in the bag. Put the bag in the microwave. For 1 to 1½ pounds of crisp tender green beans or asparagus, microwave at 100% power for 5 to 6 minutes.

—Ray L. Overton III, The Georgia Lifestyles Learning Center, Alpharetta, GA

Plastic bag presses salted vegetables

In many recipes, vegetables with a high water content, such as eggplant, cucumbers, zucchini, and cabbage, often need to be salted, pressed, and left to drain to draw out excess moisture. A colander or strainer is the best tool for draining veggies, but its semispherical shape makes pressing difficult. I like to use a gallon-size plastic bag (zip top or twist tied) filled with water to weight the vegetables. The *bag conforms to the irregular contours* and puts consistent pressure on everything in the strainer.

—Russ Shumaker, Richmond, VA

Oiling vegetables lightly and quickly

When a recipe calls for brushing vegetables with oil before grilling or roasting, I put the vegetables in a resealable plastic bag, add a little oil, and coat the vegetables by *massaging them through the plastic*. It's much faster and you won't end up with oily hands or too much oil on the food.

—Elizabeth Karmel, Chicago, IL

Marinade in a bag

I prefer to marinate in *sealed zip-top bags* because, by squeezing out all the air, I'm able to make sure all the pieces are well seasoned and in constant contact with the marinade. Also I can massage the marinated pieces on a regular basis without having to come in contact with them or the marinade.

—Bert Johnston, Talofofo, Guam

Ingredient

Tips

Cut baking powder seal so you're left with a straight edge

When I open a new can of baking powder, I use a sharp knife to *cut away a section of the seal*, leaving as straight an edge as possible. Then when I dip a measuring spoon into the can, I don't need to use a knife to level off the measure. I just swipe the spoon past the straight edge. I also do this for other dry products that have a seal under the lid, such as spices.

—Darlene Postello Sugiyama, Nanaimo, British Columbia, Canada

Keep baking powder dry and active

Don't be tempted to dip a wet or even slightly moist measuring spoon into a can of baking powder. Moisture, and even humidity, will deactivate the powder. *To test baking powder's potency*, add a teaspoon of baking powder to a $1/2$ cup of warm water. If the mixture fizzes and bubbles, the baking powder is still active. If not, it's time to get rid of it. (The strength of baking soda, on the other hand, can be tested by adding it to vinegar; if it foams, it's still usable.)

—Catherine Moulton, Dayton, OH

CHOCOLATE AND COCOA

Melt chocolate in the microwave

This is a great alternative to melting chocolate in a double boiler. Microwaves vary greatly, so you need to adjust the timing to suit your machine. Put finely chopped chocolate in a wide, shallow bowl and *heat it in the microwave on high or medium-high until it just starts to melt*, about a minute. Give it a good stir and microwave it again until it's almost completely melted, another 15 to 30 seconds. Remove the bowl and continue stirring until the chocolate is completely melted.

—Abigail Johnson Dodge, *Fine Cooking*

Melting chocolate in the microwave, take two

Heat dark chocolate on medium heat (50% power) and milk and white chocolate, which contain heat-sensitive milk solids, on low (30% power). Stir the chocolate every 15 seconds, heating until it's just melted.

—Shirley O. Corriher, *Fine Cooking*

A heating pad melts chocolate

You can melt chocolate evenly and safely and hold it at a constant temperature with a heating pad. *Line a metal bowl with the heating pad* and set a slightly smaller bowl on top. Put the chopped chocolate in the smaller bowl and turn the pad to high. Stir the chocolate occasionally. To speed melting, cover the top bowl. When the chocolate has melted, reduce the heating pad's temperature to low. The chocolate will stay melted and it won't scorch.

—Kevin Ryan, Montgomery, IL

Tips for Melting Chocolate

Chop white and milk chocolate finely. White and milk chocolates are delicate; if they get too hot, they can get gritty or scorch. Chopping them finely and stirring frequently helps melt them quickly and evenly with minimal heat.

Chop dark chocolate coarsely. It's more forgiving than white or milk chocolate, so chop it into coarse almond-size pieces. It'll take a little longer to melt than if it were finely chopped, but it means less knife work up front and less frequent stirring.

Watch out for water. Unless you're melting chocolate along with a significant amount of water or another ingredient like butter or cream, just a few drops of water (like what might be in a wet bowl) can make the chocolate seize into an unworkable mass. Be sure that all the tools that come in contact with the chocolate are bone dry before you start and don't cover melting chocolate (condensation from the lid might drip into the chocolate).

—Jennifer Armentrout, *Fine Cooking*

Chop a flat chocolate bar in no time

I use this technique when I want to break up a thin chocolate bar for baking. Lightly loosen the wrapper, then *whack it in several places with a rolling pin*, turning the pin. Unwrap the chocolate to check your progress. If you need smaller pieces, just rewrap the bar and continue hitting it with the rolling pin. If it's warm in your kitchen and the chocolate has softened, put the wrapped chocolate in the refrigerator for 10 minutes to firm it.

—Claire Larrabee, via email

Break up chocolate with an oyster knife

Most knives aren't suitable for breaking up a large block of chocolate: the blade may break if the knife isn't sufficiently sturdy. I've found that the sturdy, short blade of an oyster knife works perfectly. Hold the chocolate block firmly with one hand and the oyster knife with the other. *Dig the oyster knife straight down* into one corner of the chocolate, and pry away small shards of the chocolate, a little at a time.

—Phyllis Kirigin, Croton-on-the-Hudson, NY

Grating chocolate in the food processor

To grate chocolate without melting it (from the heat produced from processing), *freeze the chocolate and use a grating disk*. (The steel "S" blade creates pebble-like pieces of chocolate.)

—Maryellen Driscoll, *Fine Cooking*

Natural cocoa needs cooking; Dutched can stand alone

Natural cocoa is best in recipes that have many ingredients, a large amount of sugar, or where the ingredients undergo considerable transformation in cooking or baking. Dutch-processed cocoa is usually a clear winner in foods where you'll taste the cocoa unadulterated by large amounts of sugar, multiple ingredients, or cooking.

—Alice Medrich, *Fine Cooking*

Getting the lumps out

When dissolving cocoa in liquid, stir just enough of the liquid into the cocoa to *make a stiff paste*. Stir and mash the paste until it's smooth, then stir in the rest of the liquid gradually. If you'll be adding sugar to the cocoa, do it before the liquid goes in.

—Alice Medrich, *Fine Cooking*

Does the Kind of Cocoa You Use Matter?

Two types of cocoa powder are available to the home baker—Dutch processed and natural—and I have long wondered if it really mattered which I used for what.

The first thing I learned is that natural cocoa tends to be a rather inconsistent commodity, varying in flavor, color, and intensity. In the mid-nineteenth century, a Dutch chocolate manufacturer came up with a process by which he could better control and standardize the color and flavor of cocoa. The process, which involves washing the cocoa in an alkaline solution, became known as Dutch processing. The resulting cocoa is consistently darker in color, mellower in flavor, and less acidic than the natural (nonalkalized) powder.

In tasting several brands of Dutch-processed cocoa alongside a few natural cocoas, I did find it indeed to be less bitter than natural. When baking, however, any bitterness is generally mitigated by the sugar, butter, and other good things. In cakes and brownies, the Dutch-processed cocoas tend to produce moister and deeper colored baked goods—an advantage that makes it a favorite of many pastry chefs.

In baking recipes, you'll need to decide which cocoa to use based on the leavening the recipe calls for:

- Use natural cocoa—which has high acidity—in cakes made with baking soda; baking soda is an alkali and relies on an acid in the batter to produce leavening.

- Use Dutch-processed cocoa—which is much less acidic—in batter made with baking powder or eggs (or both), since these are leaveners that don't depend on an acid in the batter to work.

—Molly Stevens, *Fine Cooking*

Keep a chopstick in the flour canister

To measure flour properly, I keep a round chopstick in my flour canister (it just fits at an angle) along with a ½-cup dry measure. When I need flour, I stir it up with the chopstick to aerate it, gently scoop it up with the measuring cup, and scrape off the excess with the chopstick. (A ¼-inch dowel can also work.) If I need a larger amount of flour, I use the ½-cup measure to spoon the flour into a 1-cup measure. This method ensures that I get an *accurate* measurement.

—Melissa Gray Hizy, Pittsville, VA

Give flour a shake before measuring

Before spooning flour into a measuring cup, give the flour bag or canister a good shake. It *aerates the flour* for more accurate measuring.

—Naomi Kurkjian, Piedmont, CA

Shaking out flour

Put flour into *a salt shaker* and use this to flour a cake or muffin pan or to flour a work surface for pastry. This is a handy way to get a light, even coating of flour.

—Maureen Valentine, Sea Tac, WA

For easy-access flour, use a spice jar

I often need just a spoonful of flour for sauces or a sprinkle for rolling out pastry. Rather than haul out a large bin of flour, I now use a smaller container that's got a perfect lid for this purpose. The lids of many extra-large or value-size spice containers have one hole *for spooning* and another *for sprinkling*, and they seal shut with snap-top lids. I thoroughly wash and dry the container, then I fill it with flour.

—Elizabeth Talbert, Fort Wayne, IN

Freezing flour

Flour won't freeze solid like a block but obviously it will become cold. *Take it out of your freezer a few hours before you plan to bake* with it so that its temperature won't affect other ingredients, like yeast or baking powder.

—Dave Anderson, *Fine Cooking*

HOW MUCH PROTEIN IS IN YOUR FLOUR?

TYPE	PROTEIN CONTENT	RECOMMENDED USES
High-gluten flour	14% to 15%	Bagels, pizza crust, blending with other flours
Whole wheat flour	14%	Hearth breads, blending with other flours
Bread flour	12% to 13%	Traditional breads, bread machine breads, pizza crust
All-purpose flour	9% to 12%	Everyday cooking, quick breads, pastries
Self-rising flour	9% to 11%	Biscuits, quick breads, cookies
Pastry flour	8% to 9%	Pie crusts, pastries, cookies, biscuits
Cake flour	5% to 8%	Cakes, especially those with a high ratio of sugar to flour

—Molly Stevens, *Fine Cooking*

HONEY

Keep the honey jar closed and warm

Store honey in an airtight container at room temperature. Honey is hygroscopic, meaning it attracts moisture. If the jar is left open, the honey can absorb water from the air, causing yeast to grow and ferment the honey's sugars. Cold temperatures cause honey to crystallize. To get back to liquid form, put the jar in warm (not boiling) water until the crystals dissolve.

—Jane Charlton, *Fine Cooking*

Use a rubber band to open honey jar

I have discovered a fast and convenient way to unscrew the lid to my honey jar. By putting a wide rubber band around the lid, I can get enough of a grip to open it. I leave the band in place until the jar is empty, at which point I transfer it to the new jar. It's easier than running the lid under hot water, and the rubber band is always there when I need it.

—Verna Poole, St. Helena, CA

Putting a wide rubber band around the lid, I can get enough of a grip to open it.

Soften honey by microwaving it

When trying to get thick honey or syrup out of a jar or plastic squeeze bottle with a narrow neck, microwave the container *for about a minute*. The liquid will pour out easily. (Note from the *Fine Cooking* editors: Honey bears melt surprisingly fast in the microwave, so proceed with caution and read the next tip as well.)

—Lisa Jung, San Rafael, CA

Honey's sweet, but it can get hot

I use the microwave to soften honey, but there are two *safety concerns* readers should know about. (1) Never put any jar into the microwave if it has a metal ring around its collar; (2) For plastic honey containers, like honey bears, always loosen or remove the plastic cap before heating in a microwave. If the honey gets too hot while the cap is secure, pressure can build, causing the container to explode and create a mess in the microwave; worse, it could explode when you uncap it outside the oven.

—Bernard Roth, Santa Barbara, CA

Measure sticky ingredients easily

When I need to measure sticky syrups like honey, maple syrup, molasses, or corn syrup, I measure out the oil in the recipe first, then use the same cup to measure the syrup. The oil-coated cup keeps the syrupy ingredient from sticking so it all ends up in the batter. If the recipe doesn't call for oil, I just lightly wipe the inside of the cup with vegetable oil before measuring.

Measure out the oil in the recipe first, then use the same cup to measure the syrup.

—Kate Brick, Boston, MA

Substituting honey for sugar

Though honey is best used in recipes that call for it, you can try using it in baking recipes that call for granulated sugar *with a few adjustments*: (1) Use 1 part honey for every 1¼ parts sugar; (2) reduce the liquid in the recipe by ¼ cup; (3) add ½ teaspoon baking soda for each 1 cup honey to counter its acidity and weight; and (4) turn the oven down by 25° to prevent overbrowning.

—Jane Charlton, *Fine Cooking*

Keeping maple syrup

Once opened, maple syrup should be refrigerated. *Glass containers maintain flavor better* than plastic and metal. If mold develops, remove it, strain the syrup, and bring to a boil. Let cool and keep refrigerated. Maple syrup keeps indefinitely in the freezer.

—Sarah Jay, *Fine Cooking*

Dark Molasses Is Less Sweet, Better for Baking

A byproduct of the processing of white sugar, molasses is the syrup that's left over once the sugar is separated from the juice of the sugar cane. The sugar is extracted in three stages, and each stage produces a different grade of molasses. After the first boiling, the molasses is relatively light bodied with a sweet, mild taste. This type of molasses, sometimes labeled "mild flavor," is used as a table syrup for pancakes, biscuits, and the like.

Second comes dark molasses. Less sweet with a rich, full flavor, dark molasses is better suited to cooking. Use it in gingerbread or add a spoonful to baked beans. Look for the words *dark* or *robust flavor* on the label.

Blackstrap molasses is what's left after the final extraction. With only the faintest hint of sweetness, blackstrap molasses is very dark and bitter—definitely an acquired taste.

You often see recipes that warn against using sulfured molasses, but the truth is that sulfur is now rarely used in the processing of molasses. Once used to clarify the sugar cane juice, sulfur causes an allergic reaction in many people and most processors have stopped using it.

—Barbara Bria Pugliese, *Fine Cooking*

Choosing nuts in the shell

Look for whole, clean shells with no blemishes, holes, or cracks. Pick up a nut and shake it. Brazil nuts, hazelnuts, walnuts, pecans, and peanuts rattle freely in the shell if they're old and dry.

—Alan Tangren, *Fine Cooking*

Chop nuts quickly with a wooden mallet

Here's a great trick for chopping nuts in a jiffy. I put them in a plastic bag, close it up, and use a wooden kitchen mallet to break them into pieces. Just *three or four strikes of the mallet* and the job is done.

—Betsy Race, Euclid, OH

A nut-toasting shortcut

While preparing to toast nuts, I put a baking sheet in the oven before turning the oven on to heat. When I *spread the nuts on the heated pan*, they brown evenly and quickly.

—Annette Whipple, Ventura, CA

Toasting nuts in the microwave

To toast 1 cup of nuts, spread them out *in a single layer in a shallow bowl* or a glass pie plate. Microwave on high (100%) for 3 to 4 minutes, until they're as brown as you like them. Be sure to give them a stir every minute so they toast evenly. You can also toast sesame seeds and coconut this way; just leave them in for less time.

—Judy Rusignuolo, *Fine Cooking*

Grind nuts with sugar to prevent sticking

Making a dessert that calls for nuts? Grind the nuts with some of the sugar from the recipe so that they won't stick together or become oily.

—B. Bader, Hartsdale, NY

A better way to skin almonds

Here's a simple way to get those stubborn skins off almonds. After covering the almonds with boiling water and draining them, plunge them into an ice bath to cool and then drain again. The *ice water further loosens the skins* and stops the nuts from softening. After you skin the almonds, spread them on a baking sheet and warm them in a 350°F oven for 5 or 10 minutes to improve their texture.

—Barbara C. White, Highland Park, NJ

A glossy shell holds a moist chestnut

Look for glossy shells with no bruises and choose chestnuts that feel heavy for their size.

—Amy Albert, *Fine Cooking*

Roast chestnuts a few at a time for easy peeling

The trick to peeling chestnuts is to roast a few at a time and *peel them while they're still warm.* First, with a sharp paring knife, cut a small slit in the flat side of each chestnut. Then put just six of them on a baking sheet and roast them in a 425°F oven for 15 to 20 minutes. Peel them as quickly as you can, while they're still warm, using oven mitts if you have to. If the chestnuts are allowed to cool before peeling, the papery brown skin under the shell will stick to the nuts like glue. Repeat the roasting procedure, six at a time (or more if you're a fast peeler) until you've peeled all the chestnuts you need for your recipe.

—Betsy Race, Euclid, OH

Microwave chestnuts for easier peeling

Some people peel chestnuts by roasting them a few at a time. I use the same strategy, but I do the "roasting" in the microwave. *Cut an "X" on the curved side* of the chestnut and microwave on high, six at a time, for 40 seconds.

—Henry Troup, Munster, Ontario, Canada

Easy-to-skin nuts

Hazelnuts made me nuts until I learned how to get their skins off easily. Blanch the hazelnuts in boiling water with 1 teaspoon of baking soda for 30 to 45 seconds. Drain the nuts and dump them on a dishtowel. Rub the nuts with the towel and the skins will fall right off. Dry them completely with the towel, then roast them in a 400°F oven for about 8 minutes to bring out the best flavor.

—T. Skipwith Lewis, Marlborough, CT

No more blue walnut bread

Have you noticed the bluish cast that some walnut breads have? Walnuts contain anthocyanins next to their skins, and this causes a blue discoloration in all but very acidic baked goods. You can prevent this by *first roasting the walnuts*, which causes a chemical reaction that changes these compounds into other compounds that won't discolor.

—Shirley O. Corriher, *Fine Cooking*

Homemade walnut-flavored oil

When I moved to the United States from France, one of the ingredients I missed most dearly was walnut oil. (Now, you can buy French walnut oil in specialty shops, but it's often rancid, or on the verge of becoming so, once it's opened). Finally I came up with a flavorful, homemade version of walnut oil. Lightly toast some walnut meats, then add a flavorless vegetable oil like safflower or soybean oil and heat them gently together for a few minutes. Grind the mixture in a blender and filter the resulting mash through a sieve lined with several layers of clean cheesecloth that's been rinsed and squeezed dry. Use a ladle to press as much of the oil out as you can, then gather up the cheesecloth and squeeze until no more oil drips out. The resulting walnut-flavored oil *can be stored in the refrigerator for up to a month*.

I finally came up with a flavorful, homemade version of walnut oil.

—Madeleine Kamman, *Fine Cooking*

SHORTENING

No-stick measuring for shortening

When a recipe calls for both solid shortening and whole eggs or egg whites, use the eggs to keep the shortening from sticking to the measuring cup. Break the eggs into a measuring cup, swish them around to coat the inside of the cup, and then transfer them to the mixing bowl or to another container. Measure the shortening as usual in the coated cup. Turn the cup over and all the shortening will easily slide out.

—Kathryn H. Adams, Birmingham, AL

Use water to measure solid fats

Here's a quick and easy way to measure solid fats without mess. If your recipe calls for ¾ cup solid shortening, fill a liquid measuring cup with water to the ¼ cup line. Add the shortening, making sure it's completely submerged, until the water reaches the 1-cup level. Pour off the water and you have the shortening you need.

—Janet Morgan, Charlestown, RI

Sugar can draw out hidden flavors

A bit of sweetness can bring out other flavors in food. Just *a pinch of sugar* in a savory dish can make a big flavor difference.

—Shirley O. Corriher, *Fine Cooking*

Measuring makes a difference

Remember to *press brown sugar* into the cup when measuring. Simply scooping it up will give you a lot of air along with the sugar and an inconsistent measure.

—Joanne Chang, *Fine Cooking*

Use a measuring cup to tamp down brown sugar

When I measure brown sugar with a cup from my set of nesting measuring cups, I use the *next smaller size cup* to tamp down the brown sugar for the "packed brown sugar" called for in the recipe.

—R. Poole, via email

Getting to soft

If you find that your brown sugar has dried out and hardened, *sprinkle it with a few drops of water and microwave* it on low for 15 to 20 seconds. If you don't have a microwave, tuck a slice of sandwich bread in with the sugar to soften it overnight.

—Joanne Chang, *Fine Cooking*

Keep brown sugar soft with apple peel

To prevent brown sugar from getting hard or lumpy, put a few pieces of *apple peel in with the sugar* in its container. Replace the peel when it dries out.

—Petronella F. Gorton, Boulder, CO

VANILLA

Storing vanilla beans

Vanilla beans will dry out and become brittle if left out in the air, so *wrap them in aluminum foil,* seal in a zip-top bag, and store in a cool, dark area. They'll last this way for several months.

—Joanne Chang, *Fine Cooking*

A second life for vanilla beans

After infusing a custard or sauce with a vanilla bean and scraping out the seeds, *I bury the bean in a jar of white sugar.* Over time, a pleasing vanilla flavor and aroma seeps into the sugar, which can then be used for anything from baking desserts to making applesauce to sweetening your coffee.

—Gwen Flanagan, Bakersfield, CA

New life for dried out vanilla beans

Here's a good way to revitalize those dry, brittle vanilla beans packaged in glass or plastic tubes that have been sitting on your pantry shelf for a while. Fill the tube—bean still inside—with *light cream or half-and-half* and let it soak in the refrigerator for a couple of days. The vanilla bean will soften up; it can then be split and scraped. The bonus is the vanilla-flavored cream, which you can use for coffee or for baking.

—Lawrence A. Davis, Langley, British Columbia, Canada

Getting the most pizzazz from vanilla extract

The strength of vanilla extract will dissipate with prolonged heat, so if you're adding extract to something cooked on the stovetop, such as a custard, add it after the custard is off the stove and starting to cool. Because vanilla extract is sensitive to heat and light, keep the bottle in *a cool, dark place;* it should keep its potency for several months.

—Joanne Chang, *Fine Cooking*

Dairy and Eggs

BUTTER

Storing butter

To keep butter as fresh as possible, store it tightly wrapped away from light on a *back shelf in your refrigerator* (not in the butter compartment on the fridge door; the temperature fluctuates too much there).

—Joanne Chang, *Fine Cooking*

Score butter before unwrapping

Before unwrapping a stick of butter to store in the refrigerator, *I score it through the wrapper along the tablespoon marks* with the back of a knife. When the wrapper is removed, the indentations remain, making it easy to measure later.

—Dixie Wilson, Olive Branch, MS

Slice butter with a pastry cutter

You can use a sharp-bladed pastry cutter to slice a cold stick of butter into perfect little pats.

—Delores Jespersen, Grand Marais, MN

Candy molds for a pretty pat of butter

I collect small, flexible candy molds at secondhand shops and rummage sales, and I use them to mold butter into pretty shapes for parties or special events. I *let the butter soften before pressing* it into the molds; then I refrigerate or freeze it until firm again. The molds are so flexible that the butter pops right out. Molds have seasonal designs and themes, and this is a fun, easy way to make a party interesting.

—Melanie Walton, East Hampton, CT

How soft is softened butter?

When a baking recipe calls for softened butter, let it stand at room temperature until it's *malleable but not too soft*, 30 to 60 minutes depending on the temperature of the room. It should give slightly when pressed but still maintain its shape. The ideal is 67°F. Butter that's too soft will provide less leavening. To speed up the softening time, you can cut the butter into tablespoon pieces.

—Elaine Khosrova, *Fine Cooking*

Warm sugar softens cold butter

For people like me who love to bake on the spur of the moment, here's a way to detour the need to soften butter in advance. For recipes that call for beating the sugar with room-temperature butter—cookies, for example—just heat the sugar in the microwave first. Granulated sugar holds heat very well, and it can easily pick up enough heat in the microwave to warm the butter to about room temperature during mixing. *I microwave the sugar just long enough to warm the granules*—about 2 minutes—but not to melt them. Then I proceed with creaming the butter and sugar.

—Linda Lang, Malvern, PA

Softened butter in a hurry

To soften butter quickly, you need to increase the surface area that's exposed to room temperature. *Cut the butter into small cubes,* separate the cubes into a single layer, and let them sit on the counter. They'll reach optimal creaming temperature (65° to 68°F) in about 30 minutes.

—Jennifer Armentrout, *Fine Cooking*

Grate frozen butter

To quickly soften frozen butter, *grate the butter* onto a plate. It will soon soften to room temperature.

—Suzanne Campodonico, Menlo Park, CA

Clarify butter in the oven

It's easy to clarify butter in the oven. Put a pound of butter in an ovenproof dish that's fairly deep and not too wide. (I use a soufflé dish.) Put the dish into a 300°F oven for 1 hour. The butter will slowly melt, leaving you with clear yellow clarified butter on top and white milk solids at the bottom. Spoon off the butter, and it's ready to use.

—Jan Darbhamulla, Newark, CA

Clarify butter in the microwave by "defrosting"

It's easy and quick to clarify butter in the microwave. Just use a microwave-proof dish or jug and use the "defrost" setting. The time needed will depend on the amount of butter used. I've found that *the "defrost" setting* is also good for melting chocolate without scorching it.

—Wendy Chan, Singapore

Clarifying butter in the microwave

Making clarified butter by *removing the milk solids and liquids* from the butterfat is a natural for the microwave. After melting the butter (a stick of butter in a small measuring cup works well), let it stand for 5 minutes for the butter to separate. Skim off the foam from the top, then carefully pour the clear butterfat into another container. Discard the milky liquid that remains on the bottom.

—Judy Rusignuolo, *Fine Cooking*

Make your own buttermilk

To make a quickie buttermilk yourself, add *1 tablespoon of lemon or lime juice* to 1 cup of room-temperature whole milk. Let sit for 5 minutes, and you have sour milk, which can be substituted for buttermilk in your pancake recipe and others as well.

—Dale Conoscenti, Montpelier, VT

No matter the number, it's all the same when you bake

At the supermarket, you'll see buttermilk labeled with various percentages of milkfat: ½%, 1%, or 1½%. For baking, *they're essentially interchangeable.*

—Carolyn Weil, *Fine Cooking*

Freezing buttermilk

I don't use buttermilk often enough to finish the carton before it expires. Can it be frozen?

—Anita Hansell, Westport, CT

Sarah Jay replies: When buttermilk is frozen and then defrosted, it loses some of the creaminess it had when fresh and it separates slightly. For that reason, the National Dairy Council doesn't recommend freezing it. The change in texture would probably be noticeable in sauces, such as ranch salad dressing, and in dishes in which the buttermilk's texture is all-important, such as a buttermilk pie. But for many baked goods, frozen buttermilk is fine (powdered buttermilk is another option). When I made my favorite scones using both frozen and fresh buttermilk, I couldn't detect any real difference, but the pancakes made with frozen weren't as light and airy as those made with fresh.

Buttermilk will keep frozen for 2 months, but the longer it is frozen, the more it will deteriorate in quality. Before freezing, shake the carton vigorously. Then freeze it in small portions (½ or 1 cup) in zip-top bags; these sizes defrost quickly and are practical quantities for most recipes. Defrost buttermilk in the refrigerator and use it within the next day; if there's any left over, discard it.

Condensed Milk vs. Evaporated Milk

Last summer, I was following a new recipe for potato salad that called for evaporated milk and I mistakenly used condensed milk. Having ruined the salad, I decided it was time to figure out what was what. Both evaporated and condensed milk begin as fresh milk. The milk undergoes a vacuum process that evaporates over half the volume of the milk and concentrates the nutritive part of the milk. Evaporated milk is then poured into cans that are heat sterilized to prevent spoilage. The ultra-high temperatures of sterilization cause the milk sugars to caramelize and give evaporated milk its characteristic cooked taste. In the end, evaporated milk has the consistency of light cream and a tint that ranges from ivory to pale amber.

Condensed milk is basically evaporated milk with a lot of sugar added (up to 2⅓ cups per 14-ounce can) before it's canned. The result is a thick, gooey, and intensely sweet product. Since large amounts of sugar prevent bacterial growth, condensed milk doesn't need to be heat sterilized and has a less caramelized flavor than evaporated milk.

Despite their similar packaging and nomenclature, evaporated and condensed milks are not interchangeable. Evaporated can be reconstituted with an equal volume of water and used to replace fresh milk in most recipes.

According to food scientist Shirley Corriher, evaporated milk is good in sweet bread doughs because of its high concentration of lactose. Yeast doesn't like lactose, which means that a greater amount of residual sugars (unconverted by yeast activity) remains in the final bread, and the loaf is sweeter. Due to its high sugar content, the primary use for condensed milk is in sweets. Bakers find it especially useful in candy and fudge since the sugar has already been boiled down into a syrup, meaning fewer problems with crystallization. Condensed milk is also often used to give some bar cookies their characteristically gooey consistency. When beaten with an acid, such as lemon juice, condensed milk develops the consistency of soft cream cheese, and this mixture is sometimes used for making cheesecakes and pies.

—Molly Stevens, *Fine Cooking*

Weighing grated cheese

When a recipe calls for grated cheese by weight, I *weigh the block of cheese* before I start grating and weigh it again, at intervals, as I grate. If the cheese weighs 8 ounces to start with and I need 2 ounces for a recipe, I grate until the block weighs 6 ounces. It's much easier than grating cheese onto a scale.

—Jan Mathieu, Luck, WI

No-stick grating

Before you shred cheese with a hand-held grater, *spray the grater with cooking spray* or rub it with a little oil. This will prevent the cheese from sticking and slowing down the job.

—Mary Jane Kaloustian, Northville, MI

Grating cheese in the food processor

To grate a semisoft cheese, like mozzarella, put the *cheese in the freezer to firm* it up for 20 to 30 minutes before processing.

—Maryellen Driscoll, *Fine Cooking*

Cut goat cheese with dental floss

To cut a log of soft goat cheese into individual servings, use dental floss. Tightly stretch a length of the floss perpendicular to the log, then *gently saw it back and forth* to cut neat medallions without crushing the cheese.

—Cameron Butler, Lewes, DE

Zip up cream cheese to soften

To soften cream cheese easily without melting, seal it in a zip-top plastic bag and *immerse it in hot water*. The cream cheese will be pliable in minutes.

—Helen D. Conwell, Fairhope, AL

White vinegar extends the shelf life of cheese

To keep my cheese from getting moldy too quickly in the refrigerator, I take it out of its packaging and wrap it in a piece of cheesecloth (or good-quality white paper towel) that's been dipped in white vinegar and squeezed out. Then I put the cheese into a zip-top plastic bag, squeeze the air out of the bag, and seal it. This prevents the cheese from getting moldy for many weeks, and the *vinegar doesn't affect the flavor* at all.

—Ana Weerts, Brookfield, WI

Deep-freeze cheese

Is it all right to freeze cheese? I sometimes buy mozzarella in bulk and then realize I don't know what to do with it all.

—Martin Hammond, Newburyport, MA

Robert Aschebrock, a former grader of butter and cheese from the USDA, replies: You can freeze many cheeses if you take care to package them well, although a cheese's moisture level, salt content, and texture will also determine how well it survives the freezer.

Ice crystals often form in high-moisture cheeses (like muenster, Monterey jack, and fresh mozzarella) and in open-textured cheeses (like havarti and some blues) during freezing. These crystals force the cheese curd apart, causing the cheese to become crumbly after thawing. While the cheese's texture may suffer significantly (it will be hard to slice or shred), it should be fine for melting and cooking. Also, its flavor shouldn't deteriorate considerably.

A cheese with a high salt content (like feta) isn't a great candidate for freezing. The higher the salt content, the colder the cheese must be to freeze and the more likely ice crystals may form. After freezing, the feta will normally be suitable only for incorporating into cooked dishes.

It's easier to slice or shred cheeses before freezing rather than after. Freeze small portions of grated cheese in a double layer of zip-top bags. Tightly wrap individual pieces of cheese in aluminum foil first, then put them in zip-top bags. To defrost frozen cheese, thaw it for at least 24 hours in the refrigerator. Don't thaw the cheese at room temperature, as it will defrost unevenly and may become moist, slimy, and very crumbly.

Salt removes mold from hard cheese

If mold starts to appear on the surface of any hard cheese, such as Parmesan, aged Cheddar, or dry Jack, there's no need to trim away the mold. Just rub salt on that section and the *mold rubs right off.*

—Ig Vella, Vella Cheese, Sonoma, CA

Rescuing dried-out Parmesan

If your hunk of Parmesan dries out during storage (store it tightly wrapped in aluminum foil in the vegetable crisper), *rewrap it in a moist paper towel*, then in foil for a day before rewrapping it just in foil.

—Rob Gavel, *Fine Cooking*

Cold is best

The colder cream is, *the faster it whips*, so at least 20 to 30 minutes before you intend to make whipped cream, put your bowl and beaters in the freezer.

—Jennifer Armentrout, *Fine Cooking*

Heavy Cream vs. Whipping Cream

I used to think that heavy cream and whipping cream were the same product simply marketed under different names. Now, after a bit of research and a few tests in the kitchen, I've learned that there are differences—albeit slight— between these two types of cream.

Heavy cream is the richest type of liquid cream with a fat content of at least 36% (one local dairy I spoke to produces its heavy cream at 39%), whereas whipping cream contains between 30% and 36% fat.

In general, the more fat in the cream, the more stable it will be for whipping and for sauce making. For whipping, you need a minimum of 30% fat. While both whipping cream and heavy cream whip up quickly, I did discover that whipped cream made with whipping cream was softer, more voluminous (25% to 30% more), and more enjoyable spooned on top of desserts. The whipped cream made with heavy cream was denser and firmer—making it a good choice for piping through a pastry bag.

In sauce making, the minimum amount of fat required to prevent cream from curdling when boiled with acidic and savory ingredients is 25%, so again both creams qualify. Heavy cream, however, has the advantage here since it is a bit more unctuous and requires less time to cook down to thicken and enrich a sauce.

The final difference is that heavy cream has 5 more calories per tablespoon than whipping cream and it costs 5¢ to 10¢ more per pint.

—Molly Stevens, *Fine Cooking*

Tips for perfectly whipped cream

Don't use ultrapasteurized cream, if possible. It overwhips easily, doesn't get as thick or hold up as well, and has a slightly cooked taste. When close to soft peaks, stop the mixer and *finish whisking by hand to avoid over-whipping*. If the cream gets too stiff or curdled, fold in a little unwhipped cream to soften it. Finally, ¾ cup whipping or heavy cream will yield about 2 cups whipped cream, enough to garnish 10 to 12 desserts.

—*Fine Cooking* editors

Salvaging overwhipped cream

When whipping cream to soft, billowy peaks with an electric mixer, a few seconds of extra beating can take the cream into the stiff peak zone. There is a remedy to this, as long as you haven't gone so far as to beat the cream into butter. As soon as you notice that the cream looks overwhipped, *stop the mixer*. Pour in a bit more heavy cream and whisk by hand gently to incorporate it.

—Jennifer Johnson, New London, CT

Holding whipped cream for twenty-four hours

To hold whipped cream overnight, select a bowl a little larger than the volume of your whipped cream. Thoroughly rinse and squeeze dry a triple layer of cheesecloth. *Drape the cheesecloth inside the bowl* and over the edges and secure the cheesecloth to the bowl with a rubber band. Spoon your freshly whipped cream into the cheesecloth. Cover with plastic wrap and refrigerate for up to 24 hours before using. Some liquid will drain to the bottom of the bowl, and the whipped cream will remain firm and creamy.

—Phyllis Kirigin, Croton-on-Hudson, NY

YOGURT

A space-saving way to make yogurt cheese

I love to serve tangy yogurt cheese in the summer as a dip for raw vegetables and pita chips, but since I don't have enough refrigerator space to hold a full-size strainer to drain the yogurt, I came up with a unique method. I use a clean, 32-ounce yogurt container with some cheesecloth draped inside, the outer edges of the cheesecloth held in place with a rubber band around the rim of the container. The *cheesecloth creates a little hammock to hold the yogurt* while it's draining, and the container's lid can be snapped on to protect the contents from any strong-smelling foods in the refrigerator.

—James Koyanagi, Dawson City, Yukon Territory, Canada

EGGS

How to spot the freshest eggs

You might be surprised to learn that some egg cartons tell you exactly what day the eggs were packed—a piece of information that's a lot more specific than a sell-by date. About one-third of the eggs in the United States. are packed under the USDA's voluntary grading service. If the eggs in your market were graded by a USDA inspector, the carton will display a USDA grade shield; a three-digit code that reveals the packing date will be stamped somewhere on the carton, usually on the short side near the expiration date. The code is actually a Julian date, meaning it represents a day of the year, not a day of a month. So a carton marked *001* means it was packed on January 1; *365* means December 31. To find the freshest eggs in your store, look for the *packing date that has the highest number* (with the exception of the transition from December to January). Don't confuse the packing date with the packing plant number, which is always preceded by the letter *P*. If the carton doesn't have a USDA shield, it was packed under local regulations, which vary from state to state and it may or may not carry a packing date.

—Maryellen Driscoll, *Fine Cooking*

Float an egg for freshness

To check an egg's freshness, put it (in its shell) in a large bowl of room-temperature water. As an egg ages, it loses moisture, and the air sac inside the large end of the egg shell enlarges. The swelling of the air sac increases the egg's buoyancy. Therefore, *the older the egg, the higher it floats*. If an egg shows more than the size of a dime above the water, it's not suitable for poaching.

—Robert Danhi, *Fine Cooking*

White eggs this week, brown eggs next

I buy eggs weekly and store them in a special container in my refrigerator. I buy white eggs one week and brown the next, so if I don't use all the eggs in a week's time, it's easy to *tell the difference* between the older eggs and the fresher ones.

—Elfi Norris, Palm Coast, FL

Does Egg Size Matter?

If you happen to have a different size egg than what your recipe calls for, it's good to know when and how you can substitute. The good news is that differences in egg sizes are surprisingly small, so unless you're baking, casual substitutions are easy.

WHEN SIZE DOESN'T MATTER

If your recipe doesn't depend on the right proportions of eggs to succeed—you're making a frittata, a strata, or using a beaten egg to coat cutlets or bind fritters—use whatever size egg you have on hand. If that recipe (say, a frittata) happens to call for large quantities of eggs, you can use the substitution chart below for a little better accuracy.

WHEN SIZE DOES MATTER

If your recipe depends on the proportion of eggs to succeed (you're baking a cake, making custard, etc.), and you don't have the large eggs the recipe calls for, you'll want to measure the volume of your substitute eggs (you'll need to blend them first), and use the amount equivalent to what the large eggs would have yielded:

> **1 large egg, beaten = 3¼ tablespoons**
>
> **2 large eggs, beaten = 6½ tablespoons (¼ cup plus 2½ tablespoons)**
>
> **3 large eggs, beaten = 9⅔ tablespoons (½ cup plus 1⅔ tablespoons)**
>
> **4 large eggs, beaten = 12¾ tablespoons (¾ cup plus ¾ teaspoon)**
>
> **5 large eggs, beaten = 1 cup**

Nest for eggs

When gathering all the ingredients together before beginning to cook, eggs can be pesky—they roll around the counter and get in the way. Make a handy homemade tool to hold eggs while they await their turn by cutting a 4-egg section from *the bottom of a cardboard egg carton*. It keeps the eggs from rolling, and you can safely and quickly move all 4 simultaneously. If you find yourself using 6 eggs frequently, cut out a 6-egg section instead. The mini-carton stores easily in the utensil drawer.

—Mary Sullivan, Concord, CA

WHAT'S IN AN EGG?

Eggs are classified by weight by the dozen. Because of this, there will be slight variations in the weights of eggs in every carton. A dozen extra-large eggs weighs 27 ounces (about 2¼ ounces each on average), a dozen large eggs weighs 24 ounces (about 2 ounces each), and a dozen medium eggs weighs 21 ounces (about 1¾ ounces each).

> **1 extra-large egg yields ¼ cup (2⅔ tablespoons white and 1⅓ tablespoons yolk)**
>
> **1 large egg yields 3¼ tablespoons (2¼ tablespoons white and 1 rounded tablespoon yolk)**
>
> **1 medium egg yields 3 tablespoons (2 tablespoons white and 1 tablespoon yolk)**

IF YOUR RECIPE CALLS FOR FOUR OR MORE EGGS...

In nonbaking recipes, if you're substituting only one, two, or three extra-large or medium eggs for large eggs, simply make a one-to-one direct substitution. Beyond that, use these equivalents:

- **In place of 4 large eggs, use 4 extra-large or 5 medium eggs**
- **In place of 5 large eggs, use 4 extra-large or 6 medium eggs**
- **In place of 6 large eggs, use 5 extra-large or 7 medium eggs**

—Molly Stevens, *Fine Cooking*

Separation anxiety

It's easiest to separate eggs *when they're cold* because the yolks are firmer.

—Jennifer McLagan, *Fine Cooking*

Separating eggs smartly

If you need to separate lots of eggs, *separate each egg individually over a small bowl.* This way, you'll be sure that each white is clean before adding it to the others in your beating bowl and there's no chance that the last egg you separate will break its yolk and contaminate a bowl full of whites.

—Jennifer Armentrout, *Fine Cooking*

Separating eggs to reduce the possibility of salmonella

Never separate whites from yolks by passing the yolk between halves of the shell; instead, *use an egg separator* or a spoon to reduce contact between the egg and the outer surface of the shell. Yolks present more of a problem than the whites, as the whites contain an enzyme called lysozyme, which actually inhibits bacterial growth. Thus meringue is less susceptible to contamination than is mayonnaise.

—Molly Stevens, *Fine Cooking*

Removing egg yolk from whites

Despite my best efforts, sometimes a little yolk gets into the whites when I separate eggs. The stray yolk can be removed by touching it with a corner of a clean cloth that's been moistened with cold water. The *yolk will adhere to the cloth*, but the white won't.

—Helen D. Conwell, Fairhope, AL

And another way

If you spot a small speck of yolk in the whites, use a *clean* eggshell to scoop it out; it will attract the yolk like a magnet.

—Flo Braker, *Fine Cooking*

Egg shell grabber

The edge of a *serrated grapefruit spoon* easily grabs elusive bits of eggshell.

—Charmaine Swenson, Milaca, MN

Quickly warm eggs

To bring eggs to room temperature quickly, submerge them (still in their shells) in a *bowl of warm tap water* for 5 to 10 minutes.

—Elaine Khosrova, *Fine Cooking*

Bring egg whites to room temperature over warm water

If you need egg whites for a recipe like meringue, you'll find it easier to separate the whites from the yolks when the eggs are cold. Then you'll want to bring your egg whites to room temperature because they'll whip up better. To do this, put them in a bowl and set it over (but not touching) very warm water. When the bottom of the bowl is no longer cool, the whites are warm enough to use.

—Margery K. Friedman, Rockville, MD

CUSTOMIZE EGG WASHES FOR VARIED EFFECTS

CONTENT OF EGG WASH	EFFECT ON COOKED PASTRY
Whole egg with water	Nicely browned, slightly glossy
Whole egg with milk	Nicely browned, glossier
Egg white only	Evenly browned, slightly less brown than whole egg, very little shine
Egg yolk only or egg yolk	Browned and shiny, but less so than yolks with water cream or milk
Egg yolk with cream	Very browned and glossy, but a relatively thick egg wash that's somewhat difficult to spread neatly
Egg yolk with milk	The darkest brown crust and a touch less shiny than yolk with cream

—Molly Stevens, *Fine Cooking*

Perfectly whipped egg whites

For the best volume when whipping egg whites, *wipe down your mixing bowl and beaters with white vinegar* to ensure that they're free of any lingering traces of oil or grease that could prevent the egg whites from whipping up properly. The acid in the vinegar also negates the need for cream of tartar, so if your recipe calls for it, you can leave it out.

—Cassia Schell, via email

Picking the right bowl for whipping egg whites into meringue

Avoid using aluminum bowls and tools because any acid you add to the whites to increase stability will react with the aluminum and turn the egg whites gray. Choose a bowl to accommodate the quantity of whites to be whipped, keeping in mind that egg whites expand up to 8 times their original volume when whipped. For example, 4 large egg whites averaging 1 fluid ounce each can yield 4 cups of meringue. *Never use cold bowls*, as chilled egg whites will take longer to reach full volume. Rinsing a stainless-steel bowl in warm water before using it will hasten the whipping process, and wiping it with a bit of white vinegar will ensure a grease-free surface.

—Carole Walter, *Fine Cooking*

Reviving overbeaten egg whites

If you overbeat egg whites that are to be folded into a batter—to the point that they clump instead of blend when you fold them—there is a fix. First, use a clean spatula to scoop a quarter of the whites into the batter as directed. If the whites clump badly instead of blend as you fold, beat a fresh egg white into the remaining whites for a few seconds to remoisten them—they won't be perfect, but they should soften up. You can now fold the revived whites into your batter.

—Alice Medrich, *Fine Cooking*

Folding with a whisk

When combining beaten egg whites with other ingredients, use a whisk instead of a rubber spatula to fold in the delicate whites. The goal is to avoid deflating the whites by working quickly and efficiently, so that you have the maximum volume in your soufflé, cake batter, mousse, or whatever. When you fold with a whisk, each wire of the whisk draws the egg whites into the rest of the mixture, so only a few deft strokes are necessary to thoroughly blend the two components. With the conventional spatula method, you need to use more strokes, and you're working with a heavier utensil, so you risk overworking the whites and losing precious volume. Use the same "cutting-and-rolling" motion that you would with a spatula, and be sure to turn the bowl as you fold.

Use a whisk instead of a rubber spatula to fold in the delicate whites.

—Karen Metz, Washington, DC

Yolks smooth, thicken, and moisten

Whenever you want an unbelievably smooth texture, egg yolks are key because they contain emulsifiers, notably lecithin. An emulsifier is a compound with one end that dissolves in fat and one that dissolves in water, meaning ingredients that normally don't mix well will blend together smoothly and willingly when egg yolk is present. When a dish containing whole eggs is too dry, *switch some of the whole eggs to yolks*. I had a restaurant call me because their hot rolls were drying out near the end of serving time. When they switched half of the whole eggs in the recipe to yolks, the rolls stayed moister longer.

—Shirley O. Corriher, *Fine Cooking*

Streakless egg wash

To make an egg wash that is smooth, evenly textured, and brushes on easily, I *add a pinch of salt* to a whole egg beaten with 1 tablespoon of water. The salt breaks down the protein in the egg white so that the wash is fluid. This way I don't end up trying to brush out globs of viscous egg white on tender bread dough. The baked bread has an even color with no streaks.

—Robin Rice, Norwich, VT

Brush first, then score

If you're planning to score the surface of a loaf of bread or pastry, *first brush on the egg wash*, then score the dough so the egg wash doesn't drip into the score marks and seal them closed.

—Molly Stevens, *Fine Cooking*

A neater way to chop eggs

Use a pastry blender to chop hard-cooked eggs. The blender won't chop the eggs too finely, and it's *much easier and neater* than using a knife.

—Peggy Makolondra, Sturgeon Bay, WI

Fish, Meat, and Poultry

CAVIAR

Not just any spoon will do

When serving caviar, use a glass, bone, or mother-of-pearl spoon. Even a plastic spoon is preferable to metal, which will impart a metallic flavor.

—Amy Albert, *Fine Cooking*

CLAMS

Degritting clams

Before cooking clams, I soak them for half an hour in a mixing bowl with *water and 2 or 3 tablespoons of cornmeal*. The shellfish ingest the cornmeal and spit it out again, along with whatever dirt was inside the shells.

—June Cerrito, Wakefield, RI

When you're steaming...

Steamers, littlenecks, and cherrystones are the best for steaming. Look for hard-shell clams that are firmly shut and have a clean sea scent. When you get them home, take them out of the bag (they suffocate in plastic), put them in a bowl, cover with a wet towel, and store in the refrigerator. Though it's best to cook them as soon as possible, they'll keep this way for up to 2 days. Whatever you do, *don't soak them in water*—fresh water kills them and leaches out their flavor. Because soft-shell clams gape open, they're inevitably full of sand and should be encouraged to cleanse themselves before cooking. Soaking them in cold salt water (1 cup salt to 3 quarts water) overnight or at least for a few hours usually takes care of the sand. Then they can be stored like hard-shell clams. Shortly before steaming scrub them with a stiff brush under cold running water to get rid of any grit. Eliminate any dead clams before steaming. Give any open clams a tap; if they don't snap shut relatively quickly, throw them away.

—James Peterson, *Fine Cooking*

Steam clams and save the "liquor"

After steaming clams or mussels, there's always 1 or 2 cups of highly flavored liquid left in the steaming pot. Don't toss it out. Instead, carefully pour it into a reusable plastic container (leaving behind any sediment), let it cool, seal it, label it, and freeze it. Next time you're making rice or couscous, *use the clam or mussel "liquor" instead of water* for a flavor boost.

—John Delzani, Lakewood, OH

CRABMEAT

Checking for crab shells

There are few dining experiences as unpleasant as biting on a piece of crab shell. After years of laboriously picking over crabmeat, I've developed a technique that's quick and accurate. It's all done by ear. With an ear bent over a glass, china, or metal plate, pick up a clump of the crabmeat, 2 or 3 tablespoons in size, with your fingers. From *a height of about 6 inches, drop it onto the plate*. The crabmeat will scatter slightly and, if there is shell present, you will hear a distinct "click." If this happens, drop that clump again until you localize the guilty bit. Repeat until all the crabmeat has been checked.

—Helen D. Conwell, Fairhope, AL

Pick a frisky lobster

When held by its body, a lobster should flap its tail and wave its claws around. *Avoid lethargic lobsters* and those with short antennae or with algae growing on them, signs of long storage.

—Jennifer Armentrout, *Fine Cooking*

Tying the lobster's tail keeps it straight

The tail meat will be easier to slice into neat medallions if you tie a soupspoon or a table knife to the tail to *to keep it straight before* cooking the lobster.

—Charlie Trotter, *Fine Cooking*

Roll out the lobster

When I splurge on lobster, I don't want to waste a single delicious morsel. To get the meat out of those long, skinny legs, *I remove the leg and run a rolling pin over it*, from the "foot" up. The meat pops right out.

—Christine Adams, Charlottesville, VA

Serve lobster with infused garlic butter

When melting butter to serve with lobster, I like to add small quantities of finely chopped garlic, citrus zest, or fresh herbs to the butter an hour or two before serving. *Keeping the melted butter warm* gives the flavorings time to infuse the butter more fully.

—E. Burr, via email

Closed shells are a sign of freshness

When buying mussels, they should be completely closed or just slightly gaping; and if they smell like anything other than the sea, give them back. When you get them home, take them out of the bag (they suffocate in plastic), put them in a bowl, cover with a wet towel, and store in the refrigerator. Though it's best to cook them as soon as possible, they'll keep this way for up to 2 days. Whatever you do, don't soak them in water—fresh water kills them and leaches out their flavor. *Eliminate any dead mussels* before steaming. Look for

continued

any mussels that have opened and tap them on the kitchen counter. If they don't close, discard them. For closed mussels, press on the sides of the two shells in opposing directions. Dead mussels will fall apart. Shortly before you're ready to start steaming, scrub the mussels with a stiff brush under cold running water. If the mussels have big "beards"—black hairlike fibers that enable them to cling to things—use your thumb and forefinger to yank them off. If you steam mussels and find that one doesn't open, it's almost invariably bad, so don't take a chance and simply throw it away.

—James Peterson, *Fine Cooking*

Debeard at the last minute

Debeard mussels as close to cooking time as possible, as debearding the mussel kills it.

—Arlene Jacobs, *Fine Cooking*

OYSTERS

Choose oysters with tightly shut shells

At the market, look for oysters that feel heavy in the hand, with shells that are shut tight, a good sign that there's *a fresh, juicy oyster inside*. Don't eat any open oysters, even if they shut after being nudged. Once you hustle your oysters home, don't put them in ice, but do stash them in the refrigerator. Arrange each oyster so that its convex side faces down (the more deeply cupped half holds the flesh and liquor) and drape a wet towel over them so the shells don't dry out.

—Amy Albert, *Fine Cooking*

Prying open oysters

If you're faced with a sinkful of oysters but don't have an oyster knife to open them, you can use a *church-key type of can opener* instead. Hold the oyster with a dishtowel so that the shell doesn't cut you. Find the small opening between the shells on the narrow, hinged end of the oyster. Wedge the pointed tip of the can opener between the shells and, with a quick twist of the wrist, pry the shells apart. You're actually breaking the muscle that keeps the shell closed. Don't work too fast, though, or the shells may splinter. Slide the can opener between the shells all the way around the oyster and then pull the two shells apart.

—Pamela Lloyd Owen, Newfields, NH

Dry versus wet scallops

When you're at the fish counter, you'll often see sea scallops labeled two ways—"dry" and "wet." (If they're not marked, ask.) Whenever you can, *choose the dry* scallops. Wet scallops have been treated with a solution called STP (sodium tripolyphsphate), which helps the scallops maintain their moisture (they're made up of about 75% water when fresh). The STP solution gives scallops a longer shelf life; they don't dry out or lose their plump appearance. As a result, you'll not only pay for the added water weight (and often get scallops that are less than fresh), but you'll also have trouble browning these scallops—no matter how hot your pan or oven—because of all that excess moisture. The STP solution can also give scallops a rubbery texture and cloud the mollusk's sweet, delicate flavor.

—Tony Rosenfeld, *Fine Cooking*

Shop for scallops with your eyes and nose

Fresh scallops should appear moist but not milky. Refuse any that have a feathery white surface (a sign of freezer burn) or dried and darkened edges (a sign of age). *Always ask to smell scallops* before buying. They should smell somewhat briny and seaweedy but not offensive, sharp, or at all like iodine. If the scallops have no smell and a uniform stark white color, chances are they've been soaked in STP.

—Molly Stevens, *Fine Cooking*

Don't rinse scallops

If your scallops have any sand on them, *quickly rinse* them in cold water and pat them dry with a paper towel. Otherwise, don't wash scallops or they'll absorb water.

—Charlie Coppola, *Fine Cooking*

Peel shrimp in a jiffy

The best tool I've found for peeling shrimp is a *zip letter opener* (the small hand-held plastic kind that is given away as a promotional item). It quickly splits open the shell and separates the flesh for easy deveining.

—Doug Pryor, Key West, FL

Keeping fish fresh

Put whole fish or fillets in a large strainer set over a bowl. *Pile ice high on top* of the fish and refrigerate. The ice keeps the fish close to 32°F and, as it melts, the water continually rinses off bacteria and drains it into the bowl. When choosing a whole fish, look for shining, iridescent skin; springy flesh; clear, bright eyes with black pupils; and pink to red gills. The signs of progressing spoilage are dull opaque skin; soft flesh; cloudy, sunken eyes; and gray gills. The flesh of fillets should be firm, not gaping, falling apart, or mushy.

—Shirley O. Corriher, *Fine Cooking*

Icing fish

Fish and shellfish should be kept on ice in the refrigerator before they're cooked to keep them from deteriorating. But this is usually messy because the ice melts into a watery solution. I've found that *"blue ice"* (the packets of blue liquid coated in hard plastic that you use in coolers) is great for keeping fish very cold in the refrigerator. I keep some at the ready in the freezer for when I bring home fresh fish.

—Jerry Y. Seaward, Pasadena, CA

Keeping seafood fresh at home

I've come up with a simple way to keep seafood fresh for several days by using a large stockpot with a steamer insert. Put the seafood in the insert, cover it with ice, and set the steamer in the stockpot before storing it in the refrigerator. Replace the ice as necessary. This ensures that the seafood is both *thoroughly chilled and well drained*.

—John L. Wilson, Houston, TX

Removing fish bones

To remove the pin bones from along the center of a salmon fillet, a pair of *needle-nose pliers* works best; but in a pinch, you can use a rigid-blade vegetable peeler. First run your finger along the center of the fillet to find the row of bones and to make each bone stand up and away from the flesh. Slide the vegetable peeler over the bone so that the bone threads itself through one slot of the blade. Rotate the blade away from you just a little to catch the bone, then pull sharply to remove it.

—Randall Price, Middletown, OH

Removing fish bones easily

To locate the pin bones from a fish fillet, you usually have to run a finger along the center of the fillet to locate them, then pluck out the bones with tweezers or needle-nose pliers. It's much easier, however, to lay the fillet, bone side up, *over an upside-down mixing bowl* covered with plastic wrap. The curvature of the bowl causes the pin bones to jut out, making them easier to locate and remove. If the fillet is long, simply slide it along the back of the bowl to go over the length of the fish.

—Austin Liu, San Leandro, CA

What to look for when buying fresh tuna

The best-tasting tuna will range in color from deep red to pink. Look for moist (but not wet or weepy), shiny, almost translucent meat. This means the steak is fresh and recently cut. Cut steaks will begin to oxidize and turn brown fairly quickly. If they look dull and matte, or very brown, then they're probably old. Another sign of age is "gapping," when the meat of the muscle starts to separate into flakes. If you're in doubt about freshness, *ask for a smell;* the fish should have a fresh sea-air smell, not an overly fish odor. All tuna steaks will have a strip of darker meat running through them. This nutritious meat is perfectly edible but has a strong flavor that many people don't like. You can cut it out or better yet, choose steaks with a minimal amount of it.

—Susie Middleton, *Fine Cooking*

Less salty anchovies

For a less salty taste in the dishes you make with anchovies, *soak the anchovies in whole milk* for 10 minutes before you use them. If you like your anchovies saltier, soak them for only 2 minutes.

—Marc Malone, Waterford, CT

BACON

Roll bacon to loosen slices

Cold slices of bacon out of the refrigerator tend to stick together, inevitably causing a few slices to tear when I try to separate them. To avoid this, I curl the whole package of bacon lengthwise into a tube, then I *roll it back and forth* a few times. This loosens the slices so I can pull them off without ripping them.

—Darlene Guzman, Danville, CA

Easy-peeling bacon strips

I like to use bacon as a flavoring, but I rarely use the entire package. I've found a way to ensure that the uncooked bacon doesn't spoil by stashing it in the freezer. I *sandwich slices between accordioned layers of aluminum foil,* then fold the ends over to seal the entire package. This makes it easy to peel off the one or two slices I need, and it keeps the frozen bacon from becoming an unmanageable lump.

—Virginia Teichner, Ridgefield, CT

An easier, neater way to chop bacon

I keep my bacon in the freezer, and when I want to sauté a little, I remove *a few strips from the freezer* and cut them into small pieces with kitchen scissors directly over the sauté pan. It's a lot neater than chopping on a cutting board.

—Jane Morgan, Nashville, TN

Freezing bacon

Since the days of eating bacon at every breakfast have passed, it's difficult to keep bacon on hand. Yet I often find that I need a slice or two to add to a soup or a sauce recipe. The solution? Frozen bacon, which you can quickly and easily defrost. Start with a pound of bacon. Place two or three strips on a narrow sheet of plastic wrap. Fold the wrap over to *seal, then roll into a little ball.* Put several of these bacon packets inside a plastic freezer container for safe, fresh storage. Defrost a couple of these bacon packets, and—with eggs, parsley, and linguine or fettuccine—you can have a no-time-to-cook dinner—pasta carbonara.

—Linda Cornwell, Wyncote, PA

"Fry" bacon in the oven

When I cook a large breakfast for family and friends that involves making everything from pancakes and waffles to egg dishes, sausages, and bacon, stovetop space is at a premium, so I figured out a way to "fry" my bacon in the oven. I *drape the bacon slices over each wire* of the top oven rack and put it in a heated 350°F oven, with a baking pan on the bottom rack to catch the drippings. This isn't as messy as it seems. The bacon cooks up crisp and golden brown in a few minutes and stays warm even with the oven turned off until I'm ready to serve it. The oven rack is easily cleaned by wiping it down with a wet sponge and some dishwashing liquid.

—James Kidd, Newtown, CT

Buy steaks on sale and use them for hamburgers

To get the best ground beef for hamburgers, I take advantage of "value-pack" steaks. Most supermarkets sell packages of several steaks at a discount; sirloin and chuck are good cuts for burgers. I ask the butcher to *trim the fat from these steaks and grind them* for me. In this way, I'm assured that I'm buying freshly ground beef, and I know which cut it's from. Also, the burgers I get from these steaks are far superior to any I've tasted from packaged ground beef, and it only costs me a few more pennies per pound.

—Antoinne von Rimes, San Francisco, CA

Grinding meat in a food processor

To minimize mashing when grinding meat (like chuck for burgers), *freeze the meat* until firm before processing.

—Maryellen Driscoll, *Fine Cooking*

Look for freshness in a pork chop

The flesh of a pork chop should be *fine grained and reddish pink*. The external fat should be creamy white and have no dark spots or blemishes, which also indicate advanced age. Never buy pork that's soft, pale, pinkish gray, or wet or that has a lot of liquid in the package, a sign of improper processing. Finally, be aware that some producers "enhance" pork chops and other cuts with sodium phosphate. While this ensures juiciness, it also gives the meat a spongy texture that I find unpleasant.

—Bruce Aidells, *Fine Cooking*

Getting what you pay for when buying beef tenderloin

If you have your butcher trim out a whole beef tenderloin, be sure to *ask for the scraps* (which you have paid for)—they're perfect for a quick stir-fry.

—Katy Sparks, *Fine Cooking*

Get rid of that silverskin

If you buy a trimmed tenderloin, make sure any excess fat has been trimmed away and that the silverskin—the thin, tough, silvery membrane that runs along the surface of the meat—has been removed completely; if it's still there, it will cause the meat to curl as it cooks, and *it's tough to chew*.

—Katherine Alford, *Fine Cooking*

Remove the clear "skin" from spareribs

An old man in Louisiana who cooked meltingly tender ribs all his life taught me to always remove the cellophane-like skin from the back of ribs before cooking them. Put the ribs flesh side down and insert a fingertip into the semi-clear "skin" covering the back of the ribs. Keep pushing your fingertip in until you can grasp the skin and pull it off. It should peel off in large pieces. Repeat until you've removed it all. This makes the ribs *more tender and easier to cut* after cooking.

—Dolores G. Hart, Etowah, NC

Ask the butcher to score brisket

Some cuts of meat, such as brisket or flank and sirloin steak for London broil, must be sliced against the grain after cooking in order to be tender. One easy way to make sure you get it right is to ask the butcher to *score into the fat* before he wraps the meat to indicate the direction in which you should start slicing.

—Stanley Lobel, Lobel's Prime Meats, New York, NY

Removing sausage casings

Many recipes call for fresh bulk pork sausage, but it isn't always available in grocery stores. Most of the time I have to buy fresh sausage links and remove the casings. I find the best technique is to run the sausages under cold tap water for a minute or two, then slit the casings with a pair of sharp kitchen shears and remove the sausage meat, which will come away cleanly from the casings. The cold water softens the casings and causes the sausage fat to harden and congeal around the meat, preventing it from sticking.

Run the sausages under cold tap water for a minute or two, then slit the casings.

—Mary Malensek, Sagamore Hills, OH

Freezer bags best for pounding meat

When I pound boneless meats such as veal cutlets or chicken breasts, I find that putting the meat inside a gallon-size plastic freezer bag is much better than using sheets of plastic wrap. The *bag is stronger than the plastic wrap*, and it will contain any excess liquid or bits of meat. Even the pounding tool stays clean.

—John Wilson, Houston, TX

Try a waterless brine

With a dry brine, salt is rubbed on meat and left to sit on the meat overnight. The salt rub draws moisture out to the skin, where the salt crystals dissolve into a mild brine. Eventually, this brine also becomes absorbed by the meat. The result is *a heightening of flavor and moisture.*

—Michele Anna Jordan, *Fine Cooking*

Cutting "across the grain"

Whenever you slice raw or cooked meat, you'll get the most tender results if you cut across the grain. Look closely at a piece of meat and you'll see that the long muscle fibers run parallel to one another. Cutting across the grain means to *slice perpendicular to the fibers,* so the fiber in the cut pieces of meat become much shorter, making it easier to chew. Certain cuts of meat have areas where the fibers run in different directions; watch out for these changes as you slice and adjust the direction in which you're cutting if necessary.

—Maryellen Driscoll, *Fine Cooking*

Freezing ground meat

I save plastic lids from deli containers to use when I want to portion and freeze ground meat such as pork, beef, or lamb. I make my meat patties in the shape of hamburgers and place each one on top of a lid, then I stack the lids and patties and freeze them all together in zip-top bags. When I want to use the ground meat, I can *easily separate just the number* of patties I'll need.

—Linda Jawitz, New York, NY

Frozen meat slices better

To slice flank steak thinly for stir-fries, it's easier if you *freeze it so it's firmer*, about 15 minutes or more. This also works for slab bacon, or any meat or poultry that you need to slice before cooking.

—Gail Shem-Lee, Martinez, CA

Frozen meat for sausage

I make sausage several times a month with the meat-grinder/sausage-horn attachment to my mixer. To keep the meat from turning to mush in the grinder, I've found it best to first cut the meat into sizable chunks and *put them in the freezer until not quite frozen*. This technique is especially important for chicken breast, which is such a soft meat.

—Phillip Zook, Carrboro, NC

A quick and safe way to defrost meat

I don't like to defrost frozen meat in a microwave. Worse yet is allowing the meat to sit out at room temperature. When I don't have time to allow the meat to thaw in the refrigerator, here's what I do to speed things up: I put the frozen meat into a zip-top plastic bag and force out all the excess air. Then *I plunge the meat into a sink full of cold water.* I periodically work the package with my hands to loosen up the meat. As the water warms, I add more cold water, or throw a few ice cubes in.

—R. B. Himes, Vienna, OH

POULTRY

Blot chicken dry with a tower of paper towels

While cutting up a whole chicken for frying, I find it convenient to dry the chicken pieces by placing some on a layer of paper towels, covering them with another *layer of paper towels,* and then adding more chicken pieces, etc. My little chicken tower stays neat and dry until I'm ready to batter the pieces for the skillet. This technique is also good when cutting portions of any meat or fish.

—Ruth Moreland, Austin, TX

Getting a grip on chicken skin

I like to remove the skin from chicken before I cook it, but it can be a tough job—after a few tugs, my hand is too slippery to grasp the skin. I've found that *holding the chicken skin with a paper towel* gives me a better grip, and that I'm able to remove the skin with ease.

—Daniel Chmielowski, Juneau, AK

Pruning shears make quick work of chicken

I bought an extra pair of pruning shears for use in my kitchen. I use it to cut whole chicken into pieces. The soft handles are comfortable, and the *shears are strong* enough to slice through the toughest joints with ease.

—Shirley Schoenlein, AuGres, MI

Pound cutlets with a barbell

Recently, when my meat pounder broke, I had to find something else fast. I ended up using the *flat end of a 4-pound dumbbell* to pound the cutlets between two sheets of plastic wrap. It actually worked better than a real meat pounder because it's heavier, thus quicker, and has a wider surface, so you get a more uniform thickness to the meat.

—Darlene Wong, Toronto, Ontario, Canada

Put a lid on it

I've noticed that supermarkets have begun to sell delicate greens in large disposable plastic containers, and I recently found a use for a container lid that would have otherwise ended up in the trash. Instead of pounding boneless chicken breasts between waxed paper or parchment, which shreds, I used the plastic lid. It was large enough to cover one or two large pieces of meat and it *didn't break or shred* when I pounded on it. After use, it can be washed and used again or simply thrown away.

—Frank Faillace, Reston, VA

A marinade injection lets poultry baste itself

To tenderize and add flavor to poultry, inject marinades into the flesh before roasting or smoking. Injection kits are available in cooking-supply stores. My standard injected marinade is a strained mixture of butter or oil, wine, apple juice, garlic powder, ground white pepper (it's finer than black pepper), and salt. I inject the marinade a few times on each side of the bird and let it sit for a while before roasting. Injected poultry seems to baste itself from the inside, so I don't need to baste the poultry during roasting. The meat is flavorful and juicy throughout.

—Gary Turzilli, New York, NY

Injected poultry seems to baste itself from the inside, so I don't need to baste the poultry during roasting.

For an attractive, flavorful duck, prick the skin

For a more attractive, aromatic, and flavorful duck, use a four-pronged fork to gently puncture the skin in rows, leaving an inch or two between each puncture. The punctures *allow the duck to release juices and fat*, which caramelize and coat the skin. Puncturing the skin also prevents the internal juices from building up and pushing out forcefully, which would create skin blisters. Instead, the skin is left flat and crisp.

—Walter J. Morrison III, Buffalo, NY

Better apple coring

Are apples getting larger, or is my corer just too small? Whenever I try to core apples with my traditional corer, I end up having to remove part of the core with a paring knife. I discovered that if I cut the apple in half longitudinally first, then use the corer, I can get the whole core out. By *halving the apple*, I can see exactly where the core is and aim properly. Further, I can use the whole corer on each half, which removes a greater amount of core.

—Nancy Summers, Potomac, MD

Keeping peeled apples white and tasty

When peeling apples for pies and tarts, I prevent browning by *soaking the apples in apple juice* until I'm ready to use them. The acidity of the apple juice keeps the apples from oxidizing and turning brown, and it doesn't change the flavor the way lemon or orange juice can.

—Allan Byard, via email

Use Golden Delicious

For salads made with raw apples, choose the Golden Delicious variety. It *doesn't oxidize* and turn brown the way other varieties do.

—Jennifer Armentrout, *Fine Cooking*

Picking a ripe apricot

Ripeness cues can vary slightly between varieties, but you'll know a ripe, juicy apricot by its *fruity fragrance* and deep, uniform golden color, especially right around the stem, the portion that is the last to ripen. Don't be taken in by that seductive blush: it's just the side of the fruit that faced the sun while hanging on the tree. A ripe, juicy apricot will be firm, with a slight give when pressed. Really ripe fruit with a lot of sugar will even wrinkle a bit.

—Al Courchesne and Becky Smith, Frog Hollow Farm®, Brentwood, CA

Chopping dried apricots

I recently had to chop a large quantity of dried apricots for a stuffing, a tedious job when done with a knife since the apricots stick to one another and to the knife. (For a small amount, I find that scissors work better.) Using the food processor is a nice alternative, except that if you start the machine with the apricots already in the bowl, you will have a sticky mass of unevenly chopped apricots. Instead, turn the machine on and, with the blade spinning, *drop a few apricots at a time into the feed tube*. Continue doing this with all the apricots, and in a matter of seconds you will have evenly chopped apricots. I imagine this would also work with other sticky dried fruits as well.

—Pearl Watkins, West Hollywood, CA

AVOCADOS

Keeping halved avocados green

To store halved avocados and prevent them from turning brown, refrigerate them *flesh side down* in a bowl of water with a little bit of lemon juice. The avocados will keep beautifully for a few days this way. The same method can also be used when preparing slices of avocado ahead of time for salads or garnishes.

—Janet C. deCarteret, Bellevue, WA

Keeping cut avocados green

While preparing salad one day, I had half an avocado left over. Knowing light and air are the avocado's enemies, *I lightly sprayed the exposed flesh with vegetable oil*, wrapped the avocado half in foil, and refrigerated it. Three days later, the flesh was still perfectly green and firm. Lemon juice had never done as well!

—Linda L. Wible, Mary Esther, FL

Freezing avocados

Although avocados don't freeze well whole or sliced, I've found that nicely ripe (but not overripe) ones can be frozen for up to 5 months if they're first peeled, seeded, and mashed like guacamole with about ½ tablespoon of fresh lemon or lime juice per avocado. *Freeze the avocado mash in sealed plastic containers* with very little air space.

—Jim Peyton, *Fine Cooking*

An Apple a Day for Baking, Cooking, and Snacking

Apples can be loosely grouped into three categories: fresh apples for eating out of hand, cooking apples, and cider apples. Just about any apple can be enjoyed fresh; you only need to know what you like.

Cooking apples should be flavorful and firm. Heat breaks down an apple's structure quickly and reduces its flavor. Hard, full-flavored varieties—Gala, Braeburn, Rome, and Granny Smith—can take the heat and still retain their taste and shape.

For applesauce, a soft apple like McIntosh is a natural. Softer apples make smooth, creamy applesauce, whereas harder types give you a chunkier sauce. I like to mix a few varieties together for a more complex-tasting sauce. Leaving the skin on gives the applesauce a reddish pink tint.

Cider is often made from apples that have fallen from the tree, known as windfalls. The best cider is made by combining sweeter apples such as Empire with tarter varieties like Jonagold.

Here's a short primer of apple varieties:

- *Braeburn* can be eaten out of hand or used in cooking. Firm and juicy, it has a pleasant, sweet-tart flavor. It's harvested in late October and, if handled properly, will store well.
- *Cortland* is a good choice for a fresh fruit salad. Its very white flesh is slow to turn brown. A good all-purpose apple, it's harvested in September and October.
- *Empire* is a super-crisp eating apple that tastes similar to a McIntosh. Picked starting in September, it's best eaten raw or in salads.

Make guacamole with a whisk

I love guacamole, and after 30 years of experimenting with different tools and techniques, I've come to the conclusion that a wire whisk is a much better tool than a fork or a mortar and pestle, particularly when I'm making a big batch.

- *Fuji* is a relative newcomer to the apple scene. Sweet and juicy, it's excellent eaten fresh. It's available October through December but stores extremely well if refrigerated.

- *Gala*, a New Zealand native now grown in the United States, is a medium-size apple with a unique yellow-, orange-, and red-striped skin. It's outstanding for eating fresh, in salads, or cooked for desserts and applesauce.

- *Golden Delicious* ranges from pale green to warm yellow. The yellower the fruit, the sweeter and softer it is. Use it in tarts and salads.

- *Granny Smith* is harvested in October. It stores well, and imports make it available year round. It's a little tart for some, but it's a good cooking and baking apple. Paler green fruit is usually riper and sweeter.

- *Jonagold*, a cross of Jonathan and Golden Delicious, is crisp, juicy, and sweet, with enough tartness to make it good for cooking. Best just picked, it's harvested in late September.

- *Macoun* is a relative of the McIntosh but has a deeper carmine skin and is more versatile in the kitchen. It's harvested in late September and October.

- *McIntosh* is a favorite variety in the Northeast, where it's eaten fresh and used in applesauce. It isn't a good keeper, so enjoy it around harvest time in September.

- *Red Delicious*, with its brilliant crimson skin and unique five-knob base, is best eaten raw. Harvested in October, it's available year round, but avoid it in the spring and summer when it tends to be soft and mealy.

- *Rome* has a soft, round shape that makes it a popular choice for baked apples. It's good for cooking and baking.

—Julia Leonard, *Fine Cooking*

With a whisk, I can *mash the avocado to a perfect consistency* (leaving some small, toothsome chunks) and then stir in all the other ingredients.

—Helen M. Schwind, Glastonbury, CT

Quick-ripen bananas in the oven

If your bananas aren't ripe enough to cook with, try peeling and baking the fruit at 450°F on an ungreased baking sheet for 10 to 15 minutes until very soft. This *technique acts like the natural ripening process* and will sweeten your fruit in minutes.

—Suzan Gray, Carmel, CA

Bananas that won't turn brown

To prevent sliced bananas from turning brown, *dip them in a little white wine* before arranging them on tarts or using them in fruit salad. The acid in the wine prevents the fruit from oxidizing, but it doesn't affect the flavor.

—B. Bader, Hartsdale, NY

Save ripe bananas for baking

I don't like to waste extra bananas, so if it seems like I won't be able to eat them all before they overripen, I peel the bananas and put 2 or 3 in a small plastic bag, making sure to press most of the air out of the bag before sealing it. Then I press and mash the bananas with my hands and fingers and store the bags flat in my freezer. Now I have *mashed bananas the easy way*, ready to slip into a pancake batter or a quick bread. At a moment's notice, I can quickly thaw the frozen bananas in a bowl of warm water.

—Jeanne Schimmel, Hobe Sound, FL

Jazz up the flavor of grocery-store berries

If the berries you bring home from the store lack the perfume and flavor you hoped for, try adding *a couple of drops of rose water*, which is quite inexpensive in Middle Eastern markets. Rose water also makes perfectly ripe, flavorful berries even more luscious.

—Angela Urciuoli, Salinas, CA

Freeze berries on baking sheets

There's a simple way to preserve summer's ripe berries that requires no cooking, no jars, and, best of all, no time. Choose ripe berries without blemishes or bruises. Rinse them quickly if necessary, then arrange them in a single layer, without touching, on a baking sheet. Set the sheet in the freezer until the berries are frozen solid—this will take anywhere from 30 minutes to 2 hours. Once the berries are hard, slide them off the sheet into a zip-top freezer bag. The berries won't stick together and you can take out as many as you want at any given time. Frozen this way, these should *keep up to a year*.

—Molly Stevens, *Fine Cooking*

Freeze berries into ice cubes for festive drinks

At warm-weather get-togethers, I love to serve flavored iced teas and fruit juice drinks such as watermelon agua fresca and honeydew lemonade. To give the drinks an elegant yet simple garnish, I put *raspberries (or other summer berries) into ice-cube trays filled with water* and freeze them. Once frozen, I pop out the ice cubes, put them into glasses, and pour the drinks on top. The result is quite pretty.

—Michaela Rosenthal, Woodland Hills, CA

With blueberries, bigger is better

When shopping for cultivated blueberries, it's the rare case of bigger being better. Look for *the fattest berries you can find;* they should be grayish purple and covered with a silvery bloom. (Wild blueberries—much harder to find outside of the Northeast—should by tiny and almost black.) Don't bother sniffing: Unlike many other fruits, ripe blueberries won't be very fragrant.

—Abigail Johnson Dodge, *Fine Cooking*

WHICH FRUIT RIPEN; WHICH DON'T

Never ripen after picking	Soft berries, cherries, citrus, grapes, litchis, olives, pineapple, watermelon
Ripen only after picking	Avocados
Ripen in color, texture, and juiciness but not in sweetness after picking	Apricots, blueberries, figs, melon (besides watermelon), nectarines, passionfruit, peaches, persimmons
Get sweeter after picking	Apples, cherimoyas, kiwi, mangos, papayas, pears, sapotes, soursops
Ripen in every way after harvest	Bananas

—Jeffrey Steingarten, New York, NY

If you must wash raspberries, do it gently

Washing raspberries isn't ideal, but if you want to be safe, wash them right before using them. Fill a bowl with cold water, gently add the berries, then *lift them out with your hands*—again, gently. Let them dry in a single layer on a baking sheet lined with paper towels.

—Michelle Polzine, *Fine Cooking*

Keeping strawberries fresh

I find that if I can keep moisture away from fresh strawberries, they'll last longer. So when I bring them home from the market, I put the unwashed berries into a bowl lined with paper towels and cover them with another paper towel. I store the bowl in the refrigerator, and the berries stay fresh all week—no problem with mildew. Whenever I want berries, I take some out and wash them.

Put unwashed berries into a bowl lined with paper towels and cover them with another paper towel.

—Ruth McHugh, North Port, FL

Rinse, then hull strawberries

Leave strawberry hulls intact until after you rinse the berries or they'll become waterlogged. Keep all your berries well chilled. Remove any that are soft or moldy, as one rotten berry can spoil the whole basket.

—Sally Small, *Fine Cooking*

A drinking straw hulls strawberries

Want to hull and core a strawberry? *Push a plastic drinking straw* through the berry, bottom to top.

—Philippa Farrar, Santa Barbara, CA

CHERIMOYAS

Soft is good

Cherimoyas (or custard apples) are ready to eat when they're so soft that you could almost *poke a hole through the (inedible) peel.* Enjoy one as you would a slice of melon: chill briefly, quarter with a knife, and scoop out the flesh with a spoon to work around the large, dark, inedible seeds.

—Norman Van Aken, *Fine Cooking*

Tips for Baking with Frozen Blueberries

Fresh blueberries freeze brilliantly, and individually quick frozen (IQF) berries of both wild and cultivated varieties are widely available. IQF means the berries have been frozen individually, rather than as a clump, which makes them perfect for baking.

For most recipes, you shouldn't thaw the berries before using them. The thin skins tend to all but disintegrate, leaving a purple, juicy mess where lovely berries once sat.

Mix them into batters gently and quickly, using a few strokes as possible to avoid crushing the fruit and turning the batter a glaring lavender.

For blueberry pancakes, cook the pancake on one side and sprinkle on the frozen berries just before flipping.

In some batters, frozen blueberries can streak the batter an alarming shade of green. This occurs in alkaline conditions, such as batters with baking powder and no acidic ingredients like buttermilk, yogurt, or lemon juice. To minimize this risk, be sure the berries are solidly frozen and mix them in swiftly and gently.

—Regan Daley, *Fine Cooking*

CHERRIES

Sweet cherries to eat now or freeze for later

At the market, look for rich, uniform color. The skin should be shiny and the flesh should be juicy. The very freshest cherries should have *bright green stems*. Avoid fruits with bruises, soft spots, discolorations, or limp, brown stems. Keep them refrigerated for up to 5 days uncovered, rather than in a plastic bag. Like most tree-ripened fruit, cherries taste best if removed from the fridge an hour or so before serving so they can come to room temperature. It's easy to extend the cherry's short season by freezing them. Freeze fruits in a single layer for 3 or 4 hours, then seal the frozen cherries in doubled zip-top bags.

—Renee Shepherd, *Fine Cooking*

Picking sour cherries

Choose sour cherries that are *soft and juicy*, like ripe plums. Their thin skins are extremely fragile, so you may see a few bruises. Handle the fruits as you would delicate raspberries and refrigerate them as soon as you get home.

—Renee Shepherd, *Fine Cooking*

Pit cherries with a hairpin

I've tried many cherry-pitting devices, and most tend to mash the cherries and allow small pits to pass through. A better (and cheaper) tool is a large, sturdy metal hairpin. Simply insert the looped end of the pin into the stem end of the cherry, down to the bottom of the pit and, with a twist of your wrist, flip it out. It does little damage to the cherry's shape, and *every pit gets removed*, since you pit the cherries one at a time. To make the hairpin easier to use, you can press the ends into the flat end of a Champagne cork and use the round end as a handle.

—Rose Levy Beranbaum, *Fine Cooking*

Pit cherries neatly in a bag

When you're pitting cherries with a pitter, the juice splatters and stains everything it touches. I've found that *using the tool inside a plastic bag* contains the juice. As a bonus, the pits and stems are already gathered in the bag to be thrown away.

—Vicki McLain, Baytown, TX

Removing cherry stains

Rubbing your hands with a *cut lemon* will remove cherry stains.

—Fran Gage, *Fine Cooking*

CITRUS FRUIT

Wrap citrus in newspaper for longer storage

If you have a lot of oranges, lemons, or other citrus fruits that you want to store for more than several days, wrap each fruit individually in a sheet of newspaper. Pack them in a box or a bag, and *store them in a cool, dry place*. You'll want to wash any ink residue off the rind before using them.

—Jonathan Nickels, Longmeadow, MA

Massaging citrus fruit for more juice

To get the most juice out of a citrus fruit, first give it a massage. *Roll the fruit back and forth* on the counter, pressing hard with the heel of your hand. This will soften the fruit and crush the juice cells within the membranes. It will be easier to squeeze because the juices have already begun to flow.

—Meg Perry, Akron, OH

Microwave fruit for more juice

To get the most juice from citrus fruits, *heat them in the microwave* for 25 seconds or so before squeezing.

—Dee Ford, Louisville, KY

Remove the zest for easier juicing

To get the most out of my lemons, limes, and oranges, I use a vegetable peeler to remove all the zest before squeezing the fruit for juice. If I don't need the zest right away, it goes into a plastic freezer bag. I find that citrus is *easier to juice (especially limes) without the zest*, and the frozen peel can be used later in recipes, as garnishes, in beverages, or even to freshen the disposal. The large strips thaw quickly and they keep far better in the freezer than grated zest.

—Kathleen Wolf, Milpitas, CA

Peeling citrus with a fork

If you want a good chunk of citrus peel without disturbing the fruit inside, you can peel any citrus fruit with a fork. Starting at one pole, slip one tine of the fork under the skin of the fruit and *cut up and down through the skin* all the way back to the starting point. Make one more fork cut at a right angle to the first cut, then peel off the four quarters.

—John Ternille, Naples, FL

Easy citrus zesting

Grating zest can be a lot of work, but I think I have an easier method. I use a *sharp vegetable peeler* and a gentle sawing motion (this is important) to cut away thin strips of peel. I know I'm being gentle enough if I don't get any of the white pith. To chop the zest, I first cut the peel into strips and add a little salt (if the recipe is savory) or sugar (if the recipe is sweet), which provides friction for the chopping process (either with a knife or in an electric spice grinder) and also absorbs the zest's oils, so less flavor is lost to the cutting board.

—Russ Shumaker, Richmond, VA

Easier grating

Grating citrus zest on a box grater can be frustrating because so much of the zest gets stuck in the teeth or clings to the grater panel. A good way to avoid this is to stretch plastic film over the grater panel. I usually use the produce department plastic bag that the fruit came in. Just hold it taut over the face of the grater and grate as normal. When you're finished, pull the plastic from the grater and almost all of the zest will be on the plastic. Just shake or scrape it off. You might think that you'd get little bits of plastic in with the zest, but you don't.

Pull the plastic from the grater and almost all of the zest will be on the plastic.

—Deborah Orrill, Dallas, TX

Remove citrus zest from a grater with a pastry brush

To remove orange or lemon zest from your hand grater, simply tap a pastry brush against the outside of your grater, pushing in and out to free the grated zest from the holes. This will *clean your grater quickly* and efficiently.

—Margaret O'Halloran, Glen Allen, VA

A Microplane-type grater is the best

I always use a Microplane-type grater. Its razor-sharp teeth shave the zest rather than rip or shred it, releasing more essential oils and removing more of the zest than other graters and gadgets. You'll get at least 1 tablespoon of fine, feathery zest from each large lemon. This type of grater also *grabs only the yellow zest*, not the pith—a minor miracle in itself.

—Lori Longbotham, *Fine Cooking*

Better technique for using a rasp grater

I love the new rasp-like zester on the market. I used to hold the ruler-size piece of stainless steel at an angle with one end on the counter and then run the lemon or lime down along its grating slots, as you might grate cheese. The problem with this method is that you can't see exactly where you've just zested, an important factor if you're trying to avoid the bitter white pith that lies just below the skin of a fruit. It's much better to *hold the fruit in one hand and use a rasp like a nail file,* moving the rasp, not the fruit. Not only can you see exactly where you're zesting but you're also likely to apply less force—another way to avoid the pith.

—Joanne McAllister Smart, *Fine Cooking*

Citrus Zesting Tips

- When grating zest, you want just the thin colored top coat of the skin. Overzealous grating will result in bitter flavors.

- A citrus fruit's volatile oils are strongest just after zesting, so remove the zest just before using.

- Grate zest over waxed paper to make it easier to gather for measuring.

- Finely grated zest releases more flavor than larger strips.

- If you have more citrus fruits on hand than you can use, grate or peel the zest, juice the fruit, and then freeze the zest and juice separately. Well wrapped, they'll keep for up to 3 months.

—Lori Longbotham, *Fine Cooking*

Saving zested citrus fruit

After grating the zest from a lemon or other citrus fruit, the bare skin shrivels up and the fruit becomes hard and impossible to juice within just a day or two. A simple solution is to *wrap the fruit tightly in plastic*, then store it in the refrigerator. This prevents the fruit from drying out. I find that a completely zested lemon wrapped tightly in plastic will last for at least a week in the refrigerator.

—Leslie Revsin, *Fine Cooking*

Easy-to-squeeze lemon wedges

Try this method to produce lemon wedges that are great looking, easy to squeeze, less wasteful of juice, and have no pits. With a sharp knife, you can prepare them in seconds. First slice off each end of the lemon. The squared ends will provide a good grip to hold the lemon wedge between your thumb and index finger. Next, cut the lemon in half lengthwise. Cut out the white fibers in the middle of each half by making a V-shaped incision with your knife. Use the tip of the knife to dig out any pits remaining in the lemon. Cut each half into segments and serve.

The squared ends will provide a good grip to hold the lemon wedge between your thumb and index finger.

—J. J. Jackson, Victoria, British Columbia, Canada

Delicious Flavor Partners for Citrus

Citrus pairs well with lots of ingredients, some familiar, some less so.

- **Sweet oranges are excellent with bittersweet chocolate,** as in a dark chocolate cake with blood orange sauce. Rich, intense coffee flavorings are also complemented by sweet, fruity oranges. Nutmeg, cloves, allspice, black pepper, cumin, and anise enhance and add complexity to oranges. I like to pair oranges and pistachios, as the nut's rich, luxurious flavor holds up well to the sweet, acidic citrus, but almost any type of nut works well with orange. Basil also pairs well with orange.

- **Grapefruit and caramel are a perfect match.** The sharp bitterness of the grapefruit is tempered by the smoky sweetness of cooked sugar. Good spice foils for grapefruit are cinnamon, caraway, and rosemary.

- **The bright tanginess of lemon revives the full, complex flavors of dried fruits,** such as Black Mission figs, dried cherries, or dried blueberries. The nutty smokiness of black pepper is a wonderful way to enhance lemon, pairing sensations of the cool, sour citrus with a touch of heat from the pepper. Both mint and basil complement the brightness of lemon.

- **Limes are excellent with tropical fruits, especially papaya.** Fresh papayas sprinkled with lime juice is a traditional dessert in the tropics. Or, for something slightly more complex, try a tropical fruit compote with lime sorbet or ice cream.

—Andrew MacLauchlan, *Fine Cooking*

Easy-to-squeeze lemon wedges, part II

Here's how to slice lemon wedges that won't squirt in your eye when you squeeze them. Cut a lemon wedge, then make three or four small, vertical slits across the lemon's edge. These cuts *prevent the juice from squirting* out forcefully. When you squeeze the lemon wedge, the juice will run out gently.

—Cynthia A. Jaworski, Chicago, IL

Freeze lemons for fresh juice

To ensure you always have fresh lemon juice on hand, halve lemons, put them in a plastic bag, and freeze them. Allow the lemon to defrost overnight before you squeeze it. Not only does this method prevent you from wasting lemon halves but *the process of freezing and thawing* also seems to make the lemons very juicy.

—Nancy P. Dowd, Lunenburg, Nova Scotia, Canada

A heavy orange is a juicy orange

A ripe orange with a high juice content will be *heavy and firm*, not light and spongy. Bruises can signal that the fruit has begun to ferment. A loose peel on an orange can mean dry fruit, but it's normal on a tangerine. Look out, though, for tangerines with extremely loose, puffy peels: the fruit has likely passed its prime.

—Ethel Brennan, *Fine Cooking*

Don't judge an orange by its color

Skin color isn't a reliable sign of ripeness; in some states (Florida, for one), dyeing oranges is legal. Surprisingly, *an orange with a greenish cast* may be sweeter and riper than one that's uniformly orange.

—Amy Albert, *Fine Cooking*

DRIED FRUIT

Chopping dried fruit easily

I like to bake, but I don't like the way ingredients like figs, dates, and raisins stick to my knife during chopping. To prevent this, I *sprinkle a little flour over the dried fruit* before and after I chop. The first dusting keeps the fruit from sticking to my knife, and the second coats the individual pieces and keeps them nicely separated during mixing.

—Deborah Waldner-Khan, Waterloo, Ontario, Canada

Chopping dried fruit in the food processor

To prevent a gummy consistency when chopping dried fruit, like apricots, *partially freeze the fruit* before processing and use quick on/off pulses with the steel "S" blade.

—Maryellen Driscoll, *Fine Cooking*

Squirt lemon juice on dried fruit before processing

When chopping sticky dried fruit in your food processor, squeeze a little lemon juice on the fruit *to keep it from sticking* to the metal blade.

—Heather Darrell, Victoria, British Columbia, Canada

Separating dried fruit

When baking with sticky items like raisins and dried fruits, I roll the pieces in my hands with *just a dab of flour* before baking. This separates the pieces and keeps them from bunching together in the batter, making more uniform cookies and cakes. The small bit of flour that's on the fruit disappears during baking.

—Myrna Fox, Ponte Vedra Beach, FL

FIGS

Ripe figs are fragile and sweet smelling

A fig is ripe when it's soft and the thin skin rests close to the flesh, which is moist, fragrant, and sweet. Sometimes you'll see the skin splitting open to reveal the flesh. An unripe fig, on the other hand, is firm with a cottony white layer between the skin and the somewhat dry, undeveloped center. Coax slightly underripe figs to ripeness by leaving them on the kitchen counter for a day or two. *Store them in a single layer* rather than piled on top of one another; they're less likely to spoil that way. Avoid figs that are resting on flattened sides or that are slumped in their containers. They've probably begun to turn from too much heat during travel. (You can tell sour figs by their smell.) The tricky part about figs is that they need to be picked ripe because they won't get much better after they're picked. But with only a thin skin protecting the tender flesh, ripe figs are fragile and don't travel well. That's why the figs you find in stores are often not at their height of perfection.

—Deborah Madison, *Fine Cooking*

GRAPES

Check the stems for freshness

A reliable guide to freshness is to look at and feel the stem end of the grape bunch; it should be green and *very pliable*. Avoid bunches whose stems are toughened or brown with age. Many grape varieties have a white powdery coating that's called "bloom." This delicate natural protection helps keep the grapes from losing moisture, so wait to wash them until just before serving. Table grapes are good keepers. Store them in a loosely closed plastic bag in the refrigerator. Grapes' natural sweetness is muted by cold, so remove grapes from the fridge before serving and let them warm up to room temperature or just below.

—Renee Shepherd, *Fine Cooking*

Look for the perfume

A guava's ripeness is best judged by the strength of *its sweet, aromatic perfume*, rather than by feel. The small seeds are edible, as is the skin, which can be green, white, or even pink.

—Norman Van Aken, *Fine Cooking*

Peeling kiwi

Nothing mars the appearance of sliced kiwi more than the evidence of paring knife ridges and edges. I have found a simpler and less frustrating method using an ordinary teaspoon. To start, cut the kiwi in half. In one of the halves, insert *the tip of the shallow spoon* between the skin and the flesh. Turn the kiwi while pushing the spoon gently farther in until you hit the end. Rotate the kiwi completely at least once to make sure that all of the skin, except for a small spot at the end, is separated. Scoop out the emerald flesh, or remove the skin by peeling it back like a sock. The skin doubles as a convenient handle to hold the fruit for slicing. Repeat with the other half.

—Jürgen Richter, Mississauga, Ontario, Canada

Fragrance tells

To choose a good mango, smell it. It should have a *faintly sweet aroma*, especially around the stem. No perfume generally means no flavor. If the fruit smells sour or like alcohol, it's past its prime. Choose firm fruit that is just beginning to show some yellow or red in the skin. The skin should be tight around the flesh; loose skin means the mango is old. To ripen a mango, keep it at room temperature. When ripe, the fruit will become more aromatic, its skin will take on a blush, and its flesh will yield gently to the touch. If you want to hurry the ripening process, put a few mangos in a paper bag with a banana. Only when mangos are fully ripe can you refrigerate them but only for up to 3 days; they are a tropical fruit and don't take kindly to the cold.

—Viviana Carballo, *Fine Cooking*

No-peel mango

When I need some ripe mango flesh for a sauce or purée, or just to eat out of hand, I don't bother to peel the mango. Using a sharp knife I cut the two broad sides of the mango from the pit and, holding a mango half in the palm of my hand, I *scoop out the flesh* one spoonful at a time. This technique can also be used on other soft, ripe fruits and vegetables, such as kiwis and avocados.

—Inigo Chacon, Key West, FL

MELON

Lift it, smell it, thump it

A fully ripe melon should feel quite heavy for its size. It should smell sweet and flowerlike or richly perfumed, never unpleasantly musky or slightly fermented. The stem end is the best place to smell for ripeness, although some very aromatic thin-skinned varieties are fragrant all over. If a melon has no smell, it may be underripe, so choose another. Melon skin should be unblemished. Both netted and smooth-skinned varieties *should be without wrinkles or bumps* on their rinds. Ripe melons make a hollow sound when you tap them, rather than just a dull thud. Give it a thump with your knuckles and listen. Take melons out of the refrigerator about a half an hour before you plan to eat them because most of these fruits have a perfumed fragrance and sweetness that's dampened by the icy chill of a modern refrigerator. Plan to serve them when they're still slightly cool to enjoy their natural aroma and sweetness.

—Renee Shepherd, *Fine Cooking*

Clue to melon ripeness

A fully ripe melon should *feel heavy* for its size, smell fragrant, give a little on its stem end, and make a hollow sound when you tap it. As an additional test for honeydew and muskmelons (also known as Eastern-style cantaloupe), I shake the melon vigorously. If I hear the seeds and juice slosh around inside, I know that they have separated from the flesh and that the melon is ready to eat.

—David M. Walt, Little Rock, AR

Wash it anyway

Don't forget to *wash the outside* of a melon before cutting into it; bacteria sometimes likes to hang out on melon skin and can be dragged into the melon flesh by your knife.

—Jennifer Armentrout, *Fine Cooking*

How to Speed Ripen Fruit

When some fruits ripen (bananas and apples especially), they give off ethylene gas, which further speeds ripening. In fact, produce shippers use ethylene to ripen certain fruits (or at least to get them to change color and look ripe when they reach their destination).

At home you can use ethylene to speed ripening. This method works especially well with tomatoes, avocados, bananas, and cantaloupe. First, warm the fruit by setting it in a sunny window or microwave it for 15 seconds on medium power. Put it in a paper bag with a couple of ripe apples and close loosely. You want the ethylene concentrated in the bag, but you also want oxygen to get in to speed ripening.

—Shirley O. Corriher, *Fine Cooking*

The best way to cut a cantaloupe

To quickly remove the skin from cantaloupes or other round melons, first *cut off the ends* of the melon so you can work with a flat surface. Hold the top with one hand and carefully slice off the skin in sections from top to bottom. Turn the melon as you go. Once the melon is skinned, cut it in half and remove the seeds. This method makes it easier to cut even sections of fruit.

—Nancy Hoffman, San Rafael, CA

O L I V E S

Pitting olives without frustration

The pits of some soft black olives will slip right out. Meaty, firm olives require a bit more force. I use the side of a *heavy chef's knife*. I put the olive on a work surface, set the flat side of the knife on top, and give it a good whack. The force splits open the olive and frees the pit. Be sure to wipe the knife blade frequently because it will get oily—and very slippery—after splitting a few olives. Some chefs prefer another method. They place the olive on a steady work surface and flatten it with their thumb until they can feel the pit. This loosens the pit and usually cracks the flesh enough to squeeze or pull the pit out.

—Molly Stevens, *Fine Cooking*

Nongadget pit removal

To pit olives without the aid of an olive-pitting tool, spread the olives on a cutting board and *press down on them* in a smearing motion with the bottom of a small saucepan or skillet. The olives will crack and the pits will squeeze partially out. Finish pitting with your fingers.

—Jennifer Armentrout, *Fine Cooking*

Pit olives with a cherry pitter

Many recipes I use call for chopped, pitted Greek (kalamata) olives. I used to find it difficult to scrape the olive away from the pit. Now I use a cherry pitter, and it works wonderfully. Just position the olive as you would the cherry and squeeze. *Out pops the pit*, leaving the olive ready to be chopped.

—Joan McRae, Chesapeake, VA

PAPAYA

Pick a heavy papaya

A mottled, spotty look is okay, as long as the papaya feels *heavy for its size.* A ripe papaya should give when pressed; it should feel a little softer than a mango.

—Norman Van Aken, *Fine Cooking*

PASSIONFRUIT

Black is good

Black, wrinkly skin on a passionfruit is an indication of ripeness—*the more dimply, the better the flavor.* Rather than a fruit you'd eat out of hand, passionfruit has tasty pulp and juices; when you cut into one, be ready to catch every drop of juice. Then force the pulp through a strainer to separate it from the seeds.

—Norman Van Aken, *Fine Cooking*

PEACHES

Choose peaches with your hands, eyes, and nose

The fruit should be firm. The only soft places will be the bruises left by other people pinching the peach before you got there. A ripe peach feels heavy in the palm of your hand; it will give a little, feel more voluptuous. Look for the golden or creamy background color of the skin at the stem end of the peach. Don't be duped by a provocative blush color (varieties are being developed that are nearly 90% blush). The background color of the skin is all-important. Size is crucial, too. *Bigger is better* when it comes to peaches. Bigger peaches seem to be sweeter, more fully developed in flavor. Sniff the peach you're considering; you can smell the nectar in a riper peach. You can ripen peaches in a brown paper bag or a ripening bowl. If you've picked firm, ripe fruit with good background color at the stem end, the peaches will soften in 3 to 4 days, and a lovely fragrance will beckon you. They'll keep in the refrigerator for a couple of days longer.

—Sally Small, *Fine Cooking*

Peel not

I never peel my stone fruit. I don't think that the final result warrants the painstaking, time-consuming peeling process. In fact, I *like* keeping the skin on the fruit: it adds a deeper, richer color to compotes and baked desserts, and it helps retain the fruit's nutritional content. The tougher skins of peaches and nectarines do however need some attention. I gently prick the skin with the sharp tines of a fork several times around the fruit before I proceed with the recipe. This method *breaks up the fibrous skin* during baking yet keeps the flavors intact without bruising the flesh.

—Abigail Johnson Dodge, *Fine Cooking*

Avoiding discoloration

Once exposed to the air, peach flesh tends to turn brown quickly. To keep the color bright, *sprinkle the slices with a bit of lemon juice.*

—Sally Small, *Fine Cooking*

Peach canning shortcut

I'm lucky to live near several peach orchards, and I love to can these plentiful summer peaches for use in desserts and crisps during the winter. When canning peaches, I *peel and pit the fruit* and, instead of keeping a pot of hot sugar syrup on the stove to fill the jars, I put 1/3 cup sugar in the bottom of each sterilized jar, add the peaches, and fill the jar with boiling water, leaving 1/2 inch of headspace at the top. Then I process the jars 10 minutes longer than usual (to finish dissolving the sugar) in a boiling-water canner. This saves me a lot of sticky cleanup from the sugar syrup and reduces a step in the canning process. The sugar ultimately dissolves, and the result is a beautiful jar of summer fruit.

—Laura Dean, via email

Getting a ripe pear

Pears must be ripened off the tree. Experienced buyers can taste the "promise" of an unripened pear, but it's a tricky business. Some growers pick their fruit before it matures to catch the high prices early in the season. This immature fruit lacks sugar. It looks fine, but it will taste woody when ripe or it will shrivel and never ripen at all. You will have prettier fruit if you ripen your pears in your own kitchen. If they come wrapped in a flat, leave them there; the less handling the better. Otherwise, wrap each pear in tissue or old newspaper and set it in a cardboard box or a brown paper bag—but not plastic. You are simply trying to increase the concentration of ethylene gases that pears naturally emit without smothering the fruit. A cool (60 to 65°F), dark place is ideal. *A pear should ripen slowly*. When it yellows slightly and yields to the touch at the neck, you will have it: a ripe, juicy pear.

—Sally Small, *Fine Cooking*

Feel for ripeness

While Fuyu and Sharon varieties are ready to eat when slightly soft to the touch, Hachiyas aren't ripe until they feel soft and almost mushy. You can hasten ripening by *stashing them in a paper bag with a ripe banana* and leaving it on the counter for a day or two.

—Amy Albert, *Fine Cooking*

Give it the sniff test

Take a whiff of a pineapple before buying it—a ripe one has a *sweet fragrance* with no hint of fermentation (if you do detect a fermenty odor, move along to the next pineapple). Squeeze it: If it's rock hard, it's probably unripe. If there's a bit of give, it's probably nice and ripe. Another clue: A juicy pineapple will feel heavy for its size, but do make sure that juice isn't leaking through the bottom, indicating that the fruit is breaking down. Color isn't necessarily an indicator of ripeness. A ripe pineapple will start to deteriorate if you leave it at room temperature. For best flavor, stash your pineapple in the fridge until you're ready to eat it.

—Flo Braker, *Fine Cooking*

The Pears of Autumn

Anjou (or d'Anjou) pears are large, yellow-green, and sweet. Probably the easiest pears to get your hands on, Anjous are the workhouse pears, great for eating and cooking as long as they're a little underripe. Harder to find but also delicious is the red d'Anjou, which is slightly smaller and firmer.

Bartlett pears are best in early fall. If you find them much later, they'll probably have lost some flavor. Bartletts come in yellow and red varieties. I like to roast the smaller, bright red Bartlett whole to use in savory dishes.

Bosc pears have a long, thin neck and lightly rusted skin. I like them for cooking because they hold their shape well. Available from fall to spring, Boscs are also quite tasty for eating out of hand.

Comice pears are wonderful eaten fresh. They have a fine-grained flesh and delicate flavor. Serve them with nuts, cheese, and a glass of Sauternes for a simple after-dinner treat.

Tiny Seckels have a sweet and spicy flavor. Their thicker skin and firm flesh make them perfect for poaching and preserving.

—Frank McLelland, *Fine Cooking*

Juicing pineapple

Many people shy away from buying a fresh pineapple because they're afraid that most if it will go bad before they use it all. After I've used the pineapple I need for a particular dish, I cut the rest into 1-inch chunks and store them in the airtight containers in the freezer. This frozen pineapple can be used to make a delicious juice. Just take the pineapple out of the freezer and allow it to defrost for about half an hour. Put the semi-defrosted pineapple into a blender with some cold water (and sugar if you like a sweeter taste) and blend until the pineapple is liquefied. Strain the juice to remove the rough pulp. The juice is delicious to drink for a healthy addition to breakfast or to use in place of water or orange juice in recipes.

> The juice is delicious to drink for a healthy addition to breakfast.

—Marisa A. Valzovano, North Miami Beach, FL

When canned is preferable

Use canned or cooked pineapple *in recipes containing gelatin;* raw pineapple contains an enzyme that counteracts gelatin's firming action.

—Amy Albert, *Fine Cooking*

P L A N T A I N S

How to peel a green plantain

Ripe black plantains can be peeled like a banana, but green ones have very firm, clingy flesh and there's a trick to peeling them. (The slightly sticky substance under the skin can irritate, so wear gloves if you like.) Start by trimming the ends, then, with a *sharp paring knife*, score the skin along one or more of its ridges, bring careful not to cut into the flesh, then peel off the skin in sections.

—Tania Sigal, *Fine Cooking*

Ripening plantains

To hasten ripening, put plantains in a paper bag and leave at room temperature. Don't use a plastic bag, as the trapped humidity will cause the fruit to get moldy.

—Tania Sigal, *Fine Cooking*

P L U M S

Choose a plum that's heavy and not too soft

To find a ripe plum, hold one in the palm of your hand. It should feel heavy. There *should be some give*, particularly at the blossom end (opposite the stem end). If the plum is too soft, it's probably overripe. Hard plums will soften a little in a brown paper bag at room temperature within 2 days. But plums won't sweeten appreciably after they're picked: The sugars must develop on the tree. When the fruit is severed from the branch, a chemical reaction is triggered that breaks down the fruit's acids and changes the acid–sugar balance of the fruit. The plum *seems* to taste sweeter because of the reduced acid.

—Sally Small, *Fine Cooking*

P O M E G R A N A T E S

Pomegranate seeds add crunch to cranberry sauce

For years now, I've been adding pomegranate seeds to both cooked cranberry sauce and sweet or savory cranberry relish—they add a delightful juicy crunch. For every 2 bags of cranberries, I add the seeds of 1 pomegranate, taking care to *remove all the bitter white pith* from the seeds. I add the seeds the night before serving, which gives them time to marinate in the acidity, sugar, and salt.

—Sarah Jane Freymann, New York, NY

RHUBARB

Thinner is better

Thin rhubarb stalks are likely to be *more tender;* thick ones can be tough and stringy, so you may want to peel thicker stalks with a vegetable peeler before you cook them. A crown of bright green leaves is a good sign: they indicate that the stalks were a relatively recent harvest. Always discard the leaves before cooking, however; they contain oxalic acid, which is poisonous. Wash and dry the stalks and cut off the ends if they're soft and brown or show signs of rotting. Wrap the stalks in a damp dishtowel or paper towel and refrigerate until ready to use.

—Kathleen Stewart, *Fine Cooking*

STARFRUIT

Darker means ripe

Starfruit (or carambolas) are ripe and ready to eat when *their ridges begin to darken.* The peel is edible, so you don't need to remove it, but if you're a stickler for presentation, use a sharp paring knife or peeler to pare away the dark parts.

—Norman Van Aken, *Fine Cooking*

Herbs, Spices, and Other Flavorings

Store herbs for long refrigerator life

To keep herbs, I *sprinkle them lightly with cold water*, wrap them in a paper towel, put them in a plastic bag, breathe into the bag to blow it up, and seal the bag tightly. The extra air seems to give the herbs a booster shot of energy.

—Doris Davlin, Pauma Valley, CA

Removing water from fresh herbs

To remove excess water from fresh herbs after washing, *wrap them in a thick dishtowel* by folding it in thirds the long way. Grab an end of the towel in each hand and snap the towel 5 or 6 times by moving your hands toward each other slowly and apart very quickly. This method is faster than using a salad spinner, and it works just as well for small amounts of herbs or greens.

—Nancy Kohl, Lynn, MA

Dry your herbs at the office

If you work in a painfully dry office building like mine, consider making the dryness work for you by bringing your fresh herbs to work. My herbs *dry to a crisp in a few days with no exposure to heat or sunlight*. All you need is a bit of extra desk space.

—Joe St. Lawrence, via email

Preserving fresh herbs

When fresh herbs are abundant, gather the leaves, wash and dry them, and then *purée them in a food processor or blender* with fresh garlic and a little extra-virgin olive oil. Fill recycled 2- and 4-ounce baby-food jars with the mixture and put the jars on the narrow shelves of the freezer door. When fresh herbs are out of season, these small portions are perfect for flavoring sauces, soups, casseroles, and marinades; for topping meat, poultry, and fish dishes before baking; for filling mushroom caps; and for adding to salad dressings and simple vinaigrettes. In the last 4 years, I've enjoyed adding a variety of fresh goodness to my cooking in all seasons.

—Olive Curtis, Acme, WA

Make compound butter to use up fresh herbs

Since supermarkets sell fresh herbs by the bunch and recipes usually call for only a teaspoon of them, I combine the remaining herbs in my food processor with cold unsalted butter. Then I shape the butter into small logs, wrap them in several layers of plastic wrap, and refrigerate or freeze them. Compound butters are great for flavoring pasta, grilled fish or chicken, sauces, etc.

Compound butters are great for flavoring pasta, grilled fish or chicken, sauces, etc.

—Antoinne Rimes, San Francisco, CA

Freezing herbs

Freezing works best with delicate herbs that don't taste very good when dried, such as basil, dill, chives, chervils, and parsley. Just chop the herbs, portion them generously *into ice cube trays*, and add a little chicken broth. I do this with mint, too, but I use water instead of chicken broth so I can add the mint to iced tea and other cold drinks.

—Renee Shepherd, *Fine Cooking*

Put fresh herbs in a tea ball for soups and sauces

When adding loose herbs to a sauce, stew, or soup, instead of messing with cheesecloth and string, I put the herbs or spices in a mesh tea ball and *hook the chain over the edge of the pot*. The ball is easily retrieved, and I don't have to strain the sauce.

—Ruby Thomas, Anacortes, WA

Getting the most out of dried herbs

Rub dried herbs between the palms of your hands before using them. This *crushing action helps release their flavor*.

—Jennifer Armentrout, *Fine Cooking*

Use baby-food jars to store spices

I save money by buying my spices in bulk at my local natural-foods store, and I like to reuse baby-food jars to store spices. I paint the lids of the jars and *write the name of the spices on the top* with a black permanent marker. The stackable jars look attractive stored in my cupboard, and I can see the spices through the clear glass.

—Missy Collier, Buellton, CA

Put the date on spices to know when to replace them

I write the date on a jar or bag of spices when I first buy it, so I can easily gauge its freshness. After 6 months to a year, most spices have lost so much potency that they should be replaced.

After 6 months to a year, most spices have lost so much potency.

—Richard Forgash, Seattle, WA

Is double trouble?

Is it true that if you're doubling a recipe, you shouldn't necessarily double the spices?

—Andi Carlson, Silver Spring, MD

Pamela Penzey of Penzeys Spices in Brookfield, Wisconsin, replies: For a recipe that calls for spices per piece (e.g., ½ teaspoon seasoning per chicken breast), it doesn't matter whether you're cooking 2 breasts or 200, it will be the same ½ teaspoon per piece. In all other recipes, it isn't that simple.

If you're doubling a baking recipe, vanilla and cinnamon can be doubled, though the cinnamon may start to dominate if it's strong. Other spices should be increased by one half to two thirds. For example, 1 teaspoon allspice for one batch would become 1½ to 1⅔ teaspoons for a double batch. Strong spices, like cloves, seem to grow stronger exponentially as they are increased.

When it comes to making big batches of soups, stews, and chilis, hold back on the spices. Their flavors will grow during long cooking, especially in the company of acidic ingredients such as wine and tomatoes. There's no turning back once you've added your seasonings, so start conservatively. I taste every dish halfway through and adjust the seasoning, then again at the end just before serving.

To save flavor, keep the inner seal on spice jars

I used to often throw out jars of rarely used ground spices (like cloves, ginger, and allspice) that had become stale. Many of these spice jars were still mostly full. I've since discovered that the spices can be kept fresher longer if I don't remove the inner seal on a new jar but just *puncture a small hole in the seal* to pour out the exact amount of spice I need. The jar can then be resealed with a small piece of tape and the top tightened. This seems to limit the amount of air the spices are exposed to and keeps them fresh longer.

—Lloyd Grable, McLean, VA

Fill a pepper mill with seafood-friendly spices

Two of the least-used spices in my spice rack are whole fennel and coriander seed, even though I love their flavors. These two spices are wonderful on fish and seafood, but they're seldom called for in recipes. In an effort to use them up, I filled a spare pepper mill with the fennel and coriander seeds, plus some whole black peppercorns, and put the (labeled) pepper mill beside my stove. Now I reach for *my special pepper mill* whenever I'm cooking seafood, which is quite often. This wonderful seasoning has even found its way to the dining room table, where it's a nice addition to vegetables and salads.

—Sheila Kerr, Mansonville, Quebec, Canada

Toast spices in foil to prevent burning

I have a neater method to toast spices in a skillet. Instead of putting the spices directly in the skillet, *fold them into an aluminum-foil packet* and then heat the packet in the skillet. After 5 minutes, open and sniff. The spices are ready when you smell their aroma. Return the packet to the skillet for another few minutes if necessary. This method makes particular sense for toasting saffron, which burns easily and which is used in such small quantities that it seems like half of it never finds its way out of the skillet.

—Susan Asanovic, Wilton, CT

BASIL

Basil leaves all year

My garden produces lots of great basil during the summer that withers during the first chilly nights of fall. Here's how I freeze what I can't use, making August's harvest last through the winter. Start by removing all the leaves from the stems. Wash and dry the leaves (I like to use a salad spinner for this last step). Next, take two yards of waxed paper and lay it across a table or kitchen counter. *Spread the clean, dry basil leaves on the paper in a single layer*, leaving the last foot of paper empty. Now begin slowly rolling the paper up from the filled end—just as if you were rolling up a carpet. It's important that the leaves stay in a single layer, so this can take a few starts and stops. Roll the last, empty foot of waxed paper to seal the package. Put the rolled basil package into a plastic bag, then stow it in the freezer. When you need basil to cook with, simply unroll the paper enough to expose a few leaves, roll the paper back up, and put it back in the freezer. While the basil's color will have turned an olive green in the cold, the flavor is wonderfully preserved— better than dried basil from the supermarket.

—Margaret Kasten, Norwalk, CT

Blanching basil for pesto

There are two reasons why I blanch my basil before puréeing it for pesto. First, for a brighter green color that holds for several days. More important, however, is the texture. Blanched basil emulsifies more easily, producing *a smoother yet full-bodied sauce.* Blanching will slightly reduce the potency of the fresh basil flavor, but because it starts out so incredibly fragrant, the reduction is minimal. Just be sure to dip the leaves only briefly in boiling water, then quickly plunge them in ice water to keep them from overcooking.

—Robert Danhi, *Fine Cooking*

Make pesto go further

I learned from my Italian mother-in-law to *add potato to basil pesto* to cut down on any bitterness in the basil, to give the pesto more smoothness and body, and simply to yield more pesto. For every 2 cups of packed whole basil leaves, I add two small, boiled, peeled, and cooled potatoes (boiling potatoes are best) to the processor or blender.

—Pat Melilli, Wappingers Falls, NY

Using limp basil

When a large bunch of basil wilts and droops sooner than I'd like, I use up the leaves to *make an intense basil oil:* Use 1 part loosely packed leaves to 1 part oil. Put the leaves in a colander and scald with boiling water. Drain well and squeeze out excess water. Puree the basil with the oil in a food processor. Refrigerate for 24 hours and then strain. Store the oil in the refrigerator. This technique also works nicely with short-lived arugula. Use 1 part arugula to 2 parts oil. You can omit the blanching, but the color is better if you take this additional step.

—Susan Asanovic, Wilton, CT

Cutting chiffonade

I may be crazy, and I can't explain why this works, but if you *roll the basil* from stem to tip and cut parallel with the leaf vein, the basil does not blacken as quickly. I'm a personal chef and food appearance is as important to me as taste.

—Jackie Clark, via email

Slice basil with kitchen shears

For the thinnest chiffonade of basil, I roll up a stack of leaves and *use a sharp pair of kitchen shears* instead of a knife.

—Carol A. Vollmer, Durham, NC

Store capers in sherry

Drain your brine-packed capers and *fill the jar with sherry instead;* they'll have better flavor.

—Anne Jones, Delta, British Columbia, Canada

Freezing fresh cilantro

To avoid wasting leftover fresh cilantro, I pick the leaves off the stems and put them in snack-size zip-top bags, add enough water to cover, and freeze the bags flat on their sides. *Freezing the cilantro in water* prevents freezer burn by keeping air away from the leaves. When I need to use some, I just break off a chunk of cilantro "ice."

—Paul Vinett, Norwalk, CT

Peeling a mountain of garlic

Peeling a bulb's worth of garlic cloves is not the most enviable of tasks, but it's not a tedious as it may seem. I put the individual cloves in a bowl, pour over very hot water, and agitate the mixture with a metal whisk. The *hot water and movement both soften and loosen the skins*. I drain off the water and then easily remove the skins with a paring knife.

—Tony Rosenfeld, *Fine Cooking*

Improvise a garlic peeler from a rubber jar grip

Faced with the daunting task of peeling six heads of garlic for a pickle recipe, and not having purchased one of the new rubber tube peelers yet, I improvised using a simple round rubber disk that's sold as a gripper to remove jar lids. With practice, I was able to strip several cloves at a time by putting them in the middle of the disk, folding it in half, and rolling it back and forth with both hands. As a bonus, I found a whole head could be easily broken into cloves using the same technique. Also, rubbing cloves between your hands while wearing rubber kitchen gloves works great, too—and it eliminates sticky fingers.

Use a simple round rubber disk that's sold as a gripper to remove jar lids.

—Mickey Wilcox, Burlington, CT

Low-tech is best when removing garlic skin

My low-tech method is to *hit the garlic cloves with a brick*. The peel pops right off. So what if the skins fly around a bit. Loosen up, America. A super-neat kitchen leaves little room for creativity and fun.

—Susan Asanovic, Wilton, CT

Peeling garlic gently

One of the most popular recipes I teach is a roasted chicken stuffed with 48 unbroken cloves of garlic. Peeling all that garlic by smashing it with the broad side of a knife is not only a chore, but also ruins the presentation of the slowly roasted cloves. To peel a garlic clove quickly and easily without breaking it, simply *put the clove in the microwave and heat at 100% power* for approximately 10 seconds. The heat generated will create a burst of steam that loosens the papery skin from the garlic. Remove the garlic from the microwave, then grasp one end and gently press the clove against the counter. The garlic will pop right out of its skin. You can do several cloves at a time, just increase the time in the microwave by about 2 seconds for each additional clove.

—Ray L. Overton, III, The Georgia Lifestyles Learning Center, Roswell, GA

Blanching garlic helps peeling

To peel a few garlic cloves, I usually just press the side of a knife to crack the skin, but this can get tedious if I've got more than a dozen or so cloves to peel, especially if the cloves are very fresh and the skin is tight. For a lot of garlic cloves, I *blanch them in boiling water* for just 15 seconds, scoop them out, and then shock them in ice water. The skin slips right off.

—Robert Danhi, *Fine Cooking*

Bathe garlic to avoid the sticky mess

We use a lot of garlic at my small delicatessen on the Olympic Peninsula of Washington, and peeling it can be a chore. But I can't see buying peeled cloves when our local farmers grow so many great varieties. Fortunately, I've found a way to peel lots of garlic without making a sticky mess of my hands: I separate the cloves from the head, cut off the root ends, and loosen the skin of each clove by smashing it with the flat side of a chef's knife. Then I put all the cloves *in a big bowl of cold water* and slip them out of their skins. When you remove the cloves from the water, you'll find that your hands are no longer sticky.

—Hope Porsato, Nordland, WA

Peel garlic with wet fingers

I use a lot of garlic, and I find peeling the cloves to be a chore. The garlic juice makes the peel stick to my fingers like glue. But now I've discovered a trick that really helps. I smash the cloves first to loosen the skin, *then I wet my fingers before peeling*. This way, the peel doesn't stick to my fingers.

—Lance Kimdi, Bethel, CT

What to do when you're short on garlic

If I'm just short of the amount of garlic I need for a recipe, I fall back on the saying "*the bigger the chunks of garlic*, the gentler the flavor"—only I use it in reverse. I grate the garlic cloves on my Microplane grater, holding the garlic with a fork to keep my fingers away from the sharp blades; this gives me an intense garlic purée that yields maximum flavor, so two cloves of garlic can easily do the work of three. Just be sure not to burn the garlic when you start to cook.

—Marcy Brown, Los Angeles, CA

Instant garlic paste

Grate garlic to make an instant purée. I often use a rasp-style grater to grate garlic rather than mincing it.

—Ruth Lively, *Fine Cooking*

Grating garlic

I use *a cheese grater* with tiny teardrop-shaped holes (the same size holes for grating Parmesan cheese) to mince or finely chop peeled garlic. The grater works faster than a knife and it's easier to clean than a garlic press.

—Mary Ann Cameron, Santa Clara, CA

Mincing garlic in the food processor

To mince garlic evenly in a food processor, *drop the cloves* through the feed tube while the steel blade is running. Do the same to mince fresh ginger.

—Maryellen Driscoll, *Fine Cooking*

Salt prevents sticky garlic

When chopping fresh garlic, add a little salt; this *prevents it from sticking* to the knife.

—Rene A. Jacobus, Dayton, OH

Waxed paper for quick garlic chopping

I don't like cleaning cutting boards. If I only have to chop a few garlic cloves for a dish, *I fold a 16-inch piece of waxed paper twice,* lay it on the cutting board, and chop my garlic on top of the paper, turning the paper instead of my knife. The waxed paper is also a handy place to store garlic for 30 minutes or so (just fold over the paper), and the paper also makes it easy to carry the garlic to the waiting pan.

—Joanne Bouknight, *Fine Cooking*

Chop at the last minute

The volatile compounds that give garlic its characteristic pungency aren't released until it's chopped or crushed. Since these flavors begin to dissipate and change once exposed to air, chop garlic at the last minute before using. If you must chop garlic ahead, *drizzle it with oil to help slow the oxidation* and deterioration of flavor and refrigerate it.

—Molly Stevens, *Fine Cooking*

The thinnest garlic slices

I don't have much occasion to use *a truffle slicer* for its intended purpose, but it's essentially a small mandoline, so it comes in handy for other tasks. For example, if you run a clove of garlic over the blade, you get tissue-thin slices, which are a perfect last-minute flavor booster for sauces and sautes.

—Al Bower, Athens, GA

Marinate garlic and shallots to mellow them

I like to use finely minced garlic and shallots whenever I make salad dressing. To mellow the sharp, pungent taste of the raw garlic and shallots, I always *add a bit of lemon juice and salt* and let them sit for a few minutes before adding the rest of the dressing ingredients. This makes my salad dressing taste more mellow and complex.

—Kara Adanalian, Fairfax, CA

Removing garlic odor from hands

After chopping garlic, I run cold water over my fingers as I rub them on the flat of a stainless-steel knife (if a knife blade seems too risky, a large stainless-steel spoon works, too). The important factors seem to be *cold water and stainless steel.* A 30-second bath takes the garlic odor away.

—Jim DeMase, Greenwich, CT

Garlic Will Stick to Your Breath, But Not to Your Hands

I must draw attention to the aspect of garlic that makes would-be garlic lovers wilt—garlic breath.

- Garlic odor doesn't originate from the mouth or tongue. The sulfuric compounds that give garlic its scent and flavor get into the blood and lungs, much as alcohol does.

- Time is the only remedy for garlic breath, but chewing parsley sprigs or fennel seeds will mask it.

- Washing your hands with lemon juice and salt will kill the scent of garlic, as will rubbing your hands with used coffee grounds.

—Bob Kinkead, *Fine Cooking*

Make roasted garlic a kitchen staple

I have recently started substituting roasted garlic for raw in salad dressings, sauces, and marinades. I've come to prefer the mellowness of roasted garlic over the sharpness of raw. Roast the head by cutting off the tips and sprinkling on a few teaspoons of water, along with salt and oil, if you like. *Wrap the head in foil and roast in a hot oven* until the cloves are soft, about an hour. Then I refrigerate the garlic, wrapped in the cooking foil, and use it whenever I might have used raw. It lasts for at least a week.

—Jacquelyn Jacobi, Victoria, British Columbia, Canada

Keep roasted garlic on hand

In summer when garlic is cheap (five for $1 at my local farmers' market), I buy 50 heads and roast them all at once on foil-covered baking sheets. After the roasted garlic has cooled slightly, I snip the top off each clove with scissors and squeeze the garlic into the food processor, adding a bit of my best olive oil and then *whipping the garlic into a smooth, golden purée.* I divide the purée among a number of very small plastic containers and freeze them for use throughout the next 3 or 4 months. One container of roasted garlic is always in my refrigerator, ready to enhance bruschetta, mashed potatoes, soups, roasted meat—you name it.

—Jamie Miller, Maple Grove, MN

Roast garlic cloves individually

I'm a live-alone widow who loves to cook with roasted garlic. Rather than roast an entire head, I pick 6 to 8 large cloves (skin on), coat them with about ½ teaspoon olive oil, and set them on a piece of foil *in my toaster oven*. I bake them at 325°F for 10 to 13 minutes, turning them frequently.

—Barbara Hays Beckstrand, San Diego, CA

Convenient roasted garlic without the mess

I buy peeled, fresh garlic cloves in one-pound jars for everyday use and whole garlic bulbs for roasting. Once when I wanted roasted garlic and the local market was closed, I decided to improvise. I put a large handful (about 20) of the peeled garlic cloves on two large sheets of parchment, drizzled olive oil over them, and sprinkled them with salt. I twisted the corners of the parchment together to create a little bundle. I set the bundle into a soaked terra-cotta garlic roaster, which I put in a 350°F oven and roasted for about 30 minutes. The advantage of *using peeled garlic* is that I get buttery-smooth garlic without the work and mess of separating the soft, cooked garlic from the skins.

—Debra Sue Heaphy, American Canyon, CA

Flavor broth with roasted garlic skins

After squeezing cloves of roasted garlic, don't throw the skins away. Put them *in a small pot with some water and a little salt*, simmer for about 20 minutes, and strain. You'll have a delicious broth.

—Yvonne Mounsey, Roberts Creek, British Columbia, Canada

GINGER

Ginger stays fresh in a flower pot

To keep a chunk of fresh ginger from drying up, *I keep it covered with soil* in a small terra-cotta pot. As long as I moisten the soil with water occasionally, the ginger stays fresh for quite a long time.

—Lily Naidu, Renton, WA

Saving ginger

Rather than end up with moldy bits of leftover ginger in the crisper drawer of my refrigerator, I peel the ginger, put it whole into a jar, *cover with vinegar,* and store it in the fridge until I need a bit of it to grate or slice.

—Mary Schroeder, Seattle, WA

Vodka keeps ginger fresh

To keep ginger fresh for months, *I put it in a glass jar and fill it with vodka*. You don't need to refrigerate it, the smell is wonderful, and the ginger takes on just a hint of the vodka's flavor.

—Sheryl Hur-House, Jupiter, FL

To keep chopped ginger on hand, preserve it in sherry

Peel about a pound of ginger and chop it in a food processor. Transfer the ginger to a jar that has a lid, pour in enough sherry to cover, and screw on the lid before putting it in the refrigerator. If you run low on ginger or sherry, just add more. *The ginger keeps indefinitely.* Not only does it make ginger easily available, but you can use the ginger-flavored sherry to make great sauces and salad dressings.

—W. J. Schroeter, Santee, CA

Keep it frozen

To keep fresh ginger readily available, *I peel it and freeze it.* The root lasts many, many months and grates much more easily when it is frozen. When I need some ginger for a recipe, I shave the frozen ginger into the dish I'm creating. The grated ginger thaws almost instantly, so the cold temperature doesn't adversely affect the recipe. Then, back into the freezer with the ginger. Never thaw the root.

—Karen Tanaka, Beacon, NY, and April Mohr, Watertown, CT

Peeling ginger

When peeling fresh ginger with a paring knife, some of the usable flesh comes off with the skin, reducing the yield you get from the ginger and raising your food costs. Instead, *use a teaspoon to peel* the ginger so you don't waste any. Scrape the skin with the edge of the spoon's bowl, applying gentle pressure on the ginger. I like to push the spoon away from me as if I were scraping a carrot, but if it feels more comfortable to you, pull the spoon toward you.

—Walter J. Morrison III, Buffalo, NY

Mince ginger without a knife

To mince ginger finely in less than a second, I peel and slice coins of ginger, put the coins on a piece of plastic wrap, fold over the plastic to cover, and then I *strike the ginger with a meat mallet.*

—Leslie Revsin, *Fine Cooking*

Juicing ginger

A few teaspoons of ginger juice are delicious for *zipping up a consommé* or pouring on steamed fish. To make ginger juice without using a messy cheesecloth, finely grate a very fresh, rock-hard piece of ginger about 4 inches long. Put the grated ginger in a small bowl and press hard against the mass of ginger with the back of a sturdy teaspoon. Tilt the bowl and the juice will run off.

—Susan Asanovic, Wilton, CT

Freeze ginger for easier grating

To keep ginger fresher longer and to make it easier to grate, freeze it. First break off the lobes of the fresh root and wrap them individually in plastic wrap. Put all the pieces into an airtight bag or container, which then goes in the freezer. When a recipe calls for grated ginger, remove a piece from the freezer. Scrape off the papery skin with a serrated knife, if you want. Then start grating—*don't let it thaw*; the ginger is easier to grate when it's frozen.

—Elizabeth Mason, Dartmouth, Nova Scotia, Canada

Freeze rows of fresh ginger slices

Since fresh ginger often goes bad before you can use it all, here's a way to keep it on hand at all times. Simply peel and slice it into "coins," lay the slices in a row on plastic wrap, and fold the plastic over the cover the slices tightly. Put the package in a zip-top bag and freeze. You can take out a few slices at a time as needed—*they defrost quickly*. The consistency is slightly limp, but the flavor is still intense.

—Jayne Hollerbaugh, Tampa, FL

Frozen minced ginger

Recently when I wound up with two pounds of fresh ginger by mistake, I decided to try freezing it. I cut it into chunks and then minced it fine in my food processor. The texture was perfect. I sealed it in a plastic freezer bag and popped it into the freezer. When I needed ginger, I'd just go to the freezer and break off a piece. I found this method so convenient that now I do it all the time—and you can't tell it from fresh.

—Sharon Howard, Eugene, OR

I cut it into chunks and then minced it fine in my food processor.

Garlic press for candied ginger

I like to use candied ginger in syrup for baking and desserts, but the sticky balls are messy to chop. I use my garlic press for the job; the ginger presses into *very thin strips*, which almost vanish in cookies and cakes. They're good in stir-fries, too.

—Ruth Richman, St. Peters, Prince Edward Island, Canada

Soften candied ginger in a double boiler

When candied ginger becomes brittle and difficult to chop, I put the pieces in a double boiler for about 10 minutes. The ginger softens to just *the right consistency for slivering and finely dicing*.

—Elaine Phillips, Nashville, TN

HORSERADISH

Grating horseradish without tears

Grating horseradish by hand can produce a flood of tears, and the fibers tend to jam up in a food processor's grating attachment. Here's an easy technique that works. *Peel the root under cold running water* and cut it into $1/2$-inch dice with a sharp knife. Fit a food processor with the steel blade and start it. With the blade spinning, drop small handfuls of the dice down the feed tube. When all the cubes have been added, process 1 minute longer for finely grated horseradish. To store, add enough vinegar to make a moist paste, pack it into a jar, and seal it. It will keep this way in the refrigerator for about a week.

—Lilia Dvarionas, Kanata, Ontario, Canada

LEMONGRASS

With lemongrass, choose the freshest, heaviest, and most tender stalks

Heft is a good sign of moisture when purchasing lemongrass. Avoid those that are dried at the edges. *Store lemongrass in a plastic bag* in the vegetable bin of the fridge, where it should stay fresh for 2 to 3 weeks. If you don't use it all within that time, freeze it. To use lemongrass, peel off and discard the outer 2 or 3 layers of the stalk until you get to the tender core. Then cut off 5 or 6 inches of the woody top before cutting it up as you wish.

—Mai Pham, *Fine Cooking*

Chop mint with your sharpest knife

Like many herbs, *mint bruises easily*, and when bruised, it loses its volatile, flavorful oils. To keep bruising to a minimum, use a sharp, dry knife for chopping and slicing. Chop mint just before using it; its volatile oils evaporate quickly. These oils also fade when heated, which is why fresh mint is often added toward the end of cooking.

—Lynn Alley, *Fine Cooking*

Whisk up a bit of mustard

A small tip that keeps my dishwashing to a minimum: Instead of using a spoon to measure out mustard for my vinaigrettes, *I use a small whisk*. I dunk the whisk into the jar (if the mouth isn't wide enough, I use a fork), catching 1 or 2 teaspoons of mustard on the tines. I put the whisk in a bowl or measuring cup, pour in vinegar by eye, and whisk to combine. Then I whisk in olive oil to taste.

—Eleanor Ricci, West Palm Beach, FL

Use a mustard jar for salad dressing

Here's an efficient way to use up the last hard-to-reach bits in a mustard jar. When I start to scrape the bottom, I use the jar to mix salad dressing. My favorite vinaigrette recipe calls for a teaspoon of mustard, so I just *add all the other ingredients* to the mustard jar, screw on the lid, and shake.

—Sidney Ackerman, New York, NY

Dry mustard in cheese sauces

I've found that *a pinch of dry mustard* in my cheese sauces helps bring out the flavor of the cheese.

—Eric Corson, Epsom, NH

Grating nutmeg

I've never bought a nutmeg mill and I don't need one. Instead, I scrape off nutmeg particles *with a vegetable peeler* or even just a sharp knife. It's easier to control where the nutmeg falls this way and hence easier to gather and measure.

—Ruth Scott, Beavercreek, OH

Getting the sand out of parsley

Because parsley grows in sandy soils, it needs to be thoroughly washed. Though some people suggest washing herbs only when you're ready to use them, I use parsley so much that I wash it as soon as I get it home. Loosen the bunch and wash it in a few rinses of tepid water, then *dry it well in a salad spinner* or by blotting it with a clean towel.

—Robert Wemischner, *Fine Cooking*

Keeping parsley fresh

I keep my parsley fresh by *treating it like a bunch of flowers*. First I check the rubber band that holds the bunch together. If it's too tight, I loosen it, but I don't remove it. Then I cull any crushed, soggy, or otherwise questionable material out of the bunch. I put some water in a tall mug, stick the stems of the parsley into the mug, cover loosely with a plastic bag, and put the whole thing in the refrigerator toward the back—out of harm's way. I have fresh parsley whenever I need it. I just pluck out a few stalks, rinse, and use. I find that it lasts for a few weeks this way.

—Patricia A. Janney, Kingston, NY

Freezing parsley

If you love using fresh parsley but seem to wind up with most of it going bad in the fridge, try this method for freezing it. Wash and dry the parsley, remove the leaves, and put them in a food processor. Chop them on high speed for about 20 seconds. Put the chopped parsley in the bottom of a plastic freezer bag, roll up the bag to remove all the air, and stick it in the freezer. It will *keep for up to 6 months*. You can use the parsley frozen, even in a dish that won't be cooked—the parsley will thaw in a matter of seconds.

—Nina Rago, Tampa, FL

Pepper as memory aid

If you tend to forget whether you've salted the pot of water for boiling pasta or vegetables, add a pinch of pepper to the water along with the salt. *Pepper is easily visible* in the water so you will always know if you've seasoned the water or not.

—Pamela Reznick, Somers, NY

Add a crank handle to your pepper grinder

I turned my rotary twist-top pepper mill into one with a crank handle by screwing a small "J" hook from the hardware store into the side of the top. The added handle lets me *grind a lot of pepper* with a rotary motion in seconds rather than the slow, wrist-twisting method the old way.

—Lane Johnson, Portland, OR

To fill a pepper mill, try an envelope

When it's time to fill my salt shaker and pepper mill, I snip the corner off an envelope to make a fast, *disposable funnel.* I don't spill any salt or pepper-corns this way, and I find that it's more convenient than hunting for a real funnel, whose narrow feed tube clogs up with peppercorns anyway.

—Kit Rollins, Cedarburg, WI

A neat place for a pepper mill

When my pepper mill isn't in use, *it stands in a ramekin*, which keeps residual ground pepper from dirtying my counter.

—Peter Hyzak, Ponte Vedra Beach, FL

Crushing peppercorns

I crush peppercorns on my wooden cutting board using *the bottom of a heavy saucepan.* I hold the handle in one hand and the rim in the other, then rock the pan bottom over the peppercorns until I've got the degree of "crush" that I want. I don't try to do more than a tablespoon of peppercorns at once, because they would roll all over the place.

—Kathleen West, Havre de Grace, MD

Meat pounder quietly crushes peppercorns

For coarsely ground peppercorns, forget the hard-to-control method of crush-ing them under a pan or pot. There's a way to use your meat pounder to crush peppercorns. Group the peppercorns on your cutting board. With one hand on the handle and the other hand on the head of the pounder, slowly press a flat side of the head on the peppercorns, *crushing them with the edge.* Repeat this process, working toward you and across the peppercorns. This crushing tool is much easier to hold, and it lets you see what you're doing.

—Keith Masumoto, Chicago, IL

Crack peppercorns on a sheet pan

One popular way to crack peppercorns is to crush them on a cutting board with the bottom of a heavy skillet, but I'm always chasing whole and cracked peppercorns that have rolled and bounced off the board. Simple solution: Put the board on a rimmed sheet pan first. The peppercorns still roll off the board, but *the pan catches them*.

—Noah Thompson, Dallas, TX

ROSEMARY

Plant leftover rosemary

It's easy to turn a leftover rosemary sprig into a rosemary plant. Just make an angled cut through the sprig, at a point where a leaf meets the stem, so that you're left with a 3-inch-long cutting. Then, strip the leaves from the bottom half of this cutting, place it in potting soil in a 3-inch pot, and dampen the soil with water. Seal the pot in a zip-top bag (as in a closed terrarium, the moisture will recycle). Set the pot near a window, out of direct sunlight. In a few months, when the rosemary begins to grow, you can remove it from the bag and plant it outside, if weather permits.

Make an angled cut through the sprig, at a point where a leaf meets the stem, so that you're left with a 3-inch-long cutting.

—Irene Ong, Madison, WI

Keep it sharp with rosemary

Use a sharp knife when chopping rosemary; a dull knife would bruise the leaves and make them taste bitter. A clean cut *releases just the right amount of the potent oils*.

—Ruth Lively, *Fine Cooking*

A better way to chop rosemary

I've always found chopping fresh rosemary somewhat of a challenge because the needles tended to fly off the cutting board once you started chopping with a sharp knife. While following a recipe calling for freshly chopped rosemary and basil leaves, I decided to *fold the rosemary needles within the basil leaves* and then slice the basil "bundles" crosswise. After slicing, the two herbs can be easily chopped together.

—Joan Andrews, via email

Saffron needs moisture to release its flavor

The best way to extract flavor from saffron is to soak the threads in hot (not boiling) liquid for 5 to 20 minutes. As the saffron soaks, you'll notice the distinctive aroma indicating that your saffron "tea" is ready. I like to soak the saffron in stock or wine (rather than water) to add to the overall flavor of a dish. When adding saffron to soups, stews, salad dressing, and other recipes with a lot of liquid, you can simply toss the crushed threads in with the rest of the ingredients. I still find, however, that I get a deeper, more pervasive saffron flavor by first soaking the crushed threads, then adding them. For traditional paella, cooks first toast the saffron threads in a dry skillet to bring out the volatile flavors. I don't usually bother because I've found that this step makes little difference in the final flavor of the dish.

—Molly Stevens, *Fine Cooking*

Perfectly crumbled saffron threads

I love to cook Middle Eastern dishes, which often call for saffron. To keep my precious saffron fresh longer, I store it in a small, *airtight container in the freezer*. When I take out a pinch of saffron, the threads are quite stiff and easy to crush between my fingers so there's no need for a mortar and pestle. The spice is then ready to be added to the dish or steeped in boiling water, according to the recipe.

—Kathy Wazana, Toronto, Ontario, Canada

Pulverize saffron threads in a blender

I recently bought some Kashmir saffron that's incredibly moist and fresh. When I tried to incorporate the saffron into my challah recipe, however, I couldn't pulverize the strands because they were so moist. I found that if I put the saffron threads *in my blender along with the hot water* called for in the recipe, the saffron dissolved completely, and the liquid turned a beautiful shade of yellow. Now there are no unsightly (and wasted) strands of expensive saffron stubbornly refusing to be incorporated into my favorite recipes.

—Karen Wood, Houston, TX

Sage is best cooked

Raw fresh sage feels a little harsh on the tongue, both in texture and in flavor. If you use it raw, say in a spread, use only small, tender leaves and chop them finely. When you cook with sage, *add it early on to starchy or mild-flavored ingredients* such as grains, squashes, beans, and meats, so that they can absorb its assertive flavor. Outspoken ingredients, such as garlic or fish, can handle the bittersweet strength of barely cooked sage quite well.

—Sophia Schweitzer, *Fine Cooking*

Salt cuts bitterness, which enhances sweetness

Adding a pinch of salt to desserts can actually highlight sweetness. *Salt reduces bitterness* in a dish and this magnifies sweetness. And you can sometimes rectify a dish that tastes too salty by adding a mild acid like lemon juice or vinegar.

—Shirley O. Corriher, *Fine Cooking*

Salt helps a mortar and pestle do its job

I've always had a hard time getting dried herbs and spices—and especially red chile flakes—to crush well in a mortar and pestle. I've since found that adding some salt or sugar to the mortar really *facilitates the grinding* of the herb or spice.

—Janet deCarteret, Bellevue, WA

Stripping thyme leaves

The fastest way to detach tiny thyme leaves from a fresh sprig of the herb is to grip the stem toward the top with one hand, and use the thumb and forefinger of your other hand to run down the length of the stem, stripping off the leaves as you go. This now seems like an obvious method (it also works well with other herbs with small leaves) but until I saw it being done by someone else, I had been pulling them off one by one.

—Marian Brown, Sherman Oaks, CA

Grip the stem toward the top with one hand, and use the thumb and forefinger of your other hand to run down the stem.

Squeaky fresh

If it feels *heavy for its size* and squeaks when squeezed, you've found a fresh artichoke. Brown spots on the outer leaves of winter artichokes are okay; they're simply a sign of frost.

—Amy Albert, *Fine Cooking*

Keeping artichokes green

Cut into a raw artichoke and it will almost instantly turn brown. Although there are ways to slow the process, in my experience, no matter what you do or how quickly you do it, there's always a bit of discoloration. You can minimize browning by using only stainless-steel knives and scissors to cut artichokes, by immediately rubbing the cut surfaces with a piece of lemon, and by keeping the artichoke in water acidulated with lemon juice or vinegar until you're ready to use it. Don't use aluminum or cast-iron pots for cooking, as these will discolor artichokes as well. Also, don't cover raw artichokes with foil; use kitchen parchment or plastic wrap instead.

Minimize browning by using only stainless-steel knives and scissors to cut artichokes.

—Georgeanne Brennan, *Fine Cooking*

Save the artichoke stem

The next time you cook fresh artichokes, don't toss out the stems. Peel them down to the pale core and cook them in boiling water along with the artichokes. They're *as tender and tasty as the hearts*.

—Linda Haines, Las Vegas, NV

Testing artichokes

When boiling whole artichokes, *check for doneness by pulling on the top of an interior leaf*. If the leaf comes free under the artichoke's weight, then it's done. If it needs more coercion to break loose, then it needs more cooking.

—Diane Chesterton, Kansas City, MO

Check the bottom of the spears for age

When shopping for asparagus, choose firm stalks with tightly closed buds at the tip. The color should be vivid, with no signs of fading. Asparagus begins to lose its sweetness the moment it's cut. Check the stem ends for freshness; *the best asparagus looks freshly cut* and not at all dried out. Asparagus lasts longest if its stem ends are submerged in water.

—Seen Lippert, *Fine Cooking*

To cut or to snap?

Opinions vary about how to prepare asparagus for cooking. Unless you buy spears that have already been trimmed to the top 4 or 5 inches, you'll need to remove the tough ends. Some people simply cut the spears where the green color fades, but I prefer to snap off the ends. I hold each spear, one at a time, in both hands and bend it until it breaks naturally at the point at which it becomes tough. I think this is a more reliable trimming method and I don't mind that the snapped spears aren't all exactly the same length. Many cooks peel asparagus, especially large spears, but I never do. *If you've snapped it properly, the entire spear will be tender*, so peeling doesn't enhance tenderness, it just removes flavor.

—Janet Fletcher, *Fine Cooking*

Peel asparagus without breaking it in two

When I peel asparagus, I rest most of the stalk on the bottom of an upside-down saucepan. This way, *the tip is elevated* so I can easily grasp and rotate it as I peel, but the rest of the stalk is supported by the pot so it won't snap in two from the pressure of the peeler.

—Wayne Armentrout, McLean, VA

Tenderest green beans fall to the bottom

Rather than pay extra for slender, elegant *haricots verts*, I go directly to the green bean bin and start digging. The best beans are the smallest ones, and these young beans inevitably *collect at the bottom of the bin.* It takes a few minutes more to fill my bag, but it's certainly worth it.

—Sumner O'Keefe, Deerfield, MA

Trim beans by the handful

Here's how to quickly trim green beans: Grab a handful and, holding them loosely, tap the stem ends on the cutting board until *all the stems line up*. Then lay the beans on the board and slice off the stems in one cut. Repeat the process to remove the tips of the beans, if you like.

—Maria Reid, via email

Rinsing canned beans quickly

I use canned beans often, and one of the problems I've had is removing and rinsing the beans without damaging them. It seemed that the process of pouring the beans into a colander and rinsing them with water often left quite a few beans broken in half or with split skins. Then I tried this technique. I put the can of beans into a clean, empty sink, then I used a can opener to punch three holes into the bottom of the can, turned the can over, and opened its top. Next, I held the full can of beans under the faucet and ran cool water gently through it until the liquid draining from the bottom was clear. You can *pour the beans from the can directly* into whatever dish you're preparing. The result is nicely rinsed, undamaged beans, and a clean colander still in your cupboard.

—Clark Smith, Saratoga, CA

Keep bugs away from beans with dried chiles

To keep those nasty little pantry bugs out of your dried beans, stick a couple of *dried chiles* into all your jars or bags of beans. They'll keep the bugs away.

—Mark Thompson, Tucson, AZ

Gold-panning method works for washing dried beans

I find that washing dried beans in a colander under running water isn't always the most effective way of eliminating debris, so I figured out a new method, one that not only washes away dirt but that also helps remove damaged beans. I put the beans in a large, shallow pot or wok (to approximate a gold-panning pan), fill the container with water, and run my fingers through the beans for a few seconds. Then I swirl the container around so that the water and beans circle around the container. By tilting the pan as the beans and water slowly stop swirling, the water and debris flow off: The *swirling makes the heavier items sink* and the lighter things (like damaged beans, dirt particles, beans of a different kind that were mixed in) float so that they're easily poured off with the water.

—Jonathan Burkinshaw, Toronto, Ontario, Canada

Heavy and smooth

When buying beets, look for *smooth skins and tails* that aren't too shaggy. If they're light for their size, chances are they've been stored improperly or for too long and they may be spongy or dried out. If they still have their greens, trim them off before storing and don't wash them, as any moisture can promote spoilage. Store them loosely in a bag in your produce drawer, where they'll keep for 8 to 12 days. Red beets will stain your hands, cutting board, and dishtowels.

—Molly Stevens, *Fine Cooking*

No-grit beet juice

After boiling unpeeled beets, you're left with a delightfully colored, flavorful liquid, which unfortunately contains quite a bit of sand. To thoroughly eliminate this grit, put a *paper coffee filter in a strainer* and pour the liquid through. If you don't have an immediate need for the liquid, freeze it and use it later in your stockpot in place of water. This method also works for the water used to rehydrate dried mushrooms.

—Laile A. Giansetto, Berkeley, CA

Give broccoli a whiff

Broccoli should smell fresh, not strong and cabbagy. Look for *compact, tightly closed florets* and thin-skinned stems on the slender side. Avoid broccoli that's dried or cracked on the cut end or that has obviously woody stems, and leave behind any yellowing specimens.

—Janet Fletcher, *Fine Cooking*

Peel broccoli stems for great flavor

I have learned from my mother to use up broccoli stems as well as the head. The insides of these thick, tough stems are actually quite sweet and tender and can be cooked any way you like. Just take a sharp paring knife or vegetable peeler and carefully *peel the tough, fibrous skin lengthwise* from the stems. Then slice or chop them according to your recipe.

—Nguyen Thi Kim Loan, Fajaro, Puerto Rico

Crisping cabbage with salt

I like cabbage in coleslaw or other salads to be crisp, so *I soak the whole cabbage in ice cold water.* I dissolve a heaping tablespoon of salt in a large bowl of water, soak the cabbage for 5 to 10 minutes, rinse it briefly with cold water, and then dry it with paper towels before I grate or chop it.

—Bonnilyn Buckley, Fillmore, NY

Skewers hold cabbage wedges together

To prevent cabbage wedges from falling apart in dishes such as corned beef and cabbage, insert a wooden skewer into the back of each wedge before cooking. Be sure to remove the skewers before serving. This technique *greatly improves the presentation,* and it makes the cabbage easier to eat.

—Lynne Persinger, Houston, TX

Cook cabbage with a dash of vinegar

To *cut down on odors* when cooking cabbage, cauliflower, and other notoriously smelly vegetables, add a little vinegar to the cooking water.

—Faye Field, Longview, TX

Keeping red cabbage red

Cooking red cabbage in an *acidic liquid such as wine or vinegar* helps it retain its color. Avoid cutting red cabbage with a carbon-steel knife or cooking it in an aluminum pot, both of which also cause discoloration.

—Ruth Lively, *Fine Cooking*

Freeze cabbage for stuffing

To save time when making stuffed cabbage, *I freeze and thaw the head of cabbage beforehand* instead of parboiling it. The thawed leaves are very pliable and taste no different than before.

—Cheryl Musinski, Agawam, MA

Use a cup to make perfectly round stuffed cabbage

A coffee cup is the perfect size. Line the cups with a 12-inch square piece of plastic wrap, letting the excess hang over the edge. Line the plastic with a large cabbage leaf (or two overlapping smaller leaves). Pack in about ⅓ cup of stuffing and then fold the leaves over the stuffing. Twist the plastic for a tight bundle. After pulling the plastic-wrapped cabbage out of the cup, hold the excess plastic in one hand and twist the stuffed cabbage in the other, stretching the plastic around the cabbage tighter and tighter. *The leaves will stay tightly closed* after the plastic is removed.

—Hubert Keller, *Fine Cooking*

Avoid the green and the woody

Avoid carrots tinged with green; they can be bitter. *Cut very large carrots in half lengthwise* and look at the core. If it looks dramatically distinct from the rest of the carrot, pry it out with the tip of a sturdy paring knife. A woody core is fibrous and unpleasant.

—Molly Stevens, *Fine Cooking*

The skinny on baby carrots

Baby-cut carrots, which are actually "adult" roots *cut and trimmed to masquerade as sweet young things,* are certainly convenient, since little or no prep is required, but that's the sole reason to buy them. Since they're already peeled, they lose moisture and flavor (and probably nutrients) faster than regular carrots.

—Ruth Lively, *Fine Cooking*

Keep cauliflower florets intact

Whenever I try to separate a head of cauliflower into whole florets with a knife, I invariably slice through some of the florets. So after trimming the stem end as close to the base of the head as I can, I set aside my knife, get out my melon baller, and start scooping out the remaining stem. It takes just a few scoops to remove most of the flesh. Now *the lovely florets are only loosely attached to one another* and it's very easy to separate them, whole and intact.

—Alphonda S. Thorn, New York, NY

Keep it out of hot water

Boiling or steaming tends to bring out the one-dimensional, cabbagey side of cauliflower, and it doesn't help eliminate the water that cauliflower is so full of. That's why *roasting and sauteing are my preferred methods*. If you do find that you need very simply cooked cauliflower for part of a recipe, I suggest steaming rather than boiling, because at least the cauliflower won't absorb more water.

—Peter Hoffman, *Fine Cooking*

CELERIAC (CELERY ROOT)

Head missing?

Choose celeriac about the size of a baseball; larger ones can be woody inside. Look for *fairly evenly shaped specimens*—overly twisted roots may be tough, fibrous, or even bitter. Check the stem end; that's the first place to show any signs of spoilage. Store it in your produce drawer, where it should keep 8 to 12 days. If you're peeling and cutting celeriac more than 15 minutes before you plan to cook it, drop it into a bowl of water with lemon to keep it from turning brown.

—Molly Stevens, *Fine Cooking*

CORN

Getting corn off the cob

If you want whole kernels of corn, *dip the ears in boiling water for a minute* or two, then cool them under cold running water before you strip them. This "sets" the milk so it doesn't spurt when you cut the kernels off the cob.

—Molly Stevens, *Fine Cooking*

Stock up on fresh corn

When fresh corn shows up on farm stands, I buy a couple of cases at once. Some gets eaten right away, but the rest *gets frozen for future use* in soups, breads, and side dishes. I shuck the corn, parboil it along with some of the husks for about 90 seconds, drain it, and then cut the kernels off the cob. I line the bottom of a freezer container with husks, add a layer of corn, and alternate until the container is full. The husks divide the kernels into portions, so it's easy to defrost just the amount I need.

—Kathleen M. Larkin, Houston, TX

Cooking easy

To cook corn kernels or peas, put them in a strainer and dip the strainer into boiling water so that the vegetables are easy to fish out when they're done.

—Peter Berley, *Fine Cooking*

EGGPLANT

Plump and shiny are best

At the market, *choose a plump, firm eggplant* with shiny skin that shows no sign of slackness; over-the-hill fruits are liable to be bitter. Once the skin loses its gloss, an eggplant's quality deteriorates. Also, an eggplant with a smaller calyx—the leathery, green cap that protrudes from the stem—will often have fewer seeds than one with a larger calyx.

—Ruth Lively, *Fine Cooking*

Preserving the taste of summer

What's the best way to freeze fresh corn?

—Kim Parker, via email

Tasha Prysi replies: On my family's farm, we struggled with this question for several years. Faced with an overflow of fresh corn from my father's field, my mother tested many different methods for freezing it. Freezing the corn raw didn't work well, as the corn would become gummy when it was thawed. She discovered that cooking corn quickly and cutting the kernels off the cob before freezing best preserved the vegetable's delicate flavor and texture.

To follow her method, shuck the corn and boil it on the cob for 2 minutes. Cool the cobs under running water or in an ice bath and pat them dry. With a sharp knife, cut the kernels off the cob and freeze them in plastic freezer bags.

Fresh corn can be frozen for up to 6 months. The texture and flavor suffer slightly, but it's still well worth the effort—home-frozen corn is always much better than commercially processed corn. Do cook and freeze the corn when it's fresh (don't let it sit for more than a couple of days) to retain as much of its original sweetness as possible.

Slice eggplant with a serrated knife

Eggplant is hard to cut with a regular chef's knife unless the blade is really sharp; good, *thin slices require a sawing action.* But if you use a serrated knife (such as a bread knife), the eggplant can be sliced paper-thin with ease.

—Danny Yang, Austin, TX

An easier way to sweat eggplant

Recipes often call for salting eggplant slices and placing a weight atop them to squeeze out the bitter juices. This can be a hassle if you're preparing more than one eggplant. That's why I use a slightly different method: I cut the eggplant into slices as usual and salt them heavily on one side only. Then I reassemble the eggplant, so that the slices are stacked together with layers of salt between. *Next, I wrap the whole eggplant tightly in plastic wrap* and let it sit. The eggplant quickly starts releasing juice. After 15 minutes or so, I unwrap the plastic and rinse the slices with water. No mess, no big containers or colanders to wash. Whether you're preparing many eggplant or just a few, this is a very simple procedure.

—Dr. Salete Newton, Norman, OK

Reducing bitterness

Salt pulls out juices that carry bitter flavors sometimes found in globe eggplant. (Agricultural scientists say that the bitterness, as well as the mouth-tingle that some people get from eggplant, is caused by alkaloids, bitter-tasting compounds concentrated in and around the eggplant's seeds.) Salting may also serve to *overpower any bitter flavors.*

—Ayla Algar, *Fine Cooking*

Salt first for less oily eggplant

Eggplant soaks up oil like a sponge, but you can reduce its ability to absorb oil by *salting the cut flesh* and letting it sit for 30 minutes or more. Then drain, pay dry, and proceed with cooking.

—Ruth Lively, *Fine Cooking*

Less greasy eggplant

I like to brush a bit of egg white on eggplant slices before pan frying them or oiling them for the grill; this *seals the cut surfaces* of the eggplant and prevents them from absorbing a lot of oil.

—Leyla Ghorbani, via email

Easier eggplant

When preparing eggplant—especially for grilling—I like to leave the skin on for flavor and because it helps keep the tender flesh from falling apart, but sometimes the skin can become a chewy mess. I compromise by *scoring the entire eggplant from top to bottom* with a dinner fork. The fork's closely spaced tines leave fine "stripes" in the eggplant's skin, not unlike the way cucumbers are often left with stripes of peel. When cooked, the skin is much more manageable.

—Michael J. Wodjenski, New Milford, CT

LEEKS

Watch for sticking in the pan

Leeks contain sugars just like onions do, but they can be more prone to sticking because they contain less moisture. A good way to avoid this is to *cook sliced rinsed leeks with droplets of water* still clinging to them and just a little bit of fat in the pan.

—David Tanis, *Fine Cooking*

Use leek greens for bouquets garni

I find it wasteful to discard the top half of leeks when a recipe calls for the white and pale green part only. I put the tougher green leaves to good use by including them in my bouquets garnis. I wash the leek greens thoroughly, drain them well, and bundle two leaves, a few sprigs of fresh thyme and parsley from my herb garden, along with one bay leaf. I tie them together with kitchen twine and store them in a plastic bag in the freezer until needed. The leek contributes great aromatic flavor and helps keep the other herbs together, making it easier to fish out the whole bouquet garni after use.

The leek contributes great aromatic flavor and helps keep the other herbs together.

—Sylvaine, via CooksTalk at www.finecooking.com

Washing lettuce

Here's a quick way to wash the dirt out of "open-ended lettuce," such as red leaf, romaine, and Bibb. Cut a V-shaped wedge from the stem end of the lettuce and remove the wedge. Holding the bottom of the lettuce firmly, *run cool water into the cut area that's now exposed at the base of the lettuce.* The water will flow down through the layers of leaves, and will gently push the dirt from bottom to top. Because you've cut away the root, the lettuce leaves can be peeled away easily. Be sure to check for any stubborn dirt that might have clung to the ribs before drying the lettuce.

—Walter J. Morrison III, Buffalo, NY

Tossing lettuce for drier greens

If you put washed and dried greens in the salad bowl and discover they're still a little damp, put a paper towel in each hand and toss the undressed greens. The *paper towels will absorb the last bits of moisture.*

—Judy McCarthy, Galveston, TX

Drying and storing lettuce

Frustrated with drying each and every lettuce leaf with a paper towel, I came up with a method for drying lettuce that turned out to be a great way to store fresh salad greens and have them ready to serve on a moment's notice. Spread

Storing Greens

Preserving the quality of lettuce and other leafy greens depends on striking a balance between too little and too much moisture. For short-term storage, the more pressing concern is too little moisture, which quickly causes leaves to dehydrate and wilt. A moist environment can be created inside a sealed plastic bag; that, coupled with cold storage (40°F), slows dehydration so that plant tissue remains juicy and crisp. Adding a slightly damp paper towel to the bag is helpful because the towel adds extra humidity, but don't make the towel too damp. Too much moisture in the bag can promote decay, especially if the lettuce is stored for more than a few days.

—Linda J. Harris, Ph.D., *Fine Cooking*

the wet greens out on a clean terry towel. Roll up the towel with the wet leaves tucked inside, as you would a jelly roll. Put the roll in the refrigerator on the lowest shelf. *The towel acts as a wick, first absorbing the water* clinging to freshly washed leaves, and then gradually feeding it back as the leaves need it. Later, when you unroll the towel, you'll have crisp, unblemished, bone-dry lettuce. Just take as much as you require, roll the towel up again, and put it back in the fridge. The greens will stay fresh, crisp, and dry for up to 5 days.

—Lillian Kayte, Gainesville, FL

MUSHROOMS

Keeping mushrooms fresh

Whether your mushrooms are wild or cultivated, choose those that are firm and slightly moist with no signs of decay. They should have a woodsy scent and look fresh and alive. The best ones will feel heavy for their size. Warm air and water will cause mushrooms to decay, so keep them cool and dry. *Store your mushrooms in a basket or an open paper bag* in the refrigerator and don't clean them until you're ready to use them. They should last 4 to 5 days.

—Jack Czarnecki, *Fine Cooking*

Store mushrooms in a paper bag

Mushrooms get slimy if you leave them in a plastic produce container or bag for more than a day or two. So when I bring mushrooms home from the market, the first thing I do is *remove them from the plastic container.* I line the bottom of paper bag with a folded paper towel, arrange a single layer of mushrooms on the towel, and cover them with another folded paper towel, continuing until the bag is almost full. Before stashing the bag in the refrigerator, I fold down the top and secure it with a binder clip. Stored this way, really fresh mushrooms last for up to two weeks.

—Ruth Fairall, Eldorado, TX

Washing lots of mushrooms

To wash volumes of mushrooms quickly, *plunge them into a bath* of 2 quarts water, ½ cup vinegar, and ¼ cup salt. Briefly swirl the mushrooms around to dislodge the dirt, then lift them out of the bath. The slightly acidic saline solution forces the dirt off quickly and the vinegar also helps keep the mushrooms from darkening.

—Arthur Gordon, chef/owner, Irregardless Café, Raleigh, NC

Use a baby brush to clean mushrooms

The special brushes for mushrooms that you see in cookware stores and catalogs are rather expensive for single-use tools. I found a viable substitute in a department store for less than $2—a baby's hair brush. It has *very soft bristles* that won't abrade the mushrooms, and it works great. Mine says "It's a boy!" on it, but the mushrooms don't seem to notice.

—Russ Shumaker, Richmond, VA

Scrape portobello mushrooms clean with a grapefruit spoon

Before cooking or grilling portobello mushroom caps, I remove the unsightly dark gills from under the cap by using a grapefruit spoon. The *serrated edge on the spoon removes the gills easily*, with little or no damage to the cap. I toss the gills into my garden as compost.

—Peter Hyzak, Annandale, NJ

Keeping white mushrooms white

A *touch of lemon juice or vinegar* sprinkled on white mushrooms while rinsing will keep them bright white even when cooked. Just be sure to dry them thoroughly after rinsing.

—Molly Stevens, *Fine Cooking*

Drying mushrooms

Instead of buying expensive wild mushrooms in the winter, try drying your own while they're in season. With a needle and thread, *string the mushrooms through their stems* and hang them upside down in a warm and dry room. They'll dry out in 3 to 7 days. It's a good idea to stick the dried mushrooms in the freezer for a day or so to kill any insects that may still be on them.

—Douglas Kreidler, Olympic Valley, CA

Break up dried mushrooms for easier handling

When recipes call for dried mushrooms like shiitakes to be soaked, drained, and then chopped, I break the dried mushrooms into bite-size pieces first. The *mushroom pieces hydrate faster because they're smaller*, and I avoid the hassle of trying to slice wet, slippery mushrooms. This method won't yield a pretty julienne of mushrooms, but for many dishes it's fine and quick.

—Ana Weerts, Brookfield, WI

Stack shiitakes before cutting

When you have to slice a lot of shiitake mushrooms, the task will go a lot faster if you stack a few of them (after removing their stems) and then start the cutting.

—Kerry Burns, Van Nuys, CA

Soak dried mushrooms overnight

If you soak dried mushrooms overnight in cold water—as opposed to a quick soak in hot water—the *depth of flavor* achieved by both mushroom and soaking liquid is extraordinary.

—Barbara Tropp, *Fine Cooking*

ONIONS

Sweet onions stay fresh in refrigerator crisper

To keep sweet onions (like Vidalia, Texas, Walla Walla, or Maui) in good condition, put them in *a brown paper bag* and store them in the crisper drawer of the refrigerator. They'll stay firm much longer.

—Margaret Blakely, New Philadelphia, OH

Peeling onions easily

I hate peeling onions even more than I hate chopping them. I've added one quick-and-easy step to the standard onion dicing procedure to make peeling easier. After cutting of the stem end and the "beard" (leaving the root end intact, of course) and cutting the onion in two (vertically, through the stem and roots ends), I make a shallow cut through the peel and into the top layer or two of onion. The cut bisects each half of the onion. It's much *easier to remove the onion skin in quarters* than trying to tear it off a whole half onion.

—Jonathan Burkinshaw, Toronto, Ontario, Canada

Avoid bruising an onion when cutting

A food processor or dull knife used to slice or chop through an onion will rupture more of the onion's delicate cell structure, causing the release of more of its sulfur-containing amino acids. These come in contact with other enzymes in the onion, *creating the sulfuric acid that makes you cry* and makes the onion taste strong.

—Robert Danhi, *Fine Cooking*

A candle burns off onion fumes

A strange-but-true method for fighting off onion tears: light a candle and set it right next to the onions on the cutting board before you start chopping. The *sulfur in the flame burns off the onion's sulfuric compounds* before they have a chance to reach your eyes.

—Julie Kohl, Folsom, CA

No-tears peeling

I've found that if I hold an onion under *cold running water* while peeling off the skin, my eyes don't burn and tear up.

—Natalie Sztern, Quebec, Canada

Halt the tears

After crying my way through all the tricks in the book for cutting onions, my husband suggested I try *goggles*. I know I look silly in the kitchen with swim goggles on, but I wear them from the first slice of onion to the last and never shed a tear.

—Gretchen Allison, chef, Duck Soup Inn, Friday Harbor, WA

Another method for cutting onions without tears

If you have a stove with *a downdraft vent* and a reasonably portable cutting board, simply move your cutting board as close to the vent as possible, turn it on, and then chop, dice, or mince as you please with nary a tear. Of course, such a procedure with an overhead vent will produce disastrous results.

—Randolph Siverson, El Macero, CA

A small fan dispels onion fumes

I love to use caramelized onions in the winter to flavor my roasts and stews, and I've found the best way to peel and chop large quantities of onions without tears is to set a tiny (3- to 4-inch) electric fan (I found mine in a one-dollar store) so it blows right across the cutting board while I'm handling onions. *The blowing air dispels the onions' sulfuric compounds* before they can waft upward to irritate my eyes and nose.

—Paul Perotti, Reno, NV

Keep chopped onion in check

When raw chopped onions are added to a salad, they can turn strong and bitter if the salad sits for an hour or more, even in the refrigerator. To prevent this, *add about ¼ cup white vinegar* to a bowl of cold water. Put the onions in a strainer and quickly slosh them in the vinegar and water. Don't rinse the onions: just add them to your salad. They'll stay mild and sweet for quite a while.

—Russ Shumaker, Richmond, VA

Taming raw onions

To take the sting out of sliced or chopped raw onions, *I soak them in cool water* for an hour before adding them to my salads. The onions become very sweet.

—Eleanor Genuardi, Corona Del Mar, CA

Get rid of onion hands

If you have just finished chopping an onion and can't seem to wash the smell off, try rubbing your hands on the neck of a *stainless steel faucet*. The smell disappears!

— Michelle Kuhr, New Milford, CT

Longer-lasting scallions

To prevent scallions from quickly withering in your refrigerator, *store them in a glass of water*. Simply remove any discolored outer layers and trim the green tops, but don't cut the roots. Stand the scallions in a glass of water, cover the tops with a plastic bag, and secure the bag with a rubber band. If you change the water occasionally, the scallions will stay garden-fresh for several days. Another benefit of this storage system is that the scallions won't be buried in a produce drawer—out of sight, out of mind.

—Russ Shumaker, Richmond, VA

Keep scallions from scattering

I used to love finely chopped scallions, but I don't like chasing scallion wheels that careen off the cutting board. To make the scallions stay put, *I cut a slit down the length* of the scallion white before I start chopping.

—Diana Tarasiewicz, Grand Junction, CO

Shallot substitute

When a recipe calls for shallots but I have none, I substitute an equivalent amount of *onion plus a little garlic*. For example, if I need 2 tablespoons of minced shallot, I use 2 tablespoons of minced onion and about 1 teaspoon of minced garlic.

—Annabelle Wharton, Eugene, OR

Bigger is better

Look for medium-size parsnips. Avoid any very slender, small ones, because *they make for a lot of peeling and not a lot of parsnip.* Cut very large parsnips in half lengthwise and look at the core. If it looks dramatically distinct from the rest of the carrot, pry it out with the tip of a sturdy paring knife. A woody core is fibrous and unpleasant.

—Molly Stevens, *Fine Cooking*

Cooking easy

To cook peas or corn kernels, put them in a strainer and dip the *strainer into boiling water* so that the vegetables are easy to fish out when they're done.

—Peter Berley, *Fine Cooking*

Seeding bell peppers

To quickly remove the stem and meaty bulb of seeds from a bell pepper, *slice the pepper from the tip toward the stem*, stopping just short of the stem. Pull the two pieces of pepper apart. They'll break off from the stem, leaving most of the seeds and the stem behind.

—Ray Fairbanks, Houston, TX

Roast peppers on a chimney starter

Roasting bell peppers on the grill always seemed like a good idea but I never found a way to fit it into the flow of things. Finally I realized that I could use the heat coming out of the top of my chimney starter to roast the peppers before I started grilling anything else. When the coals in the chimney starter have burned for 10 minutes and flames are appearing on the top. I put a small grate on top of the starter and roast a pepper on it. You could also hold the pepper over the flames with tongs as you would on a gas burner. It's so easy that I almost always plan to roast a pepper or two when I'm starting up the grill.

—Carol Hiebert, Downs, IL

Torch the skin off peppers without cooking them

I love the taste of bell peppers, cooked or raw. What I don't like, though, is the texture of their skin. Many recipes call for roasting peppers before removing their skin, but this isn't very helpful if you want to use the pepper raw. I've found an easy technique for removing the skin without cooking the pepper. I set my peppers on an unlit barbecue grill and *burn the skin with my kitchen propane torch*. It takes only about 20 seconds to completely blacken the skin. Then I pop the torched peppers into a plastic bag to sweat for a few minutes before scrubbing off the skin under cold running water.

—Jim Gerber, Koloa, HI

Sweating peppers

To easily peel bell peppers, char the skins, then, instead of putting them in a plastic bag to sweat, put them in a bowl and cover immediately with plastic wrap. Let the peppers steam for 10 to 15 minutes. Take them out—*the skins should slide right off*. Pour the pepper juices that remain in the bowl into whatever you're cooking.

—Betsy P. Race, Euclid, OH

Clean roasted peppers without the mess

After roasting red peppers, I put them in a plastic bag to steam. About half an hour later, I massage the peppers through the bag to remove the blackened skin, seeds, and cores. This keeps the mess to a minimum, and, best of all, the peppers emerge clean as a whistle.

Massage the peppers through the bag to remove the blackened skin, seeds, and cores.

—Paula Wolfert, *Fine Cooking*

Ready-roasted peppers

After roasting and peeling red peppers, I lay the pieces flat in a single layer in a heavy-duty zip-top freezer bag and freeze them. Whenever I need a small amount of pepper, I simply *slide the entire frozen slab out of the bag and slice off a few slivers* with a sharp knife. They're great in scrambled eggs! I return the unused portion to the freezer. If I need to use the entire package, it's easy to thaw the peppers by submerging the bag in warm water.

—Pamela Staveley, Edgecomb, ME

Where the Heat Is

Seeds don't make chiles hot—the fire comes from the tiny capsaicin glands between the pod wall and the white spongy ribs. When you cut a chile, you rupture these glands and capsaicin spills out onto the seeds, which is why they seem to contain the heat. To minimize the release of capsaicin, make one cut through the chile, rake out the ribs and seeds, and rinse the chile well.

—Shirley O. Corriher, *Fine Cooking*

Cutting a chile without seeds and stems

I find that by *slicing off the ends* of the chile and holding it upright on the cutting board, you can slice downward from stem to tip. This allows you to cut away just the flesh and leave the veins and seeds attached to the central core. This not only saves time, but it also reduces the possibility of the chile's innards finding their way onto your skin or into your dish.

—Clyde Serda, Alameda, CA

Removing seeds from a whole chile

Use a swivel-bladed vegetable peeler to quickly remove the seeds from chiles *without burning your fingers.* Slice off the top of the chile and slide the peeler's blade inside the chile until the tip reaches the bottom. Turn the peeler in a circle to pry the seeds loose. Most of the seeds will come out when you pull out the peeler, and you can tap out any stray seeds. I like this method because it lets me remove the seeds quickly while leaving the chile whole.

—Michael Koutsodontis, Houston, TX

Seed hot chiles with a grapefruit spoon

I got tired of trying to maneuver my paring knife in tight spaces when seeding and cleaning halved serrano and jalapeño chiles, so I started experimenting. I found that *a toothed, narrow grapefruit spoon* does the trick. The grapefruit spoon also works well when cleaning and seeding other foods, including tomatoes and the body cavities of whole fish.

—John Seaquist, Peoria, AZ

Handle hot chiles with plastic bags

While seeding or chopping jalapeños or other hot chile peppers, I've often ended up with stinging eyes or a burning mouth after unwittingly touching my face. I've heard that some people don rubber gloves while working with hot chiles, but I just *cover my hands with plastic bags*.

—Sarah Richardson, Tucson, AZ

Baking soda relieves burns from hot chiles

Many times when I make a quick salsa, salad, or southwestern meal, I chop chiles without rubber gloves. Usually this doesn't irritate my hands, but on occasion they tingle and turn pink. I find that the best remedy is to put a bit of baking soda mixed with a little water in the palm of my hand or on my fingertips, and *rub the paste over my hands*, and then rinse. The irritation goes away.

—Paul-Marcel St. Onge, Chandler, AZ

Getting rid of the burn

When your mouth is on fire from overdosing on chiles, your first instinct may be to reach for water. But resist: Water won't relieve the agony; it will just spread the capsaicin compounds (the chemicals found in chiles responsible for their heat)—and the pain—around in your mouth. In 1989, John Riley, editor of the journal *Solanaceae*, found that milk is more effective at relieving the sting. It appears that *casein, a protein in milk, acts as a detergent and strips capsaicin from the nerves sending those pain messages.* In fact, any product that contains casein can bring relief: sour cream, yogurt, even ice cream. A study done one year later found that room temperature sugar water was as effective as cold milk. This may explain why some cooks say that sugar can reduce the heat in a dish that is excessively hot.

—Shirley O. Corriher, *Fine Cooking*

When chile connoisseurs talk about the heat level of chiles, they toss around really big numbers. These are Scoville heat units (SHU) and they describe pungency on a scale from 0 to over 500,000 units. The table below, from The Chile Pepper Institute, lists the Scoville levels of a selection of chiles. Keep in mind, though, that many factors, from genetics to growing conditions, will affect the heat of an individual chile. That's why the jalapeño you bought yesterday might be a lot tamer than the one you get today.

CHILE TYPE	HEAT IN SCOVILLE UNITS	CHILE TYPE	HEAT IN SCOVILLE UNITS
HABANERO	350,000	JALAPEÑO	25,000
SCOTCH BONNET	250,000	POBLANO	15,000
CAYENNE	70,000	CUBANELLE	800
SERRANO	50,000		

—Shirley O. Corriher, *Fine Cooking*

Putting the fire out

If you need to douse the burning heat of chiles in your mouth, drink milk or eat a milk-based food like cheese or ice cream, because the casein in dairy unbinds the capsaicin from nerve receptors in the mouth. Other foods that contain casein include *beans, nuts, and milk chocolate.* (Chocolate lovers, take note of this new reason to indulge.)

—Renee Shepherd, *Fine Cooking*

An olive oil bath washes away chile burn

I came up with this very effective method in a moment of desperation, based on the knowledge that capsaicin is more soluble in oil than in water: I washed a chile burn with cooking oil (I used low-grade olive oil, *the cheapest oil I had on hand)* and dish detergent. To follow my method, pour a cup or so of oil into a bowl in or near the sink. Wet your hands with the oil, squirt some detergent onto your hands, suds up (the detergent will mix with oil as well as it does with water), and rinse off with more oil. Then wash with detergent again to rinse off the oil.

—Rebecca Barr, via email

Preserving chiles easily

To keep the chiles from your garden all winter, just wash them, drop them in a glass canning jar, and *cover them with distilled vinegar*. Refrigerated, the chiles will keep indefinitely.

—Susan Asanovic, Wilton, CT

Make roasted chiles for delicious Mexican fare

In summer, I pick a variety of colorful fresh chiles at a nearby farm to roast and preserve. I use a charcoal grill to try to approximate the mouthwatering flavor of fire-roasted chiles from the Southwest. Once my roasted chiles are peeled and seeded, I keep some to use and *freeze the rest flat in freezer bags*. I use them in quesadillas, on grilled pizzas, in huevos rancheros, in salsas, and in soft tacos.

—Joe Sylvester, Papillion, NE

POTATOES

New potato or not?

Red potatoes, especially small ones, are often labeled in supermarkets as "new potatoes" but chances are they aren't new potatoes at all. Technically, a new potato is harvested from the potato vines while the leaves are still green. At this stage, the immature potatoes are thin skinned and haven't developed their full complement of starch. So regardless of their variety, new potatoes are *low in starch and high in moisture*, even if they're actually a high-starch cultivar. Since mature red potatoes and new potatoes are both low starch, they can be used interchangeably and, subsequently, the term *new potato* is used quite loosely.

—Eva Katz, *Fine Cooking*

Storing potatoes properly

The ideal storage temperature for potatoes is 45° to 50°F, but anything colder causes problems, so *don't refrigerate them*. When chilled, the starches start to convert to sugar and the potatoes will taste odd and cook differently, as the sugars will also make the potatoes brown too quickly. Even in the best of conditions, don't plan to store potatoes more than 2 to 3 weeks unless you have a proper root cellar.

—Molly Stevens, *Fine Cooking*

Can't we all just get along?

Is there any truth to the old wives' tale that potatoes and onions spoil more quickly when stored together?

—Annie Pease, Littleton, CO

Nora Olsen, a potato extension specialist at the University of Idaho, replies: Storing them together in the same place may indeed lead to premature spoilage. The main reason for this is that the two root vegetables demand different storage environments, so if they're kept together, one will suffer. Fresh potatoes should be stored in a place with cool temperatures (40° to 45°F) and high humidity (90% or higher) to keep them firm and to prevent moisture loss (which causes shrinkage). Onions, on the other hand, are best stored at even cooler temperatures (32° to 45°F) but at a lower humidity (50% to 70%). This low level prevents breakdown and rot.

Another problem with storing the two together is that potatoes contain about 80% water and some of this water is released during storage. This released moisture increases the humidity around the onions and can cause rot and decay.

Both potatoes and onions need air, so don't store either in plastic bags.

Shake potatoes clean

Scrubbing new potatoes is really tedious, but I've found that I can shake them clean using a container with a tight-fitting lid, like a large Tupperware® box or bin. Fill the container with small potatoes, *add water one-third of the way up*, seal the container, and shake vigorously. Then change the water and repeat the process until the water is clear.

—Diane Flanders, Ashland, WI

Clean potatoes without peeling

When a recipe involves unpeeled potatoes, I use a *grapefruit spoon* to clean them. The spoon's point removes eyes, and the serrated edge rubs away dirt without scraping off the peel.

—Bill Moran, San Diego, TX

A better way to peel a potato

Sometimes peeling potatoes drives me nuts: The peeled part gets really slippery. To make the job easier, I peel one end of the potato and *sink a fork firmly* into that area. I then hold the fork in one hand while a run a peeler down the length of the potato, quickly removing long strips of peel. It's so much easier than fumbling with a slippery potato.

—Willie Zee, Lincolnwood, IL

Get rid of the green

If any green appears under a potato's skin, it should be peeled off or cut away. The greenish tinge contains a mildly toxic alkaloid, known as solanine. Although you'd have to consume a lot of solanine to become sick, *it does taste bitter* and is best avoided.

—Molly Stevens, *Fine Cooking*

Vitamin C keeps raw potatoes white

Every cook knows how fast shredded potatoes can turn brown. A tablet of vitamin C (ascorbic acid) cures this problem nicely. Put a vitamin C tablet in a bowl with 2 tablespoons water; let it soften and dissolve. Shred 4 large potatoes and add them to the dissolved vitamin C, tossing to coat the potatoes, then add the other ingredients. The last potato pancake that you fry will be as white as the first one was.

Put a vitamin C tablet in a bowl with 2 tablespoons water.

—Lilia Dvarionas, Kanata, Ontario, Canada

RUTABAGAS

Don't worry about the wax

These bulbous beauties that look and taste like giant turnips are typically coated with a thick layer of wax, which extends the shelf life. Stored loosely in a bag in your refrigerator produce drawer, they will last close to 2 weeks. Look for *rutabagas that are firm and heavy with no signs of shriveling.* If they're light for their size, they may be spongy or dried out. Peel the skin (and the wax) off before cooking.

—Molly Stevens, *Fine Cooking*

"Triple-washed" doesn't always mean clean

Triple-washed produce isn't guaranteed to be free of dirt. I've washed grit out of many a bag of triple-washed spinach. Produce surfaces can carry bacteria that could make you ill, and the extra handling received by prepared produce increases the chances of contamination slipping in. So, whether it comes in a bag or not, and no matter how much of a hurry you're in, make the time to *rinse all fresh produce* well in water. And don't forget to wash items like melons and avocados that have inedible skins. Even though you don't eat the skin, you do cut through it and the knife blade can drag bacteria into the edible part.

—Jennifer Armentrout, *Fine Cooking*

Check spinach stems to gauge tenderness and age

A thin, flexibly stem indicates a tender, young plant. Choose these for salads or recipes where the spinach is served raw. Thick, fibrous stems mean more mature, tougher plants, which are best for cooking. Shop for crisp, bright green leaves with no dark, bruised patches or yellowing. I like to *buy loose leaves or bunches so I can judge their quality*. Store fresh spinach in a dry plastic bag in the refrigerator crisper, where it will keep for 2 to 3 days. Spinach stems, even of some young leaves, are fibrous, stringy, and hard to eat, especially after cooking. Remove the stems before washing. I don't bother removing the stems from truly tender, small leaves with equally tender, thin stems. Notoriously sandy, spinach must be washed carefully. Swish it in a basin of cold water, let it sit for minute, then lift it into a colander to drain. Dump the water and repeat.

—Molly Stevens, *Fine Cooking*

Stemming spinach

To quickly and cleanly stem a spinach leaf, *fold the leaf in half* and pull off the stem.

—Jennifer Armentrout, *Fine Cooking*

Squeeze spinach between plates

To squeeze excess moisture from cooked spinach, set the cooked spinach on a plate in a fairly even layer, and set an identical plate on top (bottom side down, as you would stack them in the cupboard). Press the two plates together while holding them vertically over the sink. This method is *more efficient* than squeezing the spinach handful by handful and, for those with severe arthritis, it's also less painful.

—Pamela A. Kuniecki, Park Hall, MD

How much do I need?

A pound of fresh spinach leaves *will cook down to about 1 cup.* For a side dish of cooked spinach, figure 8 ounces of raw spinach per serving.

—Ruth Lively, *Fine Cooking*

S Q U A S H

Good zucchini comes in small packages

Young zucchini is zucchini at its best. For most recipes the ideal squash is one that's still *slender and measures 4 to 6 inches long.* These zucchini have thin skin, tiny undeveloped seeds, and sweet flesh that's tender but firm. Look for firm, medium-green zucchini that are just slightly pliable. Gently scrape the skin with a fingernail; it should wrinkle easily. Refrigerated in a loose plastic bag, zucchini will last about 3 to 4 days. If a zucchini is between 7 and 10 inches long, it usually has darker, tougher skin and larger sees. I recommend that you cut these older zucchini in half and scrape out the seeds with a spoon before you cook them.

—Loretta Keller, *Fine Cooking*

Using overgrown zucchini

When I'm faced with zucchini the size of baseball bats, *I juice them.* Zucchini is mostly water, so I run the overgrown zucchini through a juice extractor. You can also shred them in the food processor with a shredding disk, then squeeze the shredded vegetables in cheesecloth to extract as much juice as possible. I use this flavorful, healthy zucchini water as a vegetable stock, as a base for a more complex stock or sauce, or as a part of the liquid in bread recipes. Sometimes I combine it with carrot juice, salt it lightly, and drink it icy cold.

—Susan Asanovic, Wilton, CT

Choose heavy acorn squash

At the market, choose a squash that feels heavy for its size. Like other winter squash, acorn squash is quite *high in water content,* so those that don't feel heavy probably have been sitting around for a while and are drying up. Although acorn squash is grown year round, the peak is October through March, when it has been cold-weather harvested and stored in the cold to develop its sugars.

—Amy Albert, *Fine Cooking*

Cool but not chilly

Store winter squash in a cool place—a dry basement is ideal. *Don't refrigerate* them, though, because they rapidly deteriorate at temperatures below 50°F.

—Odessa Piper, *Fine Cooking*

Handle squash safely

Squash skin is very tough and it can be a struggle to cut. To keep things safe, *work on a flat surface* and, to secure a solid base, trim a sliver from the bottom or one side of the squash and let it sit flat. Use a large sharp knife and keep your fingers out of the way. Insert the tip of the knife into the side of the squash and cut down, rather than attacking the squash with the full breadth of the blade. I usually don't peel any squash other than butternut because the contours are so unruly. When peeling butternut, you can use a vegetable peeler, but you might want to wear gloves, as there's a green, gluey substance under the skin that gets on your hands and seems to stay there forever.

—Ris Lacoste, *Fine Cooking*

Cleave winter squash without fear

Chopping uncooked winter squash can be difficult. A cleaver is a good tool for the job, but using one adds an unwelcome element of danger. To make this task safer and easier, *I set the cleaver blade into the skin* of the squash, then lightly tap the cleaver with a medium-size rubber mallet. This technique lets me control how quickly the blade enters the squash and saves my hands a lot of hard work, too.

—Sue Greishaber, St. Louis, MO

Another, more low-tech method

I've had some close calls—nearly slashing myself more than once white trying to stab through an obstinate acorn squash or a stubborn kabocha. Finally, following a friend's sworn method, *I dropped a big 12-pound hubbard on a concrete patio.* It broke nicely into three pieces, making it easy to scoop out the seeds. I've since used this method for any especially hard-skinned squash. Once a winter squash is cracked or cut open, remove the seeds and any particularly fibrous strings surrounding the seed cavity. I usually leave the skin on if I'm baking or steaming the squash, but otherwise I peel it before cooking.

—Georgeanne Brennan, *Fine Cooking*

Winter Squash from Sweet to Nutty

When stacks of hard-skinned winter squash start appearing at farmers' markets and roadside stands, I know that autumn is truly here. Here's an A to Z primer of the varieties you're likely to find.

- *Acorn squash* can be white, gold, or green. The white and gold have pale flesh, a grainy texture, and a bland, faintly nutty, sometimes acrid flavor. The green is my favorite: its orange-yellow flesh has a sweet, nutty flavor and smooth texture that purées beautifully and needs little seasoning beyond salt and pepper.

- *Butternut squash* has a finely grained, bright orange flesh with a rich, full, sweet flavor. Butternut, which weighs 1 to 2 pounds, is ideal for mashing, puréeing, and baking in gratins.

- *Delicata* is at its peak of flavor when the skin turns from green and white to creamy yellow streaked with orange. The slightly orange, smooth, dense flesh and nutty, nearly caramel flavor are best appreciated when the squash is simply baked. Perfect for serving two people, delicata often weighs less than a pound.

- *Hubbard squash* has dense, smooth, bright gold flesh with an intense vegetable flavor that isn't as sweet as other squashes. Excellent simply mashed or as a pie squash, hubbard is among the largest of the winter squash, weighing 12 pounds or more.

- *Kabocha* has a mild flavor and somewhat grainy texture that takes well to seasoning and is especially good in soups. Difficult to cut open, the gray or gray-green skin gives way to dry orange or yellow flesh. Each weighs 3 to 5 pounds.

- *Rouge vif d'etampes* has dark orange flesh that turns lighter orange around the seed cavity. It's slightly grainy with a fine flavor, making it a favorite for gratins and soups. Also known as French pumpkin, it can weigh from 2 to 20 pounds.

- *Sweet dumpling* is at its peak of flavor when the skin turns creamy yellow streaked with orange. The pale yellow-gold flesh is slightly grainy, with a distinctly nutty flavor. A small squash, often weighing less than a pound, sweet dumpling can be stubborn and difficult to cut through.

—Georgeanne Brennan, *Fine Cooking*

Peeling butternut squash

To peel the reluctant butternut squash before cutting it up for cooking, *microwave it for a few minutes.* The peel will be much easier to separate from the flesh.

—Betsy Schwartz, Glenville, CT

Reach for your boning knife to pare off tough skin

The boning knife's *flexible blade hugs the curves* of hard butternut squash, quickly taking off the peel but leaving the flavorful flesh behind.

—Odessa Piper, *Fine Cooking*

Serrated spoon scrapes out squash seeds

Getting the seeds and stringy fibers out of a butternut squash *goes a lot faster* if you use a grapefruit spoon with the serrated tip.

—Kim Cronin, Eugene, OR

Remove squash seeds quickly and cleanly

I scrape out the seeds and stringy ribs from halved butternut squash and other winter squash with my *ice-cream scoop.* I just sweep the scoop two or three times through the squash and press on the trigger to dump the seeds out of the scoop and into the trash. A quick rinse is all it takes to clean the scoop.

—Susan Wilson, Hanson, MA

SWEET POTATOES

Use them soon

Sweet potatoes don't keep as well as white potatoes, so use them *within a week or two after buying* them. Never refrigerate them raw, as they'll spoil even more quickly. At the market, look for firm, unblemished sweet potatoes with no soft spots or bruises.

—Karen and Ben Barker, *Fine Cooking*

TOMATILLOS

Water washes away tomatillo peels

Here's an easy way to deal with the sticky, papery husks of tomatillos. I peel tomatillos *under warm water,* and the husks come right off.

—Diana Tarasiewicz, Grand Junction, CO

Choose glossy, heavy fruit

Look for plump, glossy fruit that feel heavy for their size. A ripe tomato should *feel pliant but not mushy*, with no soft spots or cracks. Stem calyxes, if they're still attached, should be fresh and green, never shriveled or tired looking. Older and heirloom varieties often ripen from the bottom (the blossom end) to the top (the shoulders), so don't be put off if the shoulders still show a little green. If the body feels heavy, is fully colored and smooth with just a little give to it, the tomato is ripe. Don't shy away from pleated or multishouldered tomatoes either—these irregular shapes are what make many old-fashioned varieties distinctive.

—Renee Shepherd, *Fine Cooking*

Don't refrigerate tomatoes

No matter what kind of tomato, keep it out of the refrigerator. *Chilling destroys* one of the tomato's key flavor components—(Z)-3-hexanal—and it also makes the texture mealy. Ideally, tomatoes should be stored away from light at about 50°F.

—Joanne Weir, *Fine Cooking*

Useful tomato tricks

I usually don't bother to peel tomatoes, but if I must, this is the method I prefer: Stick a fork into the stem end and *rotate the tomato over the flame* on a gas stove briefly, until the skin begins to split. When it's cool enough to handle you can peel the skin off easily.

If you need tomato pulp without the skin, try this: Cut the fruit in half horizontally and grate its flesh on the large holes of a grater. The tomato is quickly reduced to a thick purée and the skin in left behind.

When slicing tomatoes, a serrated knife works best.

—Ruth Lively, *Fine Cooking*

Squeeze the seeds out of a tomato

When a recipe calls for seeding a tomato, I simply cut off ½ inch from the bottom and squeeze the tomato to release the seeds and pulp. It's *much faster than halving* each tomato and scooping out the seeds.

—Penny Cohen, Rancho Mirage, CA

Fresh and Canned Tomato Equivalents

One 28-ounce can peeled whole tomatoes equals 10 to 12 whole tomatoes, peeled (or about 2 pounds).

One 14.5-ounce can peeled whole tomatoes equals 5 to 6 whole tomatoes, peeled (or about 1 pound).

—Molly Stevens, *Fine Cooking*

Muffin tins for stuffed tomatoes

An easy way to bake stuffed tomatoes is to set them in a muffin tin. The *tin holds them upright* while they bake.

—Joyce Evelyn Yates, Moss Point, MS

Substituting canned tomatoes for fresh

When you substitute canned for fresh, *choose peeled whole tomatoes.* Stay away from crushed, diced, stewed, or any other more processed forms (unless specifically called for in the recipe) as these are typically made from lesser quality tomatoes and have a more cooked, tomato paste-like flavor.

—Molly Stevens, *Fine Cooking*

A new use for an old-fashioned potato masher

My quick way *to drain a can of whole tomatoes* is to insert a hand-held potato masher into the opened can to hold the tomatoes in place while I pour out the juice. The potato masher can then be rinsed and put away. No need to dirty a strainer or additional dishes.

—Zoe Toner, Weston, CT

Scissors chop canned tomatoes

I have found that you can do a fairly speedy and tidy job of chopping whole canned tomatoes by using kitchen shears. Rather than chop the tomatoes on a board, I keep them in the can. First, pour off the juices, then *insert the shears into the can* and start cutting up the tomatoes. For large cans, you have to chop the tomatoes in the top half of the can, remove them, and then chop those in the bottom.

—Jeannie McDermott, Roeland Park, KS

Orange juice refreshes canned tomatoes

A local restaurant chef taught me how to use canned plum tomatoes to make the best "fresh" plum tomatoes for pizza. Doctor the
canned tomatoes by slicing them once or twice and soaking them
overnight in orange juice. When I'm ready to bake the pizza, I
drain and chop the soaked tomatoes, put them on the dough, and
sprinkle on cheeses and spices. I've used plum tomatoes from my
garden, but they just don't taste as good as these.

Slice them once or twice and soak them overnight in orange juice.

—Phillip Zook, Carrboro, NC

Freezing tomato paste

In order not to waste leftover canned tomato paste, open the other end of the
can and use the lid to push the contents into a zippered plastic bag. Store the
bag in the freezer and simply *break off a chunk* of tomato paste whenever
you need it.

—Esther Whitby, Bloomington, IN

TURNIPS

What a difference a season makes

Winter turnips will be larger than their spring and summer counter-
parts. Be sure the skin is taut and the vegetable feels plump. Store them loosely
in a bag in your refrigerator produce drawer. If there are any greens attached,
trim them before storing. Don't wash them before storing, as any moisture can
promote spoilage. Expect them to last 8 to 12 days.

—Molly Stevens, *Fine Cooking*

Potatoes temper turnips

To temper the taste of mashed turnips, include *one potato for every
three turnips.*

—Tammy Hines-Dumitru, Norwalk, CT

BREAD, BREAD CRUMBS, AND CROUTONS

The best way to store bread

Crusty hearth breads are best stored in paper because this lets the bread breathe and keeps it crusty. Soft, enriched bread and rolls should be stored in plastic. *(Never refrigerate bread,* because that actually dries it out faster.) The best way to freeze a loaf is to "cater wrap" it in plastic wrap. Use two sheets of plastic wrap, one enveloping the loaf end to end, the other side to side. This is superior to plastic bags, since air can become trapped in bags, leading to moisture crystals and freezer burn.

—Peter Reinhart, *Fine Cooking*

Frozen bread revived

To make a loaf of frozen unsliced bread seem almost fresh baked, *I dip the frozen loaf quickly in water* and put it in a 350°F oven directly on the oven rack. In 15 or 20 minutes, the bread will be barely heated through and will taste fresh and chewy. I stick a wooden cake tester into the loaf to make sure the bread isn't still frozen. The reborn loaf should be eaten in a day or so, but another dunking and heating will help salvage the remainder of the loaf. I even dip and bake loaves that have never seen the freezer if they don't seem quite fresh or if their crusts need a little extra crunch.

—Joanne Richards, Portland, OR

Make bread crumbs from croissants

When I have a stale croissant or two, I freeze them in a plastic bag. Once frozen, they're easily made into crumbs by hitting the bag with a rolling pin or some other heavy object. I use the croissant crumbs to top gratins and baked pasta dishes or in a dish like meatloaf. The butter in the croissants *makes for a crisp topping* and for nice texture in the meatloaf.

—Darlene P. Sugiyama, Nanaimo, British Columbia, Canada

Grate and season bread crumbs in one step

When making bread crumbs in my food processor, *I add some freshly washed herbs and seasonings* to the stale bread before turning on the machine. This eliminates the second step of adding seasonings, and the bread crumbs absorb any moisture left on the herbs.

—Nancy J. Cruz, East Providence, RI

Make fresh bread crumbs without a food processor

A recipe called for fresh bread crumbs made by pulsing caraway rye bread in a food processor. Since I don't own a food processor, I tore each bread slice into 4 or 5 large pieces and made perfect crumbs from them by *rubbing the pieces between my palms*. Be sure to use deli-style rye bread, not the soft, fluffy type or you'll end up with bread "ropes" instead of crumbs.

—Patricia Yates, Manhattan Beach, CA

Clean the bowl—and make flavorful bread crumbs, too

After I make pesto in my food processor, I toss a few hunks of bread into the empty bowl and pulse. The *bread absorbs the oil* and basil residue from the bowl, which makes cleanup much easier. And the oil gives a wonderful flavor to the crumbs, which you can use as a savory crumb topping or breading.

—Dawn Fanucchi, Foster City, CA

Freeze homemade bread crumbs

I always have homemade bread crumbs ready whenever I need them. When I make or buy good bread and don't use it all, I get out *my food processor* and chop away. I store the bread crumbs in a heavy-duty zip-top bag in my freezer. When I need some crumbs for a topping or a breading, I just grab them from the bag.

—Mary Napoleone, Pensacola, FL

Hearty croutons from hearth breads

If you like croutons made from dense-crumbed hearth breads but don't like the hassle of trying to cut a loaf into relatively uniform cubes, *ask the baker* to slice the loaf once, rotate it a quarter turn, and slice it again. You'll get a big bag of "batons" that can easily be broken into halves or thirds in just a few minutes. Then use the bread cubes in your favorite crouton recipe.

—Lena Sims, San Diego, CA

For lighter croutons, use egg whites

I use fluffy whipped egg whites *instead of oil* as a fat-free way to get seasonings to adhere to homemade croutons. These are just as good as the ones I used to make with olive oil, but a lot lighter. After drying the bread cubes in the oven, I mix them with the whipped egg whites, toss with the seasonings, and bake the croutons until dry. Three egg whites will coat croutons from about two large loaves of Italian bread.

—Shannon R. Williams, Seattle, WA

Homemade croutons in a wok

I make croutons in a wok on my stovetop. It beats a skillet or baking sheet for three reasons: I can *toss the croutons and oil together* right in the wok, instead of tossing the bread and oil in a separate bowl. The wok holds more cubes of bread than a skillet or baking sheet. And the wok's deep bowl gives me plenty of room to stir the croutons as they brown.

—Kara Adanalian, Fairfax, CA

COCONUT MILK

Freeze that leftover coconut milk

Canned coconut milk will last indefinitely unopened, but once opened, is highly susceptible to spoilage. Refrigerate opened coconut milk and freeze what you don't use in a day or two; it will *last 2 months in the freezer.* Be aware that coconut milk will turn a very unappealing shade of gray if cooked in a cast-iron pot.

—Kay Cabrera, *Fine Cooking*

Coconut milk without the fat

I keep a bottle of imitation coconut extract in my spice cabinet for recipes that call for coconut milk. Instead of using coconut milk, I add a little of the extract to either whole or skim milk (whisking in some cornstarch or flour to prevent the milk from curdling when heated), and I get a decent imitation of coconut milk. Though it's not the same, my method avoids all the saturated fat in coconut milk.

—Ana Weerts, Brookfield, WI

I keep a bottle of imitation coconut extract in my spice cabinet for recipes that call for coconut milk.

COFFEE AND TEA

Freeze coffee or tea

Freeze leftover coffee or tea in ice-cube trays; *the cubes let you chill* your iced tea or coffee without diluting it.

—Ellen Sandberg, North Vancouver, British Columbia, Canada

The heat is on

Always add *softened gelatin to warm or hot mixtures*; adding it to a cold mixture will make the gelatin firm up immediately, creating an unpleasant stringy or lumpy texture.

—Jennifer Armentrout, *Fine Cooking*

Ingredients that don't like gelatin

Gelatin won't set if it has been combined with an ingredient containing a certain enzyme that destroys protein molecules. Notable *offenders include kiwi, papaya, pineapple, fig, honeydew melon, and fresh ginger.* Highly acidic fruits and liquids also give gelatin trouble. When using acidic juices or purées, an extra packet of gelatin may be needed for the dessert to set.

—Judith Choate, *Fine Cooking*

Cooking with miso

Always add miso toward the end of cooking and never boil it, as *high heat will destroy both its flavor* and its nutrients. For the smoothest sauces and soups, whisk miso into an equal amount of slightly warm broth until smooth, then gradually stir the thinned miso into the pot. Use 1 to 1½ tablespoons of miso for every cup of liquid.

—Thy Tran, *Fine Cooking*

Less expensive extra-virgin olive oil

For everyday cooking, I like to use extra-virgin olive oil from the Middle East and North Africa, which I buy in a Middle Eastern grocery store. The Middle Eastern oil has a fruity, complex flavor and rich green color. I find that, overall, it's comparable to Italian extra-virgin olive oils, but it's considerably cheaper.

Use extra-virgin olive oil from the Middle East and North Africa.

—David Auerbach, Durham, NC

Pouring olive oil smoothly from a metal can

I buy terrific, inexpensive olive oil in 3-liter cans from my neighborhood Italian market, but the cans are too unwieldy to use every day, so I pour some of the oil into an old olive oil bottle. The trick is pouring the oil out of a full can because a vacuum is created since there's only one pouring spout, causing the oil to "glug" out of the spout and splash all over the funnel. Avoid the temptation to punch a hole in the top of the can and use an old painter's trick instead; rotate the can so the spout is at the top, not the bottom, and pour the oil slowly. This leaves room for air to flow back into the can, relieving the vacuum and stopping the "glugging."

Rotate the can so the spout is at the top, not the bottom, and pour the oil slowly.

—Nelson Howe, Marietta, GA

PEANUT BUTTER

Use gravity to remix natural peanut butter

With nothing added to keep it emulsified, the oil in natural peanut butter tends to separate and float to the top of the jar. This is the state in which you usually find natural peanut butter in the market. Stirring the oil back in takes elbow grease, but you can get gravity to do the work for you. When you get the jar home, just *turn it upside down and leave it on the counter overnight*. Once gravity mixes the oil back in, store the peanut butter in the refrigerator, both to keep it fresh and to solidify the oil so it can't separate easily.

—Jennifer Armentrout, *Fine Cooking*

PHYLLO

Spray butter on phyllo

I like to use a spritzer to apply melted butter to phyllo pastry. I find that I use less butter than when I use a pastry brush, and the result is lighter and less greasy. I melt the butter in a pot and let the milk solids settle to the bottom. Then I pour the warm clarified butter into a *food-safe spray bottle*. I give each sheet of phyllo two or three quick sprays for an even coating. I keep the spray bottle parked in a bowl of hot tap water so the butter stays liquid. No more pastry brush with congealed butter buildup.

—Lilia Dvarionas, Kanata, Ontario, Canada

Tips for Working with Phyllo Dough

Tissue-thin sheets of phyllo dough can be frustrating to work with because they can dry out quickly and tear. Here are some tips for making your phyllo experience a happy one.

- Phyllo sheets thaw more evenly and are less likely to stick together if you let the unopened package thaw in the refrigerator overnight. You can keep unopened, thawed phyllo in the fridge for up to a month.

- Don't open the package until you have all the other ingredients prepared and you're ready to work.

- Unroll the phyllo sheets and lay them flat on a dry surface. Immediately cover with plastic wrap and then a damp towel. (Covering with just a damp towel will moisten the sheets and make them stick together.)

- Keep phyllo covered when not working with it and don't leave it uncovered for more than a minute at a time.

- Work as fast as you can.

- Use a soft-bristle pastry brush to lightly coat the sheets with melted butter or oil. Start at the edges (to keep them from cracking) and work in toward the center.

- Roll up any unused sheets, wrap well in plastic, and refrigerate for up to two weeks. Or, wrap in plastic and then foil to freeze for up to 2 months.

—Jennifer Armentrout, *Fine Cooking*

Perfect pastry cups

When making phyllo dough cups to fill with appetizers or desserts, I used to have a hard time keeping the pastry cup-shaped. Now I blind bake the pastry cups with *homemade pastry weights*. Start by cutting 6-inch squares of aluminum foil (or 8-inch, depending on your muffin tin size) and fitting each square into an empty muffin tin cup. Fill each cup two-thirds full with pie weights or dried beans, then twist the corners of the foil closed to create individual packets. Bake your phyllo dough with a foil packet in the center of each muffin cup. After baking, remove the packets with tongs and set aside to cool. You can reuse the packets within a few minutes to line another batch of phyllo cups. Once cooled, the packets can be stored for next time.

—Josephine Borut, Westbury, NY

Souping up canned stocks

For cooks who don't have time to prepare stocks from scratch, yet realize that canned stock or plain bouillon is a poor substitute, there is a simple and flavorful alternative. Begin by preparing the bouillon as directed on the package. Pour this broth (or canned equivalent) into a large pot. Add chopped carrots, celery (including leaves), and onion. For every 8 cups of broth, I use 2 carrots, 2 ribs of celery, and 1 onion. I also like to brown the flat sides of a halved onion in a frying pan and add it to the broth; this gives the stock a rich flavor and deep color. Next add about 6 parsley sprigs, a clove of garlic, and a bay leaf. Bring this mixture to a boil, then reduce the heat. Season the broth and simmer, uncovered, for an hour or so. Strain the stock through a fine sieve and cool. The result is a *much more flavorful stock* than what you started with, and it's very simple to make.

—Jeff Backhaus, West Bend, WI

Defatting canned stock

Canned stock usually comes with a teaspoon or two of fat. Separate the fat from the stock by punching a small hole in the top of the can with a manual can opener. Then punch another slightly bigger hold opposite the first one and pour the stock through the larger opening. The stock pours easily, while *the fat stays in the can*.

—Kenneth Danko, San Francisco, CA

Try a blender

After trying to remix separated tahini with limited success, I poured the entire contents of the can into a blender and blended on low speed. It came together.

—Bert Johnson, Talofofo, Guam

How to warm tortillas so they stay soft and flexible

Wrap a stack of tortillas *in a damp dishtowel*, wrap the whole package in aluminum foil, and heat in a 300°F oven. (If possible, wrap two or three smaller bundles, rather than one large bundle, and heat them all at the same time.)

Although the outside tortillas may get a bit soggy, this method keeps the rest of them from drying out. You can also heat tortillas successfully in the microwave —wrap a stack of them in a damp dishtowel and microwave until warm. Whichever method you use, bring the bundle of tortillas, still wrapped and nestled in a serving container, to the table so they stay warm and flexible.

—Jim Peyton, *Fine Cooking*

VINEGAR

Try chilling vinegar

I keep my vinegars in the refrigerator because I find that they whisk more easily into olive oil that way. It also seems to *keep them fresher longer.*

—Alice Weinstock, via email

Replace vinegar cap with a cork for drizzling

For bottles of vinegar, soy sauce, or other condiments that don't include a fitted plastic drizzle top, I improvise my own *sprinkler system with a wine cork*. Using a sharp paring knife, I carve out two narrow wedges along the length of the cork on opposite sides. Then I push the cork into the bottle. (For narrow bottlenecks, you might need to pare down the diameter of the cork.) With a shake of the bottle, I get a drizzle of vinegar or sauce.

—Isidro Blasco, New York, NY

Balsamic vinegar substitute

I have found that *Chinese black vinegar, also called Chekiang vinegar*, is a good substitute for balsamic vinegar. Made from fermented rice, this vinegar is dark and richly flavored like balsamic, but slightly less sweet. I prefer Narcissus brand made in Yongchun, in the Chekiang province, but it's often difficult to find. I usually buy Gold-Plum® brand black vinegar, which in my area costs only $1.29 for a 21-ounce bottle.

—Bill Moran, San Diego, TX

Cooking Tips

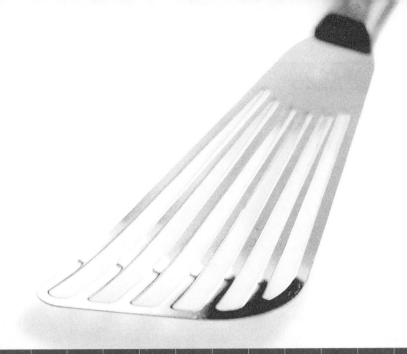

Picking a Recipe and Getting Started

Go ahead—write in your cookbook

As a child I was always taught never to write in books. Finally I learned that it's okay to write in your own personal copies of cookbooks or magazines. I *write all over the recipes*, whether I love or hate them. I note the date I made the recipe, whether it was for a special occasion or just for the family, if I changed any ingredients, if I halved or doubled the recipe, etc. I even mark the recipe with a highlighter both in the index and in the table of contents for easy reference. No longer do I find myself saying, "Now where is that recipe?"

—Ellen Sandberg, North Vancouver, British Columbia, Canada

Sticky notes keep track of favorite recipes

I cut recipes out of my food magazines and recycle the rest of the issues…but not my *Fine Cooking* magazines, which I save whole. To remind me of dishes I absolutely must prepare, or recipes that I've come to love, I *write the name of the recipe on the bottom of a sticky note* and stick the note on the edge of the recipe's page. There the note stays, standing up to remind me of favorite recipes of the past and future recipes to be discovered.

—Helene Stone, Highland Park, IL

Cross-referencing recipes

In my recipe file, I keep cards for many unusual or infrequently used ingredients that might go to waste because I only need a small quantity for a recipe—buttermilk, for example. On that card, I've listed several foods with buttermilk in it, like pancakes, biscuits, Aunt Helen's ranch dressing, etc. The card *reminds me what other recipes I use* that call for that ingredient. This prompts me to make one of those recipes so I can use up the remaining quantity.

—Mary Sullivan, Concord, CA

Read recipes through a zip-top bag

I don't own a cookbook holder, nor do I need one. When I open a cookbook or magazine to the page with the recipe I'm using, I slip it into a large zip-top plastic bag. This keeps the book open to the right page, and *saves it from spatters and spills*.

—Billie L. Porter, Newburyport, MA

Keep favorite recipes at eye level

I tape often-used recipes to the *inside of the cupboard doors* above the kitchen counter. This keeps the recipes at eye level and ready to use.

—Peg Boren, McAllen, TX

Give your oven plenty of time to heat up

Don't rely on your oven's preheat signal; it often goes off prematurely. Instead, let your oven heat for at least 20 minutes before baking or roasting anything.

—*Fine Cooking* editors

 **Baking**

Bottled water for better baking

When I bake, I use bottled spring water (most supermarkets sell it in gallon jugs). Using bottled water *eliminates inconsistencies in mineral content* or off flavors that can affect tap water.

—Margaret Kasten, Boston, MA

Mixing baking ingredients thoroughly

When mixing dry ingredients that include baking powder or baking soda, *add any dark spices to the mix last.* When you see that the spices are thoroughly mixed, you know that your rising agents have been evenly distributed, too.

—Lynn Burgess, Toronto, Ontario, Canada

Sift over a paper plate

When you're sifting flour and other dry ingredients for baking, try doing it over a paper plate. The plate is *sturdy and won't collapse* like waxed paper or plastic wrap, so the ingredients slide off the plate and into your bowl without making a mess.

—Carol M. Kuehler, Florissant, MO

Salvaging burned baked goods

Breads, rolls, and cream puffs that are burned on the bottom can easily be salvaged. Let the burned item cool, then simply *sand its blackened base* lightly with the smallest holes on a box grater until it's just the right shade of brown.

—Kate Cohen, Albany, NY

Proofing yeast in one easy step

I bake bread and pizza quite often, and I recently found a way to save washing an extra dish. When making the dough, I add all the dry ingredients—except the yeast—to the mixing bowl. I make a small well in the top and add the yeast to the well. Then I pour a small amount of measured warm water into the well, wait until the yeast and water mixture turns creamy and slightly foamy, and then continue with the recipe. Even if the recipe doesn't require proofing, I find this technique helpful because it *makes the yeast easier to incorporate.*

—Lori Miller, via email

Flour mix for robust breads

When I make robust, chewy European hearth-style bread, I don't add whole-wheat flour to white flour, as is often recommended. Whole-wheat flour doesn't give quite the right results. Instead, I add *1 part in 10 of untoasted wheat germ* (for instance, 1.6 ounces of germ for each pound of white flour). This more closely approximates the old European milling methods.

—David Auerbach, Durham, NC

Moist and fresh bread

In my work as a professional baker, I've found that *½ cup of instant potato flakes* per six cups of flour will give a loaf of bread more body and keep it moister and fresher longer. Another way I improve a loaf's longevity, as well as its rising capacity, is to add a teaspoon of malt powder (available from baking-supply stores and catalogs) to the dry ingredients.

—Pat Melilli, Wappingers Falls, NY

Nubby cutting board for kneading bread dough

A polyethylene cutting board with a nubby surface makes an excellent surface for working with bread dough or pastry. The lightly *textured surface is almost nonstick*, perfect for kneading most bread doughs. I also find that slack doughs and pastry require less flour for kneading and rolling. I stabilize the board with a damp kitchen towel underneath it.

—Margaret Hirsch, Rancho Palos Verdes, CA

Manage dough with lightly oiled hands

When handling sticky bread dough, or any type of dough for that matter, I spray my hands with a bit of nonstick oil spray. This keeps my hands dough-free, doesn't add any flavor, and ensures, in the case of tender pastry, that *I don't overwork the dough*.

—Katherine R. Perrotti, Amenia, NY

Make a nonstick surface with lecithin capsules

When I'm working with a sticky bread dough or making candy, I use lecithin—available at health-food stores in gelatin capsules—to help keep the dough or candy from sticking to the work surface. (Lecithin is the active ingredient in nonstick food sprays; since those products have oil as carriers, I prefer not to use them.) *I cut the gelatin capsule* with kitchen shears, squeeze out the lecithin, and spread it very thin. I mop up any excess with a towel, leaving a thin film of lecithin on the work surface. When finished, I scrape the surface and clean it with soap and water. Lecithin is very slippery stuff, so remember that a little bit goes a long way.

—Bill Moran, San Diego, TX

Skip the grease

I have found that there's no need to grease the bowl before putting bread dough in to rise. *If the dough is well kneaded*, you can pull it away from the sides of the bowl easily without the messy butter or oil.

—David Auerbach, Durham, NC

Plastic storage box makes an excellent proofing box

Some of the best artisan breads, like ciabatta, are made from light, wet doughs that require a long rising time. Covering the dough with towels can hinder a full rise, but the dough sticks to lighter materials like plastic wrap. To solve the problem and provide an ideal environment, you can buy an acrylic proof cover from specialty suppliers for about $50—or you can buy a clear plastic storage box of the same dimensions at your local variety store for one tenth of the price. Once you try it, you won't want to use any other method.

Buy a clear plastic storage box at your local variety store.

—Jack Sears, Port Orchard, WA

Tips for a Thick, Crispy Crust

- When kneading and shaping the dough, use only enough flour to keep the dough from sticking.

- Make sure the oven is set to the right temperature and that the thermostat is accurate.

- Bake the bread on a hot baking stone.

- Introduce steam to the oven by pouring hot water into a pan in the bottom of the oven.

- Let the bread bake long enough for a rich, brown crust to develop so that the crust can contribute to the overall taste of the bread.

- To keep the crust crisp longer, store bread in a paper bag or on the kitchen counter.

—Fran Gage, *Fine Cooking*

Creating a warm spot to proof bread

In winter, finding a moist, warm spot to proof bread dough is nearly impossible in our chilly house. So I create a *"proofing box"* by pouring about a quart of very hot or boiling water into a large picnic cooler. I set a rack in the cooler so it sits above the water, then I set the bowl with the bread dough inside and shut the lid. I find that this produces a perfect proofing environment.

—Irene Sturges, via email

Keep bread dough warm in a chilly kitchen

I usually start my bread baking early in the morning, when my kitchen is at its coldest. To create a warm environment for my dough to rise, I put the kneaded dough in a covered ceramic bowl and put the bowl in my kitchen sink. *I fill the sink with 100°F water* until it comes about two-thirds of the way up the sides of the bowl. Doing this, I've gotten reliable risings, even on the coldest mornings.

—Steve Boyle, Rural Hall, NC

Microwave proofing

The microwave is a great place to let bread dough rise. Heat a small bowl of water in the microwave and leave it there. Put the bowl of bread dough in the oven and close the door. The *hot water creates warmth* and moisture. If the dough is a little dry, leave it uncovered; if its texture is perfect, cover it.

—Theresa Overfield, Salt Lake City, UT

Measuring bread dough

Most bread recipes call for putting the dough in a large bowl and letting it rise until doubled. But how do you know when it's doubled? I solved that problem by using *4-quart plastic containers*, which are sold in restaurant-supply stores. The containers are clearly marked in quart intervals, so you know exactly when the dough has doubled—no guesswork involved.

—Maureen Fox Lucas, La Cañada, CA

Shapely bread

To preserve the symmetry of their bread, most bakeries make longitudinal slashes in the tops of the loaves before baking. This allows the loaf to expand evenly until the heat sets the gluten network of the dough. The slashing method works well at home, too, as long as your dough is robust enough to cut. But if your dough is on the softer side, as mine often is, trying to make these slashes can lead to stretching the loaves out of shape. To maintain the shapeliness of these more delicate loaves, I *poke a series of holes in the top* of each loaf with a metal skewer just before baking instead.

—Nancy P. Dowd, Lunenburg, Nova Scotia, Canada

Baking on parchment

For a crispy crust, I like baking bread and pizza on a baking stone. I used to put cornmeal on the stone to keep the dough from sticking, but my children don't like the taste of cornmeal, and I don't like the mess cornmeal makes in and out of the oven. Now I put a piece of kitchen *parchment on a wooden peel* or on the back of a baking sheet and put the shaped bread dough or rolled pizza dough on top. While it's rising, I cut away most of the excess parchment with scissors to keep it from burning or interfering with other loaves on the baking stone. When the dough is ready for baking, I slide the dough, along with parchment, directly onto the baking stone. Sometimes I remove the parchment halfway through cooking to make a slightly browner bottom crust, but more often, I leave it in place for the duration of baking.

—Deborah Patterson, Atlanta, GA

Baking at 6,000 feet

Now that I live at 6,000 feet above sea level, my doughs tend to rise too high and my cakes undercook inside. Any suggestions?

—Katy Reardon, via email

Letty Flatt, executive pastry chef at Deer Valley Resort in Park City, Utah (7,000 feet), replies: Baked goods turn out differently at high altitudes because of the lower atmospheric pressure. With less air pressure, bread doughs and cake batters rise too much or too quickly and their cell structures stretch or break, creating a coarse texture, or causing the bread or cake to fall. Also, liquids evaporate faster at higher altitudes due to the lower boiling temperature of water. Rapid evaporation makes other ingredients, such as sugar and fat, more concentrated than they are at sea level. This can also damage the cell structure, causing doughs to collapse, among other problems.

A lot of high-altitude cooking involves trial and error, with the baker having to make adjustments based on experience and the recipe's ingredients (recipes may need adjustment starting at 3,000 feet above sea level). I can't tell you exactly how to adapt every recipe, but here are some starting points.

For yeast breads, the rising dough will double sooner, and oven spring, which is the immediate rising of the dough in the hot oven, will be more pronounced. To allow for extra oven spring, put the shaped, risen loaves in the oven just *before* they double in size. You can also try to compensate for the faster rise by reducing the yeast by about 20%.

For cakes and quick breads, decrease the sugar by 1 to 2 tablespoons per cup of sugar (to recalibrate the sugar concentration). Undercooked batters may be the result of the concentrated sugar insulating the egg protein, thereby raising the temperature at which the eggs (and the batter) can set. Reducing the sugar will minimize this effect, whereas raising the oven temperature would likely just scorch the edges. If the recipe includes egg whites, whip them until they form soft peaks that just fold over—don't whip until stiff. This leaves enough elasticity in the whites for air bubbles to expand without bursting.

You can also try reducing the baking powder or baking soda by 15% to as much as 60%, depending on your altitude. When the leavening ratios are correct, the dough or batter will rise to perfect height, and not collapse, by the time the oven heat sets the expanding gas cells.

Mimic a baker's oven in your home

A *pizza stone will deliver more intense bottom heat*. Heat the oven—with the stone in it—for at least 45 minutes before baking, so it really heats up. Create steam to keep the crust moist during the initial stage of baking. This is important: you don't want a hard crust to form before the expansion is complete. Be careful with the spray bottle and aim for the loaves. Don't hit the oven's light bulb with the water or it may shatter. And don't put out the pilot light in a gas stove: I did that once and by the time I realized what had happened, I wrecked my bread.

—David Norman, *Fine Cooking*

Use a wet hand to create a brown and crunchy crust

To bake bread with a crisp crust, many recipes suggest creating steam by spraying the oven with water at the beginning of baking or setting a simmering pan of water in the oven. I've gotten the best results, however, by simply wetting my hand and running it down the length of the loaf before putting it in the oven. This technique provides *the perfect amount of evenly applied moisture* to create steam, and it produces a more uniformly browned crust.

—Mebeier via email

Steam iron makes a crusty loaf of bread

After over 30 years of trying various methods to get a perfect crust on rustic-style breads, I finally found an easy way. Using a well-heated baking stone and the steam/spray feature of my iron, I just got what I wanted: *a shiny, very crisp crust*. I spray the bread three times during the first 15 minutes of baking, using four or five bursts of steam each time.

—Ruth Ross, Northbrook, IL

Popcorn is perfect for shipping bread (and other baked goods)

Our family bakes handmade brick-oven breads for restaurants and grocers in our area, but occasionally we need to send a loaf long distance. I've found the ideal packing material: popcorn. Surrounding the bread with air-popped corn *keeps the crust intact and crisp* (plastic wrapping turns it soggy), it keeps the inside moist, and it prevents the bread from taking on a cardboard smell and taste from the packing box.

—Kathleen Weber, Della Fattoria, Petaluma, CA

Potato water for pizza dough

When I make my own pizza dough, I like to use warm potato water to proof the yeast. The starchy water helps create a wonderfully chewy crust, and the potato adds a phenomenal amount of flavor. To make potato water, use any type of potato (I like Yukon Gold). Chop the potato into large pieces, put it in a saucepan with just a bit more water than your recipe calls for, bring it to a boil, and let it simmer for at least 20 minutes. The water will be cloudy and may have small pieces of potato floating in it. Strain the water and measure it; add more plain water if necessary to get the amount required for the dough. Let the water cool to tepid before you dissolve the yeast in it. As for the cooked potato, you can cut it into thin slices to use as a pizza topping.

Starchy water helps create a wonderfully chewy crust, and the potato adds a phenomenal amount of flavor.

—Lana Baziuk, Toronto, Ontario, Canada

Use a microwave for speedy pizza dough

To make pizza dough *rise faster,* put the dough and a glass of water in the microwave and run it at 10% power for 3 minutes. Let the dough rest as long as 10 minutes and repeat. This rising technique works for any yeast dough that does not need the subtle flavors that come from a long, slow rise.

—Kathy Garrison, Lafayette, CO

Techniques for rolling pizza dough

When rolling dough, always roll from the middle away from you, then from the middle toward you. Never roll the pin from side to side. To roll evenly, give the dough a quarter turn and continue rolling. Also, *only roll just to the edges,* never past them; this would make the edges too thin and more likely to burn.

—Barbara Pepper, Salinas, CA

Stretch pizza dough over a mixing bowl

Instead of rolling out pizza dough, I stretch it over an upside-down mixing bowl. Here's how I do it: After letting the dough rest as usual, I remove it from the bowl, flip the bowl over, and dust its bottom with flour. Then I pull the dough down the sides of the bowl, give the bowl a quarter turn, pull down the dough, and so on, until I've stretched the dough to the size I want. (The dough seems to resist shrinking back up, perhaps because it clings to the textured surface of my ceramic mixing bowl.) When it's time to make pizza, *I turn the bowl over and let the dough fall onto a prepared peel*. Then I just add toppings and slide it all onto a hot pizza stone or grill.

—Rhonda Gadd, Corvallis, OR

One way to keep pizza dough from sticking to the peel

A soft moist dough produces an excellent pizza crust, but getting it to slide off the paddle and onto the hot stone can be tricky. You can use a lot of cornmeal or flour, but this doesn't guarantee the dough won't stick. My answer is parchment. Put *a piece of parchment that's a little larger than the crust* on the paddle and lay the stretched dough on top. Dress the pizza with toppings, then slide the parchment and pizza effortlessly onto the stone. About halfway through cooking, give the paper a tug and it will slide out from under the pizza. The crust comes out as brown and crisp as ever.

—Don Crane, Burnaby, British Columbia, Canada

And one more...

Our method of preventing pizza dough from sticking to the peel is to slip a length of *dental floss under the dough* and pull it all the way under using a sawing motion immediately before slipping the pizza into the oven. This loosens the dough in case it's stuck to the peel.

—John and Carla McCarthy, Loudon, TN

Keeping a crisp crust on leftover pizza and quiche

In my quest to achieve a crisp crust on leftover pizza or quiche, I've tried several techniques. Reheating in the oven tends to dry out the toppings or filling. Wrapping the pizza or quiche in foil keeps them moist, but ruins the crust. Microwaving ruins the crust, too. But if you reheat the leftovers in a nonstick skillet or sauté pan (with no oil) set over low heat, the crust always gets crisp and neither pizza nor quiche dries out in the process.

Gary Noll, Northwoods, IL

Reheat the leftovers in a nonstick skillet or sauté pan.

Punch—don't press—your biscuits

Use a metal biscuit cutter dipped in flour to punch out the biscuits in a quick motion. *Don't twist the cutter or press the dough* or you'll seal the edges and the biscuits won't rise properly. Also, don't use an overturned glass; not only will it seal the edges but it can compact the dough and make tough biscuits. As you cut, put the biscuits on an ungreased baking sheet, close together but not touching. If they're too close, their edges won't cook and the biscuits will have a cakey texture; too far apart and they'll brown too quickly and be undercooked inside.

—John Martin Taylor, *Fine Cooking*

An empty can makes a perfect biscuit cutter

When I'm making biscuits or empanadas and I don't have the right size cookie cutter, I just use the bottom of an aluminum can. My *can of baking soda is the perfect size;* I just empty the baking soda into a bowl while I'm using the can.

—Sidney Simon, Boston, MA

Getting a great scone

Chilling the butter—and keeping it chilled—is a critical step toward a delicious scone: You want it to remain in fairly large pieces and not get squashed into the flour as you mix. When the scones are thrust into a very hot oven, the butter will melt and *create a flaky texture*.

—Jacquie Lee, *Fine Cooking*

No popover pan? Try a muffin tin

If you don't have popover pans, use nonstick muffin tins. Popovers made in them will still be buttery and crisp, but just a bit smaller. *Just be sure the tins are nonstick,* as popovers will stick to aluminum tins, no matter how much you grease them.

—Abigail Johnson Dodge, *Fine Cooking*

Fill empty muffin wells with water

I often make a batch of muffin batter but only bake a few muffins at a time, saving the remaining batter to bake fresh muffins the next day. The only problem I've had is that the empty wells in my partially filled muffin tin scorch in the oven. What I now do is fill the empty wells halfway with water. This not only prevents the muffinless wells from burning, but it also *makes the oven more humid*, which for muffins seems to be a good thing.

—Ginger DeBlasio, Chicago, IL

Make your own cupcake liners

While preparing batter for cupcakes one day, I discovered I had no liners for my muffin pan. So I cut a piece of aluminum foil into small squares and molded each square on the outside of a muffin pan. Then I inserted the molded foils into the muffin cups and filled them with batter. The cupcakes baked beautifully, and *the foil peeled right off each cupcake*. I was using angel food cake batter so I didn't grease the foil, but for other kinds of cake batter, I would spray the foil with cooking spray.

—Pamela Jewett, Reno, NV

Mixing for tender cupcakes

When mixing cupcake batter (or other cake batters), it's important to beat the butter and sugar thoroughly. This creates tiny air bubbles that will expand and *help the batter rise*. When adding dry ingredients, beat only enough to incorporate them; overbeating may toughen the cupcakes.

—Greg Patent, *Fine Cooking*

Making cupcakes ahead

If you want to make cupcakes a day before serving, store them, unfrosted, in a covered plastic container. If you want to bake them farther ahead, freeze them unfrosted and uncovered, on a baking sheet. (Don't freeze frosted cupcakes—the texture of the frosting will suffer.) Once the cupcakes are frozen, transfer them to freezer bags, where they'll keep for about a week. To thaw, remove the cupcakes from the bags and set them on a flat surface. Frost them when they're completely thawed.

Freeze them unfrosted and uncovered, on a baking sheet.

—Greg Patent, *Fine Cooking*

Alternating makes wet and dry blend without a struggle

Many cake recipes tell you to alternate the addition of wet and dry ingredients. While this might seem like extra work, it's really important. If you were to add all the liquid first, the mixture would be very soupy and the emulsion of butter, sugar, and eggs would break. Adding all the flour first would create a very thick, pasty batter that would then require a lot of beating in order to incorporate the liquid. All the extra beating would toughen the cake. The *alternation of dry-wet-dry keeps the emulsion in a steady state.*

—Carolyn Weil, *Fine Cooking*

Beat the eggs briefly with a fork before adding to batter

Whisking will blend the yolks and whites so that you'll be able to dribble the egg into the batter in a slow stream as you beat. Adding unbeaten eggs one at a time to a cake batter sometimes causes the batter to collapse because you have to beat the batter too much in order to mix in the eggs thoroughly.

—Alice Medrich, *Fine Cooking*

An unconventional batter-mixing tool

When making a marble cake, I swirl the chocolate and vanilla batters together with *the tip of a knitting needle.* Because of its sleek, symmetrical shape, the needle maneuvers neatly through the batter, letting me make beautiful, tight spiral patterns that would be impossible with a spatula or knife.

—Pat Barni, Mayfield Village, OH

For a pretty cake, layer the berries in the cake batter

After making several blueberry pound cakes, I found that even when the berries were gingerly folded into the batter, their purple juices left streaks in the batter, leaving the baked cake slightly blue-gray on the inside. I finally added the blueberries in a different way: I plopped spoonfuls of plain batter into the cake pan, sprinkled a few blueberries on top, and then continued layering the batter with the blueberries. The result was *well-distributed berries and a prettier yellow cake.* The only trick is to be sure that you save enough spoonfuls of the batter to cover the top layer of berries; otherwise, they'll burn during baking.

—Louise Gallagher, San Diego, CA

It's All in the Mix

During all the stages of mixing a batter, use restraint.

- **Overbeating the butter can soften it too much, making it greasy, which will diminish its ability to trap air.**

- **Overbeating the eggs whips in too much air and creates tunnels in the finished cake.**

- **Overbeating once the flour has been added promotes gluten formation and toughens the cake.**

—Carolyn Weil, *Fine Cooking*

Don't bake a layer cake batter in a Bundt® or tube pan

Layer cakes have a lot of moisture in the batter and when confined to a deep pan, like a Bundt, they *don't bake properly*. By the time the liquid evaporates and the batter sets, the edges of the cake are dried out or, worse, the cake has fallen.

—Nicole Rees, *Fine Cooking*

Thoroughly greasing a Bundt pan

After several attempts to grease an elaborate Bundt pan with a paper towel, I still wasn't able to get the grease into every cranny of the pan. Then I tried greasing the pan with *a new makeup sponge*, and it worked great. The sharp angles of the soft, triangular sponge smooth the butter into every corner of the pan. I bought these sponges in the cosmetics area of the drugstore.

—Nanci Oliviero, Toronto, Ontario, Canada

Plastic bag greases baking pan

To grease or butter a pan, I use a small plastic bag or zip-top bag. *I insert my hand into the bag like a glove* and use my fingers to smear the butter onto the sides and corners. If I want to store the butter for next time, I turn the bag inside out before starting. When I'm finished, I pinch the bag toward the bottom and pull it right side out. Then I can just seal the bag and freeze it until the next time I need it.

—Robin Brisco, Austin, TX

Save that butter wrapper

When you unwrap a stick of butter, some butter usually sticks to the paper or foil. Don't throw the wrapper away. Instead, *fold it up and put it in the freezer*. The next time you have a recipe that calls for lightly greasing a pan, just unfold the butter wrapper and rub the pan with it.

—Mary MacVean, Jackson Heights, NY

Buttering pans

When baking, you need to butter your pans ahead of time so they're ready to use when your dough or batter is finished. But if you leave the pans sitting in a warm kitchen, the butter can melt and slide down the sides, leaving you with an unevenly buttered, and potentially sticky, pan. To prevent this problem, melt the butter and *brush the pan with a pastry brush*, then immediately put the pan in the freezer. This method allows you to get the pans ready ahead of time and it keeps the butter from melting in the heat of a warm kitchen.

—Arline Slote-Davis, Hinsdale, MA

Flouring pans with cocoa

When I grease and flour a pan before baking a chocolate cake or brownies, I'm often left with a white residue on the outside of the cake after removing it from the pan. To prevent this problem, I use cocoa to "flour" the pan instead.

—Lori Graham, Sault Ste. Marie, MI

Dusting cake pans with sugar

For a light, sugary glaze on my layer cakes, I dust greased cake pans with granulated sugar *instead of flour*.

—Suzan L. Wiener, Spring Hill, FL

Dust baking pans with bread crumbs

Instead of dusting baking pans with flour, I use *unseasoned bread crumbs*, a dusting of which is more pleasant than flour residue.

—Rick Beaudin, Bangor, ME

Release cakes from hot pans with steam

If you have trouble removing a just-baked cake from a pan that doesn't have a nonstick surface, set the hot pan on a well-dampened dishtowel for 5 minutes. *The steam it generates will help release* the precious cargo.

—Betsy Race, Euclid, OH

Colander holds tube cake while it cools

My favorite tube pan has a center hole that's too narrow to fit over a bottle neck when cooling a sponge cake. After jury-rigging various contraptions to hold up the pan, I finally gave up and set the tube pan *upside down in a large colander*. Now I always cool such cakes in a colander. The holes allow the cake to cool properly, and the pan won't get knocked over by an errant elbow.

—Joanne Bouknight, *Fine Cooking*

A rubber spatula helps free a cake from its pan

I use a narrow, 1-inch, *heat-resistant rubber spatula* to help dislodge cakes from the pans instead of running a knife around the edge. The spatula doesn't tear the cake and separates it from the pan more easily.

—Elaine Hankinson, Hayden, ID

Pain-free pound cake extraction

The trick to removing a pound cake from the pan is to do it *while the cake is still slightly warm*—15 to 20 minutes after removing it from the oven. If you try immediately, the cake will be too fragile and could get damaged. If you wait too long, try warming the outside of the pan over a flame or in a warm oven to help release the cake.

—Carolyn Weil, *Fine Cooking*

Chiffon cake *should* stick to the pan

Chiffon cakes bake in a large tube pan that doesn't get greased. As the batter bakes, it climbs slowly up the sides and stays put. I once absentmindedly greased a tube pan for a chiffon cake. It rose quickly and was unusually high. I thought, "Aha! Here's another food myth disproved!" But as soon as the cake came out of the oven, it collapsed in a heap. The greased sides couldn't support the weight of the batter, and all that had been under the top crust was a big air bubble. *Cool the cake with the center of the tube pan inverted onto a bottle.* This allows air to circulate around the cake and keeps the weight of the cake from pushing down on itself as it cools. Just be sure that you bake the cake fully; if the interior is underbaked, the weight of it may pull the cake out of the pan. The cooled cake can be a challenge to remove from the pan. If it doesn't come out after inverting it and giving it a gentle tap, run a long, thin knife around the cake as close to the side of the pan as possible. To cut smooth, even slices, without crushing the cake, use a serrated knife and a sawing motion.

—Elinor Klivans, *Fine Cooking*

Salvaging dry cake

If you have overbaked a cake to dryness, you might be able to salvage it by *imbibing it with a simple sugar syrup*. Cut off the sides and top of the cake and brush on the syrup with a pastry brush until it's well saturated; a dry cake can take a lot of syrup. The syrup will change the character of the cake, but it can be very tasty, especially if you flavor the syrup with a liqueur or brandy.

—Krista Stanley, Once Upon a Cake, Mt. Kisco, NY

Aligning cakes

I like to cut a single cake layer into two layers and fill in between them before icing the entire cake. Here's a simple method for realigning the cake layers so that the cake ends up level. Before I cut, I insert one toothpick horizontally into the side of the cake near the top, and insert another one near the bottom, directly underneath the first one. I cut the cake into two layers, spread on the filling, then set the top back on, realigning the toothpicks. This method *ensures a level cake*, yet it doesn't require a perfectly level cut.

—Betsy Schwartz, Greenwich, CT

Cutting cake layers

If you've never cut cake layers before, use two toothpicks to divide the cake into however many layers you need along the side of the cake. Do this at four points around the cake. Then, using your longest serrated knife and with a firm, slow sawing motion, cut through the cake, *using the toothpicks as guides*.

—Abigail Johnson Dodge, *Fine Cooking*

Cut clean cake layers with floss

I've found a way to cut a cake into horizontal layers easily and cleanly. Using a sharp knife, mark the desired location with a shallow cut around the circumference of the cake. Then stretch dental floss tightly between your hands and *saw gently back and forth* beginning at one point of the initial cut, gradually bringing your hands together.

—Helen D. Conwell, Fairhope, AL

Keeping it crumb free

When a cake layer must be split into layers, always place the crumb or cut side in the middle, never at the top or bottom. This way, no crumbs are visible on the outside of the cake and the surface to be frosted will be smooth and even.

—Carole Walter, *Fine Cooking*

Neat and steady cake decorating

When frosting a cake, anchor the bottom layer with *a dab of frosting or jam in the center of the cake platter*. This keeps the cake from sliding around. Also, to keep the platter clean while working, position strips of waxed paper or parchment around the bottom and slightly under the cake, letting the extra drape over the platter's edge. Remove the strips when you're finished decorating.

—Mary Sullivan, Concord, CA

Use an inverted cake pan for easier frosting

Instead of frosting a cake on a cake plate, *turn a clean cake pan upside down*, put a layer of cake on top of it, frost that layer, then put the next layer on and frost it. Put one hand inside the pan and, holding it at a comfortable level, frost the sides, which should be flush with the sides of the pan. Using a wide spatula or two, transfer the frosted cake to a serving plate.

—Phyllis Kirigin, Croton-on-Hudson, NY

A drop of blue food dye turns frosting snow white

While making wedding cakes for both my son and daughter, I learned that butter and vanilla extract produce a buttercream frosting that is off-white in color. To achieve a snow-white frosting, a friend suggested adding *one drop of blue food coloring* to each batch. It worked.

—Betsy Rice, Port Washington, NY

Glossy icing

To smooth bumpy icing (but not icing that actually has lumps in it) after a cake has been iced, pass *a blow dryer on low heat* over the surface until the bumps disappear.

—Neil Hendricks, Albuquerque, NM

Better whipped cream for frosting

When I want to use whipped cream as a frosting or filling between cake layers, *I stabilize it with gelatin*: For 1 cup of heavy cream, I use a solution of 1 teaspoon unflavored powdered gelatin softened in about 2 tablespoons cold water (microwave the mixture for a few seconds to dissolve and then cool). Add this in a steady stream while whipping the sweetened whipped cream. The stabilized whipped cream is especially useful when decorating a cake with a basketweave design or when piping out rosettes.

—Linda Wellford, Davis, CA

For a Smooth Finish, Apply a Crumb Coat before You Frost a Cake

If you've ever marveled at the flawless frosting on a professionally made cake and wondered why your frosted cakes often end up speckled with crumbs, here's a tip: Apply a "crumb coat" to your cake before you spread on the actual frosting. If you use a little bit of frosting to seal the cake's surface and secure loose crumbs, your final layer of frosting will go on much more smoothly.

Begin by brushing off any loose crumbs on the cake with a dry pastry brush or your fingers. (If you're making a layer cake, the layer should already be filled and stacked.) Then spread a very thin layer of frosting over the entire surface of the cake. With lighter frostings, this layer may be transparent. Don't worry: its role is simply to seal the surface. Fill in any cracks or divots in the cake.

After smoothing the surface of the crumb coat (don't worry if it's speckled with crumbs), refrigerate the cake for 5 to 10 minutes to let the frosting set. Before finishing the cake, clean the spatula, the rim of the mixing bowl, and the entire work area of crumbs, which have an almost magnetic way of getting into the frosting. Now you're ready to spread a smooth, crumb-free frosting onto the cake.

The simplest choice for a crumb coat is a bit of the actual frosting. Depending on the size of your cake and the amount of patching up you need to do, a crumb coat should take about $1/2$ cup of frosting. I've found that I don't need to make extra frosting, since I wind up needing less for the final layer.

As an alternative to frosting, strained preserves also make a fine crumb coat. The sleek, translucent coating that this creates is especially useful if you're planning to finish the cake with a warm chocolate glaze. Melt $1/2$ cup jelly, jam, or preserves with 1 tablespoon water until thin and smooth. Strain the warmed mixture into a small bowl and brush a thin layer onto the cake to seal the surface. Let it sit for 5 to 10 minutes to set up before applying the finish frosting. It should be somewhat tacky.

—Molly Stevens, *Fine Cooking*

Decorate cakes perfectly with melted chocolate

I've developed an anxiety-free way to decorate cakes for special occasions. I usually make a hazelnut fudge torte with a hard, smooth chocolate glaze, then pipe out decorations with melted white chocolate. Lacking both talent and confidence, I used to get nervous as I held my piping bag and started to decorate that perfect dark brown canvas. Mistakes were inevitable. Now I pipe the white chocolate onto a baking sheet lined with waxed paper. I make little stars or decorative squiggles or I write "Happy Birthday" or some other message. I do this as many times as necessary until I get it right. Once these harden, I carefully peel them off and arrange them on the cake. I never fail to get comments on how great the cake looks, and nobody guesses what a klutz I really am with a piping bag. This method should work with any icing that hardens as it dries, such as royal icing.

—Barbara Minish, Ottawa, Ontario, Canada

A thread guides your pastry bag's handwriting

Before you pipe a message in frosting on your cake, gently lay a length of sewing thread over the icing to *make a guideline*. Write the message just above the line, then gently pull away the thread.

—Lilia Dvarionas, Kanata, Ontario, Canada

A tea strainer dusts confectioners' sugar

To sprinkle confectioners' sugar on cakes or cookies, I use a mesh tea strainer. I dip the open strainer into the sugar, snap it shut, lift it out, and shake the sugar exactly where it's needed. It's *easy to wash, too*.

—Sandra Krist, Edmonds, VA

Decorate pastries with hard candies

Many people dust confectioners' sugar or cocoa onto desserts such as chocolate cakes and tortes. Another idea is to garnish a cake by *dusting it with a sugar powder made from grinding your favorite hard candy* (such as toffee or peppermint) in a clean spice grinder.

—Adam Eisner, Hadley, MA

Shake off "nut dust" with a metal sieve

I love to decorate my cakes with chopped nuts around the sides. To give the cake a more finished look, I chop the nuts, put them in a metal sieve, and start shaking. You wouldn't believe how much "nut dust" comes off. The nuts will have *a clean and shiny look instead of a dull finish*. This method works for any kind of nut. I've been told that the cakes I've entered in contests look very professional.

—Desiree Sigal, Hidden Hills, CA

Cut a cake into small portions

At a dessert party, guests may wish to sample many tarts and cheesecakes, so they may only want a small serving of each. A good way to deal with this is a traditional Scandinavian technique for cutting rich tarts into small portions. *Cut a cylinder from the center of the cake*, using a pot lid or saucer as a guide. Cut the outside ring into wedges about 1½ inches wide. When the outside of the cake is gone, you're left with a smaller round cake for tea time, another meal, or more small pieces.

—Lilia Dvarionas, Kanata, Ontario, Canada

Keeping leftover cake moist

If you have leftover cake, put it in a container or *in foil wrapping with an apple*. The fruit will keep the cake moist and flavorful.

—Faye Field, Longview, TX

CHEESECAKE

Cookie crust shortcut

When I make cheesecake or any other cake that calls for a crushed-cookie crust, I don't melt the butter as is usually called for in the recipe. Instead, I use my food processor to grind the cookies into coarse crumbs, then I add cold butter and pulse the machine a few times to incorporate it into the crumbs. I think this results in a *more even distribution of butter*. Then, when I press the crumbs into the cake pan, the heat of my hands melts the butter and makes the crust pliable and easy to handle.

—Jack Kane, Houston, TX

Freezing cheesecakes

Can cheesecakes be frozen with good results?

—Saniya Bloomer, via email

Elinor Klivans replies: A cheesecake with a high fat content from cream cheese or mascarpone and a dense texture will freeze very well. The fat in the cream cheese helps keep the ice crystals that form during freezing separated and small, which prevents undesirable icy pockets from forming. As a guideline, a 9-inch cheesecake made with at least $1^1/2$ pounds of cream cheese contains enough fat to freeze well.

It's important to cool cheesecakes thoroughly before wrapping and freezing them. Otherwise, moisture (which turns into undesirable ice) may condense inside the wrapping. Slide the molded cheesecake onto a serving plate or a cardboard circle, wrap it tightly in plastic, then again in heavy-duty aluminum foil. Wrapped in this manner, cheesecake can be frozen up to a month.

Defrost the cheesecake in the refrigerator for at least 6 hours but preferably overnight to ensure that it thaws completely. Leave the wrapping on during the defrosting so any moisture collects on the wrapper, not your cheesecake. To bring out the best flavor, let the cheesecake sit at room temperature for an hour before serving.

Easy steps for a thin cheesecake cookie crust

Pat down the crumbs with your finger, then *use a straight-sided glass to press down* and push the crumbs up the walls. Cover the crust with a double layer of plastic to prevent sticking and continue spreading the crust with your fingers.

—Rose Levy Beranbaum, *Fine Cooking*

Meat pounder smooths a crumb crust

I use my meat pounder for pressing cookie crumb crusts into a cheesecake pan or pie plate. The heavy, flat metal disk helps me get *an even thickness and eliminates marks left by my fingers*.

—Diane K. Wilson, Pacific Grove, CA

Keeping your cheesecake crack free

After you remove it from the oven, *run a thin-bladed knife between the crust and the pan sides* to prevent the cake from breaking as it cools.

—Regan Daley, *Fine Cooking*

Cutting cheesecake

To cut neat slices, use a sharp, thin-bladed *knife dipped in hot water* (shake off excess drops) between each slice. For a cheesecake without a crust, a piece of dental floss, held taut, also works (you'll need to cut across the diameter of the cake).

—Rose Levy Beranbaum, *Fine Cooking*

Cutting cheesecake, take two

To cut attractive, smooth-edged slices of cheesecake, *use fishing line instead of a knife*. Cut a piece of fishing line (15-pound monofilament) longer than the diameter of the cheesecake. Wrap the ends of the line around your middle fingers, stretch the line taught, and push it down through the center of the cake, slicing the cake in half. Let go of the line with one hand, and with the other hand, pull the line out of the side of the cake, as close to the plate as possible. You can wipe off any cheesecake sticking to the line with a paper towel. Continue to make cuts through the center of the cake until you've divided the cake into as many slices as you need.

—John Paloian, Newtown, CT

Disposable cake pans are great for giveaway cheesecakes

When I'm making a cheesecake as a gift, I line the bottom of the pan with a disposable metal cake pan. That way I don't lose the bottom when I give the cheesecake away. Cut off the sides of the cake pan and put the remaining flat circle over the removable bottom of a springform pan. Make sure you buy *a cake pan that's the same size as your springform pan* (or larger—you can always cut it down) so that you can get an exact fit.

—Gwen Roller, Columbus, OH

Cookie-dough-mixing marathon

Since I bake many different types of holiday cookies, I've discovered that it's more efficient to make all the mixes and doughs in one day. I pull out all my recipes, flour and sugar, butter and spices, and I make a big mess all at once. I put the prepared cookie doughs and mixes into separate zip-top plastic bags and label them with the following information: date, name of cookie, volume of dough, yield, storage method (freezer or fridge), baking temperature, length of baking time, shape of cookie, decorating method. The *kitchen only needs one cleaning after all the mixing*, and I can bake the cookies at my own pace over the following few weeks.

—Regina Padgett, Strongsill, OH

Fresh-baked cookies at a moment's notice

When I make cookies, I always make at least *a double batch of dough*. I bake up however many cookies I need for that day, and I roll the rest of the dough into a long tube shape, wrap it in parchment and then plastic, and freeze it. When I need more cookies, I simply pull out my tube of cookie dough, slice off as many as I need, and bake. It's a great time saver, and the taste and smell of freshly baked cookies is well worth the effort.

—Martha Breneiser, via email

How soft is softened butter?

When a cookie recipe calls for softened butter, let it stand at *room temperature until it's malleable but not too soft, 30 to 60 minutes*, depending on the temperature of the room. It should give slightly when pressed but still maintain its shape. The ideal is 67°F. Butter that's too soft will make a sticky dough that's harder to work with, provides less leavening, and spreads too much during baking. To speed up the softening time, you can cut the butter into tablespoon pieces.

—Elaine Khosrova, *Fine Cooking*

Add an egg white to shortbread

I've found that adding one egg white to a bunch of crumbly shortbread dough will make it *hold together* and handle well. It doesn't affect the flavor at all.

—S. Ryan, Redwood City, CA

Rainy days and meringue cookies

Don't try to make meringues on a very humid day. The humidity can prevent the meringues from ever getting crisp.

—Abigail Johnson Dodge, *Fine Cooking*

Getting the chocolate chip cookie you want

For a thin and crisp cookie, add more white sugar than brown sugar. Be sure the butter and eggs are at room temperature before mixing to help the cookies spread thinner as they bake. A greased baking sheet will encourage the cookies to spread even more. For a *thick and chewy cookie*, use butter and eggs right out of the refrigerator so the dough stays cool and the cookies maintain their thickness during baking; you can also use ungreased cookies sheets. To keep the cookies soft and chewy, store them in an airtight container along with a slice of bread.

—Bonnie Gorder-Hinchey, *Fine Cooking*

Making thumbprint cookies

Use a thimble of any size to make the indentations in cookies to be filled with jam or jelly. The thimble makes perfectly even indentations every time.

—Anna Victoria Reich, Albuquerque, NM

Baking perfectly round refrigerator cookies

When I started making refrigerator cookies many years ago, the roll of dough would get flat on one side from sitting on the fridge shelf, and the cookies would end up misshapen rather than round. To prevent this, I roll the dough to a diameter slightly smaller than an *an empty paper towel roll*, wrap the dough with waxed paper, and slide the wrapped dough into the cardboard cylinder. The cylinder is just the right length for the dough, and it's stiff enough so that the dough doesn't flatten when I put it in the refrigerator or freezer. When I'm ready to bake, I just slide the dough out and slice the cookies. I get perfect rounds every time.

—Maria Olaguera-Delogu, Outremont, Quebec, Canada

Mark cookie slices evenly with egg slicer

Before slicing the log of dough for refrigerator cookies, use an egg slicer to mark the length of the log. With a knife, cut through every mark for thin cookies or every other mark for thicker ones. The even spacing of the egg slicer's wires means that the cookies are always *the same thickness*. I use the slicer only to mark, not to cut, as the dough may be too hard or the log too thick.

—Isabelle Wolters, Scituate, MA

Waxed or parchment paper helps roll out cookie dough

My method for rolling out cookie dough doesn't use excess flour and *helps the cookies retain their shape*. Flatten the dough, lay it on a piece of waxed or parchment paper, and cover with another piece of paper of equal size. With a rolling pin, roll over the paper until the dough is the thickness you want. (Lift the paper frequently during this process to eliminate wrinkles.) Peel off the top piece of paper and cut out the cookies. Replace the paper to keep the dough from drying out, slide the dough onto a baking sheet, and chill until firm. When ready to bake, slide the chilled dough back onto the counter, carefully peel off the paper, and transfer the cookies to the baking sheet.

—Marianne Michener, Petaluma, CA

Flour your cookie cutters

Lightly flour the sharp edge of your cookie cutters *to prevent the dough shapes* from sticking to the cutter.

—Elaine Khosrova, *Fine Cooking*

Perfectly shaped cookies every time

Moving rolled cookies after cutting can be difficult, especially if they're rolled very thin. A great solution is to roll the dough on parchment, cut the shapes, remove the scrap dough, slide the paper onto a baking sheet, and refrigerate or freeze for a few minutes to firm the cookies. The *cookies can then be easily moved* without distorting their shape.

—Edith C. Williams, Rockville, MD

Pressing a sugar topping on cookies

I use a *hammer-type meat tenderizer to flatten* peanut butter cookie dough and also to give it a nice sugary topping. I dip the waffle surface of the tenderizer into a dish of sugar, set it on top of a cookie-size ball of dough, press to flatten it, and then bake.

—Jean Henderson, Colville, WA

Getting the drop cookie you want

To make chewy drop cookies, *underbake them slightly* so that they're still quite soft and not yet browned, but no longer look wet in the center. For crisper cookies, bake them longer, letting the cookies become lightly browned all over.

—Elaine Khosrova, *Fine Cooking*

Two ideas for streamlined cookie baking

If you bake a lot of cookies during the holidays, buy enough baking sheets so that when you take the first batch of cookies out of the oven, you have the next batch prepped and ready to go. This way, you won't have to wait for the sheets to cool down before starting the next batch. I also bought *an extra oven shelf* so I could bake even more cookies at the same time. Be sure to space your shelves evenly in the oven and rotate your baking sheets and swap their positions to ensure even baking.

—Colleen Lanigan-Ambrose, Seal Beach, CA

Lifting out lemon squares

A trick we use in our bakery is to line the baking pan with *parchment paper*, letting an inch or two extend past the sides of the pan. This makes it easy to remove the bars from the pan once they've cooled to room temperature.

—Joanne Chang, *Fine Cooking*

Electric knife slices through biscotti

When making biscotti, I slice the baked dough with an electric knife. The slices come out even, with *no crumbling edges*.

—Deborah Robichaud, Gloucester, Ontario, Canada

Cutting brownies

When cutting up brownie squares to be served, *use a plastic knife* instead of a metal one. Unlike when cutting with a metal knife, the brownies will not goop up on the plastic knife.

—Katie Benoit, Fairfield, CT

Cutting brownies II

A knife *rinsed in hot water and then dried* will cut more cleanly than a cold knife.

—Greg Case, *Fine Cooking*

Two paper plates, some cookies, and a stapler

I discovered a wonderful way to store cookies (I bake a lot of them, especially around the holidays) in my freezer. I wrap them in aluminum foil and put the package between two paper plates with the bottoms facing out, like a flying saucer. I staple the rims to seal, label the package with a marker, and stack them in the freezer. It's *easy to transport* tea sandwiches and canapés this way as well; they stack comfortably in a plastic supermarket bag without tipping over.

—Barbara Greene Ruskin, Los Angeles, CA

Tricks and Tips for Shaping Refrigerator Cookie Dough

Once your dough is mixed, make sure it's not too soft to shape. Stash it in the refrigerator for 20 to 30 minutes, until it's firm enough to handle. If it becomes too firm, just let it stand at room temperature until it's malleable.

When shaping dough into cylinders, sprinkling a thin dusting of flour (no more than a teaspoon) on the rolling surface can help make the logs easier to handle.

Moistening your hands ever so slightly can make shaping easier.

Take care not to roll the logs any longer than 10 inches. Dough that you'll roll in nuts or other coatings will lengthen when coated, so start them off slightly shorter.

Put the cylinders of dough on plastic wrap at least 6 inches longer than the length of the log.

As you wrap the log in plastic, roll tightly and tug on the ends to tighten the plastic and to smooth any creases.

To secure the plastic, twist the ends well, then roll the dough back and forth to eliminate any air pockets.

To compact the log, push the ends of the cylinder firmly toward the center.

Once in the refrigerator, turn the logs frequently. Put the logs on a level shelf or flat baking sheet in the refrigerator or freezer and turn each one every 15 minutes for the first hour. As the logs chill, the bottoms will flatten from the weight of the dough. To correct this, remold the logs by rolling them back and forth a few times on the countertop.

Or, use a cradle. If you happen to have a baguette pan, it makes a perfect cradle for chilling logs of dough. If you don't, save a few empty paper towel rolls, cut each in half lengthwise to make two cardboard troughs with rounded bottoms, and then place a log in each half for chilling.

For both of these methods, after the logs have chilled 15 to 20 minutes, turn them over once and chill until firm.

—Carole Walter, *Fine Cooking*

Cookies and convection

I just bought a new oven that has a convection feature. As an avid cookie-maker, I was wondering if it's all right to use convection heat when making cookies. Do I need to lower the heat to compensate?

—Sara Campos, via email

Elinor Klivans responds: Convection heat is perfect for producing batch after batch of evenly baked cookies. Its great virtue—even heat throughout the oven—produces nicely browned cookie bottoms and edges.

A convection oven has a fan that circulates air and creates uniform heat in the oven. Since items placed in the top or back of the oven cook at the same rate as those in the bottom or front, convection heat allows you to bake two sheets of cookies together without rearranging them during baking, as you would have to do in a conventional oven.

When baking with a convection oven, I follow the recipe's directions and its baking times, but I generally reduce the baking temperature by about 25° to compensate for the strength of the convection heat. The manufacturer's booklet may advise specific temperature suggestions for your oven, but, if not, start with this 25° deduction and try a few test batches to see what works best.

Tips for shipping cookies

Wrap varieties separately to keep flavors from mingling. Wrap the cookies in manageable-sized sleeves, then surround the sleeves in *bubble wrap for best cushioning*. Don't mix soft and crisp cookies in the same package; the crisp cookies absorb moisture from the soft cookies and become soft themselves.

—Joanne McAllister Smart and Margery K. Friedman, *Fine Cooking*

Nonstick spray helps portion sticky dough

While making gougères (cheese puffs), I had a hard time portioning the dough for the puffs; my ice-cream scoop was reluctant to release the dense, sticky dough onto the parchment. I stopped and cleaned off the scoop, sprayed it with nonstick cooking spray, and tried again. It worked like a charm—*the scoop willingly released the balls of dough*.

—Chlöe Wodjenski, New Milford, CT

For a perfect puff

Cook choux dough (the dough used for cream puffs) enough to allow the flour particles to swell and to evaporate as much moisture as possible. *The drier the dough, the more egg it will absorb* and the more puffed up the final product. For maximum puffiness, beat each egg in vigorously to incorporate lots of air into the dough. Bake the puffs until a skewer inserted in the center comes out clean, reduce the oven temperature to 250°F, and bake another 10 to 15 minutes to dry out the shells. Then puncture the baked shells with a knife to release any residual steam to avoid sogginess.

—Gay Chanler, *Fine Cooking*

Baking pastries perfectly

I learned a valuable baking technique from Chef Albert Jorant, one of my teachers at La Varenne cooking school in Paris. When baking cookies, choux puffs, or pastry cases directly on a baking sheet, slide a thin palette knife or metal spatula under the pastries to *loosen them from the sheet about halfway through the cooking time*. If you don't do this, some parts of the pastry can become stuck to the sheet and will receive more heat directly from the metal sheet. By "freeing" the underside of the pastries, the whole bottom surface of the pastry receives the same amount of heat and therefore will brown evenly, with no dark rings or edges. Chef Jorant performed this step without thinking (and without telling us students), and it was only after months of watching him work that I realized how important a maneuver it is. I've adopted this technique, and over the years it has saved many batches of pastries, I'm sure.

—Anne Sterling, Lincroft, NJ

The size of the butter chunk determines the size of the flake

The size of the butter chunk in a pie crust is critical. *Big bits of butter in the dough translate into big flakes*, as the moisture in the butter turns into steam and puffs up that section of the pastry. If the butter pieces are too small, you may get a tender pastry, but one that's more crumbly than flaky.

—Carolyn Weil, *Fine Cooking*

Flakiest pie crust

To make the flakiest pie crust, use *frozen unsalted butter* and a food processor. Cut the butter into 1- to 2-inch chunks and add them to the processor after mixing the flour and salt in it first. Process the mixture until the butter is chopped into small pieces, then add ice water. This method requires a bit more ice water than when hand-mixing with cold butter. Pulse a few times, then gather the dough into a ball and roll it out. For a 9-inch pie crust, I use 2 cups flour, 1 teaspoon salt, ¾ cup butter, and about 5 tablespoons ice water.

—Brenda Eitelman, Northville, MI

Frozen butter + box grater = perfect pastry

When I make short-crust pastry, I freeze the butter for a day or so until it's very hard. Then I *grate the frozen butter* (on the coarse side of an ordinary box grater) over the flour. This ensures that the fat is truly cold. And the flakes of grated butter mix so quickly into the flour, there's no time for it to get warm.

—Christopher Bird, Irving, TX

Give pie dough a spritz

I've always made pie dough the old-fashioned way, cutting the fat into the flour by hand rather than with a food processor. For a long time, however, I had trouble mixing in the ice water. Trickling it off a spoon invariably left me with a few wet clumps of dough sitting in a bowl of dry crumbs. I had to find a better way. So one day, I filled a clean spray bottle with ice water and *spritzed the dry ingredients* while tossing them with a fork. The ice water dispensed evenly, and my pie dough quickly came together into a workable mass that didn't crumble when I rolled it out. I now consider a spray bottle an essential pie-making tool.

—Erik Stokstad, Takoma Park, MD

Try orange juice for a tender pie crust

For a more tender and flavorful crust for fruit pies or tarts, *substitute orange juice for ice water*. It's always chilled since it stays in the fridge. The fruit flavor is only discernible as an intriguing tang, which you'll miss if you try it again with water. The acidity cuts the gluten, which is the component that makes pastry tough.

—Sara Zwicker, Braintree, MA

Easier pie crusts

For people who have warm hands or who, like me, get frustrated trying to get the flour-coated crumbs of butter to form a cohesive pie crust dough, try this method: After cutting fat into flour for pie crust dough, I mix in as much water or egg as the dough will need. Then I dump everything onto a large piece of plastic wrap. I pull the corners up above the dough and twist the package closed, leaving a bit of room to spare. It's then no problem to shape the dough into a thick disk (the plastic stretches), which is ready for rolling or for the freezer. I find this method *keeps me from overworking the dough*.

—David Armstrong, Lethbridge, Alberta, Canada

Cool surface before working with pastry

To cool your counter or board for working with pastry, keep a baking sheet full of ice on the surface until you're ready to mix, shape, or roll out your dough. Be sure to *wipe off any condensation* before you start to work.

—Tim Derikson, Houston, TX

Ice packs cool warm countertops

Before I had granite countertops, I used ice packs to cool my counters so it would be *easier to make pastry dough*. I wrapped the frozen packs in kitchen towels to keep the countertop dry. I set the packs on the counter for an hour or so before working with the dough. I still do this in the summertime; it makes working with dough much easier.

—Carole Kimball, El Cajon, CA

Roll dough on a cold board

While my freshly made pie dough rests in the refrigerator, I put a large *cutting board and rolling pin in the freezer to chill*. When I roll out the dough on the cold board, I have no problem with the dough sticking.

—Curtis McMurtrie, Bedford, MA

TO MAKE TENDER PASTRY	WHY
Blend softened fat into the flour before adding any liquid	Fat coats the proteins and prevents them from forming gluten
Instead of water, use an ingredient that is part fat, like sour cream, cream, or egg yolks	Gluten can't form without water, and the additional fat contributes to tenderness
Add acid to the dough in the form of lemon juice, vinegar, or sour cream	Acid breaks long gluten strands

TO MAKE FLAKY PASTRY	WHY
Keep the fat cold and in large pieces (pea-size to ½-inch cubes)	Large, cold pieces will remain firm in the oven long enough to create flakes
Flatten large pieces of cold fat	Chunky pieces will make holes in the crust rather than act as spacers

—Shirley O. Corriher, *Fine Cooking*

Cool hands on a cold baking sheet

Cool hands are essential for certain types of pastry work, for making pie crust or rolling out the centers of chocolate truffles, for example. My favorite trick for chilling my notoriously warm hands is to put a baking sheet in the freezer for 10 or 15 minutes. When I'm ready to work, *I take out the very cold pan* and periodically press my (dry) hands flat against it.

—Abigail Johnson Dodge, *Fine Cooking*

Flat dough rolls more easily

When I make pie dough, *I shape the dough into flat disks* instead of balls before I chill it. This makes the chilled dough easier to roll out.

—Sandy Dameron, Grandview, MO

Roll out dough between nonstick baking mats

My silicone baking mat's nonstick coating makes an ideal surface for rolling out sticky pastry and cookie dough. I put the dough on one mat, cover it with another mat, and apply my rolling pin to the top. My *rolling pin stays neat and clean.* Once the dough is the right thickness, I just remove the top mat and proceed. If the dough needs chilling, I can pick up the mats and dough and put them all in the freezer for a few minutes. I also use my baking mat to knead bread dough and to roll pastry doughs such as puff pastry and pâte brisée. Because the mat is so nonstick, you don't need as much flour for rolling and kneading, which yields a more tender result.

—Eliane Feiner, sales manager for Demarle®, maker of Silpat® liners

Rolling perfect pie crusts

Rolling out pie and tart crusts between two sheets of kitchen parchment or waxed paper has certain advantages. You use less flour, which keeps your crust from getting tough and keeps your counter clean. Measuring is also easier—I draw the appropriate size circle or square directly on the paper, using the pie or tart pan as a guide. One more tip is to use the paper *to help transfer the dough to the pan*. Simply peel off the top sheet of the parchment or waxed paper, slide your hand under the papered side, and flip the dough onto the pie pan. When the dough is properly aligned, peel off the paper. The dough is more cooperative if you chill it briefly while it's still between the sheets of the paper.

—Alice Smart, Whispering Pines, NC

Use your pizza peel as a pastry board

To roll out pie crust on a pizza peel, set the peel on a slightly dampened dishtowel to steady it, dust with flour, and roll out the dough. Transfer the dough to the pie pan by setting the pan upside down on the dough and holding the pan steady while you invert the peel. The crust is now in position and ready for trimming.

Transfer the dough to the pie pan by setting the pan upside down on the dough.

—Ann Wolthuis, Holland, MI

Roll out pastry dough with confectioners' sugar

When I roll out pastry dough for a dessert, instead of using flour to dust the rolling surface, I use confectioners' sugar. It keeps the pastry dough from sticking, and *it won't dry out the dough* or toughen the baked pastry like flour can if you work too much of it into your dough. The confectioners' sugar will cause more browning during baking—a benefit for pie and tart crusts.

—Gale Gand, *Fine Cooking*

A seam roller helps even out pastry crust

Pastry crusts that must be patted into the pan by hand tend to be uneven—too thick in some places and too thin in others. To even them out, I use a *wallpaper seam roller* that's 1¼ inches wide. It works best in a rectangular pan. Just cover the dough with plastic wrap and gently go over it with the seam roller. This gives me a consistent thickness without finger indentations.

—Ruth Clapham, Onsted, MI

A food pusher doubles as a dough tamper

I've just been given a recipe that requires pressing dough into a springform pan, and I was reminded of a trick that I use to make crushed cookie crusts in pie and tart pans. The *plastic food pusher from an electric juicer* or a food processor is ideal for tamping because it has a flat surface on the bottom and its rounded shape makes it easy to push dough into the corners and up the sides of a tart pan or a springform pan.

—Fran Enslein, via email

Keeping a pastry cloth fresh

A well-floured pastry cloth works wonders when rolling out dough, but it can get stale fairly quickly. I prevent this by keeping mine *in the freezer in a plastic bag*. The cloth gets better with use. Just scrape it clean with a dough scraper after use, fold it up, and freeze. A bonus is the cold surface for rolling out your dough.

—Ann Putnam, via email

Handling pastry lattice

Butter-based pastry dough becomes firmer when chilled, and I take advantage of this fact to make a neat woven lattice top for fruit pies and tarts. Instead of weaving soft, room-temperature pastry strips on top of the pie and ending up with uneven weaving and juice-coated pastry, *I prepare the lattice on a baking sheet or cutting board* covered with a sheet of waxed paper. First, I roll out the circle of dough (on another surface) about ⅛ inch thick and large enough for the top of the pie, then I cut the dough into ½-inch strips. I weave the strips together on the waxed paper, making sure the lattice will be wide enough for the pie or tart. I put the baking sheet or cutting board with the lattice in the refrigerator for 30 to 45 minutes, until the dough is firm enough to lift. After filling the pie or tart shell, I remove the baking sheet from the refrigerator and carefully slide the lattice off the waxed paper and place it on top of the filled shell (sometimes the lattice is firm enough to simply lift up and place on

The Keys to a Perfect Pie Dough Circle

Truth be told, a perfect circle for a pie crust isn't really necessary, since you almost always trim the circle. But I've seen some people roll out dough that in no way resembles a circle, and this becomes a problem when you try to fit the dough in the pie pan

Test the firmness of the rested dough before you roll. Press the disk with your fingers; you should leave a slight imprint. Pastry dough that is too cold will crack when rolled, while dough that's too soft will stick to your rolling surface.

Roll "around the clock" to flatten the dough evenly. When I roll, I think of the circle of dough as the face of a clock. My first four rolls, all starting from the center, go first to 12 o' clock, then to 6 o' clock, over to 3 o' clock, and finally to 9 o' clock. After those initial strokes, I roll around the clock at "hourly" intervals until my circle has stretched to the size I want. This way, I can keep track of where I'm rolling and won't favor one area over another.

Roll the dough in one direction, not back and forth, which will toughen the dough, as will flipping it over and sprinkling it with flour.

If the dough isn't spreading, stop rolling. The dough has likely stuck to the surface; use a pastry scraper to carefully pick it up and then reflour the surface underneath.

Lighten up on the rolling pin as your reach the edges of the circle. Otherwise your edges will become too thin.

Give the pastry a quarter turn frequently. Most people apply pressure on their dominant side; rotating the dough avoids this favoritism.

To even out irregularities, angle the end of the rolling pin toward the area that needs filling. This should ease the dough to where it needs to be.

—Molly Stevens, *Fine Cooking*

top of the shell). I wait 5 to 10 minutes for the lattice to soften, then I press down on the strips to seal them to the bottom crust and flute the edge.

—Mary Jane Kaloustian, Northville, MI

Always butter the pie plate and rim before lining it with pastry

Greasing the dish holds the pastry in place, decreases shrinkage, and encourages browning.

—Carole Walter, *Fine Cooking*

Chill the dough after it has been rolled and set in the pan

Most recipes have you shape the dough into a disk, then refrigerate it for a period, for the butter to get firm again and the gluten in the dough to relax. This is all well and good, except that now you're left with a disk of very hard, chilled dough that will take so much muscle to become malleable enough to roll that the dough gets overworked and cracked. I find that rolling out the dough immediately after mixing it, shaping the pie, and chilling the crust for 15 to 20 minutes before baking *produces the perfect texture*. But if the dough round seems to be getting limp or greasy as you're working, you can just pop it into the refrigerator until it's cool enough to work with again.

—Carolyn Weil, *Fine Cooking*

Chill your pie before baking

All pie crusts, whether they're to be filled first or blind-baked, *hold their shape best* in the oven if they're chilled for half an hour before baking.

—Carole Walter, *Fine Cooking*

Heating a baking sheet for a flaky pie crust

When making a pie with an unbaked crust, put a baking sheet in the oven to heat at the same time. When the oven is hot, set the filled pie directly on the hot sheet. The crust will begin to cook on contact with the hot metal, and it will be *flakier and crisp*.

—Helen D. Conwell, Fairhope, AL

Smooth pie shells

To keep a pie shell from bubbling up when you bake it empty, or "blind," it's a good idea to put in *a liner of aluminum foil* and weigh it down. Instead of using beans, though, try filling it with pennies from the penny jar. Makes cents?

—John G. Sisson, New York, NY

A heat shield for pie crusts

To prevent pie crust from browning too much, cut out the center of a disposable *aluminum pie tin* and save the resulting ring. Lay this aluminum ring on top of your crust during cooking if the edges are becoming too brown.

—Richard Simon, Lawrence, NY

When the Mercury Goes Up, Making Pastry Gets Tricky

Summer heat makes it tough to deal with pastry dough—the butter or shortening melts and you end up with a tough pie crust. If your kitchen isn't air-conditioned, here are a few tips for keeping your pies tender and flaky.

Work in the cooler early-morning hours. If you're not a morning person, measure out your ingredients the night before so you don't goof up before your coffee kicks in.

Chill your ingredients well before mixing. Measure out the flour and chill it together with the cut-up butter or shortening; cover it with plastic wrap and it'll keep for up to 2 days.

Instead of cutting in butter, try grating it. Freeze the butter, then grate it with the food processor's shredding disk or on a box grater. The shreds can simply be mixed into the flour—no need to cut them in. If you're using shortening, shape it into a cylinder, wrap it in waxed paper, and freeze it overnight before shredding.

Chill a marble or granite work surface by filling a roasting pan (or zip-top bags) with ice and setting it on the marble for 20 minutes or so. Dry the surface thoroughly before using it for pastry.

When rolling out dough, keep a baking sheet in the fridge or freezer. If the dough begins to soften, slide the cold sheet under the dough for a quick chill. Once the dough is on the sheet, it can also be covered with plastic and put in the refrigerator.

Chill your equipment: bowls, whisks, pastry blenders, rolling pins, etc. Using cold bowls and tools keeps ingredient temperatures balanced. Stainless-steel and marble rolling pins stay the coolest.

Keep a pitcher of ice water in the refrigerator for mixing into the dough and for refreshing yourself.

Handle the dough as little as possible. Your hands will quickly warm the dough, so use a bench scraper instead whenever you can.

—Abigail Johnson Dodge and Molly Stevens, *Fine Cooking*

A foil shield for pie crusts

To keep the edges of pie crust from browning too quickly, I used to wrap little strips of foil around the rim of the pie, a tedious process. Now, I simply take a *square of foil* somewhat larger than the pie, cut a big X through the center, and place it over the pie. Then I fold back the quadrants from the center and secure the edges of the foil around the pie pan.

—Carol Spier, via email

Removing a tart ring

Set the cooled tart pan on a wide, solid base that's at least 3 inches high—*a coffee can is great.* The outer side ring will slip away from the crust. To remove the bottom, set the tart on a flat surface and carefully slide a long, thin metal spatula (an offset works best) between the shell and pan bottom.

—Abigail Johnson Dodge, *Fine Cooking*

A trick for stubborn tarts

If your tart gets stuck and won't come out of the pan without breaking, put it in the freezer for 20 to 30 minutes. The tart will release cleanly from the pan.

—Mean Chef, via CooksTalk on www.finecooking.com

Leafy cutouts enhance ordinary pumpkin pies

To decorate pumpkin or sweet potato pies, *I trace pretty leaves* (oak and maple are perfect) on a rolled piece of pastry and cut them out. I might even add food color to my egg wash and paint the pastry to look like fall leaves. Then I crinkle some aluminum foil sprayed with vegetable spray, lay the pastry leaves on the foil so they look more natural, and bake them. When the pie is done, I arrange several of my fall leaves on top of my pie.

—Jan Boyd, Victoria, British Columbia, Canada

Make quick cookies from leftover pie dough

Since so many recipes for pie and tart crusts make enough for two crusts when you only need one, I often end up with spare disks of dough. While the dough will keep for several months in the freezer, I hate to let it go to waste. Instead, I turn the dough into small, *crisp, not-too-sweet cookies* to serve with coffee. I roll the defrosted dough ¼ inch thick, cut it into 1-inch rounds or other shapes, brush with egg wash, and dust with sugar or a mix of sugar and spices (such as cinnamon, nutmeg, or cardamom), or even ground nuts, and then bake at 350°F until lightly golden around the edges.

—Molly Stevens, *Fine Cooking*

Hot filling solves a weepy pie

Why does my lemon meringue pie sometimes weep?

—Steven Turk, New Milford, CT

Abigail Johnson Dodge replies: The "weeping" is probably the result of moisture forming between the meringue and the custard. An undercooked meringue is likely to blame. When the beaten egg whites aren't cooked through completely, the proteins fail to coagulate properly. The undercooked egg white eventually begin to leak moisture, which forms a puddle between the layers.

Luckily, the remedy is a simple one. Always pile your meringue topping onto a hot filling. This way, the filling begins to cook the meringue from the bottom up while the oven's heat cooks the exterior. You'll end up with a lovely browned meringue pie that doesn't weep.

Thickening the juices in a fruit pie

Some cooks use flour to bind and thicken the juices, but I find that the texture can be a bit gritty and that the flour turns the juices slightly cloudy. I prefer to use a mix of *cornstarch and quick-cooking tapioca*, which both set clear when fully cooked and cooled. Using all cornstarch would make the filling gummy and all tapioca would make it seem dry, but the two balance each other out. The cornstarch thickens while the tapioca adds texture without making the filling too gummy. If the texture of the tapioca is too pronounced, next time try grinding it to a powder in the food processor first.

—Carolyn Weil, *Fine Cooking*

Peach pies year round

I love making peach pies in winter, so while peaches are still in season, I do the following: I make the peach pie filling. Then I line a metal pie plate with plastic wrap, fill it with my pie filling, wrap it up, and freeze it. When fully frozen, I pop out the wrapped filling (you could slip it into a large zip-top bag for extra protection) and leave it in the freezer. When I feel like making a peach pie in a hurry, I simply put the *frozen molded pie filling* in a crust and bake.

—Sandi Rekis, Westbank, British Columbia, Canada

Seven Habits of Highly Successful Fruit Pies

1. *Use a metal pie pan.* The heat penetrates faster and therefore the bottom crust has a better chance of browning. But be aware that the bottom crust of a double-crust fruit pie will never be crisp—how could it be, sitting under all that juicy fruit?

2. *Use a template to cut nicely round dough circles.* I use cardboard cake circles, but a pot lid works well too.

3. *Always add a pinch of salt to your fruit fillings.* It makes the fruit fruitier and the sweetness sweeter.

4. *Don't overfill the pie.* It's tempting to pile on the berries but more fruit releases more juices, and if the level of fruit and juices is higher than the rim of the pan, the juices will leak and spill over.

5. *Chill the filled pie for 20 minutes before baking.* This lets the butter in the dough set up and the starch in the thickeners start to absorb liquid and swell, so they'll perform better in the oven.

6. *Watch the bubbles to see when the pie's done.* Juices will probably bubble out of the slits during the latter part of baking. At first the bubbles will be fast, indicating thin juices, but later they'll get lazy and slow, meaning the juices have thickened and the pie is done.

7. *Cool the pie completely before slicing.* It's tempting to dig right in, but a hot pie will be liquid inside. You need to let the pie come to room temperature so the juices can set up and cloak the fruit properly. The ideal serving method is to cool the pie, then gently heat a slice in the oven to get the butter in the crust warm and toasty.

—Carolyn Weil, *Fine Cooking*

Avoiding the dreaded shrinking meringue

When meringues are baked in the oven, the tightening of the egg white proteins causes the meringue to shrink. It also makes the meringue difficult to cut smoothly. My solution to this problem is to *add a little cornstarch paste to the meringue.* Cornstarch prevents the egg white bonds from tightening (in the same way that it prevents eggs from curdling in pastry cream) so the meringue doesn't shrink. This tender meringue with starch cuts like a dream. To add cornstarch to a meringue, you should first dissolve it in water (dry cornstarch can't access the water in the meringue—the sugar has it all) and heat it. Dissolve 1 tablespoon cornstarch in ⅓ cup water and heat it until a thick paste forms. After all the sugar is beaten into the whites and the meringue is firm, keep the mixer running and add all the cornstarch paste, 1 teaspoon at a time.

—Shirley O. Corriher, *Fine Cooking*

Slice savory tarts ahead for a neat presentation

When you're planning to serve a warm, sliced tart that can be potentially messy, like a quiche or a cheese and vegetable tart, *cut the cooled tart before you reheat it.* This will give you the cleanest, most presentable slices. Then just reheat it in the oven and you'll have a beautifully sliced tart to present.

—Julia Deane, Rowayton, CT

Deep-Frying

Use egg whites for a crisp-fried coating

When you're deep-frying and want light, nongreasy results, egg whites are ideal, either in batter coatings, like tempura, or in dishes made from heavier batters, such as fritters and hush puppies. Yolks absorb grease, but *whites dry, puff, and don't absorb much fat* during cooking.

—Shirley O. Corriher, *Fine Cooking*

Soaking and drying potatoes for french fries

I soak my cut, raw french fries in water in my salad spinner; when I get ready to fry them, I empty the water and spin dry the potatoes. It works like a charm.

—Jim Conner, Hutchinson, MN

WHAT TO DO	WHY
Adjust the temperature to the size of the food	Small thin pieces fry quickly at high temperatures, whereas large, thick pieces need a lower temperature to ensure they'll be cooked through
Keep the pieces of food uniform in size	To ensure all food will be done at the same time
Add food to fryer in batches	Adding cold food to hot oil reduces the oil's temperature; maintaining proper frying temperature limits grease absorption
For extra-crisp fried food, prefry it at a lower temperature	If the inside is cooked, the food can be fried again quickly and at a high temperature, resulting in a brown, crisp crust
Keep the surface area of the food dry	Evaporating water lowers the fat's temperature, deteriorates the fat, and causes it to spatter
Use a fat with a high smoking point	To fry food safely and with no off flavors
Be sure the frying fat is fresh	Deteriorated fats can have an off-taste, can soak into foods faster, and can burst into flames at lower temperatures

—Shirley O. Corriher, *Fine Cooking*

Making perfect french fries

First, use baking potatoes and leave the skin on. Cut them into ¼-inch-thick slices, then cut those into ¼-inch fries, then soak them in water for at least 8 and preferably 24 hours before frying. I had always assumed this simply washed away any excess starch, but food scientist Shirley Corriher offers another reason: to plump up the cells within the potatoes to result in an improved texture. *Soak them at room temperature* rather then chilling them to prevent the starches from turning to sugar, which would make the fries brown before they're cooked. Also, you want to be sure they're dry before plunging them in the oil. The uncontested hands-down best way to make french fries is to fry them once at 300°F to cook them through, then drain, then fry then again at 375°F to brown and crisp them.

—Michael Yeamans, *Fine Cooking*

Drain fried foods in a sieve

When I deep-fry potatoes, they turn out crisper if I let them drain in a sieve set over a bowl rather than on a paper-towel-lined plate. *They also cool faster.* I now use this method of draining for any deep-fried food.

—Ines Carvalho de Azevdo, Campinas, Brazil

Drain deep-fried food on paper bags

Use a brown paper bag, folded flat, to drain fried or boiled foods. *The bag absorbs excess liquid,* but it doesn't stick to the food as paper towels sometimes do.

—Mary Sullivan, Coronado, CA

Another use for a splatter screen

I love homemade fried chicken but hate to get hit with flying splatters of burning hot grease from the frying pan. As a defense, I always wear my elbow-length oven mitts, and I hold a wire-mesh splatter screen in front of the pan when turning the chicken. The *screen prevents the spatters of hot grease* from reaching my face.

—Eva Klein, Dallas, TX

Sautéing and Pan-Frying

Dry the food for the best crust

Dry the food and season it before it hits the pan. If the surface of the food is moist, *it will release steam,* which prevents the formation of a crust.

—James Peterson, *Fine Cooking*

A hot pan is key to stick-free pan-frying

To avoid having meat stick to the pan, *heat the pan first,* then add the oil, and only once the oil is hot should you add the food. To test the oil, sprinkle a few drops of cold water on it; the water should sizzle fiercely. When you first add the meat, it will stick to the bottom of the pan if you try to move it. When a good crust has formed on the bottom, the meat will easily release from the pan surface.

—Jennifer Davis, via email

Sautéing—What Separates Amateurs from Pros

Learn to sauté well and your cooking will improve dramatically. Why? Not only are properly sautéed foods delicious on their own—a well-browned exterior adds tons of flavor, as well as an appealing color—but other cooking methods, such as braising and roasting often begin with sautéing or searing (a variation on sautéing). Here are a few tips that will greatly improve your sautéing skills.

- *Dry the food.* Before putting the food in the pan, pat off excess moisture with paper towels; otherwise the food will steam rather than brown.

- *Turn up the heat.* The most important factor for a good sauté is heat—and lots of it. Though restaurant chefs may have a few extra BTUs on their burners, most home chefs don't even turn the heat to high. "People are afraid of heat," notes Gordon Hamersley, chef and owner of Hamersley's Bistro of Boston, adding, "In our house, the heat is either on or off." Put the food in the pan only when the pan and the fat in it are searingly hot (but not smoking). Then moderate the heat so the food is constantly sizzling but not burning.

- *Don't crowd the pan.* Be sure you can see the bottom of the pan between the pieces of food. Too much food will lower the temperature of the pan, creating a lot of steam, meaning you won't get good browning.

- *Let the food sit in the hot pan before tossing or turning it.* A common mistake is to fidget with the food, turning and poking at it constantly. To promote browning, leave the food alone—for as long as a few minutes for some foods—before you move it or flip it.

—Joanne McAllister Smart, *Fine Cooking*

A baking sheet is handy for dredging

When I dredge food for sautéing or frying, I set a bowl of egg wash in the center of a rimmed baking sheet. Then I scoop the flour and bread crumbs directly onto the baking sheet on either side of the bowl. This *leaves me with a clean counter* and fewer dishes to wash.

—Karen Brack, Garland, TX

Quick and convenient flour dusting

When a recipe calls for ½ cup flour for dusting pieces of fish or meat, the dusting really uses only 1 or 2 tablespoons of flour. To add convenience and avoid waste, I saved one of those square, jumbo-size, *clear plastic jars with a shaker lid* and put in 2 cups flour, 2 teaspoons salt, and 1 teaspoon ground black pepper. Whenever a recipe calls for dredging in seasoned flour, I just reach for my jar and shake some out.

—Madeline DeBlase, Stamford, CT

Perfectly shaped patties for pan-frying

To make uniform, round crab cakes, potato cakes, or falafel patties, use *a two-piece lid from a Ball canning jar*. Fill and pack the lid with the mix. Then shave off the excess with the back of a knife. Push up on the removable disk of the lid to get the patty out, slide it off the lid, and it's ready for pan frying.

—Bill Kasenchar, via email

Sautéing skin-on fish fillets

The skin on thin fish fillets, such as red snapper or trout, can shrink during cooking and cause the fillets to twist or curl as they're sautéing. To prevent this, I use a small, sharp knife to make a couple of very shallow, *1-inch-wide cuts in an X pattern* on the fish skin before I sauté them so they stay nice and flat as they cook.

—Bettina Small, Del Mar, CA

Add butter at the end of sautéing

When I'm sautéing vegetables like mushrooms or zucchini over high heat, I can use either olive oil or clarified butter (since unclarified butter would burn). But to get the buttery flavor without going though the fuss of clarifying it, I sometimes cheat: *I saute with oil but then add in butter at the end* of cooking.

—Ian Folger, Chicago, IL

Use scissors to cut chicken into stir-fry strips

I use scissors to cut the fat off chicken and to slice the meat into thin strips for stir-fries. I find that *I waste less and have better control* over the thickness of the slices. I also use scissors to cut herbs—not just chives, but also basil and parsley.

—Kathy Slavics, Eden Praire, MN

Lightly flour meat or seafood before stir-frying

One trick I use when stir-frying is to lightly coat the meat or seafood with flour (I shake off any excess) before frying it. I find that the flour helps the meat or seafood *brown more easily and keeps it moist*, and the flour thickens the sauce nicely when the liquid is added at the end.

—Jennifer Davis, via email

Add a little water to a dry stir-fry or sauté

When I'm stir-frying or sautéing something in its juices, in oil, or in its own marinade, the liquid or fat will often evaporate or be absorbed by the food. Instead of adding more oil or butter to the pan, I just add a tablespoon or two of water. This *won't affect the taste* and will add moisture to the food so it will finish cooking properly. Any residual moisture will evaporate in the end.

—Jo-Anne McArthur, Toronto, Ontario, Canada

Roasting Chicken and Turkey

Easier carving without the wishbone

For a chicken or turkey that's easier to carve, remove the wishbone before roasting the bird. You'll be able to *cut larger, neater slices of breast meat* without hitting any obstructions. To remove the wishbone, first find it with your fingers (it's behind the neck skin). Using the tip of a small paring knife, cut through the flesh just deep enough to free the bone on both sides, leaving it attached at its three points. Then hook your finger underneath and pull out the bone.

—Debra Rich, Sarasota, FL

Avoid soggy stuffing by drying the bread

If the bread isn't dried, it will become sodden, making the stuffing mushy. You can dry bread cubes by *spreading them out on a baking sheet* and leaving them out uncovered overnight or heating them in a low (275°F) oven until they feel dry, about 15 minutes. The exception is cornbread, which needs only to cool completely before being broken into large crumbs.

—Molly Stevens, *Fine Cooking*

Damming the stuffing

Instead of trussing a turkey or chicken to keep in the stuffing, I cover the stuffing with a *heel from a loaf of bread*. This seals in the stuffing and keeps the juices from dripping out.

—Betsy Schwartz, Greenwich, CT

A better way to stuff (and unstuff) a bird

Before I stuff a chicken or turkey, I line the empty cavity with *a layer of rinsed cheesecloth*—and then I add the stuffing. This makes removing the cooked stuffing much easier. Instead of digging around with a spoon, I simply grab the edges of the cheesecloth and pull out all the stuffing at once.

—Kim Marchuk, Vancouver, British Columbia, Canada

The best pan for the best results

The best pan for cooking a turkey is a heavy-duty roasting pan with about 2-inch sides. Higher sides prevent the lower part of the bird from browning and can make basting difficult. *Heavy-gauge metal* helps keep the drippings from burning.

—Molly Stevens, *Fine Cooking*

Secure legs with a paper clip

Whenever I roast a whole turkey or chicken, I can never find string to secure the legs. So instead, *I unfold a large paper clip* so that it resembles a large "C." I then secure the legs by bending the clip around the legs and pushing the clips ends into the meat at a 45-degree angle. It's quick and easy, and I don't have to worry about string or scissors.

—Bob Simms, Granada Hills, CA

Position your bird for even cooking

Start your turkey with the legs pointing toward the back of the oven, where it's the hottest. If your turkey is large, the hot air may have trouble circulating and may create hot spots. If one part of the bird is browning too quickly, rotate the pan during roasting. *Tent the bird with foil* about two-thirds of the way through to prevent overbrowning.

—Molly Stevens, *Fine Cooking*

Turning for an evenly cooked bird

To get moist breast meat when roasting a whole turkey or chicken is simple. Start the bird cooking with the breast side down. After about a third of the total estimated cooking time, turn it over and finish as usual. You can use very large forks on the neck and tail ends of the bird to flip it over, or I like to just pick it up with oven mitts–I put a square of foil on each end of the bird and hold it there so the mitts don't get wet. (Then I remove the foil.) The bird will cook evenly, with the dark meat fully cooked and the breast still moist. *The skin also browns evenly* over the whole bird.

—Kathy Bindert, Manhasset, NY

For the best basting

For basting a turkey, *a wide spoon works even better* than a turkey baster, especially at the start when there's little juice.

—*Fine Cooking* editors

TURKEY MATH

For birds under 16 pounds, figure at least 1 pound of turkey per person. For birds 16 pounds and heavier, figure a bit less since there's more meat in proportion to bone. If you want substantial seconds and leftovers, allow another ½ pound per person.

TURKEY WEIGHT (IN POUNDS)	AVERAGE SERVINGS	AMPLE SERVINGS WITH LEFTOVERS
14	14	9
16	16	10
18	20	12
20	22	14
24	26	17

—*Fine Cooking* editors

COOKING TIMES* FOR A
STUFFED TURKEY AT 325°F

WEIGHT	TIME	WEIGHT	TIME
8 to 12 pounds	3 to 4 hours	16 to 20 pounds	4½ to 5 hours
12 to 16 pounds	4 to 4½ hours	20 to 26 pounds	5 to 6 hours

*Subtract 20 to 40 minutes for an unstuffed bird.

—Molly Stevens, *Fine Cooking*

Paper-covered turkey is moister

To cook a moist turkey, roast at 450°F for 30 minutes, then reduce the heat to 350°F and cover the turkey with a tented brown paper bag. To make the tent, cut off one large side of a large brown paper grocery bag. Then *brush the bag all over with peanut or vegetable oil* until saturated. Remove the tent for the last 20 minutes of roasting to crisp up the turkey's skin.

—Virginia Teichner, Ridgefield, CT

Save stuffing from scorching

During the last hour or so of roasting, a bird's exposed stuffing often cooks more quickly than the rest of the roaster, and sometimes it burns. To keep the stuffing from scorching during the final stretch of roasting time, *cover the cavity with a small piece of aluminum foil.*

—Anne Disrude, Jersey City, NJ

How do you get it out of the pan?

To get the turkey out of its roasting pan, stick the handle of *a thick wooden spoon* in the large cavity between the stuffing (if your bird is stuffed) and the underside of the breastbone.

—*Fine Cooking* editors

Rest roast chicken on a rack, not on its juices

After roasting a chicken, let it rest on *a rack over a platter* while you make your pan sauce. This way the chicken doesn't end up sitting in its own juices and softening its nice crisp skin.

—Daniel Fredette, Herndon, VA

Don't Overstuff the Bird—And Other Tips for Safe Stuffing

Because an improperly stuffed or uncooked bird can cause illness, follow these guidelines for safe stuffing:

- *Stuff the bird just before roasting.* You can make the stuffing in advance, but bring it to room temperature before stuffing the bird because a cold stuffing will slow down the cooking. If you like to add egg to your stuffing, don't add it until just before stuffing the bird.

- *Pack the stuffing loosely.* The stuffing expands as it absorbs juices, and if it's too tightly packed, it won't cook through. I generally leave enough room to fit my whole extended hand into the bird's cavity. Any extra stuffing gets cooked alongside the bird in a casserole dish.

- *Cook the stuffing in the bird to 160° to 165°F.* Check it with an instant-read thermometer inserted all the way into the center of the stuffing. If the bird is done before the stuffing is, take the bird out of the oven but spoon the stuffing into a casserole dish and continue to bake while the bird rests before carving.

—Molly Stevens, *Fine Cooking*

Carving turkey breast

For the best-looking slices of turkey breast, and for easier carving, I remove the whole breast from a roast turkey (after it sits for 30 minutes to cool and to let the juices redistribute). I usually remove the breast after I've cut off the legs and wings. To cut off the breast, I place the knife on one side of the breastbone near the neck and cut toward the tail. As I cut between the bone and the meat, I pry the breast meat away with my hand or a spoon. I can then slice the breast like a roast, perpendicular to the grain, making the slices as thick or as thin as I like. The resulting *slices are more uniform* than conventionally carved turkey-breast slices.

—Gary Turzilli, Continental Chef, New York, NY

Rest roasted chicken upside down for juicy white meat

Most good cooks know that after roasting a whole chicken, it should be allowed to rest for 10 to 15 minutes before carving. I found that resting the chicken breast side down on its roasting rack allows the juices that would normally accumulate in its back to flow to the chicken's breast, making for *juicier, more succulent breast meat*.

—Philip May, via email

Use two skewers for kebabs

When preparing kebabs of meat, seafood, or vegetables, pierce the food with two parallel skewers. This way, the food turns in unison when you turn the skewers with tongs, rather than spinning around the axis of a single skewer. The *food cooks evenly* and the kebabs are easier to manipulate.

—Brian Patterson, Silver Spring, MD

Little metal "skewers" won't burn on the grill

I love to make hors d'oeuvres like bacon-wrapped shrimp or chicken satay on the grill. Wooden skewers always seemed to char, no matter how long I soak them in water. So, recently, I bought a few dozen *metal turkey lacers*. They're the perfect size for skewering appetizers, and they don't burn.

—Michaela Rosenthal, Woodland Hills, CA

Soak and freeze your bamboo skewers

To have bamboo skewers always ready for grilling, soak a bundle of skewers in water for 20 minutes, drain, lightly pat them dry, and then wrap them in plastic wrap. Secure with a rubber band or put them in a bag and keep them in the freezer. You'll always have *soaked skewers ready for the grill*.

—Dorothy Patton, Salt Spring Island, British Columbia, Canada

Season ahead for succulent pork chops

I buy center-cut boneless chops in large family packs, which are less expensive. Then I rub the pork chops with my favorite salt-free spice mix before sealing them in one layer in zip-top bags and putting them in the freezer. Once thawed, *the chops are well seasoned and ready for the grill*.

—Jim Moudy, via email

Parcook large onions before grilling

I love the sweet taste of grilled onions, but with their high sugar content, they often burn before they're cooked through. To prevent this, I slice the onions in half through the stem and *microwave them on high for 3 minutes*. Then I brush the onions with olive oil and set them, flat side down, on the grill over an area of lower heat. I can then forget about them while grilling the rest of my dinner, and the onions will brown slowly and stay nice and juicy.

—Diane T. Farrell, South Wayne, WI

Say you're following a grilling recipe that instructs you to build a very hot charcoal fire. "Okay, fine," you say, "but how do I know when the fire is very hot?" Believe it or not, you use your hand.

To test the heat level of your fire, hold your open palm an inch or two above the grill grate. The length of time you can stand the heat tells you how hot the grill is. (For best results, the grilling grate should be about 4 inches above the coals.) This test works for gas grills as well.

TIME HAND CAN BE HELD OVER GRILL	GRILL HEAT	TEMPERATURE
Less than 1 second	Very hot	600°F
1 to 2 seconds	Hot	400° to 500°F
3 to 4 seconds	Medium	350° to 375°F
5 to 7 seconds	Medium low	325° to 350°F

You can also tell something about the heat of a charcoal fire by looking at it. Bright red flaming coals are extremely hot—too hot for most grilling. Red coals covered with light ash are still fairly hot but suitable for high heat grilling. Coals thickly covered with yellowish ash are medium hot.

—Susie Middleton, *Fine Cooking*

An unconventional way to start charcoal

I buy cheap, bulk bags of unseasoned potato chips from my local warehouse store to light the charcoal for my grill. The chips are more affordable than fire-starting bricks, and they usually don't taste very good, so I don't feel bad about burning them. The grease-soaked chips have a large surface area to volume ratio, and they burn hot enough to start even hardwood charcoal thoroughly. Unlike lighter fluid, *potato chips don't contain any harmful additives*, and this is also a great way to get rid of old, stale chips. Just put a generous layer of potato chips under the coals and light them in various places. If you use a chimney charcoal starter, put a sheet of newspaper on the bottom grate, followed by the chips and then the charcoal; this prevents the smaller chips from falling through the grate.

—Austin Liu, San Leandro, CA

Smoke food on the grill with a hunk of wood

I never use water-soaked smoking chips while grilling because the chips produce more steam than smoke and quickly dry out and burn up. Instead, I use a chunk of hardwood around 8 to 10 inches long and about 2 inches thick. *I wrap the wood loosely in a double layer of foil* and poke holes in it for the smoke to escape. When set on the coals, the foil-wrapped wood provides a lot of smoke for a long time but it can't burst into flame because the foil prevents it from getting enough oxygen. A side benefit is that when you open the foil later on, you'll find a nice piece of charcoal to start your next grilling job.

—Vic Bastien, Tulsa, OK

Soak wood chips in fruit juice for more flavor

I get great flavors from the grill by *soaking my barbecue wood chips* in either apple juice (nice with pork), pineapple juice (try it with wood-roasted fish), cranberry juice, or orange juice (a favorite with chicken). I'll never go back to soaking my wood chips in water again.

—Grant Grizzard, Nashville, TN

Nut shells create a flavorful smoke

We save our nut shells and toss them onto hot briquettes in our grill. The smoldering shells give *a unique smoky flavor* to anything grilled or barbecued.

—Sharon R. Howard, Eugene, OR

Use that rake

A *garden rake* is handy for arranging hot coals in your grill.

—Molly Stevens, *Fine Cooking*

Avoid sticking

I lightly oil the grill just before cooking. The touch of oil helps prevent sticking; it also *leaves nicely defined grill marks* on the food.

—Molly Stevens, *Fine Cooking*

Mayonnaise keeps grilled fish from sticking

Brush a teaspoon of mayonnaise on each side of a fish fillet before grilling; it *keeps the fish moist* and prevents it from sticking to the grill. Also, although you can't see or taste the mayonnaise after grilling, if you add herbs to the mayonnaise, they'll flavor the fish.

—June Cerrito, Wakefield, RI

Prepare the grill with a potato...

To keep delicate fish from sticking when you're grilling, try this trick on a clean, hot grill. Cut a raw baking potato in half, stab it through the skin with a long-handled fork, and rub the cut surface of the potato along the hot grill several times. The *potato starch creates a sort of nonstick coating*.

—Steve Aberle, Birch Creek, AK

...Or with an onion

When my grilling recipes involve an onion, I save the *root end to clean and flavor the grill* and to prevent food from sticking. Here's how: Slice off a thicker portion of the root than usual before peeling the onion. After allowing the grill to heat up, stick a barbecue fork through the root portion of the onion. Dip the onion in a bit of olive oil flavored with garlic, then rub the cut end on the grates of the grill.

—Yaron Kaminski, Ridgefield, CT

An easier way to grill salmon

My husband and I have tried grilling salmon fillets, starting skin side up and skin side down, and we've had problems with both methods. Now we've come up with a technique that really works well. We *cut our salmon fillet into individual slices* (we call them "chops"), each about 1¼ inches wide, leaving the skin on. Then we put the "chops" on the grill on their side, with the skin facing out. (We like to use a grill screen.) We cook these pieces about 5 minutes on each side over a medium-hot fire. The skin helps hold the salmon together, and we always have delicious, moist salmon, already cut into perfect portions.

—Judy Megan, Woodbury, CT

Stick-free grilled chicken

To keep my grilled chicken from sticking, I always start grilling it skin side up. When the chicken skin starts to cook, it *releases enough fat* to keep it from sticking to the grill, so I can turn the chicken pieces over and get those nice grill marks without fearing that the chicken will glue itself to the grill.

—Beth Combs, Seattle, WA

Keep grilled chicken moist and flavorful

When I recently visited my parents in Palm Harbor, Florida, I picked up a neat barbecue tip. My father was grilling chicken and wanted to keep it moist, so he placed a *small pan of water in the grill* and added a handful of thyme and rosemary sprigs to the water. The herbs added a great flavor and fragrance to everything cooked on the grill, while the steam from the water kept the chicken moist.

—Catherine Florko, Tallahassee, FL

Grill chicken in a cake pan

Everyone knows about beer-can chicken, but what about cake-pan chicken? I rub a whole chicken, inside and out, with olive oil, crushed garlic, salt, and pepper; then I slide the tail end of the chicken over the hollow tube of a heavy-duty angel food pan. (The pan shouldn't have a removable bottom.) I pour ½ cup each of chicken broth and white wine into the pan, set it on a hot grill, and close the lid. The *chicken cooks evenly*, and the cake pan catches flavorful drippings, which you can use to make a sauce.

—Linda Hildahl, Sioux City, IA

Avoid cross-contamination

Keep a separate, *clean platter for cooked foods*. Don't reuse the container that held raw meats of fish. Keep two pairs of tongs on hand—one for handling raw meats and fish on the grill and another for removing the cooked food. If reusing a marinade for basting, first boil it for at least 1 minute to kill any bacteria it may have picked up from the raw meat and don't apply it until you have seared both sides of the food on the grill.

—Maryellen Driscoll, *Fine Cooking*

Don't crowd the grill

Leave enough room around each piece of food for *air to circulate* so that the food sears properly and so that your fire has the air it needs to fuel it.

— *Fine Cooking* editors

Save the glaze and sauce for the end

Brush on barbecue sauces and sweet glazes *toward the end of cooking.* They'll burn if they're put on early in the grilling.

— *Fine Cooking* editors

Cover grilled food for faster cooking

When grilling, take a tip from short-order cooks and keep a *high-domed lid* (like a wok lid) on hand to cover food so it cooks more quickly without having to close the whole grill. This technique helps me serve grilled steaks cooked medium rare to well done, all at the same time.

—Paul Vinett, Norwalk, CT

Use leftover hot coals to roast peppers

When you've finished grilling steaks or chicken but your *coals are still hot*, put some bell peppers on the grill to roast. Cover the grill and close the air vents (or turn off the gas). In an hour and a half to two hours, the peppers will be nicely roasted.

—Liz Bader, White Plains, NY

Getting it clean

Close the lid after grilling. This will help burn some of the residue off the grate.

—Maryellen Driscoll, *Fine Cooking*

A reminder to turn off the grill

My husband has, on occasion, forgotten to turn off our gas grill after grilling our dinner. We've solved this problem by keeping *a red plastic poker chip* with the matches. When he gets the matches to light the grill, he puts the poker chip on the kitchen counter. The chip's bright color makes it quite noticeable. We've made it a rule not to put the chip away until one of us double-checks the grill after dinner. Once we make sure the grill is turned off, we put the chip back with the matches for next time.

—Patty Ross, Kerrville, TX

Beans

Look out for "floaters"

In the process of turning from fresh beans to dried, beans sometimes shrink within their skins, creating *air pockets that may hide dirt*. You can't tell if your beans have shrunk just by looking at them, but the trapped air will make the beans buoyant enough to float. Skim off any floaters.

—David Tanis, *Fine Cooking*

HOW LONG TO COOK DRIED BEANS
ON THE STOVETOP

In general, you should have 3 to 4 cups of water for each 1 cup of beans. Count on getting 2 to 2½ cups of cooked beans for every 1 cup of dried beans. Below are approximate times for conventional stovetop cooking.

TYPE	WATER	COOKING TIME
Adzuki		
unsoaked	4 cups	90 minutes
soaked	4 cups	60 minutes
Black (turtle)		
soaked	4 cups	90 minutes
Black-eyed peas		
soaked	3 cups	60 minutes
Chickpeas		
soaked	4 cups	2 to 3 hours
Great Northern		
soaked	3 cups	90 minutes
Kidney		
soaked	3 cups	60 minutes

TYPE	WATER	COOKING TIME
Lentils		
unsoaked	3 cups	60 to 90 minutes
soaked	3 cups	45 minutes
Lima		
soaked	3 cups	60 minutes
Navy		
soaked	3 cups	60 minutes
Pinto		
soaked	3 cups	2 to 2½ hours
Soy		
soaked	4 cups	3 to 4 hours
soaked	3 cups	45 minutes

OTHER COOKING METHODS

PRESSURE COOKER (USE ABOUT 2½ CUPS WATER PER 1 CUP BEANS)
Soaked: 20 to 30 minutes; unsoaked: 40 to 50 minutes

MICROWAVE
Soaked: 50 minutes

SLOW COOKER
Unsoaked: 12 hours on low

—Shirley O. Corriher, *Fine Cooking*

Tough truths about cooking beans

If beans have been stored at high temperatures (about 100°F) and high humidity (80%), chemical changes occur that make them almost impossible to soften. You can often avoid this situation by *keeping dried beans in an airtight container* and a cool place. You may have heard the myth that salt hampers beans' ability to soften. I don't know how this rumor started, but it isn't true. The fact is that soaking beans in salted water before cooking can help rectify the hard-to-cook situation. The next time you have a recalcitrant batch of beans, try soaking them in salted water (1 tablespoon salt per gallon of water) for 2 hours. There are certain ingredients that can prevent beans from softening. Normally when fruits and vegetables are cooked, heat causes the insoluble pectic substances (the "glue" between the cells) to convert to water-soluble pectins, which dissolve. The cells then separate and the fruit or vegetable softens. Both calcium and sugar, however, hinder this conversion to pectin, so when beans are cooked with an ingredient containing these substances, such as molasses, the beans won't get overly soft. That's why Boston baked beans can be cooked for hours and still retain their shape. If you cooked the same beans without the molasses, you would have "refried" beans (bean mush). Cooking beans in "hard" water, which contains calcium, also prevents softening.

—Shirley O. Corriher, *Fine Cooking*

Eggs

A warm pan keeps scrambled eggs from sticking

Heat the empty pan first, which will expand the metal and effectively "seal" any nicks or imperfections in the pan, so your *eggs will cook on the surface*, not below it. Your pan is hot enough when you can feel the heat on the upper edge of the pan. I then spray it lightly with a nonstick cooking spray and return it to medium or low heat before adding the eggs. After you add the beaten eggs to the pan, let them sit untouched for a full minute and they will puff magnificently. The egg holds on to trapped air, which expands when heated. If you stir the egg vigorously immediately after they go into the pan, you'll stir all the air out the egg and end up with small curds and not much volume. After the eggs have puffed, gently push one edge to the center to allow the uncooked eggs to flow into the bare pan. Do this until no liquid eggs flow to the edge and you have a pan of soft mounds that still look moist.

—Shirley O. Corriher, *Fine Cooking*

Start with the freshest eggs for poaching and make sure they're cold

As eggs age, a lot of things are happening inside that porous shell. Moisture and air are moving from inside the shell to the outside environment, and vice versa. During this time, the egg white, also called albumen, thins. You don't want a thin albumen for poached eggs because it won't hold its shape as well as a thick one. A thicker white will also cling to the yolk better. Another benefit of fresh eggs: they have *a stronger yolk that's less likely to break*. Poach the eggs straight from the fridge. Adding cold eggs to hot water is a good move for a couple of reasons. Eggs are noticeably more viscous when cold and so will hold their shape better when added to the hot water. Also, starting with a cold egg will promote slow cooking so that the yolk will still be runny when the white is completely set.

—Robert Danhi, *Fine Cooking*

Get set for poaching

Getting the egg to set quickly is important when poaching. Both acid and salt make proteins in an egg denature faster, so *add a little vinegar or salt* (or both) to the cooking water.

—Shirley O. Corriher, *Fine Cooking*

Poach eggs in a steamer basket

After trying all the traditional ways to poach eggs, such as adding vinegar to water and using those silly little metal circles, my husband came up with this method. He puts my Calphalon℠ steamer basket in its pan and brings about an inch of water to a boil. He then butters four or five ramekins, cracks an egg into each one, and puts the ramekins in the steamer basket. He covers the pot and "steams" the eggs for exactly 3.5 minutes and ends up with *moist, perfectly rounded poached eggs* to use in eggs Benedict, or whatever recipe calls for them.

—Joyce Lehman-Sharpe, Longwood, FL

Poach leftover egg yolks

I recently prepared a recipe that called for egg whites, and I had several intact egg yolks left over. Instead of putting them in the fridge and forgetting about them, I *poached them in simmering water* just as I would whole eggs, until they were firmly cooked, and then I crumbled them into a potato salad.

—Jeanne Schimmel, via email

Centered egg yolk

When cooking hard-boiled eggs, *gently twirl the eggs around* while they cook. This centers the yolks and makes deviled eggs look better.

—Mary Jane Kaloustian, Northville, MI

Perfect hard-cooked eggs

For perfect cooking, start with *eggs that don't have any visible cracks.* If they've been refrigerated, warm the eggs for 4 to 5 minutes in hot tap water. By bringing them to room temperature, they're much less likely to crack in the hot water. In case small cracks do develop, add salt to the cooking water. The salt will help to speed up the denaturing of the egg white, causing less of it to feather into the water. Use at least 1 tablespoon of table salt per 2 quarts water. Overcooking causes a green layer to form around the yolk, a reaction between the iron in the yolk and the sulfur in the white. Heat speeds up this reaction, so the longer your eggs cook, the greater the chance of discoloration. Finally, the higher pH of an older egg makes the shell come off easier. That's why I don't recommend, as some cooks do, adding vinegar to the cooking water, since it would reduce the natural alkalinity of the slightly older eggs.

—Shirley O. Corriher, *Fine Cooking*

Easy-peel eggs

When I make egg salad, I find it's easier and quicker to peel the hard-cooked eggs by leaving them in the pan they've cooked in (drain the cooking water first), putting the lid on, and *shaking the pan* vigorously. You'll hear the eggs smashing against each other and against the inside of the pan. Once the sound of smashing eggshells stops, remove the pan lid and lift the eggs from the loose strips of broken eggshells, giving the eggs a quick rinse to remove any bits of clinging shell.

—Kathleen B. Jenks, Westfield, MA

Hard-cooked eggs at the ready

Many times I'd wished I had a chilled hard-cooked egg for a salad or a garnish, and now I've found a way to keep them handy. I cook the eggs as usual and crack them slightly when they're done. Then I immediately *submerge them in an ice bath* and put the bowl of ice water with the eggs into the refrigerator. There's no egg odor in the fridge because the eggs are in water. When I need an egg, I remove it from the water and peel it. This way, I can make and store the eggs several hours in advance.

—Jane Norris, Hilton Head, SC

Doughnut hamburgers?

It's always a challenge to get hamburgers to cook evenly: by the time the center is done how I like it, the edges are overcooked. I recently heard of an interesting solution from a chef on television. Shape the beef into a patty, then *poke a small hole (about ½ inch) in the center* so it looks like a doughnut. The whole patty cooks at the same rate this way and during cooking, the hole shrinks to almost nothing.

—Ned Jenkins, New York, NY

Use a potato masher to mix ground meat

I often make meatloaf because my family likes it, but I hate mixing the ingredients by hand because it's so messy. I've found that *an old-fashioned potato masher* (the kind with an S-shaped wire) works beautifully to mix the ground meat, bread crumbs, and eggs together—just gently mash the ingredients together as you would mash potatoes, scraping the bowl occasionally with a rubber spatula.

—Carol Ogren, St. Paul, MN

Melt-in-your-mouth meatballs

For extra-tender meatballs, try *soaking bread crumbs in lukewarm water* until thoroughly moist. Squeeze out the excess water before kneading the crumbs into your ground meat.

—Irene Moretti, Ridgeville, Ontario, Canada

Try short ribs in chili

I usually make chili with beef chunks that I cut myself from a steak or chuck roast. This produces *a stew with beefier flavor* than I could get using ground beef, but it also takes more time and effort to do the cutting and browning of the meat. The last time I was in the mood for chili, I tried another variation: I bought four small short ribs, browned them, and put them in with the chili to simmer. The beef flavor was wonderful.

—Jennifer Winston, LaGrange, NY

Roast meats without a rack

A tasty way to keep roasts off the bottom of the roasting pan without a rack is to *set the meat atop* several celery ribs or carrots cut lengthwise.

—R. B. Himes, Vienna, OH

SAFE BUT NOT OVERCOOKED

The proper handling and cooking of meats and poultry is crucial for preventing foodborne illness. The USDA has guidelines for the safe cooking of meats and poultry, but as a government agency, it's more interested in being foolproof than in cooking flavorful foods and its guidelines actually exceed safe cooking temperatures by several degrees, potentially resulting in dry, overcooked meat.

Although small children, pregnant women, the elderly, and people with compromised immune systems are naturally more at risk than others to foodborne illnesses and should follow USDA guidelines, most people can safely cook meat and poultry following the *Fine Cooking* guidelines below. Our guidelines adhere to the *2001 Food Code*, a set of food safety statutes issued by the FDA for food-service establishments.

Use an instant-read thermometer in the center of the food. For maximum juiciness, allow cooked meats and poultry to rest for 10 to 15 minutes before carving so their internal juices have a chance to redistribute. The larger the cut of meat or poultry, the more the internal temperature will continue to rise during the resting period (a phenomenon known as carryover cooking), so to compensate, subtract about 5°F from the temperature for larger roasts.

—Rob Gavel, *Fine Cooking*

USDA RECOMMENDED INTERNAL TEMPERATURE	*FINE COOKING* RECOMMENDED INTERNAL TEMPERATURE
CHICKEN AND TURKEY (WHOLE AND PARTS*)	
180°F (170°F for breasts)	Breast: 160° to 165°F; thigh: 170° to 175°F
BEEF, VEAL, AND LAMB (STEAKS AND ROASTS*)	
Rare: not recommended	Rare: 125° to 130°F
Medium rare: 145°F	Medium rare: 130° to 135°F
Medium: 160°F	Medium: 140° to 150°F
Well done: 170°F	Medium well: 155° to 165°F
Well done: not recommended	
FRESH PORK (CHOPS AND ROASTS*)	
Medium: 160°F	Medium: 145° to 150°F
Well done: 170°F	Medium well: 155° to 165°F

*Both the USDA and *Fine Cooking* recommend cooking all ground meats to a minimum of 160°F; ground turkey, 170°F

The best cuts for a perfect roast beef

A rib roast, cut from the loin, makes a wonderful roast. Other cuts suitable for roasting include top round, rump, and the outsize steamship round, but they are tougher than rib roast and so need to be cooked carefully and sliced thin. A boneless roast may be easier to carve, but I fine the bones add flavor and keep the meat moist. Cutting out the bones also severs the muscle fibers, so valuable juices can escape during cooking. When buying a bone-in roast, allow at least ¾ pound per person; for a boneless roast, allow ½ pound per person. Look for beef that's well marbled, meaning that it has heavy streaks of internal fat. This fat helps baste the meat while it cooks, keeping it moist and adding to its flavor. The roast should be trimmed of the bluish sinews and excess fat, but be sure you're left with a thin layer of surface fat to keep the roast moist. *The size of the pan should suit the roast* so that the meat neither stews in too small a pan nor dries and shrinks in one too large. The pan should have a heavy bottom and sides about 2 inches high, which retain the meat's drippings but don't shield the meat from the dry heat of the oven. Always keep the fat side up; as the fat renders, it also helps baste the meat. To keep the meat moist, I baste it often.

—Anne Willan, *Fine Cooking*

Freeze meat drippings from roasts for Yorkshire pudding anytime

I love Yorkshire pudding, but I don't always have on hand the meat drippings needed to make it. Consequently, whenever I make a roast, *I freeze the extra juices and fat in a mini ice-cube tray*. Now, anytime I want to cook up a batch of Yorkshire pudding, I just melt a cube of drippings in each muffin cup and proceed as usual.

—R. B. Himes, Vienna, OH

An easy way to save carving juices

When carving a steak or a grilled butterflied leg of lamb, I find I save clean-up time—and I don't lose any delicious meat juices—by carving the meat on a *cutting board set inside a rimmed baking sheet* on the countertop. Juices run off the board onto the baking sheet, and they can then be poured back onto the meat or discarded without mopping up the counter. To keep both the carving board and baking sheet from moving while carving, I lay a wet paper towel under each one.

—Elise Quimby, Bridgehampton, NY

Simulate grilling in the broiler

I use the ridged side of my cast-iron griddle pan to broil steaks. I heat the griddle under the broiler, ridged side up; when the pan is really hot, I put the steak on it. The heat from the broiler cooks the steak and the ridges on the griddle give me *nice grill marks* on the steak. The pan also lets the fat drain away.

—Steve Hunter, Norwalk, CT

Pasta

Roll pasta dough so your hand shows through

When making your own pasta, roll the dough so it is *thin enough that you can just about see the outline of your hand* through the sheet of pasta. Also, handle the pasta sheets with your wrists, not your fingers. The rolled-out dough sheets aren't fragile but to avoid puncturing or tearing them, it's best to move one around by letting it drape over your wrist and the back of your hand.

—Alan Tardi, *Fine Cooking*

Avoid the cold when making pasta

Because cold temperatures will *reduce the elasticity of the dough*, you should never make or knead pasta dough on an inherently cold surface, such as marble or stainless steel. Egg pasta dough is traditionally kneaded on a wooden surface, but many synthetic surfaces work just as well.

—Giuliano Hazan, *Fine Cooking*

The only pasta cooking tip you'll ever need

What's the secret to perfect pasta? Oil in the water? Butter? No, the only trick is to *use enough water*. For 1 pound of pasta, use 4 quarts water, with about 2 tablespoons salt; for anything under 1 pound, use 3 quarts water, never less, and 1½ tablespoons salt; for anything over a pound, increase the water by 1 quart per ½ pound and the salt by ½ tablespoon per quart. You need enough water so that the pasta moves around in the pot, which lets it cook evenly in the water.

—Bruce Weinstein and Mark Scarbrough, *Fine Cooking*

Add salt to the pasta water

Unsalted pasta will be bland, no matter how much seasoning you add to the finished dish; add enough salt to make the water taste *seawater salty.*

—Molly Stevens, *Fine Cooking*

Stick-free strategy

To keep pasta from sticking, *stir during the first minute* or two of cooking. This is the crucial time when the pasta surface is coated with sticky, glue-like starch. If you don't stir, pieces of pasta that are touching one another literally cook together.

—Shirley O. Corriher, *Fine Cooking*

Just a spritz for no-stick pasta

I'd like to offer an alternative (to pouring oil in the water) that keeps pasta from sticking without "greasing the pasta." I lightly spritz oil from a spray can (or atomizer) *over the top of the water* (a second or less—just enough to be visible on the water's surface). This floats on the surface and then lightly coats each piece of pasta as it passes through the film, without creating so thick a layer of oil that it causes a problem later.

—Liz England-Kennedy, via email

Oil the pasta pot before adding water

Many people add a bit of oil to the water before boiling pasta to reduce sticking. But I pour the oil into *the bottom of the pot* and swirl it around before adding the water, instead of the other way around. I find that when I do this, the pasta is even less likely to stick to the bottom of the pot.

—R. B. Himes, Vienna, OH

Don't rinse pasta

Never rinse either dried or fresh pasta after cooking, as *this removes its surface starches,* which add texture to the finished dish and help the sauce cling to the pasta.

—*Fine Cooking* editors

Draining pasta

After boiling pasta, I don't like carrying a heavy pot of hot water to the sink for draining. Instead, I set a colander in a large bowl on an adjacent burner and ladle the cooked pasta into it with a *Chinese wire skimmer or tongs.* I pour out the pasta water after it has cooled.

—Meri Green, Wilmington, DE

Give cooked pasta a quick dip to reheat

When I'm cooking pasta in a pot that comes with a strainer insert, I pull the insert out once the pasta has finished cooking and *rest it at an angle on top of the pot*, above the pasta cooking water, while I finish cooking the sauce. A few minutes later when my sauce is complete, I briefly dip the pasta insert back into the still-hot cooking water and drain it quickly to reheat the pasta and keep it from sticking together.

—Gary Anderson, via email

Reheating pasta, with no sticking

Pasta and its sauces aren't always ready at the same time. When I cook pasta, I drain some of the hot cooking water into a large, heatproof container before completely draining the pasta. I return the pasta to its cooking pot. When I'm ready to serve, *I pour a little of the hot water back* into the pot with the pasta, stir briefly, and drain the pasta again. In one step, the water will reheat and "unstick" the pasta. I prefer this method to coating the pasta with oil, since the oil can prevent the sauce from adhering to the pasta.

—Pamela Staveley, Edgecomb, MA

Preparing pasta ahead

In my job as chef to the governor of Ohio, I often serve pasta for dinner parties. I've always found it difficult to cook and sauce the pasta just before service, so I found a method for cooking the pasta ahead of time and holding it until I'm ready to serve it. This method works for any type of pasta, but dried pasta seems to hold up a little better than fresh. Cook the pasta—whatever the shape—in the usual manner until done. Drain it well, then toss it with oil, salt, and freshly ground black pepper. You should use just a little bit of oil and toss the pasta thoroughly so that each strand is completely coated. Put the pasta in a large, ovenproof bowl and cover with foil. Put the bowl in a very low oven—250°F. The *pasta will stay hot for up to an hour* and won't stick together. When you're ready for the pasta course, just add the sauce and serve.

—Frannie Packard, Governor's Residence, Columbus, OH

Heat your serving bowl with pasta water

Whenever I drain pasta, I put my large pasta serving bowl in the sink, under the colander. The *hot water from the pot of cooked pasta warms the bowl* while I season the pasta in the colander. After draining the bowl, which is now very warm, I put the pasta in it, toss to distribute the seasonings, and bring the bowl to the table. The pasta stays nice and hot throughout the meal.

—Carla Cimarosti, Bacliff, TX

Why bother boiling lasagna noodles?

For several years, I've been using old-fashioned lasagna noodles of the "need to be boiled" variety, but not boiling them. *I layer the dry, uncooked noodles* per the recipe and then, before baking, pour 1 cup of water around the outside edge of the pan before covering with heavy-duty aluminum foil. I usually bake it for 1 to 1½ hours and find that the noodles are tender by that time.

—Beverly Siek, via email

With baked pasta, be generous with the sauce but go easy on the cheese

Baked pasta needs *a bit more sauce* than unbaked pasta, because some gets soaked up when you bake the pasta and some just evaporates with the oven heat. The pasta should be well coated and even a bit loosely sauced before baking. A hard grating cheese, like Parmigiano Reggiano or an aged pecorino, adds body to the dish but a little goes a long way. Too much will make your pasta stiff.

—Erica DeMane, *Fine Cooking*

Manicotti "popsicles" speed cooking time

My family loves manicotti so I make it often. But trying to stuff soft, creamy ricotta into wet, slippery manicotti noodles isn't much fun. I've found an easier way; I remove the manicotti noodles from the grooved, *plastic tray and use it as a mold*, filling each groove with ricotta and shaping the fillings to approximate the size and shape of the noodles. I then put the plastic tray in the freezer. Once the filling "popsicles" are ready, I stuff them into the cooked manicotti noodles and bake them slightly longer to compensate for the frozen filling. Now I often prepare several different fillings and freeze these "popsicles" for when the craving for manicotti arises.

—Evlyn Sluis, Gibsons, British Columbia, Canada

Instant homemade "ravioli"

Sandwich fresh herbs inside ready-made *wonton or egg-roll wrappers,* then boil until tender. They're lovely when served in a light herbal stock.

—Susan Asanovic, Wilton, CT

The best pasta salad

The amount of pasta in a salad should never exceed 50% of the total dish. The greater the proportion of vegetables and proteins, the more the dish will feel like a salad. Pasta salads are *best served warm* or at room temperature within a few hours of assembly.

—Peter Berley, *Fine Cooking*

For pasta to be served cooled, make a sauce or vinaigrette that tastes too bold

Once you add the sauce or vinaigrette to chilled pasta, the starchiness and neutral flavor of the pasta will temper the sauce's flavor. Also, the flavor of food served cold will be slightly more subtle than food served warm. Taste your sauce again and again as you're making it and *don't be afraid to over-season your sauce* or vinaigrette slightly.

—Joanne Weir, *Fine Cooking*

 **Polenta**

Combine ingredients before heating them

I have a good tip for preparing polenta. To avoid the tedious stirring over a hot stove, *combine all the ingredients (cornmeal, liquid, butter) at once while they're cold.* Then slowly bring to a simmer and stir occasionally until thickened. Finish with butter, your favorite cheese, or anything else. I find this method is foolproof.

—Larry Leibowitz, Parsippany, NJ

Keeping it lump free

When the salted water is boiling, gradually *add the cornmeal in a thin, steady stream*, whisking constantly. This is important. If you pour in the cornmeal too quickly, lumps may form.

—Alan Tardi, *Fine Cooking*

A simpler path to lumpless polenta

I put all the cornmeal into a pot of cold water, turn the stove on high, and stir constantly with a whisk until the water boils. Lumps are never a problem. Once the polenta has come to a boil, *I put it in a double boiler,* cover, and cook until done, without any more stirring. This method is much less labor-intensive and the results are consistently good.

—Bill White, Stuart, FL

Even simpler yet...

May I suggest boiling 2 parts water and mixing 1 part cold water with the cornmeal? Pour it into the boiling water, give it one quick stir, and *put the lid on to let the polenta steam.* No lumps, no stirring.

—Elsie A. Harley, Seneca, SC

An old trick for smoother polenta

While living in Italy, I learned an age-old trick for making lump-free polenta. When your water is rapidly boiling, take *a plum-size piece of stale, hard bread*—preferably from a dense European-style loaf—and stir it into the water with a wire whisk until it's completely broken up. Then add your cornmeal.

—Nicole Lavezzi, Sacramento, CA

Make polenta in a rice cooker

I love polenta, but I'm not always up to the vigil required when cooking it. Now I've found a great way to *cook it without much attention*—I use my rice cooker. I whisk together 1 part polenta with 3 parts cold water in the rice cooker. I add a little salt, stir lightly, and turn the cooker on. Once the mixture starts to bubble and boil, I stir it carefully every 10 minutes or so, using a long-handled wooden spoon. Once the rice cooker goes from cooking to warming mode, I stir in butter and grated cheese, let it rest for a few minutes, and it's ready to enjoy.

—Jim Shiraishi, Miranda, CA

Resurrect polenta in a food processor

In a pinch, you can get leftover cold polenta back to its original mushy texture quickly by putting it in the food processor with a little water. *Process the hardened polenta back to a purée,* toss it in a saucepan to reheat, and it's like new. I did this once when I was desperate, and it worked out great.

—Steve Johnson, The Blue Room, Cambridge, MA

No more buildup on polenta spoons

One of the biggest problems when making polenta is that it sticks to utensils. This can easily be prevented by *buttering the spoon* or other utensil that you're using to stir the polenta while it's cooking. When it's done, remember to butter the spatula you use to spread the polenta in the pan or dish.

—T .E. Caswell, via email

Muffin tin quickly firms polenta

When I need firm polenta, I portion it into a nonstick muffin tin. When it firms, I flip the tin over and *neat, uniform, individual servings* fall out, ready for broiling, grilling, or frying.

—Tony Niro, Sault Ste. Marie, Ontario, Canada

Potatoes

Boil potatoes in a pasta pot

I boil potatoes in a pasta pot *with a colander insert* because it's much easier to drain the cooked potatoes by lifting out the colander than it is to lug a pot of boiling water to a colander in the sink.

—Colleen Lanigan-Ambrose, Seal Beach, CA

Use a fork to check potatoes

A fork or a skewer is better than a paring knife for testing the doneness of boiled potatoes. A knife's sharp tip cuts into the potato and can make it feel like it's more done than it really is. The *slightly blunted tips of fork tines* and skewers give a truer read.

—Jennifer Armentrout, *Fine Cooking*

Getting perfect mashed potatoes

Start the potatoes in a generous amount of cold water and add salt at the outset or they'll never be as tasty as they should. Don't let the water boil vigorously or the potatoes will bang around, break up, and get waterlogged, resulting in a dense, soggy mash. To dry them out, after draining, put them back in the empty pot and set over medium heat; shake the pot and stir the potatoes with a wooden spoon so they don't stick. They'll break up a bit and become noticeably

TEMPERATURES AND TIMES FOR BAKED POTATES FOR A MEDIUM-SIZE (8- TO 10-OUNCE) POTATO

BAKE IT AT	FOR
325°F	1½ hours
350°F	1¼ hours
375°F	1 hour
400°F	45 to 50 minutes
425°F	40 to 45 minutes

—Molly Stevens, *Fine Cooking*

drier, brighter, and more starchy looking. Medium- and high-starch potatoes will leave a floury film in the pot when they're dry enough. If you want perfectly smooth mashed potatoes, then get them completely mashed before you start adding enrichments. Be sure these are warm or at room temperature so they don't cool the potatoes and make them stiff. We like to *beat them in with a sturdy wooden spoon*. This last step really fluffs the mash and ensures that the ingredients are evenly distributed.

—Roy Finamore and Molly Stevens, *Fine Cooking*

Better mashed potatoes

I can't imagine mashed potatoes without butter, milk, and snipped scallions. But I've recently discovered that an added generous *spoonful of herb-and-garlic Rondelé cheese or of roasted-garlic cream cheese* (now available in many markets) adds the ultimate touch for extra richness, creaminess, and flavor.

—Marcie Graham, via email

An end to mushy boiled potatoes

When you're boiling potatoes for any recipe, try this trick to keep them firm and flaky, rather than mushy and mealy. After boiling, drain the water and leave the potatoes in the pan. Cover with a folded dishtowel and let sit for about 5 minutes. This will give the potatoes *a great texture* for everything from potato salad to mashed potatoes.

—Russ Shumaker, Richmond, VA

Don't Blame the Mayo

Whenever a mayonnaise-based potato salad is linked to a foodborne illness, chances are it was the potatoes and not the mayo that caused the illness. Commercially produced mayonnaise is usually quite safe, but there is a certain strain of bacteria (*Bacillus cereus*) that loves the cooked starches in pasta, potatoes, and rice. So whenever you're making a rice, potato, or pasta salad, cool the salad quickly by spreading it on a platter and putting it in the fridge, and keep it chilled until just before serving.

—Jennifer Armentrout, *Fine Cooking*

Spin away potato liquid

It's a tradition in my house to cook potato latkes for large family gatherings. Over the years I've found an easier way to remove the liquid from large amounts of grated potatoes and onions. First I cut the potatoes and onions into chunks and grate them in a food processor using the finest shredding blade. Then I dry the grated vegetables in a salad spinner in batches. *The spinner makes quick work* of removing the potato and onion liquid. I've found that I use much less oil to fry these drier latkes until they're nice and crisp.

—Ruth Lang Ross, Northbrook, IL

Squeezing moisture from shredded potatoes and other vegetables

I have a tip for making potato pancakes or any other recipe that requires squeezing out excess liquid from grated vegetables. *Spread the shredded vegetables on a clean dishtowel*, roll up the towel lengthwise, and squeeze out the liquid by twisting the ends of the towel.

—Michele Cook, Triuggio, Italy

Picking the best potato for baking

What you're looking for is one with a high starch content, often called a "mealy" potato. The starchier the potato, the more the inside swells and puffs up as it bakes, leaving it light, dry, and delicate. Choose potatoes with these names on the label: *russet, russet Burbank, or Idaho*. Round white potatoes and yellow varieties such as Yellow Finn and Yukon Gold are considered all-purpose potatoes. They have a moderate starch content and will do in a pinch. Stay away from low-starch potatoes, also called waxy potatoes, which will end up soggy and dense when baked. Don't use potatoes labeled Red Bliss, red, round red, or long white.

—Molly Stevens, *Fine Cooking*

The best potato salad potatoes

The best potatoes to use in potato salads are those with a low- to medium-starch content—often called *waxy or sometimes salad or boiling potatoes*. Compared to starchy baking potatoes that fall apart and turn mealy when cooked, lower starch potatoes keep their shape and remain creamy with just the right amount of tooth to hold up in salads. They also tend to have a more distinct flavor than baking potatoes. The most common are the red-skinned varieties, sometimes labeled Red Bliss. Other choices include white varieties like California long whites and Maine or Kennebec potatoes. Medium-starch options include Yukon Gold and Yellow Finn. Many specialty potatoes labeled as fingerlings, heirlooms, or "gourmet" potatoes have a low- to medium-starch content and some come in hues of rose, pink, gold, and even purple, so your salad will be pretty as well as delicious.

—Molly Stevens, *Fine Cooking*

Boil potatoes and eggs together for potato salad

When I make potato salad, I find it convenient to start boiling the potatoes in a stainless-steel pot, then add the eggs to the same pot after 15 minutes. Once the potatoes are tender, I drain off the water and leave both the potatoes and eggs in the pot to cool. When they're cool enough to handle, I peel and dice them, add mayonnaise and seasonings, and mix them in the same pot. Then I transfer the finished potato salad to a serving bowl. *One less pot* and bowl to clean.

—Kathy Walden, Rock Hill, SC

Pressure-cooked potato salads

When I'm preparing potato salads, I peel and cut the potatoes into their final shape and cook them in a pressure cooker. Not only is this faster, but it allows me to *slice cool, firm potatoes* instead of ones that threaten to lose their shape and burn my fingers.

—Marianne Smith, Johnson City, TN

Start with white wine for a lighter-tasting potato salad

When I'm making potato salad, I like to pour a little white wine or stock over the potatoes while they're still warm. I find that the *potatoes absorb less oil* this way when they're dressed, and the result is lighter and more flavorful.

—Raymond Sienko, Southbury, CT

Ice keeps potato salads fresh on a buffet table

To keep mayonnaise-based dishes such as potato salads or pasta fresh throughout a summer party, *I freeze water in zip-top bags* and put them into a large, foil-lined bowl. Then I cover the ice packs with a clean dishtowel and a large sheet of foil, making sure the dishtowel is completely covered. The salad can then be spooned on top. This also works well with hamburger condiments, fruit salad, cold cuts, and desserts.

—Angel Ryan, Bonita, CA

Rice and Other Grains

Rinse basmati rice in a strainer

Basmati (fragrant long-grain rice) should be thoroughly rinsed in a bowl of cold water to remove excess starch. Usually, this takes 3 or 4 rinses until the water is no longer milky, but clear. When I'm pouring the cold water off the rice, I often find that some of the rice winds up going down the drain. To avoid this and to streamline the process, I now put the rice in a *wire mesh strainer and submerge the strainer in a bowl of cold water.* When it's time to change the water, I simply lift out the strainer, quickly pour the water out of the bowl, refill the bowl with water, and submerge the rice-filled strainer once again. If any particles (bran or husks) float to the top, pour them off before pulling the strainer out; otherwise they'll just end up back in the rice.

—Molly Wolf, Wethersfield, CT

Use artichoke and asparagus cooking broth for risotto

After steaming or broiling artichokes or asparagus, I use the cooking water as a broth for risotto. If I'm cooking one of these strong-flavored vegetables but not making the risotto the same day, I just freeze the cooking water for another time.

—Marian Schmidt, via email

A GUIDE TO COOKING GRAINS

TYPE OF GRAIN	GRAIN TO LIQUID COOKING RATIO	APPROXIMATE COOKING TIME
Brown rice (long-grain)	1 part rice to 2¼ parts liquid	45 minutes
Brown rice (short-grain)	1 part rice to 2 parts liquid	35 minutes
Bulgur (fine or medium)	1 part bulgur to 1 to 2 parts liquid	Pour boiling water over to absorb for 15 to 30 minutes; drain excess
Couscous	1 part couscous to 1 part liquid	1 minute cooking, 8 to 10 minutes off the heat, covered
Millet	1 part millet to 2 parts liquid	20 minutes
Pearled barley	1 part barley to 3 parts liquid	35 to 45 minutes
Quinoa (rinse well)	1 part quinoa to 2 parts liquid	12 to 15 minutes
Wheatberries (soft)	1 part wheatberries to 6 parts liquid	50 to 90 minutes*
White rice (long-grain)	1 part rice to 2 parts liquid	15 to 18 minutes
White rice (short-grain)	1 part rice to 1¼ parts liquid	10 to 12 minutes
Wild rice	1 part rice to 3½ parts liquid	45 to 50 minutes*

*Soaking can reduce cooking time by half; reduce cooking liquid by a third

—John Ash, *Fine Cooking*

Perfectly cooked rice on an electric stove

I don't own a rice cooker, but I've never had trouble cooking rice in a pot on a gas stove. But when I moved to a place with an electric stove, I had to get creative. I was about to give up and buy a rice cooker (my Indian mother would not approve) when I thought of this method. *I turn on two burners: one on high; the other on low.* I start the rice and water on the hotter burner. When the water starts to boil, I immediately move the pot to the burner set on low. This simulates the quick temperature change you can achieve with a gas range, and now I make perfect rice again.

—Indrani Gardella, Los Altos, CA

A foolproof way to cook rice

I usually use jasmine rice, although I have cooked medium-grain rice for sushi this way as well. I measure out the rice and water into a pot, using 2 parts rice to 3 parts water (more or less water for old or new rice), and put the *uncovered pot over high heat* on the burner. (I don't soak or wash the rice.) I turn down the heat once the water starts boiling to avoid undue splashing, but I maintain the boil until the water has boiled down to the level of the rice and the bubbles cause crater-like pockets in the still-wet, shiny surface of the rice. I turn off the heat, leave the pot on the still-warm burner, cover the pot, and let it steam by itself for at least 10 minutes, preferably 20 minutes or more. I turn the rice into a serving dish; it comes out freely without leaving a crust at the bottom of the pot.

—Julia Tien, via email

Fluff rice with chopsticks to release steam

The best way to ensure that steamed rice remains light and the grains separate is to fluff it gently with two chopsticks as soon as it's finished cooking. Hold the chopsticks slightly apart and fluff the rice to release the steam. Cover the rice with a cloth tea towel to absorb excess moisture and *serve it quickly*. Leftover cold rice can also be separated this way to use in fried rice.

—Susan Asanovic, Wilton, CT

Reheat rice in a vegetable steamer

I have a very simple way to reheat leftover rice: I put the rice in a vegetable steamer and *steam it for a few minutes until hot*. This method works very well for most kinds of rice, as long as it isn't pilaf or a variety that remains loose and separate after cooking (in which case the rice might fall through the steamer holes).

—Olivia Duchinsky, San Diego, CA

Bring leftover rice back to life in the microwave

I sometimes cook too much rice for dinner, and I don't like to throw the extra away. But reheating cooked rice on the stovetop can be tricky. I've found that if I put the rice into a *plastic bag with a little bit of water*, close the bag loosely, and microwave it on high for 4 minutes, I get terrific results. The moisture in the bag steams and softens the rice.

—Kim Landi, Bethel, CT

Steam vegetables on top of cooking rice

When I'm cooking rice, I like to use the last few minutes of cooking time to steam my vegetables. I put the vegetables right on top of the partially cooked rice, put the lid back on, and *let them steam together.* Sliced carrots take about 20 minutes to cook, broccoli needs around 6 to 10 minutes, and sugar snap peas take less than 5 minutes. The rice and vegetables remain separate for easy serving, and I have one less pan to wash. This method works well whether the rice is cooked on the stovetop or in a rice cooker.

—Karen Olson, Bloomington, MN

Sauces and Gravy

Pork bones give tomato sauce great flavor

To give my tomato sauce a full, deep flavor, I add pork neck bones, which cost about $1.50 a pound at most supermarkets. I brown the bones in a little olive oil in the saucepot, then I remove and reserve them. Next, I cook onions and garlic in the pot, scraping up the browned bits. The pork bones go back in the pot with my tomatoes and other ingredients. You can take the bones out before using the sauce. But if I'm serving meatballs and sausage with my spaghetti, I'll serve the neckbones, too. The meat, though scant, *cooks up tender and delicious.*

—Joan McAllister, Brookfield, CT

An antacid for tomato sauce

If your tomatoes have produced an acidic tomato sauce, the solution is to add a basic ingredient, like a pinch (and I mean just a pinch) of baking soda.

—Janet Fletcher, via email

Carrot sweetens tomato sauce

Regardless of the recipe, I always add a fresh carrot or two to tomato-based sauces to counteract the acidity of the tomatoes and to *add a sweet taste* and aroma. I cut the carrots into 1-inch chunks, cook the chunks in the sauce, and then purée everything together.

—Patrizia Makohan, Bloomfield Hills, MI

Rinse pasta sauce jars with a bit of wine

If you use pasta sauce from a jar (and who doesn't, on occasion?), rinse the jar with a little good red wine, such as Cabernet, Merlot, or Zinfandel, and add it to the sauce as it's heating. The *wine helps get all the sauce out of the jar* and it adds more flavor to the finished sauce.

—Lilian Fischer, Salt Lake City, UT

Quickly thicken pasta sauce

Italian friends taught me that if your tomato sauce turns out thinner than you'd like, try adding a tablespoon or two of *dry bread crumbs*. They give body and substance by absorbing some of the sauce, without changing the flavor.

—Russ Shumaker, Richmond, VA

Toast your flour for better gravy

I brown my flour in a baking pan in the oven at 300°F for about 30 minutes, stirring or shaking the pan often. I remove the flour from the oven when it takes on a light brown color and toasty fragrance, let it cool, and store it in an airtight container. I use this *toasted flour to thicken sauces* and gravies; it gives them a deeper flavor and color and eliminates the taste of raw flour.

—Janet C. deCarteret, Bellevue, WA

Making lump-free gravy

After you've added flour to your pan juices and cooked it, stirring, several minutes, you want to add just about ½ cup of your broth, *whisking vigorously to disperse the flour* evenly through the liquid. The broth should thicken quickly and get gluey. As soon as it does, add another ½ cup of broth while whisking. Repeat until the gravy starts looking more like a smooth sauce than glue. At that point, it's safe to add the remainder of the broth all at once.

—Jennifer Armentrout, *Fine Cooking*

Adding potato water to gravy

When I make mashed potatoes and gravy, I often save a cup or so of the water in which the potatoes were boiled and add it to the pan drippings to make gravy. The potato water adds nutrients, flavor, and starch, which helps thicken the gravy.

—Tammy Hines-Dumitru, Norwalk, CT

Potato water adds nutrients, flavor, and starch, which helps thicken the gravy.

Leave out the liver

When making *giblet broth for gravy,* leave the turkey or chicken liver out, as it will make the broth bitter.

—*Fine Cooking* editors

Soy sauce boosts gravy

When making gravy, I sometimes add a little bit of soy sauce instead of salt. The soy sauce *offers another level of flavor* and gives color as well.

—Kurt Kolseth, Mundelein, IL

Fixing a thin gravy

If your gravy is too thin, thicken it with *a slurry of water and flour.* Blend 2 tablespoons flour with 3 tablespoons water and add this, a bit at a time, to the simmering gravy until it thickens. Then simmer the gravy for about 10 minutes to cook off the floury taste.

—James Peterson, *Fine Cooking*

Dried lasagna helps thicken sauces

When I need to reduce a large amount of sauce and time is short, I'll throw in a piece of dried lasagna noodle to help absorb the excess liquid. The *pasta will absorb liquid* without giving the sauce a pasty or floury flavor, which can happen if you use a lot of flour or cornstarch as a thickener. Discard the noodle once the sauce reaches the right consistency. Similarly, sliced sun-dried tomatoes (not packed in oil) or dehydrated mushrooms also work well to help absorb excess liquid, plus they add flavor to the sauce.

—Chuck Langman, Ambler, PA

Defatting a braising liquid

When braising meat for dishes, I use the following technique to defat the liquid. Set a tall, tempered glass jar, such as a canning jar, in a deep ice water bath. *(It's important that the glass is tempered;* the extreme temperature change would break regular glass.) Remove the meat from the pan and pour the liquid into the glass. Within minutes, the fat will begin to separate so that most of it can easily be removed. The tall glass jar and deep ice bath ensure that a large surface area of the liquid gets exposed to the cold water, and the glass lets you see when the fat separates. To remove even more of the fat, refrigerate the jar until the remaining fat congeals and can be skimmed off.

—Julie Ward, Menlo Park, CA

A simple onion gravy for brisket

For a wonderful, almost fat-free gravy to accompany brisket, I roast about 5 sliced onions along with a well-seasoned 3-pound piece of meat. When the brisket is done, I transfer the meat and onions to a platter, deglaze the pan, and refrigerate everything. The next day, I purée the onions with an immersion blender and add them to the deglazed drippings, which I have defatted and reheated. This gives me *a robust, slightly thickened gravy* that's a flavorful addition to the brisket, which I slice very thinly and warm up gently in the gravy.

—Jeanne Schimmel, Hobe Sound, FL

Have roux on hand for sauces

About once a month, I make a large batch of full-flavored roux, spending the time to cook it slowly to its nutty, buttery best. *I keep the roux refrigerated,* letting it soften at room temperature before using it for sauces or soups. Recently while making a sauce, I forgot to take the roux from the fridge. It was way too firm to spoon out, so I grabbed my citrus zester and scraped it along the surface of the hardened mixture. Wonderful strands of roux came through like a charm, letting me use as much or as little as needed.

—Claudia Imatt, Pleasanton, CA

Quick pan sauces

For convenient sauce making, I keep a resealable box of a *high-quality chicken broth* in my refrigerator. After sautéing meat, poultry, or fish, I pour a little broth into the sauté pan and stir over medium heat to deglaze it for a quick, delicious pan sauce. I sometimes add a bit of wine or liqueur to the pan and taste for seasoning. The box of broth will keep for a week or two in the coldest part of the refrigerator.

—Andrea Lord, Schenectady, NY

Blend away lumps in sauces and pastry cream

No matter how careful you are, sometimes your pastry cream or béchamel sauce gets lumps. Should you throw it out and start over, or just panic? Neither. Simply put the lumpy custard or sauce in a blender or food processor fitted with a steel blade and *blend the mixture* for a few seconds until it becomes smooth and satiny. Sometimes the custard or sauce will soften and thin a bit, but reheating it will restore the thicker consistency. Be sure to whisk constantly when you're reheating and keep the heat low, or it's back to the blender.

—Lyn Nelson-Joseph, Houston, TX

Waxed paper prevents skin on cream sauces

After I make a béchamel sauce or any other thick cream sauce that I'm not going to use immediately, I lay a piece of *waxed paper on the surface* to prevent a skin from forming. This also works well for storing leftover cream soups.

—Samantha Kwan, Arlington, VA

Keep sauces warm

If you want to serve a beurre blanc at your next dinner party but don't want to cook it at the last minute, make it several hours ahead of time and store it in a wide-mouth thermos. The *thermos keeps it warm* without separating.

—Maureen Fox Lucas, La Canada, CA

Stocks and Soups

The way to great homemade stock

For full-bodied, gelatinous meat stocks, *choose parts of the carcass that are rich in collagen.* Collagen is present in connective tissues (joints and tendons) and in bones. As these parts simmer, the collagen denatures (unwinds) and combines with the water, forming gelatin. Veal bones are great for stock because the younger animals have more collagen than older ones with mineralized bones. As you would expect, parts with many joints and bones, such as chicken necks and backs, are particularly good for making gelatinous stock. If there's meat clinging to the bones, all the better. Blood on the bones tends to make a stock cloudy. Soaking them for 20 minutes before making the stock will remove it. While your stock is cooking, it's important to keep the liquid at a simmer, not a boil. Boiling will cause the fat and water to form an emulsion, producing a cloudy, greasy stock. And don't stir, as this, too, will cause some emulsification of fat and water. You want all the fat to float to the top when the stock cools so that it can be scooped off. Once the stock is completely defatted, you can let it boil without fear of cloudiness. Stock will keep for 5 to 7 days in the refrigerator or 3 months in the freezer. Always reboil stock before using it. I let it boil for about 5 minutes, enough time to get it to a rolling boil and kill any lurking bacteria. If bubbles appear in a refrigerated stock, it has fermented, so discard it immediately.

—Shirley O. Corriher, *Fine Cooking*

Cook stock outside for a cleaner kitchen

I like to gently simmer my turkey, beef, and veal stocks for several hours to reduce and concentrate the liquid, but my kitchen always get steamy and greasy from fatty vapors coming off the stock, and my noisy exhaust fan does a poor job of venting the odors. Now I simmer my stocks outside on the patio, using a *portable electric burner* on a sturdy table covered with heatproof padding. To prevent injuries, I always make sure there are no kids or dogs around the house or in the backyard. Now my kitchen stays clean, cool, and odor free.

—S. Groves, via email

The best chicken for soup

I like to use a *kosher chicken* because it's salted during the processing and therefore has more flavor. I clean it and then rub the whole bird or parts with a cut lemon and sprinkle it lightly with coarse salt to boost its flavor. I wrap the salted chicken in plastic and refrigerate overnight or even for just a few hours (there's no need to rinse off the salt before soaking). This step brings out more flavor and makes the broth taste more chickeny.

—Joyce Goldstein, *Fine Cooking*

Save hard cheese and prosciutto rinds for cooking

I have a small plastic bag in my freezer that contains rinds from hard grating cheeses such as Parmesan, Romano, and even well-aged Gruyère. Also, I'm fortunate enough to be able to buy prosciutto ends at my local grocery store. I trim the skin from the prosciutto end as I use the meat and store these trimmings with the cheese rinds. Whenever I make stock, bean stew, or a hearty soup, I add a cheese rind and a piece of prosciutto skin to the pot *for a noticeable boost in flavor.*

—Maryrose Livingston, Ithaca, NY

Save vegetable cooking water for stock

When I boil sweet-tasting vegetables like corn, carrots, zucchini, and string beans, I save the cooking water to make vegetable stock. I use a large, slotted spoon to remove the vegetables from the pot, add a sliced onion, a stick of celery, a tomato, and a carrot or two (if the broth isn't carrot-based) to the pot of vegetable cooking water and simmer it, uncovered, for 25 minutes. The resulting broth—*sweet and rich with the taste of fresh summer vegetables*—can be frozen for future use in soups. I find that my vegetable broth tastes much better than the canned variety.

—Tiny Shuster, St. Johnsville, NY

Retrieving a bouquet garni

When I use a bouquet garni (a bundle of fresh parsley, thyme, bay leaf, and celery that I wrap in leek leaves) in a soup or stew, it gets soft and mushy during cooking, and it's often difficult to fish out. I tie it with an extra length of kitchen twine and attach the other end to the pot handle. When I'm ready to remove the bundle, I just *pull it out by the twine.*

—Joan Dall'Acqua, Arlington, VA

Thicken soups with flavorful liquids

When a stew or ragoût has finished cooking and the liquid is ready to be thickened, taste it for flavor. If it's just right, don't thicken it with water mixed with cornstarch. Use one of the liquid ingredients in the stew, like *a bit of the cooking broth or wine,* to make a thin paste with the cornstarch. The sauce will retain its strength and desired flavor.

—Barbara Kramer, Albuquerque, NM

Thicken soups with leftover mashed potatoes

Whenever I make mashed potatoes, I make a little extra and freeze them. Then, when I'm making a hearty, homemade vegetable soup and I need to thicken it, I just pull out a *packet of frozen mashed potatoes,* break off a couple of chunks, and add them to the soup. This adds flavor as well as thickener.

—Colleen Lanigan-Ambrose, Seal Beach, CA

A spoon prevents splashing

When transferring stock or soup from one container to another, I minimize splashing by pouring the liquid onto the back of a spoon held over the container to be filled. The *liquid follows the spoon* and any solids present go with the flow. This works well whether adding to a pot on the stove, to a stand mixer, or to storage containers for leftovers.

—Charles McEniry, Stoughton, WI

A neat trick for clarifying stock

Just add a couple of *lightly beaten egg whites* to your skimmed and simmering stock and stir it with a whisk for 2 to 3 minutes. Take the pot from the heat and scoop out the egg whites (which will now look puffy and gray) with a slotted spoon. The stock will be clear as a Rocky Mountain stream.

—Karen McLachlan, Edmonton, Alberta, Canada

Coffee filter makes a clear broth

After making chicken broth, I strain out the herbs and vegetables using a sieve. Then I strain the broth again through a paper coffee filter, which *catches all the sediment and fat* and leaves me with a crystal-clear broth.

—Leah Hitchcock, Salinas, CA

Getting more flavor from stock

This is a third-generation tip handed down. Rather than use a cheesecloth to strain chicken stock, I use a well-worn, *thin, almost transparent cotton tea towel*. This captures all the fat and particles from the bone (it works best if the broth is lukewarm, not hot, so the fat has started to congeal). I end up with a very clear, fat-free broth. I then separate the vegetables from the bones and squeeze them through the rinsed tea towel, adding these juices to the stock. This gives even more flavor to the broth.

—Sylvia Sandner, Bradford, Ontario, Canada

Defat stock quickly with ice cubes

Here's how to quickly defat stock. Toss a trayful of ice cubes into the stock, give it a quick stir, and let it sit for a minute or two. The *fat will quickly solidify around the cubes* and is easily lifted out. If you have time, cool the stock first, but this trick works even with hot stock. Repeat the ice treatment if there's any fat left. Water from the melted ice that dilutes the stock can be easily boiled off.

—Heather Jones, Port Hardy, British Columbia, Canada

Fat-free stock

It's easy to remove a large amount of fat from a stock or sauce by simply spooning it off, but it's not so easy to get that last film of fat without spooning away half of your precious stock. One method that works to remove the fat but leaves the stock is to use *a sheet of paper towel* to absorb the fat. The stock should be in a wide pan or bowl, and it should be warm, so the fat is free-flowing. Lay a sheet of paper towel over the surface of the stock. (If you have a two-ply sheet, separate it and use only one layer.) Immediately draw it up toward you and away from the stock. Have the trash can handy for the dripping towels. Repeat with new sheets until no more fat is visible on the surface of the stock.

—Blair Sanders, Dallas, TX

Damp paper towels help create fat-free stock

I have a fuss-free method for removing excess fat from homemade stock. Allow the stock to cool a bit, then pour it through a strainer lined with a *double layer of wet paper towels*. This leaves most of the fat behind in the paper towels and cuts the amount of fat left in the stock to a bare minimum.

—Jim Brookshire, Ontario, CA

Zip-top bag defats stock

If you need to quickly defat soup or stock, fill a one-gallon zip-top plastic freezer bag with the warm liquid. Refrigerate the bag for 10 minutes to allow the fat to rise to the top. Hold the bag over a large bowl, snip one corner from the bottom of the bag, and let the stock pour into the bowl. When you get to the layer of fat, pinch the corner shut. The *fat remains in the bag* and can be thrown away.

—Ray L. Overton III, Atlanta, GA

Cooling stock quickly

To quickly chill stock so that I can skim off the fat, I use my *ice-cream maker*. First I chill the container of the ice-cream maker in the freezer as I would for making ice cream. I pour some of the hot stock into the container, and after 5 minutes of occasional stirring, the fat has congealed on the surface and is easy to remove. The freezer container is usually cold enough to handle another batch of stock, and a third pass may even work. Even if I can't quick-chill the whole batch of stock, at least I've lowered the temperature of a good portion of it so that the rest doesn't need as long a refrigeration before defatting it.

—David Auerbach, Durham, NC

Cool hot soups quickly with "stock cubes"

I'm an avid soup lover who likes to serve just-cooked soups to my family and friends. Sometimes I find that the finished soup is much too hot to serve once it's ready. Since I freeze various stocks in ice cube trays, I avoid the wait for the soup to cool by taking several *cubes of stock out of the freezer*, dropping one or two in each soup bowl, and then ladling the hot soup over them. This quickly brings down the temperature of the soup but doesn't dilute the flavor.

—Diane Pietras, Levittown, PA

Quick-Chilling in an Ice Bath

The temperature "danger zone" for all food is 40° to 140°F, but food spoils most rapidly between 70° and 120°F—which is where food sits when left at room temperature. The faster you can cool cooked food below 70°F, the better off you are.

Small containers of hot food will cool quickly in the refrigerator, but anything more than a few cups won't—especially if it's thick. For example, the center of a large pot of stew left in the refrigerator overnight will still be 70°F the next morning. In addition, hot food throws off enough heat to warm up the entire refrigerator.

The solution is to make an ice water bath. Here's how.

- *Fill your sink* or any other large basin (like a roasting pan) with cold water and ice.

- *Divide large batches of food* into small, unbreakable containers, which will cool faster. Stainless steel is best. Don't use plastic—it insulates and holds the heat.

- *Set the container in the water bath* and stir the food often to speed cooling.

- *Don't cover the food* until it has cooled completely. Food will cool faster without the lid.

- *Refrigerate the food* when it reaches 70°F. Refrigerators are designed to handle food at this temperature.

—Molly Stevens, *Fine Cooking*

Cool down stocks with ice-filled bags

Here's a fast, simple way to cool down a hot stock quickly so you can skim off the fat. I came to this method after using ice cubes, which work, but this method is even better. First you'll need to fill a few heavy-duty zip-top bags with water, seal, and freeze them (be sure the bag is truly watertight; some of the new zipper bags leak). When you want to cool down a hot stock or sauce, let it rest off the heat for a minute or two, then drop one or more of these frozen bags into it. The *ice melts, but it doesn't dilute the flavor.* Refrigerate the stock, and in an hour you can usually start lifting off the congealed fat. If you're in a big hurry, just drag the frozen bag back and forth across the top of the liquid; a significant amount of fat will collect right on the bag.

—Randolph M. Siverson, El Macero, CA

Use snow to cool foods quickly

Last winter I found a culinary use for all the snow in my backyard. I wanted an easy, no-mess way to cool down a large pot of beef stew I'd just made, and the thick layer of pure white snow on my picnic table outside seemed perfect. *I set the hot pot amid the snow* on the table and packed some of the surrounding snow around the pot. I stirred the stew a couple of times, put the lid loosely over the pot, and went inside. Every 15 minutes or so, I'd give the pot a stir and pack more snow around it. In a couple of hours it had cooled down enough to refrigerate.

—Joanne Smart, Brookfield, CT

Freeze stock in flat sheets

I measure my stock into heavy-duty freezer bags, then lay the bags on the floor of my freezer so the stock hardens in flat sheets. I can stand the sheets on edge (they're space-efficient) or pile other food on top of them. Since the bag assumes the shape of the liquid, I can freeze any amount of stock and not waste precious freezer space. The *stock thaws more quickly* than when frozen in plastic tubs, and I can control how much stock I melt. Fill each bag about one-third full, press out excess air, seal it, and wipe off moisture from the exterior. To keep the bags from freezing to the floor of the freezer, lay a sheet of waxed paper, parchment, or freezer paper under them. This method of freezing also makes sense for many sauces.

—Megan Whalen Turner, Silver Spring, MD

Metal mixing bowl holds zip-top bags upright

While transferring some homemade chicken stock into gallon-size, zip-top bags for freezer storage, I found that the large stainless-steel mixing bowl from my stand mixer held the bags perfectly upright while I poured in the stock. *The bowl kept the bags neat and upright* until I could seal and label them. I didn't spill a drop of stock. This would also work with any straight-sided bowl.

—C. J. Moreland, New Canaan, CT

Folding for the best volume

It helps to first "lighten" the heavier mixture by whisking in about a quarter of the lighter one; now that there isn't such an extreme difference in texture, the two mixtures will combine more easily. Also, it's better to *put the lighter mixture on top of the heavier one*. Otherwise, the heavy base would deflate the lighter one.

—Shirley O. Corriher, *Fine Cooking*

Hot tea and iced tea are not the same

Many people make iced tea the same way they do hot tea. This method fails to acknowledge that hot and cold temperatures create entirely different flavors. Cold dampens flavor, so it's imperative to *brew iced tea to a stronger level than you would hot tea*. I prefer to make a concentrate of tea using a couple cups of water and 6 tea bags. After steeping this mixture for 15 minutes, I add 6 cups of cold water. Making a concentrate results in a more flavorful final product and lets you control the strength of the tea. You can adjust the flavor as you add more water. Once you've brewed your tea, be sure to let it cool at room temperature. Putting hot tea directly in the refrigerator will make it turn cloudy. To clear cloudy tea, try adding a little boiling water.

—Fred Thompson, *Fine Cooking*

Keep lemon curd yellow

Some saucepan materials, such as plain aluminum or unlined copper, will react with the acid in the lemons, discoloring the curd and giving it a metallic flavor. Stainless steel, anodized aluminum, and enamel all work well.

—Elinor Klivans, *Fine Cooking*

Bain-marie made easy

The hardest part of making crème brûlée is not making the actual custard but getting the ramekins and their water bath in and out of the oven without burning yourself or sloshing water all over. I find it easiest to place the ramekins in a dry pan, put the pan into the hot oven, and then add the water to the bain-marie using a curved, long-necked watering can. When it's time for the custards to come out of the oven, I use a *turkey baster to carefully remove some of the hot water* from the bain-marie before taking it out of the oven.

—Wendy Soltau, Naperville, IL

Handling hot ramekins

I love making baked custards but until recently I had trouble getting the hot ramekins out of the water bath and onto the rack to cool. Spatulas and oven mitts didn't work. Even metal tongs were hit or miss—as often as not, the ramekins would slip out of the tongs and splash back into the water. Now *I wrap rubber bands* around each of the tongs' gripping ends, and slipping ramekins are a thing of the past.

—Cassia Schell, Bay Village, OH

Handling hot ramekins, take two

I remove hot ceramic ramekins or metal molds from a water bath with rubberized canning tongs. Their grip is much more secure than regular metal tongs.

—Donna Ferries, Wilton, CT

Bake custards in small canning jars to give away

I like to bring caramel custards baked in pretty ramekins or soufflé dishes when visiting friends during the holidays, but it's a chore to collect my baking dishes days or weeks later. Now I bake my custards in *small, shallow, wide-mouth canning jars*—since the jars are relatively inexpensive, they don't need to be reclaimed. I use 8-ounce canning jars with slightly sloping sides. Canning jars are made to withstand boiling water, so I can safely bake them in a low oven in a water bath. Once the custards cool, I screw the canning jar ring and lid back on each jar, add a ribbon and a decorative label with the recipe's name, the "eat by" date, and refrigeration instructions. If you're making crème caramel, be sure to heat the jars before pouring in the hot caramel. This is easily done by putting the jars on a tray in a low oven (about 225°F) or by taking them hot from the dishwasher.

—Mary Kerr, San Carlos, CA

Make a paper template for summer pudding

Lining a round mold with bread to make a summer pudding or fruit charlotte can be tricky. Here's how to ensure your base layer of bread forms a perfect circle with no gaps. Trace the base of the mold or tin on *kitchen parchment* and cut out the circle. Fold the circle in half, then in quarters, and finally in eighths. Put the paper on a slice of bread and use a knife to cut out a triangle. Repeat this with seven more pieces of bread, and you will have eight bread triangles that form a perfect circle for the base of the mold.

—Anne Disrude, Jersey City, NJ

Loosening molds

Unmolding a frozen dessert or other chilled food that clings like glue to its container can be a frustrating mess. I like to use this method instead. Run the point of a knife around the edge of the cold mold, then invert the mold and center it on a serving platter. With a hair dryer set on high, blow hot air at all the surfaces of the mold, making several passes 6 to 8 inches from the mold. A few seconds of this and you lift the mold from a *perfectly released*, completely unblemished dessert on a dry, clean platter.

—Martin Stone, New York, NY

Make frozen desserts in zip-top bags

When I make granitas or ices, I put *the juice and sugar mixture* in a zip-top bag in the freezer. Then, instead of stirring it every once in a while, I just reach in the freezer, grab the bag, and squeeze it a few times. This breaks up the ice crystals and keeps me from dirtying up extra utensils.

—Kate Snider, Dundas, Ontario, Canada

Make perfect pancakes with a baster

Turkey basters work great for batter distribution. Try using one for perfectly round, even pancakes and crêpes. Turkey basters are also handy for filling cupcake tins—*equal batter distribution* and no messy drips.

—Erinn Casale Michalek, New York, NY

Skewer that waffle

To remove an obstinate waffle from the waffle iron, I insert two bamboo skewers horizontally through opposite sides of the waffle and gently pull them away from the iron. The waffle comes *away more neatly* than when I use a fork or spatula.

—Georganna Ulary, Red Hook, NY

Pick a fine, clear day for candymaking

Humidity can prevent your candy from setting up properly, because *sugar is hygroscopic—it absorbs moisture from the air.* So if you're cooking candy on a damp day and trying to evaporate the water, the sugar will thwart your efforts by quickly reabsorbing moisture.

—Kay Fahey, *Fine Cooking*

Don't get distracted when cooking sugar

You'll discover the mercury in the candy thermometer will hover forever at a certain place. The first time I saw this phenomenon, I thought my thermometer was broken and ran out to buy a new one. It did precisely the same thing when I repeated the procedure. It sits for minutes and then, right at the critical stage, *the thermometer suddenly surges* upward.

—Kay Fahey, *Fine Cooking*

"Butter" bread with mayo for fast grilled cheese

My neighbor created this simple shortcut for preparing grilled cheese sandwiches. When everyone's starving and *in a hurry to eat*—and the butter is cold and rock-hard—we spread both faces of the sandwich with the thinnest coating of mayonnaise instead. Our sandwiches grill up beautifully.

—Rosanne Aresty, Mamaroneck, NY

Broiling: Door Open or Closed?

If your oven is less than ten years old, chances are you should be broiling with the door closed. Most ovens sold today are built was *closed-door broilers*, for reasons of safety and smoke control. We learned this the hard way in the test kitchen when one of our ovens shut down after we broiled with the door open, and we had to call in a technician to reset the electronic controls. To find out if your oven is a closed- or open-door broiler, consult your manual or call the manufacturer. If your broiler is gas powered, you should always broil with the door closed.

—Jennifer Armentrout, *Fine Cooking*

Make crisper, theater-style popcorn at home

If you enjoy making old-fashioned, non-microwave popcorn at home and you want it as crisp as movie-theater popcorn, top your cooking pot with *a wire-mesh splatter screen* instead of the pot lid. It will keep the oil from splattering and allow all the steam to escape, producing a crisp and tender treat.

—Jim Harb, Knoxville, TN

Practice makes a perfect flip

I've often admired the way professional chefs toss food in their skillets with just a flick of the wrist. To practice that technique at home, *fill a zip-top bag with food* (rice or dried beans work well) and toss the weighted bag in a skillet until you feel confident enough to try it with real food.

—Anthony Lucas, Toledo, OH

Serving, Storage, Cleaning, *and* Kitchen Safety *Tips*

Metal spoon protects glass from boiling liquids

As a frequent tea drinker who prefers glasses to cups, I've found that if I set a metal teaspoon in the glass before pouring in the hot water, the glass can withstand the high temperature. The glass gets hot, but the heat-conductive *spoon absorbs the first blast of heat.* So far, I've never had a glass break on me using this method (and without the spoon, I have). I assume that this technique would apply to other instances in the kitchen, any time you might need to pour a very hot liquid into a non-Pyrex glass bowl or measuring cup that might otherwise crack from the heat.

—Carmen Perujo, Madrid, Spain

Honey anchors small bowls onto platters

When entertaining at home, I like to pass hors d'oeuvres on trays among my guests. Many times these tidbits are accompanied by dipping sauces in little bowls. To keep the bowls from sliding around on the platters, I put a little bit of honey on the bottom of the bowls, which *keeps them glued into place* on the platter.

—Bill Apodaca, Royal Oak, MI

Serving salad like a pro

To shape salad greens into tall stacks, lightly dress the greens and pack them loosely in a clean plastic container; pints work well. *Invert the container* onto a salad plate, lift it away, and, voila—a statuesque salad.

—Jennifer Armentrout, *Fine Cooking*

A better way to toss a green salad

Usually when I toss a green salad or a pasta salad, it ends up truly tossed about the kitchen while the salad dressing remains unevenly distributed. Now I use *two lightweight stainless-steel bowls* of slightly different sizes and put the salad fixings and dressing in the larger bowl while inverting the smaller bowl to cover the top. Clasping the top and bottom bowls together with my hands, I shake them vertically for about 20 seconds. There's no mess, and the dressing is evenly spread throughout the salad. Remove the smaller bowl and serve the salad in the larger one, which has a clean rim, free of dressing.

—Michael Bakken, Fresno, CA

A stylish way to serve deviled eggs

Deviled eggs are a timeless favorite, but they tend to tip over on a platter. I like to serve deviled eggs *on a bed of mixed whole olives* that have been tossed in extra-virgin olive oil and fresh herbs. The olives provide a colorful, pebbly nest that helps keep the eggs upright, and the match is even more delicious when I add some chopped olives or olive tapenade to the egg stuffing mixture.

—Heather Lee, Lafayette, CA

Warm your breadbasket with a heated rock

When dining, there's nothing more appealing than finding warm and fragrant crusty rolls or bread beneath the napkin in your breadbasket. Here's a way to keep buns and bread warm on your dining table. Find a *smooth, flat rock* that will fit nicely inside your breadbasket. Wash the rock and heat it in a 250°F oven for about 15 minutes before putting it in the basket, under the napkin containing the bread.

—Ross Mavis, Saint John, New Brunswick, Canada

Beverage and Food Storage

Give wine a rest

From working in the wine industry, I learned that a little planning when buying wine can truly enhance its flavor. Wine is a living liquid that needs to relax from a shipping journey filled with rapid temperature changes and movements from ship to shore, truck to warehouse, and store shelf to your home. Try this experiment: Buy your favorite inexpensive bottle of wine and *let it rest on its side* in a cool, dark place for a month, then have a wine tasting that pitches the rested wine against a bottle of the same wine that you've just purchased. The rested wine will taste noticeably better than your newly purchased wine.

—Michael Murphy, Saint John, New Brunswick, Canada

Storing leftover wine

Lubricate the cork by *dipping it into a bit of wine* and quickly tamping it down into the bottle. Also, the less air in the bottle, the better, so decant the wine into the smallest possible container.

—Rosina Tinari Wilson, *Fine Cooking*

Recorking wines

Don't pour out that half-finished bottle. Here's a gadget-free way to make it last a little longer. Pour some of the wine into a glass, dip in the cork, and tamp the cork back into the bottle so that it's flush with the top of the bottle's lips. If the cork needs further tamping, position the bottle perpendicular to a wall or a cabinet, corked end against that surface, and heave a quick hip thrust to jam the cork the rest of the way in. When you're ready to re-open the wine, use a corkscrew as you did the first time you uncorked it. The wine may not last as long as it would with a preserving gadget, but it will stay leakproof when carted home from a tasting and laid down on its side in the fridge.

Tamp the cork completely back into the bottle.

—Virginia Morisot, Ridgefield, CT

Store cooking wine in mini bottles

I buy those four-packs of small wine bottles for cooking since each is a cup, they come with screw tops, and they fit well in the fridge. *Keep the used bottles and refill them* later with leftover wine. If you fill them right to the top, there isn't much air to spoil the taste of the wine. They keep well in the fridge until the next sauce or braise.

—Paul-Marcel St. Onge, Chandler, AZ

Save those empty wine bottles

After finishing a bottle of wine, consider recycling the bottle as a *container for olive oil*. Put a pour spout in the top (the kind bartenders use in liquor bottles) and you have a convenient storage container that's much easier to work with than a cumbersome gallon tin of oil.

—Mark L. Heller, Dallas, TX

Oven mitts transport wine bottles safely

Recently, while on my way to a family dinner party I was helping to cook, I packed a large box full of food and was looking around for something to cushion the wine bottles when I saw my long oven mitts. The bottles fit perfectly *inside the oven mitts*, with just the bottle necks exposed. I stood them upright in the box. The oven mitts also came in handy during cooking later on.

—Patricia Yates, Manhattan Beach, CA

Use colored glass bottles to store oils

Since oils can become rancid more quickly when exposed to light, I use "designer" water bottles made of colored glass to store oils. The pint-size bottles are *perfect for flavored oils,* and I use quart bottles for general-purpose oils, such as olive and peanut. For easy pouring, I fit the bottles with color-coded plastic pour spouts, which are available at restaurant-supply or liquor stores.

—Bill Moran, San Diego, TX

Water bottle for accessible oils

I've come up with a way to waste less plastic and at the same time to simplify the way I sauté and fry. I buy my favorite oils in economical one-gallon containers and pour them into small water bottles—*the kind with a pull stop* on top. This lets me squirt the exact amount of oil into the pan without waste or mess. It also makes measuring into a teaspoon much easier.

—Rory Pearse, Woodside, NY

A reusable oil dispenser

I've found the perfect oil dispenser for my collection of cooking oils—an empty Worcestershire bottle. Its shape and size are perfect, and there is no risk of oil dripping down the sides. Of course, the bottle must be washed thoroughly before it can be used. If you don't have a dishwasher, mix about 2 tablespoons of dishwashing soap with about 2 cups of water, remove and soak the dripless cap, and fill the bottle with soapy water. After about 20 minutes, rinse out the bottle and the cap. When the bottle is completely dry, it's ready to use.

Try a Worcestershire bottle.

—Linda McBrearty, Portland, OR

Seasoning with soy sauce

This Christmas, I received two olive oil misters and put one to a unique use. I filled the mist bottle with soy sauce and used it to evenly season stir-fries, eggs, and grilled foods. Instead of overseasoning food with soy sauce, I now have a light, *consistent application of seasoning* and, like misting foods with oil, I now use less soy sauce.

—Gina DeVine, Carrboro, NC

How Long Will Those Leftovers Last?

Foods don't necessarily have to look or smell bad to be unsafe to eat. The general rule for most leftovers, especially those that contain meat, fish, poultry, or eggs, is four days, and that's only if you handle them properly.

Most bacteria grow best in a temperature range of 40° to 140°F—the danger zone—so make sure your leftovers cool quickly out of the danger zone. Put them in wide, shallow containers and refrigerate them partially covered until chilled, then cover them well. Any perishable food that remains in the danger zone for more than 2 hours (1 hour if the air temperature is above 90°F) should be thrown out. Use a refrigerator thermometer to be sure your refrigerator maintains a temperature below 40°F. And if you don't think you'll eat the leftovers within a few days, wrap them well and freeze them at 0°F or below. Frozen leftovers will remain safe to eat for a long time, but quality will begin to suffer within a few months.

—Jennifer Armentrout, *Fine Cooking*

Making an airtight seal on a food sack

In my kayaking class, I learned how to fold a sack so well that it's nearly airtight and watertight. Now I do this when I want to *seal up a bag* of cereal, bread crumbs, crackers, or chips. First, remove the excess air by pressing the bag shut right above the bag's contents, then fold the top edge down twice, turn the bag over, and make triangular folds on both sides of the bag, flush against the food. Fold the top edge over once more and secure with a binder clip or a clothespin.

—Zoe Hunter, Brookfield, CT

Unclutter your kitchen with bamboo steamers

I use bamboo steamers to store items that normally sit out on the counter and take up a lot of precious space. I put tomatoes, peaches, pears, and other fruits that need to ripen at room temperature in one section. In another, I put garlic, onions, and ginger—and so on. Since the *steamer sections stack vertically*, they take up very little space on the countertop.

—Drew McLaughlin, Shoreview, MN

Keeping food fresh

When covering a container of food to store in the refrigerator, put plastic wrap right *on the surface of the food* itself, pushing out as much air as possible. Then put on any additional cover. If you do this instead of stretching the plastic wrap over the top of the container, the food will stay fresh longer. Test the idea with cottage cheese—you'll be surprised how much longer it keeps this way.

—Ken Erikson, Grass Valley, CA

Colored plastic wrap identifies special dishes

While getting ready for a recent party, I covered the items I prepped in advance with green *"holiday" plastic wrap* before storing them in my always-crowded refrigerator. On the day of my party, it was easy to identify which bowls were my party dishes.

—Carol Crites, Los Altos, CA

Keeping plastic wrap off a dessert surface

Tiramisu usually calls for a generous dusting of cocoa powder or chopped chocolate on top. But since tiramisu must be covered and refrigerated before serving, I used to have trouble keeping the plastic wrap from sticking to its surface. My solution is the little *plastic three-pronged disks* that you often find in the center of take-out pizzas. I just set the disk lightly on top of my tiramisu and drape the plastic wrap over it. The disk can, of course, be washed and reused.

—Christine Cheung, Cincinnati, OH

Spaghetti "toothpicks"

Tenting plastic wrap with toothpicks keeps plastic from adhering to frosting or other sticky food, but if you don't have toothpicks, *uncooked dry spaghetti* will do in a pinch.

—R. B. Himes, Vienna, OH

Recycling butter wrappers

When you unwrap a stick of butter, don't throw out the waxy paper. Use it *instead of plastic wrap to cover food* going into the refrigerator. Not only will the paper keep refrigerator odors out of the food, but the film of butter left on the paper will also keep your food from drying out, and it will add its own nice buttery flavor, too.

—Sue Schneider, Oakland, CA

Pastry cooling racks create extra refrigerator space

When I'm cooking dishes ahead for a dinner party, I make extra storage space in my refrigerator by setting a cooling rack *on top of my food containers* so I can store more food on top. This way, I can easily make six to eight dishes ahead of time and keep them safely chilled without taking up my entire refrigerator.

—Colleen Lanigan-Ambrose, Seal Beach, CA

Save refrigerator space when entertaining

When hosting a party, I put items such as cole slaw, salad, and dips in zip-top bags and keep them all in *a large cooler filled with ice* or freezer packs. The refrigerator is then free to hold beverages, desserts, and other bulky or delicate dishes.

—Linda McLaughlin, Boston, MA

Ice cube tells if power was lost

When I return home after a long time away, I'm always concerned that a temporary power outage might have let the food in the freezer thaw and refreeze. So before I go away, I put an *ice cube on a plate* or in a zip-top bag and set it in the freezer. When I return to the house, I check the ice cube for signs of having melted and refrozen. This tells me that the food might be suspect.

—Lilia Dvarionas, Kanata, Ontario, Canada

Vacuum-sealing zip-top bags

When you fill plastic zip-top bags for the freezer, you need to remove as much air from the bag as possible to prevent freezer burn. This is easy to do for liquids, but there's a trick for dealing with solids. Put the food in the bag, *insert a drinking straw* into one end of the bag, and close the zipper up to the straw. Pinch the zipper and bag around the straw and suck out the air (yes, with your mouth). Then quickly pull out the straw and finish the zip. It's almost as good as a vacuum pack, and it will considerably extend the life of your frozen goodies.

—Russ Shumaker, Richmond, VA

Getting the air out of freezer bags

To prevent freezer burn, it's important to get all the air out of the freezer bag, but most of us don't have a vacuum-sealer. Some people improvise by sucking the air out through a straw. I prefer to put the food in the bag and immerse the

How Cold Is Frozen?

For maximum freezer shelf life, you need a freezer that holds foods at a constant temperature of 0°F or below. If you're unsure about the temperature of your freezer, test it with a freezer thermometer. Some home freezers can maintain this temperature but many don't. Among the freezers that don't are those inside the refrigerator, often called "ice-cube" compartments. These generally hold a temperature between 10° and 25°F. Also be aware that opening the refrigerator frequently causes fluctuations in this type of freezer's temperature and accelerates food spoilage. In general, ice-cube compartments are not intended to store perishable meats and fish for any length of time. Meat stored in this type of freezer should be used within 2 months and fish within 3 weeks. If you're serious about stocking up, consider investing in a free-standing freezer with its own temperature setting and a tight door seal. These freezers hold a constant temperature of 0°F or below and store food safely for much longer periods. Beef stored at 0°F can last up to 8 months.

—Molly Stevens, *Fine Cooking*

open bag up to the top edge in water. The *water pressure* forces all the air out of the bag. Then I zip the bag closed and take it out of the water.

—Matt Kaspar, Austin, TX

Liners hold more than baby's milk

Disposable baby-bottle liners are a great way to freeze leftover liquids in portions that can be more useful than ice-cube-size portions. Just pour extra buttermilk, broth (cooled first), fruit juice, wine, or any other liquid into the liner, which is *marked with measurements* and holds up to 8 ounces. No more guessing how many cubes of stock you'll need. The liner is easier to fill if you put it inside a baby's bottle, but you can also prop it up in a glass. Stand the filled liners in the door of the freezer until solid. Then store in a plastic bag. The liner tears away easily from the frozen liquid so you can put the stored broth or juice in the microwave or a saucepan, or just place the liner in a cup to thaw. One small drawback—liners can't go into the microwave. Liners are sold in boxes of 100 or more at most drugstores.

—Mary MacVean, Jackson Heights, NY

Snack-size zip-top bags work in the freezer

I find that snack-size zip-top bags (they're about half the size of the sandwich bags) are very convenient when I want to freeze small amounts of anything: leftovers from a can of tomato paste or coconut milk, for example. I also use the snack-size bags to freeze portion-size amounts of stew, stock, or tomato sauce. To keep the small bags organized in the freezer and to protect them, I *store them all together* in one large heavy-gauge freezer bag.

—Anita Pandolfi, South Britain, CT

Milk cartons are good freezing containers

I use empty milk cartons to freeze stocks and soups. Thoroughly washed, they make excellent freezing containers. Use *strong tape to close up the spout* and store the cartons standing up, if possible (at least until the contents freeze). The cartons expand in the freezer without cracking or pushing off the lid, and the outside can be peeled away to expose the contents for quick thawing.

—Deborah Easson, Utterson, Ontario, Canada

Mix and freeze extra dry ingredients

If you have favorite baking recipes that you make often, mix together an extra batch or two of the dry ingredients and freeze them in a zip-top bag. This *saves time and keeps the ingredients fresher* than if they were in the kitchen cabinet. It's especially helpful for breads that call for more than one kind of flour—you'll no longer have to lug out 3 or 4 bags of flour each time you bake.

—Michael Feldman, Hendersonville, NC

Double-wrap foods to avoid freezer burn

The best way to prevent freezer burn is to use a double-wrap system. Wrap foods in plastic, then seal them in an airtight plastic bag. This initial layer keeps moisture from escaping (and thus the food from drying out), while the second layer prevents oxidation. *To keep ice crystals from forming* on ice cream, put a layer of plastic wrap directly on the surface of the ice cream.

—Shirley O. Corriher, *Fine Cooking*

Flat-freezing vegetables without sticking

When you flat-freeze vegetables, you want to keep the produce from sticking to the pan or baking sheet. Line a jelly roll pan or baking sheet with a linen dish-

Tips for Better Freezing

Check your freezer temperature. Ideally, home freezers operate at about 0°F and can freeze food quickly. Poorly operating freezers and ice-tray compartments will freeze food slowly (between 25° and 31°F), resulting in larger ice crystals and poor texture in your frozen food.

Wrap food tightly. Limit moisture loss and prevent freezer burn by sealing food tightly in moisture- and vapor-proof wrap. Freezer burn occurs when the moisture from the surface of food evaporates. Be sure to use plastic bags that are specifically for freezer use, nonpermeable plastic wrap, or containers, and squeeze or burp out as much air as possible before sealing.

Freeze food quickly. Set the food on the freezer's lowest shelf, which is usually colder than the upper shelves. When the food is frozen solid, it can then be moved to another shelf. Adding too much food to the freezer can warm it up, so only add about 10% of the freezer's capacity at a time.

Don't exceed the expected shelf life of a food. Even foods that freeze well deteriorate if left in the freezer too long. Label and date frozen foods.

—Shirley O. Corriher, *Fine Cooking*

towel and spread out the produce on the towel in one layer. Freeze the produce until hard, then transfer to storage bags. *The towel absorbs any excess water* and prevents your fruits or vegetables from sticking to the pan.

—Susan Asanovic, Wilton, CT

Store ground beef flat in freezer bags

Although I try to use only freshly home-ground beef (or any other meat), there are times when I prefer the convenience of preground beef. I'll grind a large quantity of beef and divide it into smaller portions. After putting a portion of the ground meat into a zip-top freezer bag, I gently flatten the bag until the meat is quite flat, then seal the bag. This allows for a *perfect vacuum seal*, makes for quicker defrosting, and makes freezer storage much more efficient.

—Richard G. Avramenko, Red Deer, Alberta, Canada

Freezing meat efficiently

When I buy meat in bulk, I put small portions into plastic sandwich bags, labeling and dating each with a permanent marker. Then I put these small bags into a big freezer bag and label it chicken, beef, or whatever. When I need meat, I take out a small bag or two, but I leave the bigger bag in the freezer. Not only does this save me money on freezer bags, but my meats also get *double protection from freezer burn.*

—Desiree Mendoza, Veradale, WA

Keeping order in the freezer

To avoid frozen chaos in my chest-style storage freezer, I bought 4 *plastic file-folder crates* (like the old milk crates) from an office-supply store. The crates stack up and are well-ventilated. Getting to the bottom of the freezer is now just a matter of lifting out one crate. To further organize, each crate holds a different category of food: poultry, beef, fruits and vegetables, and breads. The crates left enough room at the top of the freezer for 2 large, shallow bins that hold leftovers and other items that I plan to use soon.

I keep a running list of what goes in and what comes out.

—Paul St. Onge, Chandler, AZ

Keeping inventory of freezer food

I've used one of your reader's tips about using stackable crates in the chest freezer and then storing foods by category. To help keep track of what's in there, I keep a running list of what goes in and what comes out. When I put food in the freezer, I add it to the list, noting the quantity, the date it went in, and the date it would expire, and when I take something out, it gets crossed off. I keep the inventory list on my fridge, along with a food storage chart. This way, nothing gets lost or forgotten in the freezer, and when I don't know what to make for supper or when I'm rushed, I check the list, decide what I want, and go fetch it. This list reminds me when I'm running low on certain foods, and when there is something that needs to be eaten or else tossed out.

—Carole Villeneuve, Chelsea, Quebec, Canada

Labeling frozen foods changed my life

Everyone knows that you're supposed to label a bag or container of food with the date and contents before sticking it in the freezer, but I never bothered to

The Safe Temperature Zone
for Food

Close to 90% of all foodborne illness is caused by something we can control—temperature.

The range at which bacteria can survive and grow enough to make us sick is between 40° and 140°F. The extremes of the danger zone are much less dangerous than the center, however. Bacteria growth rate slows dramatically below 70°F and above 120°F. The real concern is keeping food below 70°F (room temperature) and above 120°F.

COOL FOOD QUICKLY SO BACTERIA CAN'T GROW

Obviously, we can't avoid the danger zone altogether, or we wouldn't be able to cook or cool food. But we can move the food rapidly through this zone by heating and cooling it as quickly as possible. Here are a few tips:

- **Defrost food in the refrigerator. It takes longer but prevents the food from sitting at room temperature.**
- **Defrost food under cool running water (below 70°F) if you're in a hurry.**
- **Cook the food immediately if you defrosted it in a microwave. Microwaves heat unevenly, and parts of the food may rise above 70°F during defrost.**
- **Chill food to just below 70°F in an ice bath before refrigerating. (Refrigerators do a poor job of chilling large amounts of food.)**
- **Divide large amounts of food into smaller batches to speed chilling.**

—Molly Stevens, *Fine Cooking*

do it until I went to a stationery store and bought some *white adhesive labels* and put them in my silverware drawer along with a pen. At first it seemed like a hassle, but I've finally disciplined myself to go to the drawer before the freezer. I can't express the satisfaction I get from grabbing a container of unidentifiable something from the freezer and knowing definitively what it is and when it went in. If you're still not labeling your frozen foods, just do it.

—Carol Spinelli, Atlanta, GA

Labeling freezer bags neatly

I like to buy bulk packs of fresh meat and poultry and portion the meat into plastic bags to freeze. I always filled the plastic bags with meat first, and then, with wet and sticky hands, I'd take a permanent marker and try to write the contents on the equally wet and sticky bags. It finally dawned on me that I was doing things backward. Now *I write on the clean, empty bags* first, then fill the bags.

—Madeline DeBlasi, Stamford, CT

Thaw food quickly without gimmicks

You can thaw frozen foods quickly with a heavy aluminum frying pan. Fill the pan with hot water and wait a minute or two for the pan to warm. Pour out the water and set the frozen food in the pan. When the pan cools, repeat the heating process with hot water and turn the food over to thaw it from the other side. *Aluminum is an excellent heat conductor* that quickly transfers its stored heat into the frozen food. This method works just as well as those expensive thawing trays advertised on television.

—Robert Ponsi, Eustis, FL

Kitchen Organization

Opening food cans safely

I keep my manual can opener near my refrigerator door so I can grab a refrigerator magnet to fish out the *sharp-edged can lid* without having to worry about cutting my fingers.

—Ken Fruehstorfer, Palantine Bridge, NY

Make a homemade utensil rack

I have a small kitchen and a large collection of utensils. I like the look and convenience of hanging my kitchen tools, but the racks on the market were so expensive that I bought some hardware to make my own. I mounted large cup hooks in a row under the upper kitchen cabinets about 3 inches from the wall, then pushed a 4-foot aluminum rod through the hooks and hung some small "S" hooks on the rod to hang the utensils on. Now my *gadgets are instantly available*, I gained drawer space, and the display looks cool.

—Shirley Hooper, Kuna, ID

Key hanger holds measuring spoons

I've transformed a piece of hardware meant to hang keys into a handy place to hang measuring spoons and cups. I love having these items so accessible.

—Patricia Ryan Madson, El Granada, CA

Organize your measuring tools

For handy measuring and quicker conversions, I hang a row of measuring cups on the *inside of an upper cabinet door*. A set of measuring spoons (that have been separated from their ring) hangs below the cups, and a table of equivalents is taped above. If you do this, just remember to position the cups and spoons so that they won't knock against the inside shelves when the cabinet door is shut.

—Jean Linton, Adell, WI

Deli container holds twine

We've discovered an easy and inexpensive way to keep our butcher twine clean and handy. We take a *clear plastic container* from the deli counter that's big enough to hold the twine (pint-size), cut a hole in the middle of the lid (two slash marks with a knife works), and fish the twine through. We haven't chased a ball of twine since.

—Bill Apodaca and Cheryl Keller, Royal Oak, MI

Rolling pin rack

To keep my 6 rolling pins from rolling around in my cabinet, I've converted a rack that's meant to hold waxed paper and aluminum foil into a special rolling pin rack. The "wrap stacker" is made of plastic-coated heavy wire. My cabinet is now better organized, and I have easy access to the pins.

Convert a rack that's meant to hold waxed paper and foil.

—Fran Datko, Weston, FL

A neat spot for a sifter

I always keep my flour sifter in a disposable round aluminum pan rather than directly on the shelf. *The pan keeps the sifter's flour and sugar dust* contained so my shelf stays neat and clean.

—Matt Guagliardo, Kendall Park, NJ

Storing dish brushes out of sight

I've discovered a great place to store my sturdy vegetable and dish brushes: the *dishwasher silverware basket*. It's a logical and convenient place to stash those unsightly brushes and dish pads, and the brushes are always there and always clean from being run through the dishwasher with the soiled dishes. No more searching in the scary cabinet under the sink for my dishwashing tools.

—Denise Scott Jackson, Grandville, MI

A neat way to store dish detergent

Tired of the bottle of liquid dish soap—goopy and slippery with spilled detergent—that sat on my kitchen sink, I bought a small, empty plastic bottle *with a pump dispenser top* and filled it with dish detergent. The filled bottle now looks neat and clean on my sink, and the convenient dispenser top never spills its contents.

—Evelyn Evans, Brewster, NY

Rubber wineglass mats keep kitchen tools anchored

I bought some thin foam Grip Liner® mats to line our wineglass shelves, but I'm just now discovering how versatile this material is. I can store my damp, just-washed glasses on the mats to dry, and I use pieces of the mat under cutting boards and mixing bowls to keep them from sliding on the counter. A piece of the mat makes *a great lid-opener* for the most stubborn jar. Used as a drawer liner, the mats keep my kitchen hand tools and cutlery organized, preventing them from sliding around in the drawers.

—Sadie McAllister, Little Rock, AR

Save cabinet space by nesting pans

To save storage space in my small kitchen, I keep all my pans in three stacks in my kitchen cabinet. My saucepans, sauté pans, and frying pans nest inside one another, resulting in compact stacks that take up only the shelf space of three pans. If a pan has a nonstick finish, I'll throw in a couple of sheets of paper towels to keep the coating from getting scratched. (Nonskid shelf liners work great, too.) Whenever I'm shopping for a new pan, I look for one that can be stacked with my old pans.

Nest pans into compact stacks that take up only the shelf space of three pans.

—S. Schieving, via email

Hang pans with their lids

I hang much of my cookware on a pot rack mounted on my kitchen ceiling. Many people don't realize that the lids of most high-end cookware companies (such as All-Clad®, Calphalon, and Sitram®) can be inverted and slid onto the long handles of their pans before hanging—thus *saving space*. Now you won't have to hunt for that elusive lid for the pan you're using.

—Adam Eisner, Hadley, MA

Lid holders

Hang onto those racks you once used to organize *long-playing record albums*. They make terrific holders for pot and pan lids so the lids don't clang around in your kitchen cabinets.

—Don Silvers, Los Angeles, CA

A drying rack keeps pot lids organized

After trying various ways to store the lids of my pots and casseroles so they were accessible yet organized, I finally hit upon a method that works for me. I bought a *dish-drying rack* (the kind you would put on your counter next to the sink) and set my lids in it, arranged by size. The rack sits on a shelf next to my pots and pans. Now the right lid is at my fingertips.

—Stacey Ballis, Chicago, IL

Create a spot for hot pot lids

To solve the problem of where to put hot, dripping pot lids, I made a lid rack *for the back of my stove.* I cut a piece of wood the width and length of my stove and put a few grooves in it. I rest the grooved board on the back of my stove and set pot lids there when they're still hot. Storing the hot lids on their sides allows condensation to drain off so I avoid burning myself, plus it keeps my limited counter space clear.

—Howard Cheung, via email

Organize magazines by seasons, not titles

As a culinary professional and an avid reader, I save many cooking magazines. I used to save all of one title in binders for each year, but now I save mixed titles in separate binders or boxes for each month. Now when I'm looking for information about a seasonal food or *particular holiday*, all of the information is together. As I flip through the monthly files, I often find foods that pair well with the one for which I had originally sought information.

—Tim Furst, Frederick, MD

Store trash bags at the bottom of the trash bin

To save time and storage space, I store clean trash bags at the bottom of the trash container, *underneath the bag* that's in current use. They don't take up much room, and I never have to search for the bags.

—Lega Sammut Medcalf, Limington, ME

Keep produce bags in a paper towel tube

Everyone has trouble figuring out what to do with all of those plastic bags you take home from the produce department. We've discovered that an empty paper towel tube is the perfect holder. Just *stuff the bags* in one end and pull them out the other. You can also wrap your rubber bands on the outside of the tube to keep down the clutter in your kitchen drawer.

—Bill Apodoca and Cheryl Keller, Royal Oak, MI

Handling dishtowels

In my kitchen I use many more dishtowels than paper towels, sometimes racking up 4 or 5 dirty dishtowels in a day. Instead of constantly running the used towels to the hamper down the hall, I keep them in a *tiny round hamper* (from the dollar store) in the corner of my kitchen. The added benefit is that while the towels in the hamper may not be clean enough to reuse to dry dishes or wipe a counter, they can be used to mop up spills on the floor or cooking splatters from the stovetop. Every two days I dump the dishtowels from my little hamper into my big hamper to be washed.

—Sandra Leshaw, Riverdale, NY

Crease-free tablecloths

Instead of keeping my tablecloths folded and stored on a shelf, I drape them on a large clothes hanger and *hang them in the closet.* There are fewer creases this way, so they look good even if I don't iron them—and I get to spend more time working on the meal.

—Kelly Danek, Westminster, CA

A cardboard box safely transports food

I often bring hot cooked food to family gatherings, and I've found that the best way to travel with it is to place the container in a small cardboard box *lined with sheets of newspapers*, with some scrunched-up newspapers wedged in around the dish if necessary. The cardboard box then goes into my car's trunk so the food is on a level surface. This helps me transport hot foods safely, and any spills are neatly contained in the box.

—Gwen Webster, Laramie, WY

Use plastic manicotti trays for transporting éclairs

I have a tip for transporting cannolis and éclairs. Whenever I buy dry manicotti shells, I save the plastic trays that hold the shells in the box. I then use these trays when I bring éclairs or any other similarly shaped dessert to a friend's house. I can *stack the plastic trays* into a rectangular glass dish and transport them without breaking even one.

—Caryn Tentarelli, Fogelsville, PA

 **Cleaning**

Nonstick spray without the mess

When spraying a skillet, cookie sheet, or pan for baking, hold it over the open *door of your dishwasher.* This way, there will be no greasy mist on the sink, stovetop, or counter to clean.

—Lilia Dvarionas, Ottawa, Ontario, Canada

Make cooking cleanup much faster and easier

All recipes tell you to have your ingredients measured out and ready to use before starting to cook. Since I live alone and have no dishwasher, I make clean-up easier by using paper *muffin and cupcake liners* or the small, flat-bottomed paper cups you might find at water coolers, to hold ingredients such as chopped herbs, garlic, and spices. The little cups are even great for the small amounts of liqueur some recipes call for. After cooking, just throw the bits of paper away. This is a lot faster than having lots of little bowls to wash, dry, and put away.

—Al Politowski, Hoboken, NJ

Pastry scraper cleans counter

Keep your pastry scraper handy after you've finished rolling out your pie crust or kneading your bread and use it to *clean off your counter;* it's especially efficient at scraping off bits of hardened dough.

—Lily McCafferty, Newton, MA

Waxed paper makes cleanup a breeze

When I'm baking or cooking, I often lay a piece of waxed paper on the counter for easy cleanup. When measuring flour or sugar, any excess falls on the paper and can easily be collected by lifting the corners of the paper and pouring it back into its container. Waxed paper is useful when separating eggs while making angel food cake—put the broken shells on the paper in a pile—when you're done, just wrap the shells up in the paper and discard; no need to wipe the counter. It's also great for grating cheese on the counter, or setting wooden spoons during cooking…you get the idea.

—Yvonne Wai, Bella Coola, British Columbia, Canada

Easier cleanup after making bread

Here is how I make cleanup easier after making bread dough in a stand mixer. After removing the dough from the bowl, *I use a pastry brush to brush the flour dust from the mixer arm and base* into a small dish or bowl. I use this small pile of flour to finish the dough by hand before the first rising. I'm also careful to soak the mixing bowl and the dough hook in cold water. Warm or hot water would cause the flour to stick; cold water helps it slide right off.

—Natalie Slater Cornwell, Quincy, IL

Quick baking cleanup

A friend once showed me the best way to clean up the flour that's left on the counter after dusting or kneading dough. Instead of making a gooey mess with a damp sponge, try sweeping up the dry flour with *a small whisk broom*, especially one with soft bristles.

—Paisley Close, San Diego, CA

A cleaner stovetop and better fried foods

I always use a spatter screen to minimize the mess when pan frying, but a fine spray of greasy steam always seems to get through the screen to coat my cabinets and stovetop. Now when I fry, I place a *paper towel on top of the spatter screen* to absorb the grease and moisture coming off the frying food. This helps the food crisp up better and results in less cleanup.

—Josie Grable, New York, NY

A baking sheet helps keep the stovetop clean

Last month I finally bought the professional-style, six-burner stove of my dreams. It's twice the size of my old stove, with twice the amount of surface to clean. Now when I cook, *I cover the unused burners* with baking sheets to keep them clean. This makes cleaning the stove a breeze.

—Lori Lewis, New York, NY

Dish soap protects stove from boil-overs

As a home beer brewer, I used to get annoyed at how my stovetop turned black during the long boiling period. Then I learned this trick, which I now use whenever I'm cooking something that threatens to boil over or make a mess of the stove. Dab some dishwashing liquid on a paper towel and spread a thin film of soap on the stovetop before cooking. Afterward, use a wet towel to wipe off any marks. *No scrubbing necessary.*

—Jim Basara, Falls Church, VA

A drop of oil protects stainless-steel stoves

My professional-style stainless-steel stove looks and works great, but the brushed metal finish shows every fingerprint and smudge. To keep it looking great, after cleaning the trim with soapy water, I wipe it with the same cloth I use for polishing my furniture with lemon oil. You can't see or feel the oil on the metal, but it *protects the finish from blemishes.* A drop of mineral oil or baby oil also works well. Wipe the oven with a dry cloth afterward, if you want.

—Margaret Hirsch, Rancho Palos Verdes, CA

Salt prevents oven fires

If ingredients bubble over onto the oven floor when baking, you can *stop them from smoking* by tossing salt on the mess. When baking is finished, immediately scrape up the spill with a spatula.

—Mary R. Sullivan, Concord, CA

Self-cleaning oven cleans grill racks, too

Whenever I use my oven's self-cleaning feature, I also put the black, heavily encrusted racks from my charcoal and gas grills in the oven to clean; *they always come out like new.* Just be sure your grill racks are sturdy enough to withstand the extremely high heat of the self-cleaning cycle.

—Mimi Christie, Ramsey, NJ

Steam helps clean the microwave

Before cleaning the interior of your microwave, bring a *cup of water to a boil in the microwave* and boil it for an additional minute or two. The condensation from the hot water is enough to loosen most cooked-on splatters. Carefully remove the hot water and wipe the inside of the microwave clean.

—Mary Anne Meyer, Vermillion, SD

Keep baking soda handy for kitchen chores

I got tired of going to the pantry every time I needed a dab of baking soda to clean something at the sink and, because my hands were usually wet, the box of baking soda always got wet. Now, I keep the baking soda handy by putting it *in a glass shaker bottle* that once held grated cheese and that has a lid full of large holes. Now the bottle is next to my sink, ready to remove odors, food stains, coffee and tea rings from my dishes and kitchenware.

—Sara Burns, Grass Valley, CA

Scrub with a salt paste

I use a handful of kosher salt mixed with a few drops of water to scrub vegetables and fruits like potatoes, apples, citrus fruits, whole fish, and skin-on poultry. *I treat the salt like sandpaper* to exfoliate the surface of the foods, then I rinse them well under cold running water and blot dry with paper towels.

—Lorie Vu, Las Vegas, NV

Vinegar removes dirt from vegetables

To remove excess dirt from home-grown vegetables, add about ¼ cup vinegar to a basin of cold water. Submerge the vegetables in the water and *soak for several minutes*. Slosh vigorously, rinse well, and drain. The vinegar cuts through and loosens the dirt without affecting flavor.

—Russ Shumaker, Richmond, VA

Scrub vegetables with sponge pad

I use the *bristly side* of a plastic scouring pad (a clean one that's just for this purpose) to scrub vegetables. It's ideal for potatoes, carrots, or beets. Often, I don't even have to peel them afterward.

—Peri-Lyn Palmer, Redwood City, CA

Keep scouring pads dry on netting from fruits

To keep small dish scrubbies and scouring pads *dry, clean, and rust free*, I recycle those elastic-rimmed nets from the tops of blueberry and other fruit cartons and put them over an interesting cup that I found at the flea market. This keeps the pads out of the puddle of water that always collects under them in a dish. Each net lasts for a few months as long as you rinse it and the cup occasionally.

—Michele Mannella, Pittsburgh, PA

Keeping bleach solution in a spray bottle

I keep a spray bottle of 10% bleach solution (1 part bleach to 9 parts water) under my kitchen sink. It's very handy to use in conjunction with soap and water to *disinfect cutting boards and countertops* after preparing meats and to help avoid cross-contamination. I also spray the bleach solution on my kitchen sponges to keep them fresher longer.

—Janet de Carteret, Bellevue, WA

Deglazing cleans pots and pans

Here's how to make cleanup easier when your skillet or other pan has a caked-on residue in the bottom. After cooking, remove all the food and set the pan on the stovetop until it's hot. With the pan still on the flame, *deglaze it with water*. Almost all the residue will be lifted up from the bottom.

—Jim Harb, via email

Steam-clean a Pyrex pan

Cooking in Pyrex can have a serious drawback: scrubbing off cooked-on bits afterwards. To make the job easier, I fill the pan halfway with water, cover it with plastic wrap, and microwave it for 5 minutes. Then I let the dish sit for a few minutes, covered, so the steam can go to work on the gunk. When I pour off the hot water, I am able to wash the pan with *a minimum of elbow grease*.

—Julia Robinson, Nashville, TN

Drying a spinner basket

Here's a fast way to dry a salad spinner basket: After washing, *return it to the spinner* and give it a whirl. The water flies off the basket and onto the outer bowl, which is much easier to towel-dry than the basket.

—Vicki McLain, Baytown, TX

Fingernail brush for hard-to-clean tools

I keep a small, stiff fingernail brush with my dishwashing supplies. I find that it's terrific for cleaning my garlic press, cheese and ginger graters, sieves, and any other tool with tiny *pesky holes and crevices*.

—Beverly Elliott, Philo, CA

Clean the garlic press with a sink spray nozzle

I have a separate spray nozzle on my sink (the kind with a plastic or metal hose) that's terrific for cleaning out the garlic bits wedged tightly in the little holes of my garlic press. I hold the garlic press open and aim the sprayer directly at the holes in the press plate. The *tiny, powerful jets* of water quickly blast the stubborn garlic right out of the press.

—Josie Grable, New York, NY

Getting that pastry brush really clean

To clean my brushes, I put a few drops of dish detergent in a Pyrex or other heatproof cup, fill it with *almost-boiling water*, and soak the brush for about 15 minutes, working it around a little to dislodge and dissolve any congealed fat or other gunky particles. I then pour the water out and repeat the process two or three more times. This has kept my collection of brushes in near-new condition for many, many years.

—Carole Walter, *Fine Cooking*

Bottle brush cleans cookie cutters

I have a lot of intricately shaped cookie cutters. I used to struggle with a sponge to *dislodge cookie dough* from the cutters' many nooks and corners, but now I use a bottle brush to clean them.

—Rose Barvenik, Trumbull, CT

Film of oil keeps plastic from staining

Storing tomato-based soups or sauces, such as marinara sauce or chili, in a plastic container often leaves a red stain. I've found that if *I lightly spray the container* with cooking oil before pouring in the sauce, the container washes out like new.

—Elaine Kovacs, Garland, TX

Getting storage containers clean

Foods that are tomato-based or high in fat tend to leave a greasy film in plastic containers. There are a couple of easy solutions for getting rid of the film. First, wipe the container with a paper towel to pick up some of the greasy residue. Then, make a *thick paste of baking soda and water*, rub it inside the container, rinse it out, and wash the plastic in hot, soapy water. You can also try washing the containers with white vinegar instead of, or in addition to, this paste.

—Sophie Hudson, senior product manager, Tupperware Corp.

Newspaper absorbs odors from plastic

To remove the odor from a plastic container in which I've stored cut onions, I borrow an old trick from my mother. I wash the container and stuff it with a crumpled piece of newspaper. In a few days (with the lid closed), the *newspaper has absorbed the odor*.

—Eric Feinstein, Ossining, NY

Cleaning oil and vinegar bottles

Cleaning unusually shaped oil and herb vinegar bottles is sometimes tricky. Add some *uncooked rice to the soap* and hot water in the bottle and shake. The rice will help rub off stubborn residue.

—Sylvie Parent, Rimouski, Quebec, Canada

Getting the coffee out

When using an upright Braun®- or Krups®-type coffee grinder, turn the grinder *upside down* while you're still grinding. Stop grinding, lightly tap the grinder on the counter once or twice, and take off the cap. All the ground coffee or spices are in the cap and ready to be dispensed.

—Erin J. Donahue, Westerly, RI

Cleaning coffee grinders

Grinding fresh coffee beans is an essential part of my weekend coffee ritual. After grinding the beans, I use a rather unorthodox tool to clean the grinder: an old-fashioned *bristle shaving brush* (about $1 at a bargain store). It does the job as effectively as a more expensive culinary brush.

—Isabella Losinger, Burnaby, British Columbia

Clean your coffee grinder with rice

I like to clean my coffee grinder with rice. I put in ¼ to ½ cup long-grain white rice and grind it to a powder. The *grinding loosens the coffee residue*, and the rice powder absorbs the oils.

—Michael W. Wood, San Jose, CA

Coffee between two paper filters is less messy

To keep cone-shaped coffee filters from collapsing and spilling grounds into the brew, or spattering the hard-to-clean area of the coffeemaker, I add *a second filter* on top of the measured coffee.

—Jean Linton, Adell, WI

Clean spice grinder with bread

I love to grind whole spices like cloves, coriander, and nutmeg in my coffee grinder, but cleaning up between batches has always been a problem. To eliminate leftover flavor from the ground spices, I put about three-quarters of a slice of bread in the mill and process. The *damp bread crumbs* pick up even the finest spice particles. In just a few seconds, the inside of the mill is clean and shiny, ready for the next batch of spices.

—Fredric A. Rhoads, Austin, TX

Keep a pastry brush for the spice grinder

I love to cook with freshly ground spices, but I always find that some spices get left behind in the grinder. To get out every last bit of bit, I use a *2-inch pastry brush* reserved just for this purpose. Now I can get a clean sweep.

—John Cecil, Austin, TX

Make the blender clean itself

After using the blender to mix, purée, or liquefy food, *use it once more* to start cleaning it. Fill the pitcher halfway with hot water and add detergent. Cover and blend for a few seconds. Rinse out the pitcher with fresh hot water and dry (depending on what you've blended, you may still need to disassemble the blade).

—Edith Ruth Muldoon, Baldwin, NY

Cold water removes cheese from a food processor bowl

After shredding mozzarella cheese in my food processor, I stumbled on the fact that if I treated the cheese clinging to the dirty blade and bowl as I do candle wax, it would be easier to clean. Sure enough: I found that hot water only spreads, stretches, and gums up the cheese (especially in the blade holes). Using very cold water helps the cheese harden and come right off.

Use very cold water; the cheese hardens and comes right off.

—Ana Weerts, Brookfield, WI

A spatula quickly cleans mixing bowls

Whenever I make a yeast dough in my stand mixer, the mixing bowl is always encrusted with the sticky residue of the dough. I used to scrub the bowl in water with a brush or sponge and then spend more time cleaning the cleaning utensils, but I'm wiser now. I just *soak the bowl in cold water* and dish-washing liquid for a half hour, then I scrape a rubber spatula around the inside of the bowl to remove the dough before quickly washing.

—Anne Yodice, Wantage, NJ

Make less of a mess with your stand mixer

I have a large stand mixer with metal arms that hold the work bowl in place. When I do a mixing job that involves adding ingredients while the mixer is running, I always put a large sheet of *waxed paper between the bowl* and the base of the mixer to catch any spills and to keep the mixer base clean. I make sure the sheet is large enough to cover several inches of counter space on either side of the mixer. This helps keep cleanup to a minimum.

—Marian Cabello, Portland, OR

Keeping a food scale clean

I store and use my electronic scale in a *large plastic zip-top bag*. This keeps the scale clean and dry, and I don't have to worry about food becoming trapped between the balance platform and the display base. The bag is easy to wipe clean after each use, and easy to replace when it's torn or old.

—Calli Barry, Honolulu, HA

Cleaning pasta machines

I have found that the most effective tool for quickly cleaning a stainless-steel pasta machine is a 1-inch brush. The *bristles can get into the little crevices* where flour likes to hide. I set the machine on the widest setting available to clean the rollers.

—Carla Brownlee, Ottawa, Ontario, Canada

Clean appliance crevices with a toothbrush

I like to keep an old toothbrush near the sink for *cleaning the crevices* of items like food processor attachments and the meat mallet. I store it along with my other scrubbers and sponges in a flowerpot with an attached saucer, so that the scrubbers can drain between uses.

—Stephanie Daval, Princeton, NJ

Hands-off cleaning for a pizza stone

I have found the best way to clean my pizza stone is to *leave it in the oven* during the self-cleaning cycle. Make sure you can leave your racks in during the high-heat cleaning and put the stone on one of the racks in the middle of the oven. I usually use the shortest clean cycle. All you need to do is wipe up the dust with a damp paper towel once the oven has cooled completely (be sure the stone is cool, too). I know there are some brands of pizza stones that cannot be left in the oven, so it's best to check with the manufacturer.

—Karen Grappone, Hillsborough, NJ

An easier way to wash wineglasses

While having a new baby has mostly hindered my attempts at cooking, it did give me a good cleaning tip. The long, *narrow brush designed for cleaning baby bottles* also works great for cleaning wineglasses that you can't put in the dishwasher.

—Lea-Anne Jackson, Atlanta, GA

Cleaning your pizza stone

Due to frequent use, my pizza stone as become a blackened mess. How can I clean it?

—Laura Hyatt, Rocky Point, NY

P.J. Hamel, senior editor of King Arthur Flour's "The Baker's Catalogue," responds: I would never clean it. The stains give it character! As for gunk, scrape it off while it's hot with a baker's bench knife or other metal straight-edge. You can also try scrubbing (when cold) with a paste made from kosher salt and warm water, using a scrubby sponge.

What you never want to do is use soap, vinegar, or anything that you don't want associated with your bread or pizza. The stone will absorb it, then give it off later, no matter how thoroughly you rinse it.

If you're set on keeping your stone clean, put a piece of parchment between the stone and whatever you're baking. The parchment won't hurt the stone's ability to give your baked goods a great, crisp crust. (Know that parchment can char at temperatures of 400°F and higher.)

Soak pans in dishwasher detergent

I use automatic dishwasher detergent and hot water to soak my stainless-steel, ceramic, and glass (but not nonstick) pans. The *powerful detergent* makes quick work of even the hardest cooked-on mess.

—Lane Johnson, via email

Toss sponges into the dishwasher

The last items that go into my dishwasher before I turn it on are my kitchen sponges. They come out fresh and clean, and *they last longer.*

—Lisa Jung, San Rafael, CA

Wash your faucet after handling raw meat

When I go to wash my hands after handling raw meat or poultry, I always run my soapy fingers over and under the faucet and its handles and give it a quick rinse as I rinse my hands. This *eliminates any cross-contamination* in case the faucet came into contact with the raw meat.

—Drew Dupuis, St. Louis, MO

Lemon helps dissolve calcium deposits

If you live in an area with high calcium content in the water, as I do, unsightly calcium deposits can build up around the sink faucets and other places. The mild acid in lemon juice seems to dissolve the calcium, so every time I juice a lemon or other citrus fruit, I rub the squeezed half over these areas. This saves future scrubbing with abrasive cleaners or chemicals, and the "fresh lemony scent" is genuine.

The mild acid in lemon juice seems to dissolve the calcium.

—Angie Newton, Twickenham, England

Sort waste products easily

For easy cleanup, I hook the handles of *a plastic grocery bag over the drawer beneath the counter* where I'm chopping vegetables. As I clean and chop vegetables, I scrape discards into the bag. When I'm done, I remove the bag and dump the debris in my compost pile. I hook a second bag over another drawer for noncompostable waste. And on a third, I hook a bag for recyclables.

—Lynda Breeze, Simi Valley, CA

Old newspapers keep trash bags from dripping

When I empty the trash bin, I always put some folded *newspapers in the bottom* of the new trash bag to soak up moisture from kitchen trash. A few sheets of newspaper also go into the bottom of the trash bin. This keeps the filled bag from dripping when I take it out of the kitchen.

—Thai Moreland, New York, NY

A no-mess way to discard used oil

Like many people, I pour greasy pan drippings and used cooking oil into an empty soup or vegetable can. Once the fat cools, though, I put the can in a small plastic bag, seal it with a twist-tie, and *store it in the door of my freezer*. I add more used fat or drippings to the can until it's three quarters full. Then on garbage day, I toss the can (still in the plastic bag) in my regular garage. It's a "no mess" way to handle a messy job.

—Helen de la Cerna, Altadena, CA

Use flour to clean up cooking oil spills

If you spill grease or oil in the kitchen, the best way to clean it up is to sprinkle the spill generously *with flour and use a dough scraper* or spatula to scrape it up. This way, you aren't leaving a greasy residue and it takes a lot less effort (and fewer paper towels) to clean up the mess.

—Jennifer Denlinger, Clermont, FL

Bleach absorbs fish odors

I love frying fish, whether pan-fried catfish or deep-fried shrimp. And I don't usually mind the smell while I'm cooking it or eating it. What I do mind is when I leave the house and return only to find that the house still smells like fish hours or even a day later. A friend offered this tip: put out *a little bowl of bleach* while frying. (It doesn't matter where you put it, just don't put it somewhere where it might be mistaken for water, or where a curious child or pet might come upon it.) I don't know how it works exactly, but the bleach winds up with a coating of scum on top of it, and the fishy smell disappears. One warning: Use a glass bowl; bleach can corrode a metal one if it's left in it for too long.

—John Martin Taylor, *Fine Cooking*

Erase cooking smells with an air cleaner

When my puny kitchen fan died recently, I was desperate to find a way to get rid of the persistent cooking smells that hung in the air. My eyes lighted on the huge, round air cleaner I keep in the living room for a family member with allergies, and I lugged it into the kitchen and plugged it in the next time I did some cooking. It did an amazing job, *getting rid of even the strongest,* fishiest smells. Now, I won't cook salmon without it.

—Joan Lord, New York, NY

Neutralize odors with citrus

If you have a garbage disposal, *toss in some orange and lemon peels* to remove kitchen odors.

— Marie Carpenter, Stamford, CT

Reduce broiling smoke

To reduce smoke and cooking odors when broiling, put a few slices of *stale bread in the broiler pan* under the rack to absorb spattering fat. Just be sure the rack is positioned an inch or two above the bread.

—Betsy Race, Euclid, OH

Natural copper cleaner

For a quick and natural way to clean copperware, just mix a solution of about *2 parts salt to 1 part vinegar or lemon juice,* rub it lightly onto the copper, and then rinse. Be sure to wear rubber gloves if you have any cuts or nicks on your hands, because the combination of acid and salt is not soothing!

—Inger Skaarup, Kansas City, MO

Toothpaste takes out tough stains

For stubborn stains on my countertops, pots, and pans, I rub out the stain with a dab of toothpaste *on a soft, wet sponge*—it almost always works. I also like knowing that toothpaste isn't overly abrasive, that it rinses easily, and that it's safe for my teeth and therefore safe in the kitchen.

—Ana Weerts, Brookfield, WI

Baking soda removes coffee and tea stains

To quickly clean coffeepots and teapots, don't use dish detergent. Just fill the pots with very hot water and baking soda, leave them in your kitchen sink for a few minutes, and then rinse with cool water. Your pots will be sparkling clean and *untainted by detergent perfumes.*

—Jean Zimkus, Woodbridge, CT

Be Prepared to
Prevent Kitchen Fires

A few years ago, a dinner guest left a plastic bottle of vegetable oil on the stovetop after helping me with the cooking. As we ate, the bottle melted and within minutes, a good grease fire was under way. Fortunately, we were able to smother the flames before they spread. There was no real damage—but the episode made me realize how important fire safety should be to every cook.

YOU CAN STOP MOST FIRES BEFORE THEY START

More house fires begin in the kitchen than in any other part of the home, and over 75% of kitchen fires start because people walk away from the kitchen. The lesson is obvious: pay attention while you're cooking. But there are also precautions that will help you avoid fires and to control those that may occur.

Fires need fuel. Deprive them of this and there's no fire. Small kitchen fires become larger house fires when food, oil, or greasy buildup begins to burn and the flames then spread to counters and cabinets. You can reduce risk by keeping kitchen surfaces and range hoods clean and free of debris. Avoid having towels, curtains, paper bags, and other flammable material near the stove or oven. Don't wear loose-fitting clothing while you're cooking: this way, there's nothing to dangle over an open flame.

KEEP A COOL HEAD, BUT DON'T BE A HERO

If you do have a kitchen fire, don't panic. Keep in mind that you should never try to fight a spreading fire by yourself. If a fire reaches cabinets, counters, or curtains, leave the house and call the fire department. But if you spot a small fire as it starts, there are a few simple methods to stop it.

All fires need air, and if you can take away a fire's air supply, it will die. Smothering a fire can be as simple as putting a lid on a burning pot, stomping on a burning dishtowel, or covering the fire forcefully with towels. Water is a great way to extinguish *some* fires, but can be deadly for others, so don't automatically think of dousing the flames.

EACH TYPE OF FIRE NEEDS A DIFFERENT RESPONSE

Basically, there are three types of fire: grease, electrical, and paper (which includes cloth, wood, plastic, and rubber).

Grease fires are the greatest hazard in kitchens. Cooking oils all have a temperature limit (generally 425° to 500°F), called a flash point. When heated beyond this point, oil will burst into flames. If you reuse oil for deep-frying, be aware that as the oil get old, this flash point drops, making it more highly flammable. Also, be aware that unrefined oils, such as extra virgin olive oil and nut oils, break down and catch on fire at a much lower temperature.

Never throw water on a grease fire—it will splatter and spread. Instead, smother the flame with a lid or a kitchen towel. Throwing baking soda on a small grease fire will extinguish it, so keep a large, opened box of baking soda close to the stove. Salt works too, but not as effectively. The best response is to throw baking soda on the fire *and* cover it with a lid.

Electrical fires can result from faulty wiring, overloaded outlets, or malfunctioning appliances. Never throw water on an electrical appliance until you unplug it. If an electrical fire starts, immediately unplug the appliance. Once the appliance is unplugged, the fire is no longer electrical, and you can then safely smother the flames by dousing with water or using a towel or fire blanket. To help prevent electrical fires, keep your appliances in good condition and replace old appliances as they become worn out.

Paper fires may be the most obvious to deal with. To put out burning food, paper, wood, cloth, or plastic, use water and smother the flames. For example, pour water on a fire in a trash can or stomp on a burning cardboard box.

DON'T RELY ON EXTINGUISHERS

Fire extinguishers are sold for home use but they aren't ideal for kitchen fires. People are often injured by relying on a fire extinguisher instead of calling the fire department. The dry chemical solution found in most home extinguishers is highly pressurized. Even the smallest fire extinguisher has enough force to blow a good-size pot and its contents right off the stovetop. If you're trying to subdue some burning oil in a wok, the force of the fire extinguisher could splash burning oil across your kitchen and anyone in the way. Fire extinguishers are best used to put out wood and paper fires or to knock down a fire in order to escape a burning house. Fire blankets are also very effective for smothering small fires. Most important, install smoke detectors on all levels of your home and check their batteries regularly.

—Molly Stevens, *Fine Cooking*

Handy
Kitchen
Techniques

Trussing a *Chicken* or *Turkey*

You don't have to truss, but the finished bird will look neater if you do.

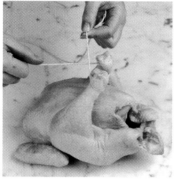

1. Starting under the legs, draw a length of kitchen string up and over the legs.

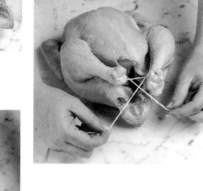

2. Cross the string between the legs and pull the ends to draw the legs together.

3. Keeping the string taut to pull the legs toward the body, run each end over the thighs and wings and tie securely at the neck.

Boning a *Chicken* Breast

If you need a reason to learn how to bone a breast, just compare the price of boneless breasts against those of bone-in breasts in the supermarket. If the bone-in breast halves you buy are still attached, cut them apart at the breastbone, with either kitchen shears or a chef's knife. For taking out the smaller bones, a boning or paring knife works best.

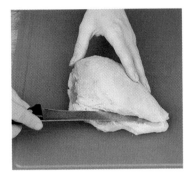

1. With a sharp boning knife, begin cutting between the meat and bone along the narrower side of the breast.

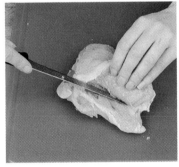

2. Gently pull back on the meat as you continue slicing the meat away from the bone.

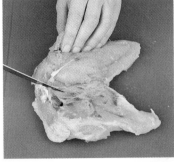

3. When you reach the wing joint, maneuver the knife over and around the joint as you continue to pull back on the meat.

4. At this point, you should be able to feel a spur of the wishbone in the breast meat. Scrape and cut around the wishbone to free it from the meat, then finish cutting the breast completely free of all the bones.

How to Turn a *Whole Chicken* into Ten Serving Pieces

Packaged chicken parts are often poorly trimmed, randomly sized, and more expensive pound for pound than a whole chicken. By cutting up a chicken yourself, you get more evenly sized pieces for grilling, frying, sautéing, or stewing. A sturdy chef's knife and a washable cutting surface are the only tools you need. As a bonus, the leftover chicken back is a great addition to the stockpot—you can freeze it until you're ready to make stock.

1. Pull out each of the wings and cut through the first joint, leaving the meatiest portion of the wing attached to the breast.

2. Hoist the chicken off the surface by the end of the drumstick to loosen the leg. Slice through the skin to expose the leg's interior.

3. Forcefully bend the leg away to expose the joint. Insert the knife point between the ball and socket to separate the joint.

4. Cut the leg away from the body as close to the backbone as possible. Repeat steps 2 through 4 for the other leg.

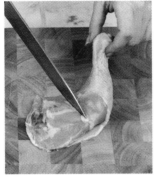

5. Follow the line of fat that divides the drumstick from the thigh to cut down through the joint that separates the two parts.

6. Starting at the tail end, cut through the ribs to free the backbone. Chop through the collarbone to completely cut off the back.

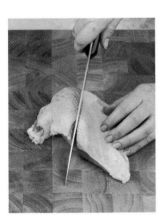

7. Flatten the breast with your hand, then cut down through the breastbone with some force to separate the halves.

8. Divide each half breast in half again; cut at an angle to make two evenly sized pieces.

How to Split and Partially Bone a *Chicken*

By following these directions, you'll end up with two partially boned chicken halves (the process is also known as spatchcocking), perfect for cooking on the grill or under a brick with incredibly moist results.

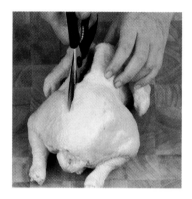

1. Place the chicken breast side down on the cutting board and remove the backbone using kitchen shears or a sharp chef's knife. Starting at the neck end, cut along one side of the backbone.

2. Now turn the bird so the tail end is facing you and cut down along the other side of the backbone.

3. Cut a short incision in the middle of the top of the keel bone (this has cartilage on the top end) and flatten the chicken. The keel bone should partially pop out. Trim the rest of it away with a paring or boning knife.

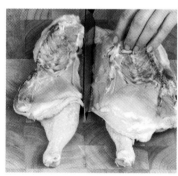

4. Cut the bird completely in half.

5. Cut off the first two wing joints on each side with a chef's knife or cleaver.

6. Slide a sharp paring knife under the ribs on both chicken halves and carefully cut them out.

Butterflying a *Chicken* Breast

You'll want to butterfly a chicken breast for one of two reasons: first, to get a very thin, even cut that you can cook up quickly in all sorts of ways on the grill or in a sauté pan. You can also butterfly a breast if you intend to stuff it. Butterflying is best done with a boning knife.

1. Starting with the thicker side of the breast, hold a sharp knife parallel to the cutting surface. Slice the meat almost completely in half, stopping about ¼ inch from the other side.

2. Open the breast like a book and pat the new surface to make the cutlet evenly thick.

Carving a *Turkey*

You'll want to carve your turkey using a long carving knife or a chef's knife. A large fork will help keep the bird in place, but a table fork will do in a pinch.

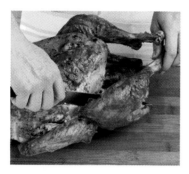

1. Slice down and back to where the thigh attaches to the bird. Bend the thigh away from the breast. Slice down through the joint to separate the leg, twisting the knife a little until the leg comes off.

2. Place the thigh on the cutting board skin side up with the knee facing away from you and cut through the joint that separates the drumstick from the rest of the leg. (The joint is always a bit farther into the drumstick than you think.) Separate the two.

3. Cut the thigh meat away in strips by sliding the knife along the side of the large thigh section parallel to the bone. Slice the drumstick or serve it whole.

4. Make a horizontal cut just above the wing, straight into the turkey as far as you can go. This cut allows the breast meat to fall from the bird as you slice.

5. Slice the breast meat on the diagonal, parallel to the breastbone. Hold the fork against the breastbone as you carve the slices. Lift off each slice, holding it between the knife and fork. Continue carving until you've sliced all the meat from one side.

6. Cut into the joint above the wing to remove it. Or leave it on for now—it helps stabilize the turkey on the platter. Repeat the carving on the other side of the bird.

Trimming a *Tenderloin*

Pork, beef, and lamb tenderloins all have an area of connective tissue known as silverskin for its silvery white appearance. Silverskin doesn't dissolve when the tenderloin is cooked, so it needs to be trimmed away.

After trimming any visible fat, position the tip of a boning knife ½ to 1 inch from one end of the visible silverskin. Push the tip under a strip of silverskin ½ to ¾ inch wide. Angle the knife slightly up toward the silverskin as you slide the knife down the tenderloin, freeing the silverskin. Use your other hand to hold the silverskin taut as you cut. If your knife isn't extremely sharp, you may need to use a slight sawing motion to work down the tenderloin. Once you've cut all the way under the end of the strip, turn the knife around and cut off the end that's still attached. Repeat until all the silverskin is gone.

Butterflying and Rolling
a Boned *Pork Loin*

Butterflying yields a rectangle of meat of fairly even thickness, good for grilling flat or for spreading with seasonings or a stuffing, then rolling up as a roast. Use a medium to large chef's knife to do the slicing.

1. Make a horizontal slit in the loin, cutting almost through to the other side. Open the meat flat, like a book, so it's an even thickness.

2. If stuffing, use a spoon to spread the filling over the meat.

3. Roll up the stuffed loin so it forms a tight cylinder. (Depending on the shape of your loin, it might be easier and more attractive to spread the stuffing over only half the loin, then to fold the loin closed again—essentially, closing the book—then to fold the stuffed loin in half upon itself.)

4. Tie the meat with kitchen string at even intervals to maintain the shape of the roast.

Trimming a Rack of *Ribs*

Start by scraping away any excess fat with a small knife; a little fat is fine, but too much will cause your fire to flare up if you're grilling the ribs.

1. On the bone side of the rack cut a horizontal slit in the tough membrane just below the rib tips. Wiggle your finger beneath the membrane to get it loosened, then pull.

2. Find the skirt—the meaty flap that curves down the bottom of the bone side—and trim off the thick white membrane on its edge.

3. Using a chef's knife, cut off the rib tips—but save them for the grill. Feel where the first large rib bone ends and cut horizontally—you're cutting cartilage, not bone.

4. Cutting off the tips just makes the ribs easier to handle—you won't have that floppy part sitting on top.

Carving a Leg of *Lamb*

Carving a leg of lamb is simply a matter of cutting as many slices as you can from the meaty section until you hit bone, then turning the leg and repeating on the other side. Use a carving or chef's knife for this.

1. Lay the shank flat and slice the meat at the end of the leg. Keep slicing until you meet bone, 2 or 3 inches in.

2. Turn the leg so the thick, meaty edge faces up. Carve at a shallow angle relative to the bone. When you run out of meat, rotate the leg 180 degrees and repeat on the other side.

Carving a *Rib Roast*

For a large roast, you'll need a fork to hold it in place. Try not to pierce the roast with it, rather, press it against the meat.

1. Hold the ribs with a towel and slice along the inside of the ribs, using a carving or chef's knife. Keep the knife close to the ribs so you don't cut into the meat. Remove the ribs completely.

2. Put the rib-less roast cut side down and slice across the grain.

Debearding a *Mussel*

Pull the beard—a clump of fibers attached to the mussel meat that sticks out from the shell—out with with your fingers. If it's especially stubborn, grab it with a kitchen towel and pull.

Removing Pin Bones from a *Fish Fillet*

Use tweezers or pliers to remove the slender pin bones from the fillets of fish such as cod or salmon. If you run your fingers gently down the center of the fillet, you'll feel the prick of the bones. Pin bones should be pulled out in the same direction as the grain of the fish.

Shelling a Cooked *Lobster*

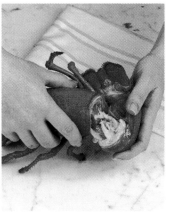

1. Twist off the tail. Grab the head section (called the thorax) with one hand, the tail with the other, and twist. The parts should separate easily.

2. Use the heel of your hand to press down on one side of the lobster tail. Press until you feel a gentle crunch.

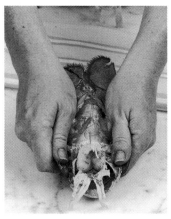

3. Pull the sides of the lobster tail away from each other with both hands. The back of the shell should crack and the tail meat pop out. The orange you see mixed in with the meat is called the coral, or roe, of the lobster and can show up anywhere in a female lobster.

4. Snap the claws off where they join the body.

5. Begin to pull the pincer off each claw by bending the pincer gently from side to side. Then pull the pincer straight out. Most times the cartilage-like "butterfly" will pull out of the claw along with the pincer.

6. Crack into the the claw with an a dull knife. The knife should go in about ¼ inch. Rotate the knife in both directions to split the claw open so you can pull out the meat. You can also do this with a cracker or even your hands.

7. Cut the small claw sections with scissors. Use your fingers to coax out the meat.

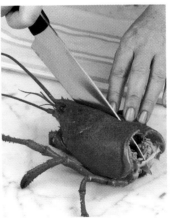

8. Forage for more meat and the tomalley, the lobster's liver, in the head section. Split it open with a knife.

9. Throw away the head sac, shown here. Spoon out the green tomalley as well as the coral, if you find any (as there is here) and use a cocktail fork or a toothpick to harvest any meat.

Cracking a Cooked *Crab*

1. Flip the crab over so the apron is exposed (by the shape of its apron, you can tell this crab is a male, or "jimmy"; the apron of a "sook," or female crab, looks more akin to the U.S. Capitol, rather than the Washington Monument of the jimmy). With a knife or your thumb, pop off the apron.

2. Turn the crab over and pry off the top shell.

3. Scrape or pull off and discard the gray-colored spongy gills, which are called dead man's fingers. Scrape out the rest of the innards, called the devil, and discard. The yellow stuff is called the mustard, which is the crab's fat and is quite tasty.

4. Break the crab in half. Gently push down on the back of the shell where the back flipper legs are located to start loosening the meat.

5. Break the claws off the body. Break and separate the legs away from the body. Every place where the legs were connected to the body is a cavity full of meat. Use your fingers or a small knife to get at it. The biggest prize is the large lump of meat from the back flipper. With practice, you can remove it, whole and attached to the back flipper, by breaking the back flipper away while holding your thumb against the cartilage.

6. Each of the smaller legs has a little bit of meat attached to it. Use your fingers or a small knife to get at it.

7. Break the joints around the claws. Using crackers or a mallet, crack the claws. Remove the meat.

Peeling and Deveining *Shrimp*

1. Use your fingers to pry open and pull back the first few sections of shell, starting at the large end.

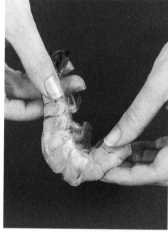

2. Remove the rest of the shell by gently tugging on the very end of the shrimp's tail.

3. To expose the sand vein, make a shallow cut along the shrimp's back.

4. Gently lift out the vein with the tip of your knife.

Cutting a *Chiffonade*

Cutting a chiffonade is a classic technique for slicing leafy vegetables and herbs. Greens cut into a chiffonade don't discolor or wilt as quickly as when they're chopped.

First remove any fibrous ribs and tough stems. Cut larger leaves, such as cabbage, in half lengthwise and cut out the center rib. Stack 3 or 4 leaves, with the larger ones on the bottom, then roll the stack across (not from the base of the leaves) into a tight cylinder. Hold the cylinder securely and slice it neatly into shreds with a sharp knife.

Chopping an *Onion*

Onions, shallots, and garlic are chopped the same way.

1. Cut an onion in half through the root end and remove the peel. Place it on the cutting board and make lengthwise vertical cuts (thin or thick, depending on how finely or coarsely you want it chopped) that go almost, but not, through the root.

2. Now make horizontal cuts parallel to the board, again being careful not to cut through the root end.

3. Now cut across the width of the onion, making cuts as thin as you wish.

Prepping *Leeks* for Easy Washing

After cutting off the tough green top, slice the leek lengthwise without cutting through the bottom layers. Fan open the layers while rinsing out the grit under lukewarm running water, then submerge them in lukewarm water, shaking vigorously. Leave the leeks for 5 to 10 minutes so that any remaining grit settles in the bottom. Lift the leeks out, pat dry, and slice as the recipe instructs.

Julienning a *Carrot*

1. Peel, then, using a sharp knife, square off the sides of the carrot to make a rectangular section of whatever length you need.

2. Slice lengthwise into ⅛-inch-thick slabs for julienne.

3. Stack a few slices and cut them into ⅛-inch-wide strips for julienne.

Seeding a *Bell Pepper*

Because of their puzzling shape, bell peppers can be difficult to cut into even slices. This method produces the best results.

1. With a chef's knife, cut off the top of the pepper just below the shoulder so you remove the entire stem end, exposing the ribs inside the pepper.

2. Squarely cut off the narrow bottom. The pepper will now be shaped like a cylinder.

3. Set the pepper on one end and make one vertical slice to open the cylinder.

4. Set the pepper cut side up and work the knife along the inside of the pepper (with the blade parallel to the work surface), removing the ribs and seeds while unrolling the pepper so that it lies flat. Now you have a neat rectangle that you can cut up as you wish.

Trimming an *Artichoke* for Steaming

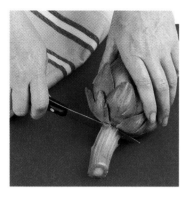

1. Slice off the stem. Rub the exposed base with lemon juice to prevent browning.

2. With a serrated knife, cut across the artichoke, removing about a third of the top.

3. With scissors, cut off the pointed tip of each outer leaf.

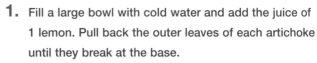

Preparing *Artichoke* Bottoms

1. Fill a large bowl with cold water and add the juice of 1 lemon. Pull back the outer leaves of each artichoke until they break at the base.

2. Remove the leaves until you reach the pale yellow-green, tender inner leaves. With a sharp knife, slice off all but 1 inch of the stem.

3. Cut across the leaves just above where they join the base. Reserve these for steaming another time, if you like.

4. With a small knife, pare the stem and the base, removing any dark green parts. If you like, cut the stem and base in half.

5. With a melon baller or a spoon, scoop out and discard the hairy choke and prickly leaves inside. Immediately drop the trimmed artichoke bottom into the lemon water to prevent browning.

Trimming *Baby Artichokes*

1. Trim the outer leaves by pulling downward so they break off at the base; keep pulling them off until you get to the core of pale green leaves.

2. Trim the stem with a sharp paring knife and shave off the the rough areas around the base.

3. Cut off the top ½ inch of the artichoke.

4. Halve the artichoke, if you wish, and rub all the cut surfaces with lemon to prevent browning or place them in a bowl of lemon water.

Coring and Slicing an *Apple*

Many people core apples and pears by cutting them into quarters, then cutting the core out of each quarter. While that method works well enough, it results in awkwardly shaped pieces. Here's a faster, neater way of getting rid of the core. If your recipe calls for peeling the apples, do it before you slice.

1. Hold the fruit upright, try to judge where the core is, and slice off two opposite sides as close to the core as possible.

2. Rotate the fruit and slice off the two remaining sides to get a rectangular core piece and four flat-sided pieces of fruit (two wide and two narrow).

3. The side pieces will now lie obediently on your cutting board for slicing or dicing.

Coring a *Pear* to Poach Whole

Using a corer, paring knife, or nonswivel peeler, remove the core from the bottom of the pear.

Coring *Pear* Halves

1. Peel if necessary, then cut the pear in half vertically and scoop out the seeds with a melon baller.

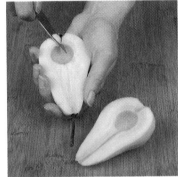

2. Cut out the flower end with a paring knife.

3. Cut out the stem.

Cutting Segments from an *Orange* or Other *Citrus Fruit*

These neat segments, also known as supremes, are great in a salad.

1. Slice off both ends of the orange with a small knife. Stand the orange on one of its cut ends and slice off the skin in strips. Try to get all the white pith off, but don't sacrifice too much of the sweet flesh to do it.

2. Working over a bowl to catch the juices, cut the segments free from the membranes, letting them fall into the bowl. Once all the segments are free, squeeze the empty wheel of membranes to get the last of the juice.

Zesting a *Citrus* Fruit

1. *Using a hand grater.* Use the grater's smallest holes and don't press hard enough to scrape the white pith. A pastry brush helps free the zest from the grater.

2. *Using a zester.* A five-hole channel zester makes quick work of zesting. Its shallow blade, dragged against the peel, won't go any deeper than the zest.

3. *Using a rasp-type grater.* This tool is ideal for creating fine feathery zest. Its shallow, sharp teeth allow you to efficiently zest an entire fruit without removing any of the bitter pith. (Hold the rasp in one hand and gently pull the fruit over the teeth of the rasp.)

Pitting a *Peach* or *Nectarine*

1. Using a small sharp knife, start at the stem end of the fruit and cut through to the pit. Run the knife all the way around the fruit, keeping the blade up against the pit and finishing where you started.

2. Hold the fruit in your hands with the cut mark parallel to your palms and gently twist in opposite directions until one half comes free from the pit. Set that half aside.

3. Remove the pit from the remaining half by loosening the pointed end with your fingernail or the tip of a knife. If the pit doesn't come free, don't force it. Instead, cut off a few sections from the half and you'll be able to wiggle the pit free.

Pitting a *Plum*

1. Make two vertical cuts on either side of the center of the plum, about ¾ inch apart.

2. Set aside the two cheeks for slicing and trim a wedge from each side of the center piece. Discard the pit.

Cutting a *Mango*

The mango contains a large, flat seed that doesn't separate readily from the juicy flesh, so the flesh needs to be cut away from the seed. Mango flesh can be slippery, so leaving the skin on until you've dealt with the seed will help your grip.

1. Balance the mango on one of its narrow sides, then slice off one of the wide sides of the fruit. Try to cut as close to the seed as possible, usually about ¾ inch from the center. Repeat with the other wide side, then slice off the remaining narrow pieces of fruit.

2. To dice a mango, cup one of the unpeeled pieces in your palm and use a paring knife to score the fruit into the size of dice you want. Be careful not to cut through the skin of the fruit (or into your hand).

3. Use your fingertips to pop the mango inside out, then use the paring knife to slice the dice away from the skin.

Pitting an *Avocado*

1. To neatly remove the pit from an avocado, leaving it perfect for stuffing, slice the avocado in half lengthwise around the pit. Twist the two halves in opposite directions and pull them apart. You'll have one pit-free half. Cover your nondominant hand with a kitchen towel. Place the avocado half with the pit in the palm of that hand. Very carefully but firmly chop the blade of a chef's knife into the pit. The knife should stick in the pit.

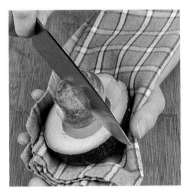

2. Use the knife to twist the pit out of the avocado. To dislodge the pit from the knife, scrape it off against the edge of the sink.

Peeling a *Melon*

Don't forget to wash the outside of the melon first; bacteria present on the skin can be dragged into the melon flesh by your knife as you peel off the skin.

1. Cut off the melon's top and bottom ends.

2. Stand the melon on one of the cut ends and slice off the remaining skin in strips, taking care to hug the curves so you're trimming only the skin and not the flesh. A flexible knife works well for this. Cut the melon in half, scoop out the seeds, then cut the flesh as you like.

Peeling and Coring a *Pineapple*

1. With a sharp knife, lop off the top and bottom of the pineapple and stand it on the cutting board. Shave off the peel, exposing the juicy flesh. Don't worry about getting the eyes of the pineapple at this point.

2. The eyes tend to run in spiral stripes around the pineapple, like a barber pole. Make an angled cut on both sides of a stripe of eyes, creating a v-shaped channel under them. Use the knife tip to flick out the stripe. Repeat to get the remaining stripes. Cut out any leftover eyes individually with the knife tip.

3. To core the pineapple, cut it lengthwise into quarters, then cut the core out of each quarter. If you want pineapple rings, cut the whole peeled pineapple into slices, then use a knife or small biscuit cutter to cut the core out of each slice.

Hulling a *Strawberry*

Be sure to rinse strawberries before you hull them, or they'll absorb water and become soggy.

To hull a strawberry, hold a paring knife at an angle and, with the tip, carve out a small cone-shaped wedge from the top of the berry, removing as little flesh as possible. If you have an underripe strawberry with large white "shoulders," trim away the flavorless white part entirely.

Chopping *Chocolate*

You'll need a heavy chef's knife and a stable wooden cutting board. Don't try to cut big chunks; just cut off a bit at a time, putting the pressure on the heel of the knife.

The Stages of *Whipping Cream* and *Egg Whites*

When cream or egg whites are whipped, air gets trapped inside and causes them to foam, grow in volume, and become stiff. Recipes usually instruct you to whip egg whites or cream to a particular firmness, or peak stage. These photos show you what those stages should look like. We show sugar-stabilized egg whites, but the characteristics of each stage apply to cream as well.

1. **Soft peaks** barely hold their shape. The peaks flop over immediately when the beaters are lifted.

2. **Medium peaks** hold their shape pretty well, except that the tip of the peak curls over on itself when the beaters are lifted.

3. **Stiff peaks** stand straight up when the beaters are lifted.

Clarifying *Butter*

The objective in clarifying butter is to remove the milk solids and water it contains. By doing this, you can subject the clarified butter to much higher cooking temperatures without it burning, a boon when you want to pan-fry cutlets in butter, for instance. Do not leave the stove while you're doing this—the milk solids can burn in a matter of seconds.

1. Over medium or medium-low heat in a heavy saucepan, melt the butter and let it cook until it begins to bubble gently. Remove the pan from the heat and set aside for a few minutes to let the milk solids and water settle to the bottom. Skim off any foam that remains on the surface of the butter.

2. Ladle or carefully pour off the clear, golden clarified butter, leaving behind the milky looking bottom layer—the milk solids and water— which you can discard.

When Things Go Wrong, Substitutions, *and* *Equivalents*

THE PROBLEM	POSSIBLE CAUSES	FIX-IT TIPS FOR NOW OR NEXT TIME
Cake batter looks curdled	Either the ingredients weren't of the same temperature or they were too cold. The eggs and/or liquids may have also been added too quickly.	Don't worry about a curdled-looking batter—the final height of the cake may be shorter, but it will turn out fine. Generally, all ingredients should be at the same temperature for best volume, and adding the eggs and liquids gradually creates a better and more stable emulsion.
Sponge or angel food cake falls	Though disturbing a foam cake during baking can make it fall, as will under-baking or overbaking it, the most likely culprit is overbeaten egg whites. Overbeaten egg whites are grainy and deflate easily; the egg proteins are overworked and no longer capable of expanding and holding air.	Next time, stop beating the whites once they form stiff, shiny peaks. For extra-stable egg foams, beat a portion of the recipe's sugar into the whites, beginning when they reach soft peak stage. If you moved the cake during baking or slammed the oven door last time, take it easy next time.
Layer cake or quick bread falls	Cakes fall for many reasons, but the most common reason is that the pan was overfilled: If the batter reaches the top of the pan and still needs to rise, it will collapse. Stale or the wrong type of leavening could also be at fault. Though atrocious mixing will do it, you'd have to really abuse the mixing method to make a cake fall.	Never fill layer cake pans more than half full and leave an inch at the top of loaf pans. Start with fresh leavening (6 months for baking soda and 1 year maximum for baking powder) and don't make substitutions. Measure carefully and don't skip steps in the mixing method.
Cake, muffin, or quick bread has poor volume	Poor volume is a result of tempera-ture (ingredients were too cold) and improper mixing (fat and sugar were insufficiently creamed or eggs were incorporated too quickly). Overmixing can develop gluten in the batter, resulting in a tougher cake with poor volume. Using the wrong type of or expired leavening will do the same.	For maximum volume, start with room temperature ingredients. To best incorporate air, cream the fat and sugar for the time specified and beat in the eggs one at a time. Use fresh leavening and don't make substitu-tions. Don't beat the batter for long once all the liquid has been added.

THE PROBLEM	POSSIBLE CAUSES	FIX-IT TIPS FOR NOW OR NEXT TIME
Muffin or pound cake doesn't peak	The amount of batter in the muffin cup or pound cake pan is key: underfilled muffin cups or loaf pans won't bake up with a nice peak. Too low a baking temperature will cause the batter to spread outward rather than up, a problem especially seen in muffins. Insufficiently creamed or aerated batters will also not peak.	Fill muffin cups especially high, a little over three quarters full, and loaf pans to within an inch of the top. Bake muffins at 375° to 425°F. Be sure to cream ingredients for the amount of time specified and add the ingredients as indicated.
Muffins are dry and/or tough	The wrong flour may have been used. Also, overmixing after the last ingredients are added can develop the gluten in the batter, resulting in a tough muffin. (Muffin recipes typically contain less sugar and fat than other cakes; both interfere with gluten development and contribute to tenderness.) Finally, the muffin may simply be overbaked.	Next time use a low-protein all-purpose or pastry flour. After the liquids are added, mix quickly and gently, stopping when the batter is just combined, then let it rest in the muffin pan for 10 minutes before baking to relax the gluten. Start checking them for doneness at least 10 minutes before the end time specified in the recipe.
Fruit-filled muffins burn and stick to the tin	The tin was not adequately greased and floured, allowing the sugary, ripe fruit to stick to the pan.	Stubborn scraping to loosen the muffin is the only way to salvage them. Next time, generously grease the pan, covering every nook at the bottom and even around the top edge. Also flour the pan for best insurance against sticking. Turn muffins out of the pan while warm—before the juices from the fruit solidify.
Biscuits, shortcakes, or scones are dense, with poor volume	These need a hearty kicky of leavening since they have little or no eggs or a creaming phase for aeration—inadequate or stale leavening makes short biscuits. These foods also get their lift from cutting fat into the flour, then folding the dough into layers before cutting: the pieces of fat melt and leave air holes behind, then steam gives the air pockets a lift, creating layers. If the fat is completely ground into the dough or high-protein flour is used, the baked good will be dense.	Biscuits need about $1\frac{1}{2}$ teaspoons of leavening per cup of flour, including no more than $\frac{1}{4}$ teaspoon of baking soda per cup. Use the right flour: all-purpose, pastry, or cake flour mixed with all-purpose. Cut in very cold fat and use the least amount of liquid needed to get the dough to come together. Try folding the dough to create layers and let the dough rest 15 minutes before cutting and baking in a hot (425°F) oven.

THE PROBLEM	POSSIBLE CAUSES	FIX-IT TIPS FOR NOW OR NEXT TIME
Rolled biscuits or scones are dry	Adding too much liquid will make them seem drier and cakey rather than moist and rich. Also, there may not be enough fat in the recipe.	Next time add the liquids gradually, stopping when the dough is still shaggy in places. Press the dough into a disc to see if it has enough liquid, then add more if necessary. Never skimp on fat when making biscuits or scones.
Cake texture is grainy; coarse crumb	Poor texture in a cake is usually attributable to either overmixing or undermixing the batter. The most frequent undermixing error is not creaming the fat and sugar long enough or adding the eggs too rapidly; both create poor structure. Overmixing usually occurs after the flour goes in and the remaining wet ingredients are added.	Follow the recipe instructions: Creamed mixtures should look light and fluffy; and if, ideally, all the ingredients are at room temperature, when the eggs are added slowly, the batter will not curdle. Add dry and wet ingredients alternately, always beginning with the dry. The fat coats the flour first, preventing the liquid from developing too much gluten as it comes in contact with the flour.
Cake or quick bread has tunnels	Either the batter was overmixed after the wet ingredients were added or the flour used was too high in protein. In both cases too much gluten developed, making the batter tight and dense. Too much leavening may have also been used. In any of these cases, the air bubbles created by mixing or by chemical leavening continue to expand after the cake structure starts to firm, resulting in tunnels.	When the last ingredients have been added and the batter looks relatively homogenous, stop mixing. Be sure you are using cake flour if it's specified and certainly avoid bread flours, with their high protein content. Be especially careful not to develop too much gluten in batters leavened with baking soda, since soda does most of its work in the batter stage before the cake or quick bread even reaches the oven.
Sides of cake collapse	All-purpose flour was substituted for cake flour or the batter contained too much liquid. Cake flour is uniquely processed to hold more liquid, sugar, and fat than other flours, and caved-in sides are a sure sign that the flour can't hold the amount of liquid in the recipe. If the proper flour was used, then too much liquid is at fault.	Don't substitute one type of flour for another in cake recipes. Be precise about measuring both the flour and the liquids.

THE PROBLEM	POSSIBLE CAUSES	FIX-IT TIPS FOR NOW OR NEXT TIME
Pound or Bundt cake has thick, dark crust	The oven temperature was too hot and/or the cake was overbaked or a dark metal or glass pan was used, both of which conduct heat more readily, which will cause the edges to brown and form a thick crust.	Rich pound and Bundt cakes take a long time to bake through to the center. Next time, try reducing the oven temperature by 25°F and, if you don't use a heavyweight or light-colored metal pan, consider dropping the temperature even further.
Quick bread, muffin, or cake is gummy overall or has rubbery layer at bottom	Buttermilk, fruit purée, sour cream, and yogurt can all make cake gummy when used in excess. Also, the cake may not have had enough egg or flour. Inadequately drained carrots or zucchini will also make a cake heavy.	Don't improvise when measuring, as too much of something may not be a good thing. If the recipe says to drain the carrots, don't skip this step. If you repeat the recipe and still get a gummy texture, either reduce the fruit or dairy products or add more egg and flour to compensate.
Jelly-roll cake will not roll	The eggs were underbeaten or overbeaten or the egg foam was deflated when folded into the dry ingredients. Flexibility for these cakes comes from a higher egg to flour ratio, since egg proteins remain flexible even after they are cooked. If the cake had too much flour from inaccurate measuring, the cake will not stretch as easily. Also, if the cake is not trained while still warm (see right), it will break when rolled.	If the jelly-roll is merely cracking, it is possible to cover the cracks with frosting. For cakes that break, however, there's no quick fix. Next time be precise when measuring the flour and take care not to deflate the egg foam. Also, while the cake is still warm, roll it up in a towel and let it cool to set the shape.
Layer cake is too fragile to cut or assemble	The cake is still too warm to cut. Delicate layer cakes are heavy in sugar, liquid, and fat and have less flour and eggs than sturdier cakes, like pound cake. This makes them especially hard to handle.	A quick chill in the refrigerator will solve the problem, since cold cake is firmer and easier to slice and frost. For an easier cake to work with next time, you can add more flour or egg to the recipe, but the moist, delicate crumb will certainly be compromised.
Cheesecake forms cracks in top	It is overcooked.	Next time, remove the cheesecake from the oven when just barely set. If this problem recurs, try baking the cheesecake in a water bath (using a waterproof cake pan, of course).

—Nicole Rees, *Fine Cooking*

THE PROBLEM	POSSIBLE CAUSES	FIX-IT TIPS FOR NOW OR NEXT TIME
Pie dough is still dry even after adding all the cold water specified	Pieces of fat cut into the flour were left too large. Dough needed to be kneaded briefly. Flour required more hydration due to type or seasonal variability.	First, try mixing the fat into the dough with your fingertips. If still dry and crumbly, add more cold water, 1 tablespoon at a time. When the dough just starts to look like it's coming together, stop and knead briefly to form a cohesive mass. Small pieces of fat should be visible in the dough.
Pie dough or short (sweet) dough is too sticky to form into disk	Ingredients, room, or dough is too warm. Also, too much liquid may have been added.	Chill sticky dough 10 to 20 minutes before trying to form it with well-floured hands. Next time, start with cold butter and shortening. When making pie on hot days, grate frozen butter into the flour or freeze all the ingredients briefly. Keep the water ice cold in the refrigerator until needed.
Chilled pie dough cracks when rolled out	Dough was too cold or not kneaded enough, making the edges of the dough disc ragged and dry. Also, the dough may not have rested enough to allow the flour to hydrate evenly.	If there are many cracks and the edges seem dry, gather the dough into a ball. Chill for 20 minutes and try again: the rolling should be easier now that the dough has been mixed more from handling. One or two cracks can be fixed by brushing with water and rolling the edges together to seal. Next time, allow the dough to warm up slightly if very cold and roll as evenly as possible near the edges to prevent cracking.
Pie dough/sweet dough sticks to counter and tears	Dough or countertop is too warm. Insufficient flour was used on rolling surface and pin. Dough was not rotated or flipped while being rolled.	Slide a long spatula under the dough to loosen, then slide the dough onto a floured sheet of parchment paper or cutting board. Chill and try again. Next time, start with cold dough. Roll sweet doughs between sheets of floured parchment. If necessary, chill, parchment and all, until firmer. Remember to flour while rolling and rotate dough frequently.

THE PROBLEM	POSSIBLE CAUSES	FIX-IT TIPS FOR NOW OR NEXT TIME
Crumb crust too mealy to press into pan	Crumb mixture doesn't have enough butter and/or sugar.	Drizzle in melted butter just until mixture clumps when squeezed, then press into pan. The crumb crust may need more sugar: Sugar melts readily in the oven and helps set the crust—don't skimp on recipe requirements.
Baked pie crust is tough	Dough was kneaded too much after the water was added. Or dough was not relaxed after rolling.	Next time, stop mixing as soon as the dough just begins to come together after the water is added. Do not rush the process. Then, after rolling, let the dough rest in the refrigerator for at least 25 minutes to allow the flour to hydrate and the gluten structure to relax.
Baked pie crust is crumbly and mealy	Fat and flour were overmixed in dough: Visible pieces of fat should remain in the dough. When baked, these pieces will melt, leaving air pockets behind, making the crust flaky. Also, the dough may have contained too much fat.	Next time, stop cutting in fat when most of the pieces are pea size. Some pieces will be smaller, but the baked crust will resemble crumbly shortbread if the fat is thoroughly mixed in. If still crumbly, reduce the amount of fat by 2 or 3 tablespoons for a double crust.
Blind-baked pie/tart shell is misshapen, puffed on the bottom with sides that have caved in	Dough was not allowed to relax before being fitted into pan or was stretched when fitted into pan. Pie weights were not used to stabilize dough during initial baking.	Next time, let the dough rest after rolling and before fitting into pan; this relaxes the gluten and prevents shrinking. Gently push dough into corners of pan—do not stretch dough or it will contract during baking! Line the cold pie shell with parchment and fill with pie weights (or dried beans and rice) to give the crust support until its structure sets.
Edge of blind-baked pie crust falls off during baking	Shaped dough was not firmly chilled before baking. Crimped dough edge extended too far over pan edge. Also, the oven may not have been hot enough to set the crust quickly.	Next time, freeze the crust until firm before baking to set the structure and prevent the edges from collapsing. A hot oven performs much the same function: Start crusts off at 425°F, then reduce the temperature by 50°F after 15 minutes if the crust is browning too rapidly.

THE PROBLEM	POSSIBLE CAUSES	FIX-IT TIPS FOR NOW OR NEXT TIME
Pie browns poorly	Crust was underbaked or contained bleached flour. Doughs that include an acid such as lemon juice or vinegar to make rolling easier brown less readily.	Next time, use unbleached flour for the crust. Add milk or sugar to facilitate browning if you use an acid in the dough.
Bottom crust is soggy and pale	Not enough heat was directed to bottom crust. Or the cut fruit and sugar sat too long before the pie was assembled, causing the fruit to release its juice before baking. For custard pies, the shell was not adequately prebaked.	For crisp crusts, bake pies and tarts on a preheated sheet pan situated near the bottom of the oven. Next time, don't let the fruit and sugar mixture sit more than 15 minutes before baking. Prebake the crust for custard pies whenever possible.
Pie/tart is burning at edges before filling is cooked	The heat is not penetrating to the center of the pie or tart before the edges are set. Also, the filling may be very cold.	Cover edges of pie crust with foil to prevent burning. Let ice-cold fillings warm a little before filling pie or tart shell.
Fruit in filling disintegrates and is mushy	Pie was overbaked, the fruit was very ripe, or the wrong apple variety was used.	Next time, be prepared to reduce the baking time for ripe, juicy fruit. Don't use eating and sauce apples for pies.
Fruit filling is sour	Not enough sugar was used; the fruit was not ripe.	Always taste the fruit before adding sugar and adjust accordingly. If the fruit is really unripe, consider adding extra juice and flavorings such as vanilla.
Fruit filling is too stiff even though the correct amount of thickener was used	Fruit was not ripe and released little juice during baking.	Underripe fruit may require more sugar, added juice, and a longer baking time to allow the fruit to soften. Always assess the ripeness of the fruit before you begin.
Fruit pie has cooled to room temperature, but juices are thin and runny	Filling contained too much sugar. The fruit was juicier than anticipated, or insufficient thickener was used. Filling wasn't cooked to a high enough temperature to set the starch.	Next time, taste and assess the sugar content of the fruit. Very ripe fruit will produce runnier (but still delicious!) pies that require more starch to set juices. To make checking the progress of the filling easier, cut vents in top of pie. The pie is done when the filling is bubbling at the center.

THE PROBLEM	POSSIBLE CAUSES	FIX-IT TIPS FOR NOW OR NEXT TIME
Tapioca granules don't dissolve, leaving hard lumps behind	Either the tapioca in the filling was exposed to the heat of the oven in a lattice or open-top pie or the pie was underbaked.	Tapioca needs to be covered to dissolve and thicken effectively—double-crust pies are the best use for this starch. Or purchase it in gel form.
Custard pie, like pumpkin, cracks while cooling	The filling was overbaked or the filling contained more starch than needed to set the custard.	Next time, remove the pie from the oven when custard is just barely set. If it still cracks, reduce the starch in the recipe by one quarter.
Cooked custard, pudding, or curd filling seemed thick in baked shell, but is thin and runny the next day	Filling was not sufficiently cooked: An enzyme in eggs will slowly break down the starches in the gel if not denatured by cooking.	Completely cook custards going into baked shells: Stir custards often, making sure the heat penetrates evenly throughout the pan, and cook until it bubbles gently at the sides.
Quiche is watery instead of creamy and set	The most likely cause are the vegetables in the filling. Vegetables release water as they cook, which destroys the perfect creaminess of the egg custard. However, if the quiche also seems tough and watery, then it is overcooked.	Next time, thoroughly sauté or precook the vegetables to be used in the quiche, draining them on paper towels, if necessary.
Meringue topping pulled away from side of pie during baking	Meringue was not pressed or spread carefully against crust. Meringue shrinks slightly as it bakes and will pull away from an edge if not firmly adhered.	Next time, spread the meringue along the edge of the pie crust first before piling the remainder high onto the center of the pie.
Meringue topping weeps underneath	The meringue failed to cook through because the pie wasn't hot when it was applied.	Next time, place the meringue directly on the hot filling for even heat penetration from all sides.
Meringue topping forms beads on exterior	Meringue is overcooked: the egg proteins are no longer capable of holding liquid and have squeezed out sugar and water.	No quick fix here, just bake the meringue more carefully next time. In general, higher heat for a shorter period is better for a meringue topping.

—Nicole Rees, *Fine Cooking*

THE PROBLEM	POSSIBLE CAUSES	FIX-IT TIPS FOR NOW OR NEXT TIME
Cookie dough is sticky and difficult to roll and cut	The dough probably became too warm. In particular, doughs rich in butter and egg are especially difficult to handle if not kept very, very cold.	A quick chill in the refrigerator or freezer will make most doughs behave—butter solidifies quickly. For ease of handling, roll the dough between sheets of parchment paper, then chill. You can add more flour as a last resort if chilling doesn't do the trick.
Dough sticks to springerle mold, tears, and won't stay together when turned out of the mold	The dough is too warm.	Keep the dough as cool as possible, leaving the portion you aren't working with in the refrigerator. Use a fine mesh sieve to dust flour over the mold or, even better, dust the dough that will be pressed against it.
Slice-and-bake cookies are not perfectly round	Refrigerating a quickly hand-formed log often creates imperfections. Also, the pressure of slicing can flatten the bottom of the log.	Roll the log a couple times *throughout* the chilling process to work out inconsistencies of shape. Rotate the log while you are working to prevent an uneven shape. If the dough feels uneven and bumpy when you begin, let it soften for a few minutes and roll it against the counter until it evens out. Refrigerate once more, then begin slicing and baking.
Cookies are unappealingly white, pallid	Recipes that contain mostly white ingredients (bleached flour, cake flour, shortening, granulated and confectioners' sugar) will make lighter cookies. Cookies containing baking powder will brown less than those made with baking soda, so be sure not to confuse the two. Also, your oven may not be hot enough.	Try increasing the oven temperature by 25°F to see if you get better results. Using unbleached flour in your next batch will take your cookies up a shade; and substituting a little butter, margarine, or butter-flavored shortening for some of the white shortening will impart a golden hue (but watch the spread! See next tip).

THE PROBLEM	POSSIBLE CAUSES	FIX-IT TIPS FOR NOW OR NEXT TIME
Rolled cut-outs spread, blurring shape	The dough was too warm going into the oven—the edges of cold dough will firm and set in the oven before the center of the dough warms, which inhibits spread and creates defined edges on cut-outs. Cookies rich in butter, molasses, honey, and a lot of leavening may not be suitable for detailed cut-outs, so beware when adapting recipes to a new use.	A quick chill before baking is an easy fix: Just pop the cookie sheet, with cut-out dough and all, into the refrigerator or the freezer if you have room. If this doesn't solve the spreading, knead a small amount of flour into the dough. Flour is a guaranteed fix, but use it as a last resort, since the finished texture and flavor will change.
Cookies brown too much, but are not overbaked	An overly hot oven can make cookies brown before they are baked through, but browning is often an ingredient issue as well. Molasses, honey, corn syrup, dark brown sugar, milk products, and baking powder all encourage browning. Substituting dark brown sugar for light can dramatically change the color of your cookie.	For a quick fix, try reducing the oven temperature by 25°F. If you don't see better results, next time substitute some lighter ingredients, like bleached flour or granulated sugar, or reduce the amount of liquid sugars (molasses, honey, corn syrup) in the recipe.
Cookies are pale on top and burnt on bottom	An oven that runs too hot; the use of dark, heavy baking sheets; the placement of baking sheets on the bottom rack of the oven, or any combination of these 3 things will cause your cookies to burn only on the bottom.	If you don't bake often, get an oven thermometer. It will save you lots of guesswork. Choose lighter baking sheets for your cookie baking or a double-pan (stack an extra pan underneath) to better insulate the dough. Always, always rotate pans from the top to bottom rack (and back to front) midway through if the oven has hot spots for even color and texture.
Cookies don't spread enough	Recipes high in shortening and flour but lean on sugar are more resistant to spread in the oven. A change in flour type or brand can cause this—both cake and bread flours absorb more liquid than other flours. A too-cool oven is another possible culprit. Leaving out or using expired leavening makes for leaden cookies, as does adding too many nuts or chips.	Before you start next time, scrutinize your flour and leavening, making sure you have the appropriate, fresh ingredients on hand. Try holding back 2 tablespoons to ¼ cup of flour at the end of the mixing. Before adding the last of the flour, bake a test cookie to check the texture. This will also help you decide whether to increase the heat a little. Adding extra chips is fine, but don't double the amount.

THE PROBLEM	POSSIBLE CAUSES	FIX-IT TIPS FOR NOW OR NEXT TIME
Gingerbread ornaments/house cut-outs are too soft and cakey	Many gingerbread cookie recipes have generous amounts of molasses, which keeps baked cookies soft and contributes to a cakey texture. They are delicious to eat but tend to be too delicate to handle if not thoroughly baked.	For firmer cookies that will stand up to being frosted, hung, or assembled into a house, return the cookies to the oven and bake until well done to compensate for the softening effect of the molasses. Next time try adding more flour to the dough to accomplish the same thing, or reduce the amount of molasses slightly.
Chocolate chip cookies spread too much	Recipes based on the Toll House® recipe are rich in butter, sugar, and egg, all of which contribute to spread. A change in flour can alter spread, even just a brand change. A too hot oven or too warm dough is a secondary cause. If a recipe calls for lots of chips and nuts, but you leave out the nuts, your cookies will be flatter and wider.	Chilling the dough before baking might fix the cookies. If not, stir a small amount of flour into the dough. Flour is a guaranteed fix, but also a last resort, since the texture and flavor will change. Adjust the oven temperature, if necessary, and be sure you've added the amount of chips and nuts specified.
Chocolate chip cookies are too crisp and thin	Recipes generous in butter and sugar but lean on egg and leavening create crisper cookies. Was the leavening left out or the flour mismeasured? Did you use smaller eggs than specified?	First, try chilling the dough to firm up the butter and slow down spread. If this doesn't do the trick, beat in half an egg (or a whole one if the recipe contains no egg and calls for at least 2 cups flour) and 2 tablespoons flour. Bake a test cookie before adding more flour.
Chocolate chip cookies are too cakey and/or dry	The most common cause is using a different flour than usual, such as cake flour, and measuring flour with too heavy a hand. Using larger eggs than called for can make cookies cakey, as will the addition of milk or more milk or other liquids than specified.	Next time try holding back 2 tablespoons to $\frac{1}{4}$ cup of the flour at the end of mixing. Before adding the last of the flour, bake a test cookie to check the texture. Make sure the eggs are the right size and omit the milk if you prefer denser cookies.

THE PROBLEM	POSSIBLE CAUSES	FIX-IT TIPS FOR NOW OR NEXT TIME
Oatmeal cookies are crumbly and dry	Classic oatmeal cookies have a lot of oats, which can be drying to the finished cookie and make them more susceptible to overbaking. Mismeasuring flour can also tip the balance from crisp-chewy to dry. Using all granulated sugar for the brown sugar will create a drier cookie, too, since the molasses in brown sugar provides moisture.	Try removing the cookies from the oven before the centers are set—you'll be surprised at how much the cookies will firm as they cool. Next time hold back ¼ cup of flour and/or ½ cup of oats and bake a test cookie; add more if necessary. Most oatmeal cookies call for some brown sugar—be sure to add the right amount and the right type.
Peanut butter cookies are too crumbly	Flour is likely at issue here, but changing brands of peanut butter will also affect texture.	Next time try holding back 2 tablespoons to ¼ cup of the flour at the end of mixing. Before adding the last of the flour, bake a test cookie to check the texture. Be sure to use the type of peanut butter called for, since added sugar and salt will affect the texture and flavor of your cookies.
Biscotti are hard and tough instead of crisp	Biscotti that are cut while too soft will compress and have a tougher bite. Adding too much flour for ease of handling can also toughen these cookies. Using the wrong, too little, or expired leavening will have the same effect.	For a quick fix, try drying out your baked, sliced cookies further in a 300°F oven—this will minimize toughness. Next time cool the baked cookie log longer before slicing to prevent compressing, and use a sharp, serrated knife. Avoid kneading in more flour when shaping the cookies, and do not use leavening more than a year old.
Drop sugar cookies or ginger snaps do not have cracked tops	Baking powder and soda give these cookies their characteristic cracks, so stale leavening is probably at fault here. Also, the right amount of flour is necessary to allow the dough to expand, crack, and set at just the right time—too much flour will prevent this from happening. Check oven temperature, too, since a hotter oven is sometimes better for these cookies.	Next time, make sure you have fresh leavening on hand before you start baking—baking soda is not usually tightly sealed and loses its power faster than baking powder from exposure to warm, humid air. Hold back 2 tablespoons of the flour and bake a test cookie before deciding to add it to the dough. This will also let you know if you need to boost the heat in the oven.

THE PROBLEM	POSSIBLE CAUSES	FIX-IT TIPS FOR NOW OR NEXT TIME
Shortbread tastes pasty instead of buttery	It may be underbaked or the oven temperature may be too low. Another possibility is that you added too much cornstarch or confectioners' sugar.	Return underbaked shortbread to a 350°F oven until it begins to turn golden. Flour and starch need to be cooked thoroughly to lose their cereal flavor and let the toasty flavor of the butter shine.
Shortbread crumbles when cut	The shortbread is no longer warm. Shortbread is prized for its sandy, crumbly crisp texture, but this makes it difficult to cut when cool.	Use a serrated knife to gently saw the shortbread into pieces. Next time score the shortbread before baking or when it first comes out of the oven and cut through while it is still warm.
Blondies or brownies are dry and hard	Assuming all the ingredients that create chewiness (butter, eggs, and sugar) were measured correctly, overbaking is the danger with bar cookies. Too much flour or changing types of flour can make bar cookies dry, too.	Next time start checking for doneness 10 minutes before you expect them to be done. For chewy bar cookies, a skewer inserted two-thirds of the way to the center should come out clean, but the center should be barely set. Be precise with flour measuring.
Brownies are too cakey	Some recipes are more cakey than fudgy, but if your brownies seem both cakey and a little dry then they are also overbaked. Cakey brownies tend to have more flour than other types, and any mistakes in measuring flour will be evident as dryness. Cakey brownies often contain leavening, which provides a lighter texture. Using larger eggs than specified can create a dry, spongy texture in combination with too much flour.	Next time start checking for doneness 10 minutes before you expect them to be done. For chewy brownies, a skewer inserted two-thirds of the way to the center should come out clean, but the center itself should be barely set. Be precise with flour measuring. If your recipe contains leavening and you prefer fudgy brownies, try omitting it. Also try reducing the flour by 2 tablespoons to ¼ cup for a moister, fudgier brownie. Be sure to use the right size eggs.
Baked hard meringue cookies or dessert shells are chewy and slightly soft	Either the meringues were undercooked and the remaining moisture caused them to lose their crunch or the meringues picked up moisture from the air due to improper storage. Rainy weather could also be at fault, since humidity quickly softens even the most perfectly crisp meringues.	Spread the meringues on a parchment-lined baking sheet and bake in a 225°F oven until dry and crisp, at least 20 minutes. On rainy days, let the meringues cool in the oven after the heat is turned off—you can even let them sit overnight. Place them in airtight containers when completely cool.

—Nicole Rees, *Fine Cooking*

BAD BREAD BLUES

THE PROBLEM	POSSIBLE CAUSES	FIX-IT TIPS FOR NOW OR NEXT TIME
Dough will not come together in mixer and appears soupy or shaggy	The salt was omitted. Salt tightens the structure of dough and without it doughs with a large amount of water may not come together. Also, the dough may require more mixing (kneading)—when dough looks shaggy, this is usually the problem. If too much liquid or not enough flour was added, the dough may look soupy and will need more flour.	Taste the dough to see if the salt was omitted—if so, add now and continue kneading. A dough high in water may form a ball when the mixer is running, then slump when the mixer is stopped. That's OK—if it is shiny, glossy, and elastic, it's done. Otherwise, keep kneading or mixing, adding more flour after a minute or two if necessary. Let the dough rest 10 minutes and try kneading again. Next time, if the recipe gives weights for ingredients, use a scale for best results.
Dough looks good, then loses cohesiveness	This problem usually occurs only when making bread in a stand mixer. The dough is kneaded for too long at too high a speed, overheats, and the nice gluten structure that was developed breaks down.	Overmixed or overheated dough looks rough, loses elasticity, and can rarely be salvaged. Next time, check dough frequently during mixing for a good gluten window. When the dough can be stretched to form a transparent, thin sheet, stop kneading. In general, knead on medium speed rather than high unless the recipe specifies otherwise.
Dough will not form gluten window	A gluten window, the thin sheet of transparent dough formed by stretching a small portion of dough between the fingers, is a sure sign that the dough has been mixed enough. Not all doughs will make one, though, such as rye and whole grain breads. For other doughs, however, lack of a gluten window usually indicates the dough was not kneaded long enough or that the flour may have poor protein quality.	First, try increasing the speed of the mixer for 1 minute. Check to see if the dough feels stretchier and more elastic; if so, knead for another minute or two to finish up. Just watch carefully to make sure you do not overmix. If you don't see any sign of improvement, add small amounts of flour while continuing to mix, checking for a gluten window frequently. Next time, make sure to use bread flour or a high-protein flour.

THE PROBLEM	POSSIBLE CAUSES	FIX-IT TIPS FOR NOW OR NEXT TIME
Baked loaf's crust is too dark	The oven temperature was too hot or perhaps the amount of sugar in the bread was excessive for that baking temperature.	Next time, reduce the temperature and bake longer. If it still browns too much, and contains a fair amount of sugar, try reducing the amount of sugar (including honey or molasses) by a quarter.
Baked artisan loaf's crust is too soft	Adequate heat and steam are needed for a crisp yet chewy artisan crust. Using steam during the first 5 to 10 minutes of baking not only helps the bread expand without breaking but develops the crust: During baking, minerals are precipitated out of the bread as steam. As they condense and settle back on the crust, they increase crispness and flavor.	Use a baking stone for a crisp crust, or bake near the bottom of the oven. Be sure to preheat the stone with the oven and start the bread at a high temperature (425 to 500°F) for the first 10 minutes. Use a spray bottle filled with water to create steam in the oven during the initial 5 to 10 minutes of baking time.
Crust is too thick	There are two possible causes: The loaves were not covered while rising or the bread was baked too hot or too long.	Next time, cover the loaves with a flour-dusted cloth or sheet of oiled plastic wrap to prevent them from drying. Reduce the oven temperature by at least 25°F and use the thumping test to see if bread is baked through (it will sound hollow when tapped on the bottom).
Bread tastes bland	The dough was allowed to rise too quickly at too high a temperature, or it contains insufficient salt.	Next time, refrigerate the shaped loaves overnight—this allows lactic acids to develop in the dough, which contribute greatly to flavor—or increase salt by at least ½ teaspoon per loaf.
Bread stales quickly	The dough was allowed to rise too quickly at too high a temperature or the bread was baked too long. If the baked loaf was stored improperly, it will, of course, deteriorate rapidly.	Next time, increase the amount of water (up to ½ cup) and rise cooler over a long period of time. Reduce the baking time. Cool the baked loaves on a rack. Store in a paper bag, placed inside a loosely closed plastic bag, to best maintain freshness.

THE PROBLEM	POSSIBLE CAUSES	FIX-IT TIPS FOR NOW OR NEXT TIME
Baked sweet bread (stollen, cinnamon rolls) texture is dense, gummy, or doughy and has poor volume	Most likely it is underbaked, or the dough was not given enough time to rise. Doughs rich with fat and sugar take longer to rise and may require more yeast to get the job done. Also, the dough may contain too much sour cream, buttermilk, yogurt, or fruit purée.	Be sure to give sweet doughs plenty of time to rise, and up the amount of yeast by 25% to make sure the dough at least increases to 1½ times if not double its original size. Make sure the rolls or bread are baked through. Use an even hand when measuring rich dairy products—too much is not a good thing.
Sweet dough crust is too brown, but the sides and bottom are still pale	The amount of sugar or milk in the dough was too great for the baking temperature and/or length of the bake.	Next time, either reduce the amount of milk and/or sugar or drop the oven temperature by 25°F. If top browning is still an issue, try making two smaller loaves, which will bake through in a shorter time.
Pizza or foccacia crust is not crisp	The oven temperature was too low or the toppings were too high in moisture.	Preheat a baking sheet or baking stone at 450°F and reheat the pizza for 5 to 10 minutes to crisp up the bottom. Next time, bake at 425° or 450°F. If you don't have a baking stone, bake flat bread nearly through, slide off the pan onto the bottom oven rack, and finish baking there for the last 5 to 10 minutes. Prebake pizza crusts halfway before adding toppings to prevent sogginess, especially if adding vegetables.

—Nicole Rees, *Fine Cooking*

THE PROBLEM	POSSIBLE CAUSES	FIX-IT TIPS FOR NOW OR NEXT TIME
Candied citrus peel is bitter	Undercooking is the likely cause, since raw citrus peels are bitter. If you've removed the peel with its white pith still attached, that can also result in bitterness.	If you have not yet dusted the cooled peel in sugar, you can boil the peel in one or two changes of water until it is tender and no longer bitter. If pith is the culprit, there's nothing you can do except be more careful when peeling next time.
Candy (any type) has lumps	These lumps are sugar crystals that have resisted melting due to uneven or rushed heating in the beginning of the candymaking process. The melted sugar may have also crystallized accidentally from too much stirring, the introduction of crystals from the side of the pan, or contact with a spoon carrying sugar crystals.	Cooled candy cannot be saved. However, if lumps are detected in the pot, just add a little water to encourage the lumps to melt. The cooking time will be extended since the extra water will have to boil off. Wash down any crystals that form on the side of the pan with a wet pastry brush or cover the pot briefly to allow steam do the job. Avoid stirring after the sugar is melted and smooth.
Candy (any type) does not set up properly and/or is sticky	Warm, humid, and rainy days wreak havoc on candymaking. Under heat, sugar, or sucrose, breaks down into glucose and fructose. Fructose is hygroscopic, attracting moisture from humid air and potentially making candy sticky.	If you are determined to make candy on a rainy day, cook the candy a little more than directed, at least 5°F more. Keep the windows closed and cool the candy in the driest place in the house. Store in airtight containers as soon as completely cooled.
Fudge or fondant is grainy	The sugar may not have been thoroughly melted initially. The fudge may have been disturbed before it was cool enough to beat, or it may not have been beaten long enough.	Generally, grainy candy is difficult to save. The determined cook can start over, returning the candy to the pot and heating slowly back to the soft ball stage. If the candy contains milk, however, it may curdle or break if this is done. Next time, wash down crystals that form on the side of the pan with a wet pastry brush or cover the pot briefly to let steam do the job. Avoid stirring after the sugar is melted and smooth.

THE PROBLEM	POSSIBLE CAUSES	FIX-IT TIPS FOR NOW OR NEXT TIME
Fudge becomes overly stiff when beaten	The fudge may have cooled too much during beating.	Stir in a few drops of warm cream or half-and-half at a time until the desired consistency is reached.
Fudge does not set up	The fudge was beaten before it had cooled sufficiently or was not adequately beaten.	Next time, cool fudge to 120°F before beating, then beat vigorously until it is no longer glossy.
Divinity is too soft to hold shape when dropped from a spoon	The divinity is not cooked enough.	Place soft divinity in a bowl set over simmering water. Cook, beating constantly, until it holds its shape when dropped from a spoon.
Divinity is too stiff	The sugar syrup poured into the beaten eggs was cooked past the appropriate stage or not enough syrup was added.	Add drops of hot water to the divinity, beating constantly, until it softens.
Caramel is too grainy	The sugar may not have been thoroughly melted initially. The melted sugar may have also crystallized accidentally from too much stirring, the introduction of crystals from the side of the pan, or contact with a spoon carrying crystals.	See the advice for fudge or fondant that is grainy.
Taffy is too stiff to pull and shape	The taffy was cooked to too high a temperature or has cooled too much to work with easily.	Butter your hands and work surface to prevent sticking. Try gently warming the taffy under a hot lamp or in the microwave at 10-second intervals at low power to soften. If it still won't budge, it is unsalvageable.
Peanut brittle is too thick	The peanuts added to the candy were cold, causing the brittle to set up too quickly.	Next time, warm the peanuts in the oven for a few minutes before stirring them into the candy. Buttering the sheet will also facilitate spreading the brittle as thinly as possible.

THE PROBLEM	POSSIBLE CAUSES	FIX-IT TIPS FOR NOW OR NEXT TIME
Toffee is grainy and doesn't set up	The sugar may not have been thoroughly melted initially. The melted sugar may have also crystallized accidentally from too much stirring, the introduction of crystals from the side of the pan, or contact with a spoon carrying crystals.	Break the candy into small bits and reheat slowly to the temperature specified in recipe—even 5° to 10°F higher in humid conditions. Although this may actually take longer than making a new batch of candy, you will have at least not wasted your ingredients. Next time, be sure to wash away crystals that form on the side of the pan with a wet pastry brush or cover the pot briefly to let steam do the job. Avoid stirring after the sugar is melted and smooth.
Toffee or peanut brittle is sticky when cooled, bends before it breaks, and sticks unpleasantly to teeth	The toffee or brittle was not cooked to the proper temperature. Also, rain and humidity are the enemy of candies that start off crisp and crunchy, causing them to absorb moisture from the air and soften.	Break the candy into small bits and cook it slowly until it reaches the proper temperature—even 5° to 10°F higher in humid conditions. This can take longer than making a new batch of candy, but at least you will not have wasted your ingredients.
Caramel sauce is too thick to pour when cold	Needs more liquid.	Warm the sauce over low heat. Slowly stir in heavy cream until the desired thickness is reached.
Caramel sauce is too thin	Contains too much liquid.	Place the sauce over medium heat and reduce slowly to desired consistency. Caution: If the sauce contains milk, not heavy cream, it may break if held at a high heat for too long.
Caramel sauce lacks flavor and is too sweet	The caramel was not allowed to darken sufficiently. Sugars break down during the caramelization process, making the candy more flavorful as it darkens and less sweet.	Next time, cook the caramel until deep amber in color, rather than golden. The darker color is essential for a deepness of flavor that will stand up to the addition of cream and butter.

—Nicole Rees, *Fine Cooking*

CHOCOLATE CONUNDRUMS

THE PROBLEM	POSSIBLE CAUSES	FIX-IT TIPS FOR NOW OR NEXT TIME
Chocolate forms hard, grainy lumps during melting process	If chocolate is improperly melted (over too high a heat or left in the microwave too long at high power), it may burn, forming small, hard lumps that float in the melted chocolate.	Taste the smooth portion of the chocolate. If it does not taste burnt, strain the chocolate to remove the lumps and proceed with the recipe. Next time, be sure to finely chop the chocolate for more even melting, monitor your heat level, and stir often, whether you use the microwave or the stovetop.
Chocolate seizes suddenly, forming a single, grainy mass	If even a small amount of water gets into the melting chocolate, it will seize. Steam created from melting chocolate over hot water could be the source.	If you needed pure chocolate for a recipe, then you will have to start over, but the chocolate can be saved for another use. Ironically, though a little liquid will make chocolate seize, larger amounts are fine: Melt cream or another liquid into the seized chocolate to create a delicious dessert sauce.
Chocolate ganache breaks or appears curdled	Though chocolate ganache can break (the cocoa butter separates out) if it is agitated or stirred too vigorously, the problem most likely lies with the ratio of chocolate to cream. Intense chocolates, such as bittersweet with its high percentage of cocoa solids, require more cream or a touch of sugar before they smooth out.	To bring the ganache back into a stable emulsion, pour 1 to 3 teaspoons of warm heavy cream on top of the broken ganache right in the saucepan. With a whisk, begin to stir the cream into the uppermost layer of the ganache. Start with very small circles, then move outward and deeper once the cream has formed a smooth ganache in the center.
Whipped chocolate ganache becomes hard and grainy	Ganache that has been overbeaten will harden and seize easily. Often the ganache seems pliable at first, but within a few minutes will become stiff and unworkable.	Melt a portion of the hardened ganache and stir it into the remaining seized whipped ganache until smooth, adding a little warm heavy cream if necessary. Let the ganache rest in the refrigerator or a cool room for at least 6 hours. Whip briefly with an electric mixer until fluffy. For perfect whipped ganache, stop beating once it forms soft peaks; it will continue to firm up as it sits.

THE PROBLEM	POSSIBLE CAUSES	FIX-IT TIPS FOR NOW OR NEXT TIME
Chocolate mousse mixture seizes when melted chocolate is folded in	Seizing can occur when warm chocolate comes in contact with cold ingredients, like cold whipped cream.	Next time try stirring the melted chocolate into a small portion of the mousse, then folding in the remaining mousse. Or melt the chocolate with an equal amount of cream from the recipe. Let this cool, then incorporate it into the mousse.
Unable to form sizeable chocolate curls using vegetable peeler	Using a peeler to shave delicate chocolate curls is hard work if the bar of chocolate is too cool—good chocolate that is well tempered may seem brittle at temperatures under 70°F.	To make chocolate more pliable, set the bar under a warm lamp or heat it gently in the microwave (5- to 10-second bursts). Just soften it enough to glide a peeler across it with minimal pressure.
Chocolate on chocolate-dipped fruit won't set up or softens if not kept cold	The chocolate was not tempered if it won't set up. If the fruit was cold to begin with, or the dipped fruit was placed in the fridge to force it to harden, the coating will soften as soon as it is removed from the refrigerator.	For best results, temper the chocolate to ensure that it will crystallize properly. If you do not have time for tempering, add 1 tablespoon of vegetable shortening to the melted chocolate to stabilize it. Use clean, dry, and cool—not cold— fruit pieces.
Cocoa butter separates from chocolate during tempering	The chocolate was heated too harshly: Beyond 130°F, the cocoa butter will separate from the chocolate liquor.	You'll have to start over. Next time check the temperature of the melting chocolate with a chocolate or instant-read thermometer (don't use a candy thermometer—it's meant for measuring a higher range of temperatures).
Tempered chocolate is streaky instead of shiny or the tempered chocolate did not set up	There are four major crystal formations in chocolate, and the goal of tempering is to allow only one of those forms to dominate the chocolate's structure—otherwise the chocolate won't be shiny and hard when it cools. If the thermometer is not precisely accurate or if room is unusually hot or cold, the chocolate may not set properly.	Tempering requires patience and precision. Chocolate must be melted to near 120°F (but not over), then cooled to 80°F. Milk and white chocolate must be heated back up to 85° to 87°F, and bitter chocolate to 87° to 90°F. For nearly foolproof tempering, if the chocolate you begin with is in temper (shiny, with a nice snap when it breaks), save a portion and stir it into the melted chocolate. This acts as the seed, encouraging the formation of the right crystals. Work in a draft-free environment that is moderate in temperature.

—Nicole Rees, *Fine Cooking*

SAUCY SITUATIONS

THE PROBLEM	POSSIBLE CAUSES	FIX-IT TIPS FOR NOW OR NEXT TIME
Cream will not form peaks after whipping	Cream cannot be beaten into a stable foam unless it is cold. If the room is hot, it will be more difficult to whip the cream. Cream that is cold but will not hold air may not have a high enough fat content.	Place the mixing bowl, cream, and beaters in the refrigerator and try beating again in 15 minutes. Next time, chill the bowl and beaters or whisk ahead of time. Be sure the label says heavy cream for reliable results—it should have a fat content of at least 36%.
Whipped cream is grainy	Whipped cream that is beaten beyond the stiff peak stage quickly becomes overmixed and grainy. If beaten even further small hard lumps of butter will begin to form.	If the cream is merely grainy, pour in more heavy cream (at least a quarter of the total amount) and beat only until soft, smooth peaks can be formed. Once hard lumps of butter have formed, the cream cannot be saved.
Crème Anglaise has small lumps	See "Egg-gravations" on p. 374.	
Sauce or gravy is too thin	If it was a cornstarch-thickened sauce, it may have been boiled too long, causing the starch to lose its thickening capacity. A roux made with flour will weaken as it browns in the pan, reducing its ability to gel.	For every cup of sauce, mix 1 teaspoon of cornstarch with 1 to 2 tablespoons of water and stir quickly into the warm sauce. Bring to a boil to cook the starch—then let it simmer 30 to 60 seconds to eliminate the flavor of uncooked starch. For the same amount of flour-thickened sauces, knead 2 teaspoons of butter into 2 teaspoons of flour and follow the same procedure, letting it simmer at least a minute or two after it reaches a boil.
Sauce tastes pasty	The starch, probably cornstarch or flour, has not been cooked adequately.	Simmer the sauce a few minutes longer to cook off the raw taste of the starch. Cook cornstarch sauces gently, reducing the heat once they reach a boil. Flour-thickened sauces need to cook for a few minutes longer.

THE PROBLEM	POSSIBLE CAUSES	FIX-IT TIPS FOR NOW OR NEXT TIME
Pan gravy is lumpy	When cold liquid was added to a roux, the flour didn't dissolve properly. Inadequate whisking also lets lumps form.	If the sauce is thick enough to use, simply strain it to remove the lumps. For a too-thin, yet lumpy sauce, thicken as directed for a sauce that is too thin, then strain the gravy.
Pan gravy is bitter	The browned bits of flavor on the bottom of the pan were burnt.	Sorry, there's nothing you can do once you've made the gravy. Next time, however, taste the browned bits before making the gravy in the roasting pan. If most taste too burned, scrape up some of the pleasant-tasting bits to add to a gravy made in a clean saucepan.
White pan gravy has a skin on it	Any sauce made with milk or other dairy products will form a skin—the result of the protein casein separating from the sauce.	If the sauce is in the pan, first try gently reheating it to melt the skin. Transfer the gravy to a serving container and place plastic wrap directly against the surface of the sauce to prevent a skin from forming.
Pan sauce of reduced wine is bitter	Either the flavorful bits on the bottom of the pan were burnt or the wine was not good.	Sorry, with charred flavor and bad wine, you'll have to start over. If the sauce is pungent from too much wine, but the wine is good, whisk in reduced stock or butter to mellow out the flavor.
Pan sauce of reduced wine has separated	The sauce doesn't have enough water—too much may have evaporated while the sauce was kept warm.	Stir in a little warm water and see if the sauce comes together. Adding cream, which is a stable emulsion already, may also do the trick.
Cheese sauce or fondue is stringy, grainy, or oily	High heat will cause a cheese sauce to break. Stringy sauces, for which the cheese refuses to smooth out, don't have enough flour or lemon juice or the liquid in your recipe may have evaporated. Also, the cheese may have curdled from high heat or too much stirring.	Over medium-low heat stir in a little lemon juice and/or flour to reduce stringiness. If the sauce is simply too thick and gloppy, add more liquid, whether it be wine, milk, or cream. If the sauce won't smooth out, you're out of luck and will have to start over. Next time reduce the heat before stirring in the cheese.

THE PROBLEM	POSSIBLE CAUSES	FIX-IT TIPS FOR NOW OR NEXT TIME
Mayonnaise looks separated	The emulsion has broken. You may have added too much oil or added it too quickly. Another culprit is the oil itself: Unrefined oils are more resistant to emulsifying than refined ones.	If the problem mayonnaise was made with unrefined oil, discard and begin again. If not, you can try to re-emulsify your mayonnaise. If you have a blender or food processor, process the sauce to see if high-speed agitation will bring it back. If that doesn't work or you don't have the machinery, try the following: Start with a whole new egg or an egg yolk mixed with 1 tablespoon of water or lemon juice, and slowly whisk the broken mayonnaise into it.
Beurre blanc, béarnaise, or hollandaise sauce has oil accumulating around the edge of the pan	The sauce is about to break. Separation occurs when the cooking temperature is too high.	Get it off the heat quickly, then whisk gently until the sauce cools a bit and comes back together.
Beurre blanc sauce looks broken	The heat was too high. Once beurre blanc passes 130°F, it will break.	Remove the pan from the heat. As the sauce cools, whisk in a little heavy cream until the sauce comes back together.
Beurre blanc sauce congealed into grainy mass while cooling in pan	If left to cool too long, the sauce can form a crystal structure, making it grainy.	You'll have to re-emulsify the sauce: Start with a tablespoon or two of warm cream and slowly whisk the sauce into it over low heat.
Béarnaise or hollandaise sauce is broken	After oil begins to accumulate around the sides of the pan, the emulsion will break if the heat remains too high. Besides high heat, adding too much butter or adding the butter too quickly can cause curdling.	Remove the sauce from the heat. Stir in a little water, lemon juice, vinegar, or cream until the sauce comes back together. Reheat very gently over low heat if necessary.
Hollandaise sauce is lumpy and thick	The heat was too high and the sauce cooked too fast, causing the egg proteins to scramble.	If the sauce is otherwise thick and smooth, you can strain out the lumps, but a scrambled sauce cannot be saved.

—Nicole Rees, *Fine Cooking*

THE PROBLEM	POSSIBLE CAUSES	FIX-IT TIPS FOR NOW OR NEXT TIME
Beaten egg whites are grainy and won't fold into batter	The egg whites are overbeaten, causing the proteins to contract and squeeze out water.	Sorry, once egg whites are overbeaten, they cannot expand and hold air to contribute to a cake or soufflé's volume—dump them in the garbage and start again. Next time, beat the egg whites just until they are shiny; overwhipped eggs become visibly dull and grainy.
Egg whites won't form stiff peaks	If you can't get the egg whites to form a stable foam, then there is fat present in the bowl or on the beaters, usually in the form of a small bit of yolk that broke into the white, but a greasy bowl will also compromise the egg foam.	Start over with a squeaky clean bowl and yolk-free egg whites.
Beaten meringue is grainy	Meringue, a simple mixture of egg whites and sugar, should be smooth for optimum volume and stability. Sugar particles have not dissolved if the meringue is grainy, which means that egg whites were too cold or that the meringue was not beaten slowly enough to allow the sugar granules to dissolve.	Set the grainy meringue over—not in—another bowl filled with hot water; whisk vigorously until the meringue feels smooth between your fingers. Remove and beat 30 seconds to a minute at high speed for maximum volume. Next time, add the sugar to soft-peak-stage egg whites 1 tablespoon at a time so the sugar dissolves without deflating the egg foam.
Pie meringue weeps or forms beads	See "Pie Pitfalls and Tart Tribulations" on p. 352.	
Cooked eggs are discolored	Eggs cooked in reactive metal pans will discolor; cast iron can impart a reddish tinge and aluminum (not anodized) will turn eggs gray.	Sorry, there's nothing you can do except use a stainless, anodized aluminum, or another nonreactive pan the next time.
Hard-boiled egg cracks in water	Cold eggs placed in rapidly boiling water are prone to cracking; the pressure of the hot water causes existing fissures to expand.	Next time, start the eggs in cool water. Bring the water and eggs to a boil together for a more gentle cooking method.

THE PROBLEM	POSSIBLE CAUSES	FIX-IT TIPS FOR NOW OR NEXT TIME
Hard-boiled egg has green layer around yolk	The eggs are overcooked. When an egg is heated for a prolonged period, a chemical reaction takes place between the yolk and the white, causing green iron oxide to form.	Next time, watch the clock closely. Don't boil eggs longer than 20 minutes and be sure to cool promptly by rinsing in cold water.
Scrambled eggs are watery and tough instead of creamy and fluffy	The eggs were overcooked, causing the protein network to become tighter and squeeze out moisture.	Next time, cook the eggs slowly over gentle heat, stirring often, but not too vigorously. Turn off the heat when the eggs are just barely set—the hot pan will finish cooking the eggs through.
Omelet sticks to pan	Eggs stick to the pan if they are cooked at too high a temperature. Omelets require the right amount of fat to grease the pan, the correct cooking temperature, and an effective swirling motion to distribute the eggs evenly.	If one portion of the omelet is stuck to the pan, simply flip the other half onto the stuck portion and pry the omelet loose with a spatula. Serve it torn side down to hide the damage. If the omelet is stuck completely, stir the eggs and pretend the intent was scrambled eggs. Garnish with chopped herbs or scallions or grated cheese to further the deception.
Omelet is over-cooked on outside but undercooked on inside	The omelet contains too many eggs or too much filling. Another possibility is that the eggs may not have been adequately swirled in the pan and set before the filling was added.	Next time, consider the pan-to-egg ratio before you begin, which is traditionally 2 eggs for an 8-inch pan. An omelet of this size will be easy to swirl and cook quickly and evenly, avoiding a tough exterior and runny interior.
Poached eggs are misshapen and uneven	Older eggs have runny whites and delicate yolks that break easily, making them a poor choice for this cooking method. Rapidly boiling water can also cause an egg to set in an irregular shape.	Next time, start with the freshest eggs possible. Use gently simmering water with a little added vinegar and salt, which will help set the eggs even faster.
Crème Anglaise has lumps	The eggs may have not been tempered before being added to the hot cream mixture. Or the sauce was cooked over high heat, or at too high a temperature.	If the eggs are scrambled, the sauce is not thick enough to use so you'll need to start over. Next time, whisk about one-third of the hot cream mixture into eggs before returning it to the pot to finish cooking. Cook over medium heat. Crème Anglaise is set well below boiling: It is done when a path can be drawn across a sauce-coated spoon and remain clear.

THE PROBLEM	POSSIBLE CAUSES	FIX-IT TIPS FOR NOW OR NEXT TIME
Pastry cream has lumps	Pastry cream can be lumpy from the eggs scrambling over too high a heat, or it may have lumps of flour or cornstarch that did not dissolve during cooking. The eggs may have not been tempered before being added to the hot cream mixture.	If the pastry cream has thickened properly and lumps are the only concern, simply press it through a wire mesh strainer to make it perfectly smooth. If it's completely scrambled, you need to pitch it and start again. Next time, whisk about one-third of the hot cream mixture into the eggs before returning it to the pot to finish cooking over medium heat.
Baked custard (flan, pots de crème, crème brûlée) cracks or curdles	These custards contain little or no starch and thus set at a lower temperature than pastry cream. As a result, they are easily overcooked. Baked custards continue to cook for a few minutes after being removed from the oven—they are considered done when the center is just barely wobbly.	Next time, be sure to bake the custards in a water bath (a pan filled with warm water) to better insulate the custards and allow for even, gradual heat penetration. Remove from the oven and the water bath when they are just barely set.
Soufflé falls immediately when pulled from oven	Though all soufflés are ephemeral, recipes with little or no starch are especially fragile. Also, the egg whites may have been overbeaten and unable to set the structure of the soufflé.	Next time, make sure the soufflé base is thickened properly. Adding 2 tablespoons of additional flour will strengthen the structure. Seek out recipes that include chocolate or cheese, as these ingredients also stabilize a soufflé's structure. If the soufflé didn't rise much before it fell, then be careful not to overbeat the egg whites next time: the egg whites should be glossy and firm, not grainy and dry looking.
Quiche is watery instead of creamy and set	See "Pie Pitfalls and Tart Tribulations" on p. 352.	
Mayonnaise looks separated	See "Saucy Situations" on p. 371.	

—Nicole Rees, *Fine Cooking*

THE PROBLEM	POSSIBLE CAUSES	FIX-IT TIPS FOR NOW OR NEXT TIME
Pan-seared meat sticks to pan	The pan wasn't hot enough or the meat was not ready to be turned. Insufficient fat in the pan can also cause the meat to stick.	If the meat isn't overly browned, continue cooking—it will release much easier once it has seared. Next time, be sure to preheat the pan and check that the pan is evenly coated with a small amount of fat to prevent sticking.
Pan-seared meat isn't browned	Either the pan was not hot enough when the meat went in, or the meat was overcrowded in the pan. Overcrowding will cause the temperature of the pan to drop, and the meat will end up steaming rather than searing.	To avoid cooking the meat beyond the desired doneness, brown it fast by running it under a hot broiler. Next time, preheat the pan for 3 to 5 minutes before searing, and don't crowd the meat in the pan for maximum browning.
Herb and spice coating on meat is now stuck to bottom of pan	Some of the coating always sticks to the bottom of the pan, but if you lose most if it, then there was either too much coating on the meat, not enough fat in the pan, or the heat was too low.	If you plan to make a pan sauce, then the flavor will be recovered in the end. If not, sprinkle the finished meat with herbs to replace what was lost. Next time, use more fat in the pan and more heat, and tap excess spices from the meat before you cook it. Sear, turning only once, and finish cooking the meat in a 425°F oven.
Garlic is burned before rest of sauté is done cooking	The garlic was minced too small or the heat was too high. Garlic cooks lightning fast, owing to its size and softness, and will become bitter if it browns.	Though the flavor of the burned garlic may have infused the sauté, you may be able to pick out the darkest, most bitter pieces. Next time, use larger pieces of garlic over a lower initial heat; turn the heat up only when other foods are added to the pan. The best bet, however, is to ignore the directions and add the garlic later in the recipe. The volume of food in the pan will act as a buffer and cook the garlic more slowly.

THE PROBLEM	POSSIBLE CAUSES	FIX-IT TIPS FOR NOW OR NEXT TIME
Sautéed onions are cooking unevenly: Some are crisp, some are too brown, and some remain nearly raw	The onions have not been stirred often enough. A pan full of raw onions will collapse into less than a third of its volume when cooked—the trick is cooking the onions so that they caramelize evenly.	If some are getting too dark, pour in a little water: this will deglaze the pan, coating all the onions in flavor. Cover the pan and continue cooking; the onions will soften and cook through without burning.
Sautéed mushrooms aren't browned	The pan is not hot enough and there were too many mushrooms in the pan. Mushrooms release liquid as they cook, which will change the cooking method from sauté to steaming if the pan is too crowded.	Pour off excess liquid (but reserve if you are making a sauce) and cook the mushrooms over medium-high heat until they brown. Next time, preheat the pan before you start, and cook the mushrooms in batches to avoid over-crowding the pan.
Stir-fried vegetables are sticking to the pan and burning on the bottom	The pan wasn't hot enough and/or there wasn't enough oil in the pan. In addition, the vegetables may not have been tossed or stirred well enough to be evenly coated with the oil during the initial stage of cooking.	You can't repair overcooked food, but you can add a little oil to the pan to help prevent the remainder of the vegetables from sticking. Next time, preheat the pan. Once the pan is hot, swirl in the oil and then add the vegetables in small batches, removing and repeating as many times as needed to prevent overcrowding. Be sure to toss the vegetables often.
Stir-fried vegetables are unevenly cooked: Some are crisp, others too soft.	Each food was not cut into uniform-size pieces. Also, vegetables that cook quickly were cooked with vegetables that cook slowly.	You'll have to live with this one. Next time, cut your vegetables into the same size pieces and begin with the longer-cooking foods (onions, potatoes, broccoli), adding quicker-cooking ones later (peas, zucchini, eggplant). Hurry slow vegetables along by adding 2 to 4 tablespoons water to the hot pan once the vegetables have begun to color and soften. Cover the pan, letting the food steam and quickly soften over high heat. The water should evaporate within a minute.
Coating falls off fried food	The coating (flour or crumbs) was too thick.	Next time, tap off excess coating before frying and let the food rest a few minutes after is has been coated.

THE PROBLEM	POSSIBLE CAUSES	FIX-IT TIPS FOR NOW OR NEXT TIME
Fried food has tiny black specks	One of the ingredients in the coating, such as a spice or sugar, is burning, leaving charred particles in the oil.	Unless you want to heat a pan with fresh oil, there's nothing you can do except keep a close eye on the heat to make sure the burning doesn't accelerate. Once particles begin to burn, the oil degrades and may impart off-flavors to the finished food.
Fried food browns on outside but is undercooked in middle	The frying oil is too hot, or the food was cold when immersed in the pan. The pan may also have been over-crowded, especially when cooking fried chicken.	Hold off on frying the next batch until the oil has cooled down and you've checked the temperature with a thermometer made specifically for frying. The fat should not be above 375°F—many oils will degrade quickly and smoke at higher temperatures. Before you cook the next batch, let the food warm up a little if it is cold.
Fried food is greasy and soggy	Either the cooking oil was not hot enough or too much food was added to the pan at once, thus cooling the frying oil. When the temperature is too far below 350°F, oil will enter the food faster than steam (generated by the pressure of the heat on the food's moist interior) will escape, causing the food to take in too much fat.	Sorry, there's nothing you can do besides discard the greasy batch. Next time, monitor the oil's tempera-ture with a special thermometer for frying. Adjust the heat accordingly on the stovetop to maintain the correct temperature or consider investing in a batch fryer with an automatic temperature control.
Fried potatoes (french fries) or plantains (tostones) are not crisp enough	The temperature of the oil may not have been high enough, or you did not fry the potatoes twice. Also, you may have overcrowded the pan, slowing the cooking process.	Using a frying thermometer, check to make sure the oil is at the proper temperature. Fry in small batches to ensure quick and even cooking. The best french fries and tostones are twice-fried: Fry at 300° to 325°F until veggies just soften the first time; drain and cool briefly, then fry at 350° to 375°F until crisp and golden.

—Nicole Rees, *Fine Cooking*

INGREDIENT	SUBSTITUTION
Allspice, ground	2 parts ground cinnamon plus 1 part ground cloves
Aniseed	Fennel seed
Apple pie spice (1 teaspoon) plus ⅛ teaspoon ground allspice	¾ teaspoon ground cinnamon plus ¼ teaspoon ground nutmeg
Arrowroot	Cornstarch (as long as chilling or freezing is not involved)
Baking powder (1 teaspoon)	¼ teaspoon baking soda plus ½ teaspoon cream of tartar OR ¼ teaspoon baking soda plus ½ cup sour milk, buttermilk, yogurt, applesauce, or mashed banana
Brandy (2 tablespoons)	1¼ teaspoons brandy extract
Bread crumbs, dry	Cracker crumbs, matzo meal, crushed corn flakes
Buttermilk (1 cup)	1 cup plain low-fat yogurt OR 1 cup minus 1 tablespoon milk plus 1 tablespoon lemon juice or white vinegar
Capers	Chopped green olives
Cayenne pepper (⅛ teaspoon)	3 to 4 drops hot pepper sauce
Cheese, cottage	Ricotta or farmer cheese
Cheese, goat (fresh)	Feta cheese
Chile paste	Red pepper flakes, cayenne pepper, hot pepper sauce
Chinese egg noodles	Fresh or dried angel hair, spaghetti, or thin linguine
Chocolate, semisweet (1 ounce)	1 ounce unsweetened chocolate plus 1 tablespoon sugar
Chocolate, unsweetened (1 ounce)	3 tablespoons natural unsweetened cocoa powder plus 1 tablespoon melted butter
Cornstarch (1 tablespoon)	2 tablespoons flour or 4 teaspoons quick-cooking tapioca
Corn syrup, light (1 cup)	1 cup sugar plus ¼ cup water
Corn syrup, dark (1 cup)	¾ cup light corn syrup plus ¼ cup molasses
Cream, heavy (1 cup)	Whipping cream or, if not using to make whipped cream, ¾ cup milk plus ¼ cup melted butter
Crème fraîche (1 cup)	½ cup sour cream plus ½ cup heavy cream
Currants	Dark raisins
Dates	Dark raisins

INGREDIENT	SUBSTITUTION
Eggs (1 large egg)	2 egg whites or ¼ cup egg product
Fish sauce (1 tablespoon)	2 teaspoons soy sauce mixed with 1 teaspoon anchovy paste
Flour, cake (1 cup)	1 cup all-purpose flour minus 2 tablespoons
Flour, self-rising (1 cup)	1 cup all-purpose flour plus 1½ teaspoons baking powder and ½ teaspoon salt
Garlic (1 medium clove)	¼ teaspoon garlic powder
Herbs, chopped fresh (1 tablespoon)	1 teaspoon dried leaves
Jicama	Water chestnuts or a tart apple
Lemongrass	Substitute an equal amount of lemon zest
Lemon juice	White wine vinegar or lime juice (though if lemon juice is called for in quantity in the particular recipe, substituting could quite significantly affect the taste of the dish)
Lemon peel, grated (1 teaspoon)	1 teaspoon lemon extract
Lime leaves, Kaffir	An equal amount of lime zest
Mango, green	Granny Smith apple
Mascarpone	Cream cheese
Milk (1 cup)	½ cup evaporated milk mixed with ½ cup water OR 1 cup water mixed with 3 tablespoons powdered milk
Mustard, dry (1 teaspoon)	1 tablespoon prepared mustard
Mustard, prepared (1 tablespoon)	1 teaspoon dry mustard mixed with 2 tablespoons wine vinegar, white wine, or water
Orange juice, blood (1 cup)	½ cup lemon juice mixed with ½ cup lime juice
Orange liqueur (1 tablespoon)	1 teaspoon orange extract
Orange peel, grated (1 teaspoon)	1 teaspoon orange extract
Pancetta	Blanched bacon
Pine nuts	Slivered blanched almonds
Poultry seasoning (1 teaspoon)	¾ teaspoon ground sage plus ¼ teaspoon ground thyme
Pumpkin pie spice (1 teaspoon)	½ teaspoon ground cinnamon plus ¼ teaspoon ground ginger plus ⅛ teaspoon ground cloves plus ⅛ teaspoon ground nutmeg
Rice wine	Dry sherry

INGREDIENT	SUBSTITUTION
Salt, table (1 teaspoon)	1¼ to 1½ teaspoons kosher salt (you need more to achieve the same saltiness because of kosher salt's larger flakes)
Shallots	Scallions, white part only, OR white onion
Shortening, vegetable (1 cup)	1 cup (2 sticks) plus 3 tablespoons butter; if using to bake cookies, you may want to add just a bit more flour to the cookie dough to keep the cookies from flattening out, if that's important to you
Shrimp paste	Dried salted anchovies
Sour cream	Plain yogurt
Sugar	For every 1¼ cups sugar, you can substitute 1 cup honey plus ½ teaspoon baking soda (to counter its acidity and added weight). For every 1 cup honey used, you need to reduce the liquid in the recipe by ¼ cup and, if you are baking, reduce the oven temperature by 25°F to prevent excess browning.
Sugar, brown	Light and dark can be used interchangeably; to make your own, pulse in a food processor 1 cup white granulated sugar and 3 to 4 tablespoons molasses to yield 1 cup
Sugar, palm	Maple syrup or light brown sugar
Sugar, superfine	Equal amount of regular granulated sugar pulsed in a food processor fitted with a steel blade 30 to 60 seconds
Tomatillo	Green tomatoes plus a little lemon juice
Tomatoes (1 pound fresh)	One 14-ounce can peeled whole tomatoes with their juice
Vanilla bean (2-inch piece)	1 teaspoon vanilla extract
Vinegar, sherry	Balsamic vinegar
Yeast (1 teaspoon active dry)	¾ teaspoon instant OR 2 teaspoons fresh yeast

BAKING PAN SUBSTITUTIONS

If you don't have the exact size baking pan called for in a recipe, in most cases you can substitute a pan with the same volume capacity. Just make sure your substitute pan has sides that are of a similar height. A pan with taller or shorter sides will affect the rate of cooking and could ruin something like a cake. Also, be careful about substituting for a tube pan. If it's a delicate cake, such as angel food, the tube in the center of the pan is critical for proper cooking. To measure any pan not found on this list, fill it with water to within 1/4 inch of the rim and measure the volume of water

CAPACITY OF STANDARD BAKING PANS

SQUARE PANS		ROUND PANS	
8 x 8 x 2 inches	8 cups	8 x 2 inches	7 cups
9 x 9 x 2 inches	10 cups	9 x 2 inches	8 cups
		9 x 3 inches	12 cups
RECTANGULAR PANS		10 x 2 inches	10 cups
11 x 7 x 2 inches	8 cups		
13 x 9 x 2 inches	12 cups	SPRINGFORM PANS	
		9 x 2½ inches	10 cups
LOAF PANS		10 x 2¾ inches	15 cups
8½ x 4½ x 2½ inches	6 cups		
9 x 5 x 3 inches	8 cups	TUBE PANS	
		9 x 3 inches	10 cups
		9½ x 4 inches	16 cups

MEASUREMENT EQUIVALENTS

VOLUME EQUIVALENTS

To convert liters to cups, multiply the number of liters by 4.22675 (1 liter = about 4¼ cups; 2 liters = about 8½ cups); to convert cups to liters, multiply the number of cups by 0.2368.

1 tablespoon = 3 teaspoons = ½ fluid ounce = 14.8 milliliters

¼ cup = 4 tablespoons = 2 fluid ounces = 59.2 milliliters

⅓ cup = 5 tablespoons plus 1 teaspoon = 2⅔ fluid ounces = 78.9 milliliters

½ cup = 8 tablespoons = 4 fluid ounces = 118.4 milliliters

1 cup = 16 tablespoons = 8 fluid ounces = 236.8 milliliters

1 pint = 2 cups = 16 fluid ounces = 473.6 milliliters

1 quart = 2 pints = 4 cups = 32 fluid ounces = 947.2 milliliters

1 gallon = 4 quarts = 8 pints = 16 cups = 3.79 liters

WEIGHT EQUIVALENTS

To convert grams to ounces and pounds, divide grams by 28.35 for ounces; divide grams by 453.6 for pounds. To convert ounces and pounds to grams, multiply ounces by 28.35; multiply pounds by 453.6.

1 pound = 16 ounces = 453.6 grams

2.2 pounds = 1 kilogram

OVEN TEMPERATURE EQUIVALENTS

To convert from degrees Fahrenheit to Celsius, subtract 32 from the Fahrenheit temperature, then multiply by 5 and divide by 9. To convert degrees Celsius to Fahrenheit, multiply the Celsius temperature by 9, divide by 5, then add 32.

FAHRENHEIT (F)	CELSIUS (C, ROUNDED)	GAS MARK
225	110	¼
250	120	½
275	140	1
300	150	2
325	170	3
350	180	4
375	190	5
400	200	6
425	220	7
450	230	8
475	240	9

A common kitchen quandary—a recipe calls for mincing a large clove of garlic and all you have are what seem like small cloves—how much garlic do you need to mince? Or maybe you're making a pie that calls for 7 cups of sliced apples. How many apples do you need to buy at the store? This chart give you the answers so you can be all the more prepared in the kitchen—and the supermarket.

DRY GOODS	WEIGHT	VOLUME
Beans, black	6½ ounces	3 cups cooked; 1 cup uncooked
Beans, kidney and Great Northern	6½ ounces	2¾ cups cooked; 1 cup uncooked
Rice, arborio	7 ounces	2⅔ cups cooked; 1 cup uncooked
Rice, long-grain white	6½ ounces	3 cups cooked; 1 cup uncooked
Rice, medium-grain	6¾ ounces	3 cups cooked; 1 cup uncooked
Couscous	6½ ounces	3½ cups cooked; 1 cup uncooked
Penne, uncooked	1 pound	8 cups cooked
Spaghetti, uncooked	1 pound	8¾ cups cooked
Almonds, hazelnuts, and peanuts, whole, shelled, 1 cup	5 to 5½ ounces	1 cup coarsely chopped; 1 cup plus 2 tablespoons finely chopped; 1¼ cups ground
Pecan and walnut halves, 1 cup	4 ounces	¾ cup plus 2 tablespoons coarsely chopped; 1 cup finely chopped; 1 cup ground
Breadcrumbs, fresh from about 2½ slices sandwich bread, with crust	2¼ ounces	1 cup
DAIRY		
Cheddar	2 ounces	½ cup lightly packed, coarsely grated
Parmesan	½ ounce	¼ cup lightly packed, finely grated

DRY GOODS	WEIGHT	VOLUME
FRUITS AND VEGETABLES		
Carrot, 1 medium	2½ ounces	½ cup coarsely grated; ⅓ cup small (¼-inch) dice; ½ cup ¼-inch slices
Celery, 1 medium rib	2¼ ounces	⅔ cup small (¼-inch) dice; ⅔ cup ¼-inch slices
Garlic, 1 large clove	¼ ounce	1 teaspoon paste; 1½ teaspoons minced; 1 tablespoon coarsely chopped
Leek, 1 medium	6 ounces (3 ounces white and pale green parts only)	1 cup medium (½-inch) dice; 1½ cups ¼-inch slices
Onion, 1 medium	8 ounces	1⅓ cups minced; 1⅓ cups medium (½-inch) dice; 2⅓ cups thin (⅛-inch) slices
Bell pepper, 1 medium	7 ounces	1 cup fine (⅛-inch) dice; 1⅓ cups medium (½-inch) dice; 1½ cups thin (⅛-inch) slices
Potato, red, 1 medium	5 ounces	1 cup medium (½-inch) dice
Potato, russet, 1 medium	12 ounces	2¼ cups medium (½-inch) dice
Shallot, 1 large	¾ ounce	3 tablespoons minced
Tomato, 1 medium	5 ounces	1 cup medium (½-inch) dice
Mushrooms, white	8 ounces	3 cups thin (⅛-inch) slices
Olives, kalamata, ½ cup whole	3 ounces	scant ½ cup pitted and coarsely chopped
Parsley, flat-leaf (Italian), 1 small bunch	3 ounces	½ cup lightly packed, chopped
Apple, 1 medium	7 ounces	1⅓ cups medium (½-inch) dice; 1 cup thin (⅛-inch) slices
Lemon, 1 medium	5 ounces	4 to 5 tablespoons unstrained juice; 2 tablespoons zest grated with a rasp; 1 tablespoon zest grated on a box grater
Lime, 1 medium	4 ounces	3 to 4 tablespoons unstrained juice; 4 teaspoons zest grated with a rasp; 2 teaspoons zest grated on a box grater
Orange, navel, 1 medium	10 ounces	6 to 7 tablespoons unstrained juice; 2 tablespoons zest grated with a rasp; 1 tablespoon zest grated on a box grater

Bruce Aidells is the author of *Bruce Aidells's Complete Sausage Book* and *Bruce Aidells's Complete Book of Pork.*

Amy Albert is a senior editor at *Fine Cooking.*

Katherine Alford, the former director of instruction at The Institute of Culinary Education, is a senior writer for the Food Network.

Ayla Algar, the author of *Classical Turkish Cooking,* is the Mellon Lecturer in Turkish at the University of California at Berkeley.

Lynn Alley is the author of *Lost Arts,* a cook's guide to making handmade ingredients.

Dave Anderson, known as Famous Dave, is the author of *Famous Dave's Backroads & Sidestreets.*

Pam Anderson is the author of *How to Cook Without a Book* and is a contributing editor to *Fine Cooking.*

Jennifer Armentrout is the test kitchen manager at *Fine Cooking.*

John Ash is the author of several cookbooks, including *John Ash: Cooking One on One.*

Karen and Ben Barker are chefs/owners of the Magnolia Grill in North Carolina.

Rose Levy Beranbaum is the award-winning author of *The Cake Bible, The Pie & Pastry Bible,* and *The Bread Bible.*

Peter Berley is the author of *The Modern Vegetarian Kitchen* and *Fresh Foods Fast.*

Joanne Bouknight is the author of numerous books, including *The Kitchen Idea Book* and *Taunton's Home Storage Idea Book.*

Flo Braker is the author of *The Simple Art of Perfect Baking* and *Sweet Miniatures* and is a past president of the International Association of Culinary Professionals.

Georgeanne Brennan has written several cookbooks, including *Potager: Fresh Cooking in the French Style* and *Great Greens.*

Ethel Brennan is the author of *Citrus* and *Herbes de Provence.*

Kay Cabrera, former pastry chef at the Gallery Restaurant at the Mauna Lani Bay Hotel in Hawaii, is a freelance pastry chef for area caterers and restaurants.

Greg Case is the owner and pastry chef of G. Case Baking Co. in Somerville, Massachusetts.

Viviana Carballo is a food writer in Miami, Florida.

Gay Chandler is a dessert caterer and pastry chef in Flagstaff, Arizona.

Jane Charlton is the author of *A Taste of Honey.*

Joanne Chang is the chef/owner of Flour, a bakery and café in Boston.

Judith Choate is a cook and food writer.

Charlie Coppola is a partner in Manchester Seafood in Tiverton, Rhode Island.

Shirley O. Corriher, a food scientist and former contributing editor to *Fine Cooking,* is the author of the award-winning *CookWise.*

Jack Czarnecki is the author of *Portobello Cookbook* and owner of The Joel Palmer House in Dayton, Oregon.

Regan Daley is author of the award-winning cookbook *In the Sweet Kitchen.*

Robert Danhi is the corporate chef for Two Chefs on a Roll Company.

Erica DeMane is a chef, writer, teacher, and author of *Pasta Improvvisata.*

Tasha DeSerio, formerly a cook at Chez Panisse, now teaches and writes about cooking.

Abigail Johnson Dodge is a contributing editor to *Fine Cooking* and author of *100 Great Fruit Desserts* and *The Weekend Baker.*

Tom Douglas is chef/owner of four restaurants in downtown Seattle and author of *Tom Douglas' Seattle Kitchen* and *Tom's Big Dinners.*

Maryellen Driscoll is *Fine Cooking's* editor at large.

Kay Fahey is a writer in Reno, Nevada.

Roy Finamore is a cookbook editor and co-author of *One Potato, Two Potato.*

Janet Fletcher is the author of many books, including *Fresh from the Farmers' Market*.

Margery K. Friedman specializes in making custom wedding cakes in Rockville, Maryland.

Fran Gage is a teacher, writer, consultant, and author of *A Sweet Quartet: Sugar, Almonds, Eggs, and Butter*.

Gale Gand received the James Beard Award for Outstanding Pastry Chef and is the author of *Just a Bite* and *Gale Gand's Short and Sweet*.

Rob Gavel is a graduate of the Culinary Institute of America and a former intern at *Fine Cooking*.

Maggie Glezer is the author of *Artisan Breads*.

Joyce Goldstein is a culinary consultant and author of *Italian Slow and Savory*.

Bonnie Gorder-Hinchey is the director of culinary services with the Seattle food marketing communications firm Publicist Dialog.

Linda J. Harris, Ph.D., is a food safety specialist at the University of California, Davis.

Giuliano Hazan is a cooking instructor and the author of *The Classic Pasta Cookbook*.

Martha Holmberg is the former publisher of *Fine Cooking* and the food editor of *The Oregonian*.

Peter Hoffman is the chef/owner of Savoy in New York City.

Steve Hunter is the art director of *Fine Cooking*.

Dana Jacobi is the author of *The Best of Clay Pot Cooking* and *The 12 Best Foods Cookbook*.

Arlene Jacobs is a chef/instructor at The French Culinary Institute.

Sarah Jay is the managing editor of *Fine Cooking*.

Michele Anna Jordan is the author of several cookbooks, including *The BLT Cookbook*.

Madeleine Kamman is the author of many cookbooks, including the award-winning *The New Making of a Chef*.

Elizabeth Karmel is the author of *Taming the Flame*.

Eva Katz is a recipe developer and food writer in Jamaica Plain, Massachusetts.

Hubert Keller is chef/owner of Fleur de Lys in San Francisco and the author of *The Cuisine of Hubert Keller*.

Loretta Keller is the chef/owner of Bizou in San Francisco.

Elaine Khosrova is a recipe developer and a food writer living in New York's Hudson Valley.

Bob Kinkead is the chef/owner of Kinkead's in Washington, D.C., and the winner of the James Beard Award for Best Mid-Atlantic Chef.

Elinor Klivans teaches baking across the country and has written numerous cookbooks, including *Bake & Freeze Chocolate Desserts*.

Ris Lacoste is the award-winning executive chef of 1789 Restaurant in Washington, D.C.

Jacquie Lee is the co-owner of The Garden Baker in Ukiah, California.

Julia Leonard is a cook and writer who lives in Manchester, Massachusetts.

Seen Lippert is a chef consultant at Yale University in New Haven, Connecticut.

Ruth Lively writes about cooking and gardening.

Lori Longbotham is the author of several cookbooks, including *Luscious Chocolate Desserts*.

Andrew MacLauchlan is the author of *New Classic Desserts* and *Tropical Desserts*.

Deborah Madison is the author of the award-winning *Vegetarian Cooking for Everyone*.

Jennifer McLagan is a food stylist and the author of *Bones*.

Alice Medrich is the author of numerous books on chocolate, including the award-winning *Cocolat* and *Bittersweet: Recipes and Tales from a Life in Chocolate*.

Frank McClelland is the chef/owner of L'Espalier in Boston.

Susie Middleton is the editor of *Fine Cooking*.

Jan Newberry is the former managing editor of *Fine Cooking* and author of *Super Smoothies*.

David Norman is a chef at Hart & Hind Ranch in Rio Frio, Texas.

Greg Patent is the author of *Baking in America*.

Brian Patterson is the hospitality manager of the American Medical Association's Federal Affairs Office and a teacher at L'Academie de Cuisine in Bethesda, Maryland.

James Peterson is a former contributing editor to *Fine Cooking* and author of *Classic French Cooking*.

Jim Peyton is the author of *Jim Peyton's New Cooking from Old Mexico*.

Mai Pham is the chef/owner of Lemon Grass Restaurant and Cafes in Sacramento, California.

Odessa Piper is the chef/owner of L'Etoile in Madison, Wisconsin.

Michelle Polzine is a pastry chef in San Francisco.

Barbara Bria Pugliese is a baker at Take the Cake Bakery in Guilford, Connecticut.

Susan Purdy is the author of *The Perfect Pie, Have Your Cake & Eat It Too*, and *Let Them Eat Cake*.

Nicole Rees is a professional pastry chef and baking-science expert. She is the co-author of *Understanding Baking*.

Peter Reinhart, CCP, is a baking teacher at Johnson & Wales University and author of *American Pie: My Search for the Perfect Pizza*.

Leslie Revsin authored many cookbooks, including *The Simpler The Better*.

Tony Rosenfeld is a contributing editor to *Fine Cooking* and a restaurant consultant.

Judy Rusignuolo develops new products and recipes for Best Foods in New Jersey.

Sophia Schweitzer writes about food, wine, and fitness from her home in Hawaii.

Tania Segal is the chef-owner of Tania's Table, a catering company in Miami.

Jackie Shen is the executive chef for Lawry's in Chicago.

Renee Shepherd is a gardening cook and seed cataloguer.

Sally Small grows fruit for the Pettigrew Fruit Company in Walnut Grove, California.

Joanne McAllister Smart is the co-author of *Bistro Cooking at Home* and a former *Fine Cooking* editor.

Dorette Snover is a food writer in Chapel Hill, North Carolina.

Katy Sparks is the executive chef of Compass in New York City.

Molly Stevens is a contributing editor to *Fine Cooking* and the author of *All About Braising*.

Kathleen Stewart runs the Downtown Bakery in Healdsburg, California.

Alan Tangren is a pastry chef and former forager at Chez Panisse.

David Tanis is a chef and author who cooks and lives in Santa Fe, New Mexico.

Alan Tardi is the former chef/owner of Follonico in New York City.

John Martin Taylor, owner of Hoppin' John's, an online culinary bookstore, is the author of *Hoppin' John's Lowcountry Cooking* and *The New Southern Cook*.

Fred Thompson is the author of *Lemonade, Iced Tea*, and *Crazy for Crab*.

Thy Tran is the co-author of *The Williams-Sonoma Kitchen Companion*.

Barbara Tropp authored several cookbooks, including *The China Moon Cookbook*.

Charlie Trotter is the chef-owner of Charlie Trotter's in Chicago.

Norman Van Aken is the chef/owner of Norman's in Coral Gables, Florida. He has won the James Beard Award, Robert Mondavi Award, and Food Arts Silver Spoon.

Carole Walter is the author of *Great Cakes* and *Great Pies & Tarts*.

Carolyn Weil, a former pastry chef, is a food writer and teacher.

Bruce Weinstein and **Mark Scarbrough** are contributors to numerous magazines. Weinstein is the author of nine books, including *The Ultimate Ice Cream Book*. Scarbrough writes the "Report from New York" for *Passport Newsletter*.

Joanne Weir is an award-winning cookbook author and the host of *Weir Cooking in Wine Country* and *Weir Cooking in the City* on public television.

Robert Wemischner is the author of *The Vivid Flavors Cookbook*. He teaches professional baking and culinary arts classes in Los Angeles.

Anne Willan, the founder of L'Ecole de Cuisine La Varenne in Burgundy, France, and La Varenne at The Greenbrier in White Sulphur Springs, West Virginia, is the author of dozens of cookbooks.

Rosina Tinari Wilson is a senior editor at *Wine-X*.

Paula Wolfert is the award-winning author of five cookbooks, including *The Slow Mediterranean Kitchen*.

Michael Yeamans is the executive chef of Rouge in Los Angeles